PLOTINUS

THE ARGUMENTS OF
THE PHILOSOPHERS

Editor: Ted Honderich
Grote Professor of the Philosophy of
Mind and Logic, University College London

The purpose of this series is to provide a contemporary assessment and history of the entire course of philosophical thought. Each book constitutes a detailed, critical introduction to the work of a philosopher or school of major influence and significance.

*available in paperback

PLOTINUS

Lloyd P. Gerson

London and New York

First published 1994
by Routledge
11 New Fetter Lane, London EC4P 4EE

Simultaneously published in the USA and Canada
by Routledge
29 West 35th Street, New York, NY 10001

First published in paperback 1998

© 1994 Lloyd P. Gerson

Typeset in Times by
Ponting–Green Publishing Services, Chesham, Bucks
Printed in Great Britain by
TJ International Ltd, Padstow, Cornwall

Printed on acid free paper

British Library Cataloguing in Publication Data
A catalogue record for this book is available from
the British Library

Library of Congress Cataloguing in Publication Data
Gerson, Lloyd P.
Plotinus/Lloyd P. Gerson.
p. cm. – (Arguments of the philosophers)
Includes bibliographical references and index.
1. Plotinus   2. Neoplatonism.
I. Title.   II. Series.
B693.Z7G47   1998
186'.4–dc21   97–50000

ISBN 0–415–05662–4 (hbk)
ISBN 0–415–17409–0 (pbk)

To my wife
Theresa Krystyniak Gerson

Contents

CONTENTS

PART II

Acknowledgments

It is a great pleasure to acknowledge the assistance generously given to me by colleagues, students, and friends. Earlier versions of the entire typescript were read by John Bussanich, Gary Gurtler, SJ, Michael Wagner, John Rist, Eyjölfur Emilsson, and Mark Reuter. Their extensive comments were enormously beneficial. Brad Inwood, Doug Hutchinson, and Joseph Owens discussed with me many points of detail. Richard Sorabji provided me with a number of acute comments on an earlier version of part of chapter III delivered at a conference in New Delhi in 1993. In the academic year 1991–2 the Toronto Greek Reading Group worked its way through Plotinus' treatise III.7, "On Eternity and Time." All those who participated were of great help to me in learning to better understand Plotinus' difficult idiom. Abigail Cinader helped with the proofreading and editorial tasks. A grant from The Social Sciences and Humanities Research Council of Canada relieved me of most teaching duties during 1991–2 when the largest part of this book was written.

The *Enneads*

The following is a list of the treatises comprising the *Enneads* with the titles that appear in Porphyry's edition. The chronological ordering is indicated in brackets.

Introduction

1 The Life and Writings of Plotinus

We are fortunate in possessing a fascinating document, *The Life of Plotinus*, written by the philosopher Porphyry, a pupil and associate of Plotinus for the last eight years of his life. The basic facts contained in this *Life* can be quickly recounted.

Plotinus was likely a Greek born in Egypt in AD 205. It is possible, though, that he came from a Hellenized Egyptian or Roman family. In his 28th year, Plotinus discovered in himself a thirst for philosophy. This led him to Alexandria and the school of Ammonius. Little is known of this enigmatic figure, who may at one time have been a Christian and who wrote nothing. After some ten or eleven years with Ammonius, Plotinus conceived a desire to study Persian and Indian philosophy. To this end he attached himself to a proposed military expedition of the Emperor Gordian III to Persia in about 243. The expedition was, however, aborted when Gordian was assassinated by his troops. Plotinus evidently abandoned his plans to travel east and instead reestablished himself in Rome in 245, where he remained until his death in 270/271.

Porphyry tells us that during the first ten years in Rome Plotinus lectured on the philosophy of Ammonius, although he wrote nothing. These lectures were open to all and were evidently a considerable success. Porphyry himself arrived in Rome in 263. He reports that by this time the first 21 of Plotinus' treatises had been written. There is no way of telling for certain where reliance on Ammonius leaves off and where Plotinus' own thought begins in these works, although for reasons to be discussed presently, the degree of originality is likely to have been high. The remainder of the 54 treatises of the *Enneads* (by Porphyry's counting) were then written during the last eight years of Plotinus' life.

Since Plotinus is generally thought of as something of an ethereal figure, it would be a pity not to say a bit about his admirable character as this is revealed by Porphyry. We are informed that many people were personally devoted to him even up to the point of naming him guardian for their children upon their death. As Porphyry tells us, he proved himself to be "holy and god-like" in this role. Porphyry also recounts several quaint legendary events concerning Plotinus which, for want of a better word, testify to his superior spirituality. Although Plotinus did not absent himself from public affairs, he never, says Porphyry, made any enemies among Roman officials. Modesty, rectitude, compassion, and gentleness seem to have been evident in his dealings with other people. This will be important to remember when we come to consider some of Plotinus' more severe claims in ethics.

Porphyry tells us with a measure of pride that Plotinus entrusted him with the task of editing his works after he died. There may have been another edition done by his friend and personal physician, Eustochius, but if there was, it is lost. We should note first of all that probably owing to Plotinus' foresight in choosing an editor, especially one as able as Porphyry, we possess everything Plotinus wrote. There is no record of any work written but not extant. Among the ancient Greek philosophers, the only other one we can say this about is Plato. In his edition, Porphyry ordered the works in a fashion that is both perspicuous and somewhat misleading. He eschews a chronological ordering, though this is, happily, attested in the *Life*. Instead, he orders the works according to theme, ascending as it were from the earthly to the heavenly, from the supposedly easier material to the more difficult. *Ennead* I contains treatises on what Porphyry calls "ethical matters"; *Enneads* II–III contain treatises on natural philosophy or cosmology, with some rationalizations for the inclusion of III. 4, 5, 7, and 8. *Ennead* IV concerns the soul; V Intellect or νοῦς; and VI being, numbers, and the One. The thematic unity of *Enneads* I, IV, and V is somewhat greater than the rest, but even there an expectation of systematic treatment will be disappointed.

As for the division into six groups of nine treatises each (hence, the word *Enneads*, from the Greek word for the number nine), Porphyry just says that it gave him pleasure to see the work divided according to the "perfect" numbers 9 and 6. We know, however, that several works divided into individual treatises so as to make the numbers come to 9 times 6 most likely belong together as single works. This is so for VI.4 and VI.5; IV.3–5; III.8, V.8, V.5, and II.9; VI.1–3; and III.2 and III.3. So the number of individual works is really 45 rather than 54. As can be seen, only in the fourth instance was the division seriously disruptive, so seriously in fact that it was only fairly recently that scholars have come to believe that they were in fact one work.

These works vary in size from a couple of pages in Greek to over a hundred. They appear frequently to be occasional and related to Plotinus' public teaching. Indeed, Porphyry suggests as much. Thus, Plotinus will raise a question at the beginning of a treatise and consider various answers. It is natural to associate these with the results of actual recent discussions. Plotinus will then proceed to give his own determination of the matter. In this regard, one might usefully compare the tradition of *Quodlibetal* questions such as is found in Thomas Aquinas. I think the complaint that is sometimes made that it is difficult to discover where Plotinus stands on an issue is relevant more to the beginning than to the end of these works and is answered by their dialectical nature. Understandably enough, though, Plotinus, like Aristotle, will occasionally come down on one side of an issue with some hesitation and even diffidence.

In the school meetings, of which the writings are perhaps a partial record, Plotinus would have had read out works by Platonic and Peripatetic commentators. This suggests first of all that the original texts of Plato and Aristotle were already known to the pupils and that the commentaries were the starting-point for discussion. Was the aim of the discussion a correct interpretation of an original text or the solution to a philosophical problem? We know that Plotinus considered himself simply a disciple of Plato. "Neoplatonist" is a term of art and indicates a measure of critical revision that may have in fact occurred but of which Plotinus is seemingly unaware. If Plotinus had commentaries on Aristotle read and discussed, it was evidently not because he approached Aristotle with the eye of a neutral scholar. Thinking that the doctrines of Plato embodied wisdom, Plotinus correctly recognized that the greatest challenge to this position came from Aristotle. The reading of the Aristotelian commentaries was, I suggest, part of a definite strategy: to understand the essence of Aristotelian objections to Plato in order to provide their proper responses.

Porphyry tells us that the *Enneads* are full of concealed Stoic and Peripatetic doctrines. In particular, Aristotle's *Metaphysics* is concentrated in them. A measure of what this means can be gleaned from the admittedly incomplete *index fontium* of the edition of Henry and Schwyzer. There are at least 150 direct references to the *Metaphysics* and perhaps a thousand references to other texts of Aristotle. There are as well many hundreds of references to Stoic doctrines, most of which are difficult to identify because the original texts are lost. These facts show what I regard as a fundamental feature of the *Enneads*: they are contributions to a rehabilitation or defense of Platonism against its opponents. The originality of Plotinus that I mentioned a moment ago is in how the defense is constructed. For more often than not, it consists in appropriating distinctions and terminology that are Aristotelian and Stoic. And in using these to construct the defense, Plotinus arrives at conclusions that frequently go beyond what could be called a plausible interpretation of Plato based on the writings of Plato or even on the oral tradition.

An additional and sometimes overlooked facet of Plotinus' Platonism is that Plotinus leans heavily on Aristotle for an understanding of what Plato's doctrines actually were. For one thing, Plotinus' Plato is sharply distinguished from Socrates, following that perfectly natural distinction in Aristotle. Nothing in the *Enneads* is derived from or depends on what we have come to recognize as especially Socratic. More importantly, Plotinus follows Aristotle in holding that Plato had an unwritten doctrine of principles. Indeed, Plotinus appears to rely on Aristotle for understanding what that is.

Some effort is expended in the *Enneads* in order to show that this unwritten doctrine is at least consonant with that which appears in the dialogues. Finally, Plotinus will frequently accept as authoritative an interpretation of Plato by Aristotle, an interpretation which Aristotle himself thinks leads a Platonic doctrine to shipwreck. Plotinus, however, will typically attempt to show that what Aristotle thinks is a disastrous consequence of a Platonic position is in fact true and even necessary. The alternative Aristotelian position is what ought to be rejected. And yet where Plotinus judges that Aristotle is really not in disagreement with Plato, he will quietly adopt Aristotle's terminology, distinctions, and even his explicit conclusions.

In the light of the above, I have frequently begun my treatment of Plotinian doctrines with the reasons why Plotinus rejects the Aristotelian alternative. I have found this approach enormously illuminating. Plotinus is primarily a Platonist, not an anti-Aristotelian. But his Platonism is in many respects filtered through his struggle with Aristotle.

2 Some Problems in Reading Plotinus

I list here four problems that have in my opinion impeded the critical appreciation of Plotinus' work. I mention them with the hope that precipitous judgments of Plotinus' arguments may be forestalled.

(1) Owing to his dates, Plotinus is not easy to incorporate into the curricula of courses in either ancient or medieval philosophy. This means that he has received less attention by the people who potentially could write about him in a philosophical manner.

(2) A related point is that the root system of Plotinus' philosophy is enormously tangled and extensive. Yet, the fruit of his philosophy is obscure and only harvested with difficulty. That Plotinus is a highly "derivative" philosopher in the way that, say, Hegel is and Wittgenstein is not is obvious upon a simple perusal of the *index fontium* of Henry and Schwyzer's edition. This means that an enormous background is very nearly essential to appreciating and judging fairly much of what he says. And the advantage that we sometimes have in interpreting other philosophers by the explicit developments of their disciples is mostly lost in the case of Plotinus, for from Porphyry to Proclus and then on into Arabic and Christian scholasticism it is usually very difficult to see straightforward use made of arguments that are uniquely those of Plotinus.

(3) Plotinus' philosophy is in some sense systematic, but his works are anything but that. There is no single treatise which one could go to in order to discover anything like a definitive statement of his views on a central question. Since the treatises are frequently, as we have seen, occasional pieces written in response to questions or problems raised in classroom discussion, there is no plan of orderly exposition according to which they are produced. This fact is no doubt related to Plotinus' conviction that the true

system of philosophy has already been developed by Plato. Hence, it requires considerable effort and patience to assemble all of the evidence regarding Plotinus' position on a philosophical problem. It is quite a challenge to arrive at a point at which one can feel confident that all the relevant evidence has been canvassed. I should say here, though, that I am very sceptical about claims regarding a development of Plotinus' thought in the *Enneads* following the chronological ordering. I think that the fact that we have a relative chronology has just been a temptation to search for such schemes. There are certainly variations in nuance and emphasis, but I have not detected any substantial alterations in doctrinal content throughout the *corpus*. Accordingly, in this book I have felt free to draw on texts everywhere in the *Enneads* as evidence for an interpretation. I should add that my anti-developmentalist position is in fact the dominant view among Plotinus scholars today.

(4) The *Enneads* are written in a highly compressed, often obscure style, where dialectic, exegesis, allegory, and technical argument are often mixed together in a distressing fashion. It is an exotic work, both in form and content. I am conscious of having suppressed this exotic quality in two respects. First, I have been very selective in discussing Plotinus' arguments. Occasionally, presumably for polemical reasons, Plotinus will indiscriminately evoke a veritable avalanche of arguments against a position. I have chosen from among these the arguments I regard as the most philosophically interesting and have left aside ones that I judged to be of only marginal philosophical interest. I am not confident that my judgment always corresponds to what Plotinus' own would have been about the relative merits of his arguments. Second, I have kept mostly silent about some very exotic topics, such as magic, astral bodies, and guardian angels, which undoubtedly do have some place in a complete picture of Plotinus as a thinker. I do not, though, think that they have a place in a philosophy book, or at any rate a contemporary philosophy book. I do not wish to act as an apologist for Plotinus regarding his interests. He is certainly a child of his own age, as is the author of this book and all of his readers. But these issues are distractions from the philosopher's concerns.

Owing in part to the nature of Plotinus' writings, I have allowed myself what I hope is a not too excessive measure of repetition in my exposition of his thought. I have treated some complex issues from different perspectives in different parts of the book. For example, Plotinus believes that matter and evil are the same thing. But I have treated matter within the context of Plotinus' metaphysics of the sensible world and evil within the context of his ethics. Accordingly, as in this case, I sometimes deal with the same texts more than once and repeat interpretative claims. I hope that this is helpful and not just irritating. I have also thought it well to make rather extensive references to the text, even when this means citing the same texts in different places. For I have found that one cannot have too many signposts to guide one through the labyrinth of Plotinus' philosophy.

3 A Note on Terminology and Translation

Plotinus' vocabulary is laden with ambiguous terms. For example, the term νοῦς is used to refer to (1) a fundamental ἀρχή or principle of the universe; (2) the intellect of the soul of the universe; (3) an individual human intellect in its discarnate state; (4) the highest part of a human soul in its incarnate state. One cannot always be confident as to which of these Plotinus is referring on a particular occasion. It is not, I think, desirable for an interpreter simply to avoid the issue by always using νοῦς instead of trying to say which of the four meanings he thinks is present in a passage or argument. The ambiguities between (1) and (2), (1) and (3), and (3) and (4) are especially troublesome. When I write "Intellect" with a capital "I" as a translation for νοῦς, I am always referring to (1). When I write "intellect" with a lower case "i," I mean either (2), (3), or (4). Which of these it is in particular should be clear from the context. Nevertheless, I wish I were more confident than I in fact am that I have always been able to interpret Plotinus correctly in this regard. A similar but slightly less acute problem exists for his use of the word ψυχή or soul. I write "Soul" for the principle and "soul" for individuals or when Plotinus is referring generally and indefinitely to psychic properties. I capitalize "One" and "Good" when Plotinus uses these words, roughly, as proper names.

Translating the texts of the *Enneads* is in general exceedingly difficult. The best complete English translation presently available is that of A. H. Armstrong in the seven volumes of the Loeb edition. The quotations from Plotinus in this book are mainly taken from Armstrong's translations, with my own modifications where I found these to be necessary. I judged it less confusing to the reader familiar with Armstrong's work to rely on his terminology rather than to introduce my own.

Part I

I

An Argument for the Existence of a First Principle of All

General accounts of Plotinus' metaphysics typically assert that his system contains three "hypostases," the One (τὸ ἕν), Intellect (νοῦς), and Soul (ψυχή). Such a division is misleading. First, as Plotinus explains, these are the only three "in the intelligible world", that is, in contrast to the sensible world (II.9.1.15–16).[1] He also says that the three are "in us" as well as in nature (V.1.10.5–6). Second, the above statement gives the impression that ὑπόστασις is a technical term reserved for primary entities in the system. This is false. Plotinus speaks often of the ὑπόστασις of a variety of things such as wisdom, matter, love, numbers, relations, time, motion, and so on.[2] In the majority of passages, the term means simply "extra-mental existence" or "existents" in the plural.[3] When Plotinus raises a question about the ὑπόστασις of X, he is generally not in doubt that X exists in some way, but he is intent on arguing that some opponent's account of that existence is false and that a better (i.e., Platonic) one is needed. Such an account of the existence of X is usually understood by Plotinus according to traditional categories of material/immaterial; independent/dependent; generated/ungenerated; particular/universal. Thus, one opponent, say, a Stoic, will hold that the ὑπόστασις of X is material and dependent, while Plotinus wants to argue that it is in fact immaterial and independent.

It is more helpful and accurate to refer to the One, Intellect, and Soul as ἀρχαί or principles, as Plotinus frequently does (see II.9.1.12–16; V.1.9.23–4; V.2.1.1; V.3.15.27; V.3.16.7, 13, 38; V.4.1.12; V.8.7.44; VI.8.9.5; VI.8.19.16; VI.9.5.24; VI.9.6.35, etc.).[4] The One, Intellect, and Soul are principles in three ways.

First, they are principles of explanation or starting-points for solving the inventory of philosophical problems inherited from the tradition to which Plotinus is attached. Thus, if Plotinus is giving an account of, say, voluntary action or memory or evil, he will appeal to his three principles as providing the conceptual framework for his account. These principles are supposed to enable him to interpret phenomena correctly. They are fundamental explanatory categories.

Second, they are principles in the sense of paradigms. Like Platonic Forms,

Plotinus' three ἀρχαί are identitatively whatever it is that participates in them is predicatively. Nevertheless, Plotinus' paradigmatism is more complex than Plato's. For Plato, Forms alone are paradigms. For Plotinus, however, although Intellect is the locus of Forms, the One and Soul also serve a paradigmatic function. Thus, the notion of image or copy is expanded beyond its basic Platonic reference to the instances of Forms.

Third, they are actual causes of some sort. Plotinus shows no interest in merely notional or theoretical paradigms. The three ἀρχαί of Plotinus are first causes in distinct kinds of explanation. They function in his arguments as explanatory entities, adduced to account for specific kinds of data. These ἀρχαί are ordered in terms of scope. Thus, the first ἀρχή, the One, includes within its causal scope the second and third ἀρχαί, Intellect and Soul. And the second includes the third in *its* causal scope. These causes overlap, but they are irreducible. They can be severally adduced to explain various features of the same things, but their causality is not identical. That is why Intellect and Soul are not just inferior manifestations of the One. The ἀρχή One is the cause only of its proper effect.

Plotinus' argument for the existence of an unconditionally first principle of all belongs to a long tradition of philosophical theology. To call this first principle "god" (θεός) is uncontentious within this tradition.[5] Among the arguments definitely known to Plotinus were Plato's and the Stoics' design arguments, Aristotle's argument for an unmoved mover based on the eternity of motion, and the ubiquitous argument *ex consensu gentium*.[6] Plotinus does not employ any of these arguments, opting instead for a different and original approach. Actually, he confidently alludes to a plethora of unnamed demonstrations of the first ἀρχή.[7] Perhaps he believed that, since he has at least one good argument, there *must* be others. Or perhaps he believed that one basic argumentative strategy is variously nameable depending on the particular type of data employed. In any case, the most direct line to Plotinian metaphysics goes through the argument for the existence of a first principle. Here is the passage containing the beginning of the argument:

> For there must be (εἶναι) something simple (ἁπλοῦν) before (πρὸ) all things, and this must be other than all the things which come after it, existing by itself, not mixed with the things which derive from it, and all the same able to be present in a different way to these other things, being really one, and not a different being and then one; it is false even to say of it that it is one, and there is "no concept or knowledge" of it; it is indeed also said to be "beyond being" (ἐπέκεινα οὐσίας). For if it is not to be simple, outside all coincidence and composition, it could not be a principle (ἀρχή); and it is the most self sufficient, because it is simple and the first of all: for that which is not the first needs that which is before it, and what is not simple is in need of its simple components (τῶν ἁπλῶν) so that it can come into existence from them. (V.4.1.5–15)[8]

At first glance, this passage looks like the statement of a banal analytic truth masquerading as a metaphysical argument. The existence of complexes entails the existence of simples. This certainly does not seem promising. But notice that the argument explicitly distinguishes the "simple" that is "before" a complex and a simple component. It is of course only the latter that is entailed by the existence of a complex. So, we are left to wonder, where is the argument for the existence of the former?

A clue is contained in the next line of the text, where Plotinus claims that "such a thing [i.e., 'something simple before all things'] must be one alone: for if there were another of this kind, both would be one." The only reason given for this claim is that if there were two, both would be one. Presumably, this means "specifically one," since it would be nonsense to claim that there cannot be numerically two things because then they would be numerically one. But what is wrong with saying that two things are specifically one, differing *solo numero*? We must not suppose a sort of Leibnizian reply from Plotinus based on the principle of the identity of indiscernibles for the obvious reason that Plotinus is talking about the uniqueness of the absolutely simple first principle of all, not the uniqueness or identity of any individual, which of course may be complex. This uniqueness is supposed to follow from its being the sort of thing it is (τὸ τοιοῦτον), namely, one or simple.[9] Evidently, unqualified simplicity is thought to be incapable of duplication.

Let us ask first of all what unqualified simplicity is supposed to mean. Minimally, this means that it has no predicates (III.8.10.29–35). We cannot say of the unqualifiedly simple, claims Plotinus, that it is one or even that it exists. Why would this entail a denial of simplicity? I suggest that the only complexity that would be entailed in such a proposition as "the One exists" is a real distinction grounded in reality between *what* exists and its existence. A mere conceptual distinction between whatever it is that "it" means and what "exists" means would not entail complexity. As we shall see in the next chapter, there are many possibilities for non-redundantly referring to the One so long as these are understood to be merely conceptually distinct ways of referring to that which is unqualifiedly simple.

If unqualified simplicity entails an absence of a real or extra-mental distinction between whatever it is that the name "One" refer to and its existence, then we might construct the following argument to show why it may be supposed that the One is utterly unique as well. Let there be two unqualifiedly simple things, A and B. In that case, each one will have no predicates. They will both exist, but we cannot say of each "it exists." Then how could we establish that there are two? Presumably, the only way we could refer to two existents is by referring to *what* it is that exists in each case. But if in each case we cannot distinguish what it is from its existence, we can make no such reference. We might say simply that "exists" is not a referring expression but that referring expressions are needed to refer to the putative duo. Nor does it even seem possible that we can conceive of what it would mean for there to be two such unqualifiedly simple existents. To conceive of each is to conceive of what each is. Even an "I know not what" is *something*.

Perhaps it will be said that the reason why we cannot conceive of more than one unqualifiedly simple thing is that we cannot conceive of even one. Plotinus is actually sensitive to such an objection. After all, if the One is "beyond being," then it is apparently beyond conceivability so long as conceivability is taken to belong to all and only that which has being in some sense. I think we shall better understand Plotinus' highly creative and nuanced response to this problem if we suppose that the One's being "beyond being" does not mean that it has no nature or essence at all or that it is a blank ontological place-holder or bare particular. Rather, its essence is identical with its existence and therefore it is unqualifiedly simple. By contrast, if in everything else essence or nature or "whatness" is really distinct from existence, then what each thing is can be conceived of apart from its existence. If the One is identical to its existence, conceiving of it is impossible.

In claiming that the first principle of all is unique Plotinus can draw on many arguments of his predecessors for support. For example, Plato argued for the uniqueness of every Form.[10] Still, every Form will share in some characteristics with every other Form, such as eternality, immateriality, oneness, and so on. Thus, Forms are not unqualifiedly unique; they may be nevertheless the same in some respects. A more pertinent model for Plotinus is Aristotle's argument in the *Metaphysics* that the first immovable mover is one both in number and in formula.[11] The reason given for the uniqueness of the unmoved mover is that since it is unqualified actuality, it has no matter. The unspoken premise is that matter is necessary for multiplication within a single kind. This cannot be the reason why Plotinus thinks that the ἀρχή of all is unique. As we shall see, he assumes without question that a multitude of immaterial minds can exist that are yet one in kind. Hence, the composition of act and potency which, for Aristotle, allows multiplication within a kind in some cases and whose absence disallows it in one case only is only analogous to the composition *within* immaterial entities that is absent from the One and guarantees *its* uniqueness.

My explanation of how one might understand the claim for the uniqueness of the absolutely simple still leaves me with the task of showing that this is what Plotinus means and the further task of showing that even if there can be no more than one unqualifiedly simple thing, we have in fact reason to believe that there is at least one.

Consider the following passage:

> if an individual thing loses its oneness (τὸ ἕν)[12] it will not exist at all. We must therefore see if the individual one and individual being are the same thing, and universal being and the universal oneness. But if the being (τὸ ὄν) of the individual is a multiplicity, but it is impossible for

oneness to be a multiplicity, they will be different from each other. At any rate "man" and "living being" and "rational" are many parts and these many are bound together by oneness. "Man" and "one" are therefore different, and one has parts and the other is partless. And, indeed, universal being, which has all the beings in it, will be still more of a many and different from oneness, and will have oneness by sharing and participation. But being also has life; for it is certainly not a corpse; being therefore is many things. But if it is Intellect, in this way too it must be many; and still more if it includes the Forms. For the Idea is not one, but rather a number, both each individual one and the total Idea, and is one in the way in which the universe is one. (VI.9.2.15–29)[13]

This is the main text I adduce in support of the claim that Plotinus understands complexity in the way that I have sketched above. Let us begin with the apparent allusion this passage makes to Aristotle's claim in the *Metaphysics* that "one man and being a man and a man are the same" (4.2.1003b22–34. See also 10.2.1054a9–19, 11.3.1061a10–18).[14] As Aristotle carefully notes, he is not claiming that "being" and "one" are the same in λόγος or formula. That is, he is not claiming that there is no conceptual distinction between being and one. He is claiming rather that being and one are extensionally equivalent; everything that can be said to be is one and vice versa. "Being" and "one" indicate two different ways of considering "the same thing." Further, there is something like a one-to-one correspondence among the many senses of being and of one (see 7.4.1030b10–13). Primary being is primarily one; derivative being is derivately one.

In our passage Plotinus is arguing that being and oneness are "different from each other." Apparently, he is arguing that being and oneness are more than conceptually distinct, and not that "being" and "one" are different in meaning but with an identical reference. This can mean one of two things. Either "being" and "oneness" refer to independent objects so that what "being" refers to exists separately from what "oneness" refers to or else "being" and "oneness" refer to really different parts or features of the same thing. The former possibility is explicitly excluded by Plotinus himself in the chapter prior to our passage. There he asks rhetorically, "what could anything be if it were not one? For if things are deprived of the oneness which is predicated of them they are not those things" (VI.9.1.3–4). Plotinus unequivocally denies that "being" can refer to that of which "oneness" is not predicated. In this he agrees with Aristotle. So, we are left with the second possibility, namely, that "being" and "oneness" refer to really distinct features within the same thing. Nothing is actually "deprived of one," but what something is can be considered in thought apart from its oneness.

Aristotle himself provides ample precedent for the sort of distinction here at issue. A substance and any one of its accidental attributes are really distinct. "Man" and "pale," for example, have really distinct referents

7

because their distinction is not based on a concept but on an irreducible difference in reality. But "man" and "pale" do not refer to different things altogether because, though the man could exist without being pale, the paleness of this man could not exist apart from the man. I should add here a point that will concern us later. Generally, if there is a real distinction within one thing, it follows that there is an asymmetry between the really distinct referents. The man could exist apart from his paleness, but his paleness could not exist apart from the man. If this man's paleness could, *per impossibile*, exist by itself, then "pale man" would not refer to one substance but rather to something more like a heap or a contiguous collocation of two or more substances.

Plotinus then can be taken to be arguing that there is a real distinction between being and oneness in any one being. What are his reasons for thinking this? The first reason he seems to offer is that if the being of an individual is a multiplicity but it is impossible for oneness to be a multiplicity, then being and onenesss will be distinct, that is, really distinct within this individual. As he goes on to explain, "man" and "living being" and "rational" constitute a plurality of parts which together are bound together to make one individual. The unity these parts possess must be really distinct from these parts.[15] The interpretative puzzle facing us is that the being of the individual seems perfectly adequate in accounting for its unity. Even if the parts are a multiplicity or plurality, each part must after all be one and all the parts together of the multiplicity make another one. They comprise "one multiplicity." That is precisely why Aristotle says that "one" is just a different way of looking at a being, for example, considering the same being along with others of the same kind.

For Plotinus' argument to make any sense we have to show that he is using "being" in such a way that it can refer to what is deprived of oneness. Consider the following example. The whale is an aquatic mammal. Let us assume that "whale" names a natural kind and that it is possible to give an exhaustive inventory of all of its essential parts. Is the whale one? I do not mean the word "whale" or my concept of the whale, but the natural kind. It would seem that it cannot be one, so long as we refuse to identify the natural kind with any instance of it. But is not the whale one kind of mammal? Yes, but only within a conceptual schema of our making. In itself, the whale is indeterminate as to number and therefore as to existence. Apart from some existence, it is merely a nature. But to identify this nature with any instance of it would be to eliminate the possibility that there should be another individual of the same natural kind. Such a move seems quite gratuitous. If the being of the natural kind is identified as what it is, then unity is not an attribute of that being.[16]

This, however, leaves us with the being of the individual which Plotinus supposes is really distinct from its own unity or oneness. What is the reason for supposing that being and oneness are really distinct in the individual? The reason is apparently that nothing in the individual's nature determines or explains why an individual exists. No statement describing what a man is is equivalent to a statement asserting that one man exists. There is a real distinction between what a man is and what makes an individual man exist because the statement "one man exists" gives two objectively different pieces of information – what exists and the existence of what exists. Alone, however, "one man" does not refer to anything real as opposed to conceptual any more than does "man."

It will be noticed that I have alternated between speaking of a real distinction between being and oneness and a real distinction between essence or "whatness" or "nature" and existence.[17] In defense of this move, let us begin by noting that if "being" in our passage did not refer to essence alone but included existence as well, there would be no grounds whatsoever for holding that being and oneness were really distinct. Plotinus has already agreed that whatever exists is one. Second, Plotinus holds that the first principle of all preserves (σῴζει) all things in existence (VI.7.23.22–4).[18] That is, it is supposed to be that which gives composites something which does not come from them but which comes from outside, namely, their existence. Since this first principle is perfectly incomposite and called, among other things, "the One," it appears that the unity it gives to things which are one and the existence which it gives to them are the same thing.[19] If this be doubted, let us recall that "One" is strictly speaking no more legitimate a description of *what* the ἀρχή of all is than is any other term. To think of the One as nothing but the cause of oneness as opposed to being the cause of existence is to think of the One as an essence like a Form or as that whose nature is oneness, not as that which is "beyond being."[20] Finally, an imputation of scholastic anachronism in applying the language of essence and existence to Plotinus' metaphysics is really beside the point if that language accurately elucidates what is going on in the arguments. I claim that it does.

Plotinus says that "One" is strictly speaking an improper name (ὄνομα) for the first principle (V.5.6.26–30). This is an odd thing to say if a name is understood merely as a label or a proper name. Plotinus, however, perhaps following Plato in the *Cratylus*, thinks that a correct name reveals the nature of what is named. He rejects "One" as the correct name presumably because its nature is not oneness. Rather, it is one in the sense that it is simple and unique. To suppose that the One is the cause of oneness is, it seems, just the error Plotinus is warning against in saying that "One" is not a correct name for the first principle.[21]

Many texts have been mentioned already in which Plotinus says or implies that the One is the cause of oneness in whatever is one. I have argued that these texts should not be taken to mean that the One usurps the role of a Form of Unity. If this is so, then we need to ask just what the One is meant to be the cause of when it is said to be the cause of oneness. My answer is based in part on an analysis of the simplicity and uniqueness of the One. Owing to this simplicity and uniqueness, the One cannot be a complex cause, a cause of different features of things. But the One is in some sense the cause of all that is complex, even the minimally complex Intellect. If, as I have also argued, the simplicity of the One is a result of the identity of essence and existence in it, then minimal complexity follows from a lack of identity of essence and existence. As I shall show in chapter 3, Intellect is the principle and cause of essence. This makes it reasonable to infer that the One is the cause of existence of whatever exists. Indeed, a number of texts already referred to can be interpreted in this way. The main reason for refusing to interpret them thus is the false assumption that the One is the essence of oneness. As we proceed, I shall try to show that the hypothesis that the One is the cause of existence is confirmed by many other things that Plotinus has to say about the One's causal activity and the relation of everything else to it.

Plotinus does not appear to distinguish the cause of coming into being of whatever has such a cause from the cause of its being sustained in existence (see VI.7.42.11; VI.7.23.20–4).[22] Of course, there is no coming into being in the sense of temporal beginning for eternal Intellect or even for Soul, which is not in time but of which time is an attribute. But even for individual contingent composites, the cause of their being is identical at every moment of their being. If this were not so, then a limitation would be introduced into the One which is inadmissible on the basis of its absolute simplicity. Either the One would be thought to be unable to "reach down" all the way to contingent beings or else it would be thought to delegate the role of cause of being to some other principle. The former case implies an illicit limitation in power. The latter would mean that the One refrains from doing something that it could do, and this too implies limitation, albeit self-limitation, and hence, complexity.

On the hypothesis that the real distinction between being and oneness is a real distinction between essence or "whatness" and existence, we still have to ask whether Plotinus has actually given any serious reason for believing in this real distinction and also how the real distinction is supposed to function in an argument for the existence of a first principle of all.

The reason for the first claim is the argument for the unicity of the absolutely simple. From the premise that there can be at most one un-qualifiedly simple thing in which essence and existence are indistinct, Plotinus can infer immediately that in a given plurality at least one thing must be such that essence and existence are really distinct in it. Hence, any thing we like is either something in which essence and existence are really distinct or else it is in fact the first principle of all, in so far as the first principle is defined as that in which essence and existence are not really distinct. Thus, any plurality as such provides the requisite datum for an argument to the One. This fact may account for the utter generality of the data to which Plotinus appeals. Whatever we point to which has a nature or an attribute which another thing could possess is a case of something in which essence and existence are really distinct. Whatever is such that we can say of it "so and so exists" is apt for an explanation of its existence.

The apparent assumption of the possibility of identity in difference should give us pause even if it does not trouble Plotinus in the slightest. What if we took a rigorously nominalist line and refused to allow generally that two things can have the same attribute? Then of course there could not be two first principles, if these are supposed to differ *solo numero*. But more importantly, in so far as the argument for a real distinction depends on the *possibility* of two things differing *solo numero* so long as they are composites, this argument seems to be defeated. Plotinus did not intend to demonstrate the absolute uniqueness of everything, but only of the first principle. If the absolute uniqueness of everything is deduced as a consequence of a nominalist position, then there might be one first principle, but this would not entail that essence and existence were really distinct in everything else. A conceptual distinction would suffice.

What Plotinus needs to show is that two things cannot differ *solo numero* when they are incomposites, that is, where essence and existence are merely conceptually distinct in them. This amounts to showing that it is possible for two composites so to differ. Thus, he must show merely that it is possible that there should be two Xs which are identical in so far as they are Xs but are really different in their existence. Then, there would be a real distinction within each X. Plotinus' confident acceptance of the Platonic principle of identity in difference makes this something less than a serious problem for him. I do not suspect that he for one moment countenanced the claim that it was impossible for two things to be identical in any respect while remaining numerically two. Evidently, this is because he believed that the phrase "identical in some respect" is not nonsensical.

It would seem that the only way one could show it to be impossible that two things could be identical in any respect is by constructing a theory of properties according to which the identity and the individuating conditions for properties are the same. Thus, no two properties could be the same, for what makes them each one ensures that they cannot be identical. From this it would follow that there would be no grounds for positing a real distinction between essence and existence within one individual. What a thing is and the fact that it is would be merely two different ways of referring to the same individual. And just as the distinction between essence and existence within an individual would be merely conceptual, so would the identity of properties of several individuals.

I believe that Plotinus does have an argument which shows in general that the identity and individuating conditions for something cannot be the same. I shall consider this argument within the context of his criticism of Aristotelian and Stoic category theory. For the moment, let us assume that Plotinus' argument for the unicity of a putative first principle is no stronger or weaker than a claim that "identity in some respect" is possible. Hence, in so far as his argument for a real distinction within one individual depends on showing that there could only be one incomposite first principle, that argument rests on a premise not yet established. Notice, however, that if Plotinus is committed only to showing the possibility of identity in difference – as opposed to its actual occurrence in any particular case – then refuting him requires the formidable task of showing the *impossibility* of identity in difference. And this seems to require one to go beyond an ad hoc stipulation of the meaning of "identity."

If Plotinus can establish the impossibility of there being more than one incomposite being, then composite beings exist within any plurality, say, among the objects in a room. This of course still leaves us with the central question of why this fact should lead us to think that the unique, absolutely simple first principle actually exists. What is there about the datum of a real distinction between essence and existence in one individual that requires an inference to an incomposite ἀρχή? The texts make it quite clear that it is precisely the existence of a composite being that is the explanandum and that Plotinus wishes to argue (1) that this existence requires a causal explanation and (2) that only if there is a unique, simple, first principle is this explanation provided (see I.7.1.20–2; I.8.2.2–4; II.3.6.16–17; V.3.12.19–20; V.3.15.11–12, 28; V.3.17.10–14; VI.5.10.2; VI.7.23.22–4).[23]

There is no straightforward, concise cosmological argument for the existence of god in the *Enneads* based on the datum of complex entities. It is possible, though, to piece together most of the elements of such an argument. First, Plotinus thinks that his first principle must be uniquely self-sufficient, which means that everything else, whether it be eternal or temporal, cannot be self-sufficient (V.4.1.12–15). This claim implies that the causal argument for a first principle does not depend on temporal attributes such as generability and destructability. The existence of anything at all whose existence is really distinct from its essence is in need of a causal explanation. If this explanation is in every case only that which is incomposite and there is only one incomposite, then it is the same explanation for all. It is clear enough that Plotinus thinks that for everything else besides the first principle existence could not be explained by essence, for if it could, then such things would be self-caused and hence in no need of another cause of their existence.[24] But only the first principle is self-caused, for only that which is unqualifiedly simple is self-caused (VI.8.14.41: αἴτιον ἑαυτοῦ).[25]

At this point the possibilities are three: either the existence of a composite depends on another composite, or it depends on the one and only one incomposite cause, or it depends on nothing. The first possibility is excluded only by the cryptic principle often repeated by Plotinus, namely, that oneness is prior to multiplicity (see III.8.9.3; III.8.10.15–16; V.3.12.9, 12–13; V.3.15.12–13; V.3.16.12–13; V.4.1.5; V.6.3.22; V.6.4.6). It seems that by "prior" he means "causally prior" so that the multiplicity depends for its existence on oneness. To this principle must be added the claim that

12

the oneness upon which the multiplicity depends for its existence cannot be the oneness of any of its parts (V.6.3). It would be perfectly reasonable to say that a whole could not exist without its parts. But Plotinus evidently wishes to claim more than this.

I interpret his meaning as follows. Either the part is inseparable and dependent on the whole, in which case it is not incomposite: that is, it will share the compositeness of the whole. For example, a part of a divisible body is itself divisible, in which case it is not incomposite. Or else the part is separable, like the marbles in a bag, in which case the whole does not have existence distinct from the parts. So, one contingent existent could not depend on another contingent existent for its existence, because if it did, the supposed explanans would efface the explanandum. That is, if composite A depended *now* on composite B for its existence, then composite A would not be a separate existent. The composite A/B would become the explanandum. In other words, a composite which was a putative cause of the existence of another composite would in fact either be identical with the explanandum or it would not be so, in which case it would provide no explanation at all. Its being not identical with the explanandum means that it exists independently, that is, it is another existent. Since independence here must be a symmetrical relation, the explanandum can exist independently of the putative cause of its existence. And that just means that the putative cause of its existence is no cause at all. The real internal distinction of essence and existence in composites means that we could not tell the difference between one contingent existent causing the existence of another and there being one contingent existent with parts. In the latter case, the whole indeed could not exist without the parts, but the parts are not the cause of existence of *another* existent, namely, the whole.

The possibility that the existence of a composite depends on nothing or that it is inexplicable is not considered as a serious one by Plotinus. If this possibility amounts to the claim that it is impossible that there should be an explanation of the existence of a composite, it is difficult not to share Plotinus' diffidence. How could such a thing be shown? If, however, the claim merely amounts to the assertion that, though it is possible that there should be an explanation, there is in fact none, then Plotinus' obvious reply is that he has an explanation at hand and its adequacy needs to be addressed, not by saying that there is no explanation but by showing why his explanation is not satisfactory.

The argument for the existence of a unique, incomposite first principle is, therefore, only as good as the explanation it provides for the relevant data. In order to understand and assess this explanation properly we shall have to explore the supposed operation of the first principle on the explananda. Two points should be mentioned in this regard which will concern us more fully in due course. First, Plotinus will have no recourse to an inscrutable divine mind whose purpose in causing the existence of composites transcends human understanding. Accordingly, it is not open to him to claim that the existence of the first principle is established because without it composites could not exist but that this is as much as we can say. He cannot isolate final and efficient causality in what might be taken to be a self-serving manner.

Second, the operation of the first principle is crucial to the explanation because this first principle is not merely a first principle of understanding but rather a cause of existence. It may well be that cognitional discrimination requires a principle of unity to be employed, but for Plotinus this fact would be posterior to the need to postulate a cause to explain the existence of everything else. Hence, again, efficient causality is implicated in the explanatory process. Furthermore, owing to the efficient causal role of the first principle in explaining the existence of everything else and owing to the real distinction between essence and existence, essential causality and efficient causality are not easily joined in one first cause. Wherever there is essence or οὐσία, existence is really distinct from it. The first principle can perhaps cause an essence to exist; but as for its being an essential cause, that is another matter.

For the moment these questions can be left aside. From the postulate of a unique incomposite first principle Plotinus deduces a number of entitative attributes, those that pertain to it apart from its causal relations with anything else. Accordingly, it is with the deductions from Plotinus' primary hypothesis that we may begin.

II

The Attributes of the One

1 The Entitative Attributes of the One

Plotinus tells us that the One is above all predicates (III.8.10.29–35; see also V.3.13).[1] Hence it might seem pointless to try to speak about its entitative attributes, those which it has considered in itself apart from anything else. What Plotinus means, however, is that nothing can be said of the One that implies composition, that is, I hold, the composition of essence and existence. Such would be the case wherever the attribute was really distinct from the subject of which it is predicated. For example, accidents are really distinct from their subject, which means that the One can have no accidental attributes. Nor can it have essential attributes if having these is taken to imply that essence is really distinct from existence, which of course it would if the essence were shareable by more than one being. So, in a sense the One could be said to have a unique essence, unrepeatable outside of itself so long as this were merely conceptually distinct from its existence. Nevertheless, Plotinus quite reasonably eschews essentialistic language in reference to the One, both because such language might be understood to apply to an essence really distinct from its existence and because essentialistic predication is only usefully employed in contrast to accidental predication.

It is sheer confusion to deduce from the denial of all predication of the One that it does not exist at all. But this is not so because Plotinus thinks that existence is a special type of predicate. Rather, the reason for the denial of predication is the unique incompositeness of the One, which I have argued is to be understood as the identity of its essence and existence.[2] So, although there are no legitimate predicates said of the One if these imply compositeness, we can still speak truly of it by making conceptual distinctions regarding it, for conceptual distinctions imply no composition in that to which they apply. That is, we can legitimately describe the One from different perspectives or negatively or in the different ways that other things are related to it.[3]

Plotinus further specifies the conditions for referring to the One:

How then do we ourselves speak about it? We do indeed say something about it, but we certainly do not speak it, and we have neither knowledge nor thought of it. But if we do not have it in knowledge, do we have it not at all? But we have it in such a way that we speak about it, but do not speak it. For we say what it is not, but we do not say what it is; so that we speak about it from what comes after it. (V.3.14.1–8. See also III.8.9.16–19; V.3.13.1–5; VI.9.3.49–54; VI.9.5.34)

The contrast between "speaking it" and "speaking about it" is, as the passage shows, primarily the contrast between positive and negative predication. The former is proscribed just in so far as it implies compositeness. The latter approach accordingly would seem to be limited merely to saying that the One is incomposite. Does not *that* say it all? No, for "what comes after it" is not merely the class of composites different from their incomposite ἀρχή, but also the effects of the causal activity of that ἀρχή. We can know of the One both whatever follows from incompositeness and whatever follows from its being a cause of its effects (see V.3.14.7–8; V.5.6.20; VI.9.3.49–51).[4]

These limitations actually leave us with much scope for the deduction of attributes in some sense of the first principle or ἀρχή of all.[5] From the incompositeness of the One follows its simplicity (see II.9.1.8; V.2.1.4; VI.7.37.19; VI.9.5.24, etc.).[6] This means, above all, that, owing to the identity of essence and existence in the One, any further complexity is excluded. Thus there can be no complexity in essence, for essence is not distinct from existence. What is *not* excluded is the sort of complexity implied in the One's being related variously to composites. For example, the unqualifiedly simple first principle can be the cause of the existence of different things. How this is possible without entailing internal complexity remains to be seen. Further, the simplicity of the One is not to be equated with emptiness or complete abstractness, like a mere conceptual place-holder. It is not lacking anything possessed by any complex; on the contrary, it possesses everything, but not in such a way as to entail complexity (V.3.15.27–31).[7]

From the simplicity of the One Plotinus deduces its self-sufficiency (I.8.2.4–5; II.9.1.9; V.4.1.12–13. See also V.3.13.18; V.6.2.15; V.6.4; VI.7.37.31; VI.8.7.46; VI.8.15.25–6; VI.9.6.16, 24). What is not simple depends upon its components as a condition of its existence. That which is uniquely without components is self-sufficient. That that which is not self-sufficient depends not merely upon its components but ultimately upon the One for its existence comes under the heading of the One's operational attributes. To say that the One is uniquely self-sufficient is as much as to say that it is uniquely necessary being in the strongest sense of "necessary." Although other things may have no beginning and no end to their existence necessarily, they are still dependent on the first principle. Thus, the One is necessary *a se*, whereas other things are necessary *ab alio*.[8] The transcendence of the One should be understood principally as self-sufficiency. And conversely the immanence of everything else in the One is to be identified with their dependence or self-insufficiency.

The One is also perfect (τέλειον) owing to its own essence (οὐσία) (V.6.2.13. See also V.1.6.38). This implies that essence in everything besides the One entails imperfection. An essence is of course not imperfect relative to itself. The imperfection consists in the limitation in existence that the essence entails. To be *this* is to be not *that*. The One has no such limitation. This is why the One does not have an essence in the way that anything else has an essence. Its essence is not really distinct from its existence and so cannot be conceptualized. To speak of the One as having an essence is to speak analogically.[9] The perfection of the One derives from the fact that there is eternally no gap between what the One is and what it can or will be.

The notion of perfection is common currency in Greek philosophy. Perfection is typically relative to kind. Something is perfect to the extent that it achieves or fulfills its nature; it is imperfect in so far as it fails in this regard. The term "perfect" is in one sense inappropriately applied to the One in so far as that implies that it has a nature which is distinct from existence. Plotinus' explanation of the One's perfection as owing to οὐσία shows the natural connection in Greek philosophical vocabulary between the terms τέλειον and οὐσία. We might say that the One is analogically speaking perfect because it is analogically speaking an οὐσία. The meaning is that in the unique first principle, where essence and existence are only conceptually distinct, there can be nothing that this first principle could be that it is not. And perhaps more importantly there is nothing that it can do that it does not, at least in so far as acting is interpreted as directed to a goal not yet achieved.

The feature of eternal achievement in the One's perfection is expressed as power (V.4.1.23–6).[10] The One is the most powerful of all beings precisely because there is no impediment to its being or acting. Supreme power would also follow from self-sufficiency, since an impediment would involve dependence of some sort. Does this mean that the One is unimpeded, say, by the laws of logic? Yes, in its internal activity. The One is "beyond" logic, for it is "beyond οὐσία" wherein the eternal truths of logic are grounded. Such constraints as the One experiences appear as it operates "externally," where οὐσία becomes relevant to determining what and what not the One can do.

The One is evidently eternal. I say "evidently" because Plotinus does not actually say that it is. Nevertheless, he does with sufficient clarity distinguish limited temporality, everlastingness, and eternity and attribute the latter to what is subordinated to the One, namely, the second ἀρχή, Intellect. It is undeniable that the One is eternal, if only because whatever is eternal is for Plotinus superior to what is in time in any way and because that upon which the eternal depends obviously cannot itself be in time (see I.5.7.22–30; II.4.5.26–8). But the attribute of eternality may be deduced for the One indirectly from its perfection. Whatever is in time or measured by time is imperfect just in the sense that there are things it can be that it is not now or is no longer. Even if it does not otherwise change, it cannot perfectly possess whatever it has. This is so because it cannot now have the future possession. Whatever the first principle is, it is eternally in the sense that temporal predicates do not apply to it, even analogously, in so far as these are taken to imply the possession of attributes whose future possession would be an enhancement.

The One is infinite. This means that it is without form of any sort (V.5.6.5 and VI.7.32.9, ἀνείδεον).[11] This attribute is deducible immediately from the fact that the One is the ἀρχή of all form and hence does not share in that of which it is the ἀρχή (V.5.6.1–5, 8–10). Further, what is absolutely incomposite cannot be finite, because anything finite is analyzable into what is limited and the limiting principle. Hence, all and only finite things are not absolutely incomposite.[12] That the limiting principle is form itself follows from the fact that what differentiates one Form from another cannot be the One, but is owing to the Forms themselves.[13] Hence, it follows that what is limited in the composite is the existence possessed by participating in the One.[14] We shall need to return at some length to this extraordinary inversion of the traditional notion of form as perfecting as opposed to limiting.

The One is everywhere or omnipresent (πανταχοῦ) (III.8.9.25; III.9.4.1; V.5.8.24; V.5.9.18–19, 22–3; VI.4.3.18; VI.5.4; VI.8.16.6).[15] What this certainly does not imply is pantheism. Plotinus' preferred way of making this point is to add that the One is nowhere as well (III.9.4.3–9; V.2.1; V.5.12.47–50). Plotinus is here evidently extending the account that Plato gives of participation, for example, in the *Phaedo*. Plato says there that all beautiful things are beautiful by means of beauty and tall things tall by means of tallness (100d7–8, e5–6). He in fact characterizes this type of causality by the words "presence" (παρουσία), the inverse of participation, and "association" (κοινωνία). And yet in the same dialogue Plato tells us that the Forms exist "by themselves" or separately in the sense at least that they are independent of sensibles (79ab).[16] So, it is reasonable to infer that "everywhere" and "nowhere" are analogous to "present" and "separate."

It might be thought that if this is not explaining the obscure by the more obscure, it is at any rate not very illuminating. Perhaps. It is clear enough, however, that just as Plato wants to say that all beautiful things are beautiful because they participate in the eternal Form of Beauty, so Plotinus wants to say that everything participates in the One, which is yet eternal and not really related to anything. Nothing could exist if the One were not somehow present to it.

The entitative attribute of the One perhaps most frequently mentioned by Plotinus is its goodness (see I.3.1.3; I.7.2.2–4; II.9.1.5–6; III.8.11; V.4.1.32–4; V.5.9; V.6.5; V.9.2.23–7; VI.2.11.26–7; VI.5.1.18–20). Clearly, Plotinus thinks that he is following Plato, who, in the *Republic*, posits a Form of the Good "beyond οὐσία."[17] It is equally clear, though, that in a number of respects the One is not equivalent to the Form of the Good in the *Republic*. First, Plato does not explicitly claim that the Form of the Good is the cause in any sense of the demiurge or divine mind. It is explicitly said only to be the cause of the being and knowability of the Forms. Second, Plato does not even analogously attribute "personal" attributes to the Form of the Good as does Plotinus. Third, Plato evinces no reticence or qualification in calling his first principle an Idea even though it is "beyond οὐσία." This is quite unlike the case with the One, as we have seen. Finally, Plato is silent about any causal relation between the Form of the Good and anything else besides Forms. On the contrary, his sketchy remarks suggest that this Form is only indirectly related to what participates in the other, subordinate Forms. I shall argue, however, that the proper effect of the One's activity is the existence of everything else.

One reason why Plotinus blithely conflates the Form of the Good and his own primary ἀρχή is his belief that Plato himself identified the former with the subject of the first hypothesis of the second part of the *Parmenides*, namely, an ineffable "one" having neither essence nor any other predicate (see V.1.8.23–5). The exact interpretation of Plato's meaning in the second part of that desperately difficult dialogue is to put it mildly a matter of considerable dispute. Nevertheless, there is very little to be said for the identification of the subject of the first hypothesis with the Form of the Good. I do not wish thus so cavalierly to dismiss an entire tradition's interpretation of Plato. I wish merely to set it aside, for to say that Plotinus was inclined to identify the Form of the Good and "the one" of the first hypothesis of the second part of the *Parmenides* is ancillary to the analysis of his own arguments for his own principle. Even if Plotinus thought that Plato meant what he himself meant, we cannot go to Plato to find out what Plotinus meant, for this would be circular reasoning on behalf of establishing what Plotinus means.

In any event, Plotinus' One is also the Good or goodness itself. It does not of course have goodness as an attribute. The basic meaning of ἀγαθόν in Plotinus is unexceptional in Greek thought. It refers primarily to whatever is a goal of action and object of desire. Derivatively, it refers to whatever is thought instrumental to such a goal. What is exceptional, given the metaphysical principles and arguments already developed, is the idea that goodness is locatable uniquely in a single (infinite) nature. Since the One is that nature in which all existing things participate, identifying the One with goodness unifies all things in terms of final causality in addition to efficient causality.[18] Even though, in a derivative sense, things possess their own goods, unqualified goodness can only be some sort of condition in which a unique goal is attained. What attainment is supposed to consist in is far from clear.

The last entitative attribute of the One I shall discuss is also perhaps the most obscure and difficult. The One possesses some sort of life, more particularly a cognitive life (see VI.8.16.12–29; V.1.7.12; V.4.2.12–26; VI.7.39.1–2; VI.8.18.26).[19] It even possesses will or βούλησις in some sense, although this is not the result of deliberation (VI.8.13.1–8, 53. See also VI.8.21.1–5). This will is identified with its activity. Of course, these attributes are to be understood with the crucial qualification that their application is not to be taken to imply compositeness in any way. But it is here precisely that one wants to say that compositeness is unequivocally essential to having life or will, in which case such attributes may be merely gratuitous or honorific as applied to the One, but philosophically groundless.

I think it is fair to say that Plotinus would have found intolerable and implausible the hypothesis of a first principle of all which did not manifest intelligence, even analogically. It is perhaps worth noting that, Plotinus' protestations notwithstanding, Plato himself, in positing the Form of the Good, evidently eschewed cognitive attributes in his first principle.[20] Furthermore, in rejecting Aristotle's identification of a first principle with Intellect or with its activity, Plotinus might have been expected to reject "personal" characteristics altogether for the first principle of all.[21] He does not in fact do this unqualifiedly owing to his adherence to a far-reaching principle, namely, that a cause must in some sense "contain" its effects.

Since the primary effect of the One's activity is that everything else exists, the One must contain everything else within it in some way.[22] This containment is just causal dependence. But the One must also be the sort of thing upon which everything can be causally dependent. So, if life of any sort exists owing to the One's causal activity, the One in some sense possesses life. More precisely, it has within itself that in virtue of which life is produced. The possession of whatever it is that produces life legitimates a conceptual distinction of life within the One in some way.

There are many deep problems here. First, if the One is the cause of the existence of all things, it is the cause of the existence of, for example, spatially extended things. But the One is in no sense an extended magnitude. Second, it seems that the principle that the cause must contain its effects does not entail that the cause has the attributes of its effects, even analogically. For example, if organic matter evolved from inorganic matter, in what sense can we say that the inorganic is organic? We might indeed suppose that the One is like the "singularity" of modern-day cosmology, whence arose the galaxies and all that they contain. But it would be nonsense to attribute cognitive attributes to the singularity.

Plotinus' response to such objections begins by pointing out that, unlike the singularity, the One is the cause of the existence of everything else *now*. Furthermore, the fact that the One is the cause of the existence of everything else now does not imply that it is the cause of the essence of everything else. The second ἀρχή, Intellect, will explicitly be given this role. Hence, the One does not have to have magnitude to be the cause of the existence of things with magnitude. But the obvious response to this defense is that Plotinus cannot have it both ways. Either the One is exclusively the cause of existence, in which case it only need have existence in some sense, not life, or else it is the cause also of the essence of everything else, in which case, on the posited principle, it must have not only life but, say, magnitude as well.

What Plotinus obviously needs is a way to distinguish non-arbitrarily among attributes those which the One may and those which it may not possess, all the while holding on to the claim that the One is the cause of the existence of everything regardless of the attributes they possess. He needs to be able to show that neither magnitudes nor life could exist without the activity of the One, but that this fact entails something like the possession of a life in the One without magnitude.

The reasoning leading to the conclusion that the One possesses a sort of cognitive life is Aristotelian and not Platonic. It departs from Aristotle, however, in refusing to identify the first principle of all with Intellect. Aristotle argued that the ἀρχή of all is a final cause and is self-absorbed thinking. The crucial step in Plotinus' alteration of Aristotle's argument is in his insistence that if the good is achieved by thinking, then there is a distinction between the Good in itself and the good that is achieved by thinking.[23] The justification for this step, as we shall see more fully in the next chapter, is that thinking is essentially a complex activity and so is not unqualifiedly self-explanatory. Merely focusing on the fact that thinking is in some sense an achievement indicates the requisite complexity and hence the distinction between the goal and the state or activity in which the goal is achieved.

The next step depends upon recognizing the relation between the dependent and the independent as one of image to model or, as we shall see presently, as one between secondary and primary activity (ἐνέργεια). Strictly speaking, the ἀρχή of life is Intellect. Accordingly, in one sense to attribute life or cognition to the One with the qualification οἷον is to denominate the cause from the effect on the basis of virtuality. The One is virtually whatever it produces just in the sense that it has the power to do so. But evidently Plotinus means more than this in attributing certain forms of cognition to the One.

When in the *Metaphysics* Aristotle identifies primary activity and ultimate object of desire with a cognitive life, he provides no argument for this startling inference (12.7.1072b14ff.).[24] Probably, Aristotle conjectured that the only plausible candidate for perfect activity was Intellect itself. If Plotinus had settled for an unreflective Platonizing response to Aristotle, he might have asserted just that Intellect cannot be the primary ἀρχή of all and that the One must be absolutely without cognitive attributes. But in identifying the One with activity, he is perhaps as much as Aristotle assuming that perfection and cognition go together.

The One neither thinks of itself, as does Aristotle's god, nor thinks of anything else, which would of course be inferior to it. From these denials it follows that the One does not think at all. For Plotinus, however, this conclusion is not to be understood as a denial of a perfection to the One. This is so because thinking implies an imperfection, specifically, non-identity between thinker and object of thinking. Since thinking is goal-directed, and since thinking is a kind of identification between subject and object, even perfect thinking is not unqualified perfection, because a residual duality between subject and object must remain. To move from this conclusion to the further conclusion that the One is beyond cognition altogether requires the premise that all cognition entails the imperfection of thinking. Just as it is wrong to assume that because the One is beyond limited essence it has no essence or does not exist, so it is wrong to assume that because the One is beyond Intellect and Intellect's activity it has no cognition. But this still gives us no positive reason for attributing cognition to the One other than that the term ἐνέργεια is used in such a way as to entail it.

2 The Operational Attributes of the One

The central operational attribute of the One is that it is or has activity, although predictably enough, Plotinus adds that the One is above activity (cf. VI.7.17.10; VI.8.16.16; VI.8.20.15).[25] In order to appreciate this key concept, it is necessary to begin with the reasons for holding that activity is an operational attribute at all, rather than merely an entitative one.

The background to Plotinus' use of the term ἐνέργεια is to be found in Aristotle. Plato does not use the term at all. In the *Metaphysics* Aristotle identifies being in the primary sense with ἐνέργεια, particularly the unimpeded thinking of the divine (12.6.1071b19–20; 7.1072b26–7). Aristotle is led to this conclusion because he has argued that being in the primary sense is separate form, and form is contrasted with matter or potency. Hence, primary being must be unqualifiedly without potency. Plotinus agrees with Aristotle that the first principle of all must be without potency. So much is deducible from the One's perfection. Indeed, if there were no more to the matter than this, then the attribution of ἐνέργεια to the One would add little to its hypothesized perfection.

There is, however, a related distinction in Aristotle. In *De Anima* Aristotle distinguishes implicitly between first and second actuality (ἐντελέχεια) in an organic individual. The soul of an organic individual, its form, is its first actuality (2.1.412a27–8). The operations of the individual are second actualities. The relevance of the distinction to Aristotle's natural philosophy is clear. The form of an organic individual marks it as a member of a biological class. Yet every member of the class manifests the form uniquely. For example, it is owing to the possession of a human soul that individual humans are human, but every individual will possess unique anatomical, physiological, and psychological attributes. When a man is asleep, he engages in distinctively human sleep because sleeping is an actualization of a human life. But sleeping is not essential to being a human. That there be second or secondary actualities follows from the fact that a biological individual is necessarily enmattered. In the case of god, though, there is evidently no distinction between first and second actuality, because in god potency is unqualifiedly absent and the limitation imposed necessarily by our not being able to actualize all our second actualities at once must be excluded. Aristotle makes it abundantly clear that a perfect ἐνέργεια can have nothing to do with anything outside itself. To have activity outside itself would be to allow a wedge between what the first principle is in itself and what it does outside itself. Such a wedge would require that the former be in potency to the latter.

It is sometimes said that Plotinus' One is just Aristotle's god removed into ineffable transcendence to the *n*th degree. This seems to me to be quite mistaken.[26] Plotinus combines the Aristotelian distinction of act and potency with the distinction of first and second actuality in a most remarkable way. He distinguishes between the ἐνέργεια τῆς οὐσίας and the ἐνέργεια ἐκ τῆς οὐσίας (V.4.2.27–33. See also II.9.8.22–5; IV.5.7.15–17, 51–5; V.1.6.34; V.3.7.23–4; V.9.8.13–15; VI.2.22.24–9; VI.7.18.5–6; VI.7.21.4–6; VI.7. 40. 21–4). The first he calls the activity which is the thing itself and the second the activity which comes from the thing. The latter is a necessary consequence of the former, but different from it. For example, the heat in a fire is its first activity and the heat radiating from the fire is the second (V.3.7.23–5. See also IV.5.7.13–15; V.1.3.10).[27] The application of this distinction to the One comes in two passages whose importance cannot be overestimated.

> All things which exist, as long as they remain in being, necessarily produce from their own essences (οὐσίας), in dependence on their present power, a surrounding reality directed to what is outside them, a kind of image of the archetypes from which it was produced: fire produces the heat which comes from it; snow does not only keep its cold inside itself. Perfumed things show this particularly clearly. As long as they exist, something is diffused from themselves around them, and what is near them enjoys their existence (ὑποστάντων). And all things when they come to perfection produce; the One is always perfect and therefore produces everlastingly; and its product is less than itself. (V.1.6.30–9. See also IV.8.6.8–12; V.4.1.27–34; VI.8.18.51–2)[28]

> In each and every thing there is an activity of the essence (ἐνέργεια τῆς οὐσίας) and there is an activity from the essence (ἐνέργεια ἐκ τῆς οὐσίας); and that which is of the essence is each thing itself, while the activity from the essence derives from the first one, and must in everything be a consequence of it, different from the thing itself: as in fire there is a heat which is the content of its essence and another which comes into being from that primary heat when fire exercises the activity which is native (σύμφυτον) to its essence in abiding unchanged as fire. So it is also in the higher world; and much more so there, while it [the One] abides in its own proper way of life, the activity generated from

the perfection in it and its coexistent activity (συνούσης ἐνεργείας) acquires existence (ὑπόστασιν), since it comes from a great power, the greatest indeed of all, and arrives at being (τὸ εἶναι) and essence, for that [the One] is beyond being. That is the productive power (δύναμις) of all, and its product is already all things (τὰ πάντα). (V.4.2.28–39. See also II.6.9.14–24; II.9.8.22–5; IV.5.7.51–5; V.1.6.34; V.3.7.23–5; V.9.8.13–14)

There are a number of features in these passages which will require close attention. Let us begin with the apparent claim that from a primary activity a secondary activity can be deduced, a claim far more puzzling that the opposite. Why should we suppose that this is universally the case? Even presuming that being and primary activity are extensionally equivalent so that everything that exists has such an activity, still it is difficult to see why this should entail that there be a secondary activity. A moment's reflection will allow us to see that Plotinus cannot unqualifiedly maintain both that every thing that exists produces another activity outside it and that the series of producers is finite. But Plotinus does in fact believe that the series of producers is finite. Neither of course is he committed to holding that, say, the smell of the perfume emitted from the perfume's first activity is itself a primary activity with yet another activity emitting from it.[29]

Even more important, however, is Plotinus' apparent assumption that the primary activity of the One has a secondary activity which is outside of or at least distinct from it. By contrast, Aristotle has argued that if perfection is an activity, then it cannot have a further activity outside itself, for this would entail potency in the first activity in relation to the second and hence would contradict the claim that the primary activity is perfect.[30] It must not be thought that Aristotle's claim can be avoided simply by considering not the actuality of an agent and a patient, but rather the actuality of a substance and its accidents. Since an accident is an actualization of a substance, the substance is in potency to it. Indeed, precisely because the One is supposed to be perfect, it has no accidents. So, we need to inquire why Plotinus thinks that perfect activity implies external actualization.

For a concept of external actualization we naturally look back to Plato. There are at least three relevant passages. First, there is the famous text in the *Republic* regarding the Form of the Good which produces knowability, existence and being in the other Forms (509b6–10). And though this text does not clearly distinguish between what the Form of the Good is or does in itself and what it produces outside itself, the analogical representation of it by the sun and the unique attributes it possesses, such as being ἐπέκεινα τῆς οὐσίας, make it reasonable to conclude at least that some such distinction is in harmony with Plato's intention.

The second relevant text is the description of the demiurge in the *Timaeus*. The demiurge is good and so without grudging (φθόνος) (29e. Cf. *Phaedrus*

247a7). He desires that the world should be as much like himself as possible. And so he creates order out of chaos. Notice that in the demiurge benevolent desire cannot be capricious or transitory. He is permanently well-disposed – but here one hesitates – well-disposed to what? Not to a non-existent creation, or to the inchoate heaps of disordered quasi-elements which represent the necessity the demiurge must *overcome*. Reflecting on an answer to this question, it is natural enough for Plotinus and indeed for an entire tradition to surmise that the demiurge or ἀρχή of all or God or the gods are essentially benevolent in the sense that their goodness is always overflowing. They are naturally beneficent. Whether the result of this overflowing goodness is an adjunct to a product or the product itself, the idea that good is diffusive of itself (*bonum est diffusivum sui*) can be traced back to this text.

The last text that should be mentioned is from the *Symposium*, where Diotima declares that the work (ἔργον) of love is birth in beauty (206b). More precisely, all men love to possess the good everlastingly and in their possession of it they produce beauty, particularly, as the passage goes on to say, the beauty that is true virtue (212a). So here, though it is not goodness that is itself diffusive, it is the association with goodness that spontaneously or better, naturally, results in production.

As suggestive as these three texts undoubtedly are, they do not quite amount to the distinction between ἐνέργεια τῆς οὐσίας and ἐνέργεια ἐκ τῆς οὐσίας as this is applied to the One. The Form of the Good works exclusively on the other Forms; these other Forms are, if anything, the causes of the being of their participants. And this would reflect a causal series which, as we shall presently see, is to be rejected as explicative of Plotinus' intentions. The demiurge, which neither in Plato nor Plotinus is equivalent to the Good or One, quite explicitly works on a preexistent chaos, whereas for Plotinus there is no room for an independent ἀρχή "from below." So, the pressing question is not merely why Plotinus endorses the axiom of the diffusiveness of goodness but why he reinterprets this, using or perhaps misusing an Aristotelian concept of ἐνέργεια.[31]

I answer this question as follows. Plotinus rejected the primacy of Intellect as postulated by Aristotle because the activity of Intellect implies complexity and that which is complex cannot be the ἀρχή of all. We shall consider this argument in detail in the next chapter. For now, we need to focus on the claim that the rejection of the primacy of Intellect implies the rejection of the primacy of οὐσία, implicitly identified with Intellect by Aristotle. Since οὐσία represents limitedness or distinctness in nature, the immediate consequence is that the ἀρχή of all is going to be beyond οὐσία and so beyond limit (V.5.6.5, 14–15; V.5.11.2–3; VI.7.32.9).[32] This much could be inferred alone from a reaffirmation of Plato's account of the Form of the Good in opposition to book 12 of the *Metaphysics*. It is Aristotle who identified primary οὐσία with activity; it is Plotinus who reasoned that if the ἀρχή of all is beyond οὐσία, then it is beyond the kind of activity that is οὐσία, not beyond activity *tout court*. As we have seen, that the One is beyond essence does not mean that it is beyond existence or being altogether. Suggestions to the contrary are just misunderstandings of Plotinus' so-called "negative theology." What Plotinus rejects in reference to the One is language that implies limitedness or complexity.

We might suppose that at this point in the reasoning, Plotinus had to ask himself whether or not activity was so tied to οὐσία that to attribute it to the One was wrong. There is a text which clearly indicates his answer:

> Nor should we be afraid to assume that the first activity is without οὐσία, but posit this very fact as his, so to speak, existence (ὑπόστασιν). But if one posited an existence without activity, the principle would be defective and the most perfect of all imperfect. And if one adds activity one does not keep the One. If then the activity is more perfect than the οὐσία and the first is most perfect, the first will be activity. (VI.8.20.9–15)[33]

It is not too difficult to see why this must be so. The reasoning leading to the positing of an ἀρχή of all in the first place is reasoning from effect to cause (see V.3.15.12–13, 28; V.3.17.10–14; VI.4.10; VI.7.23.22–4; VI.8.18.6–7). The first cause is not an essential cause. The ἀρχή of that which possesses essence is οὐσία itself. And οὐσία does not explain the datum that the One is needed to explain. The only kind of cause that the absolutely first cause can be is an efficient cause. Thus, for the One to be the ἀρχή of all it cannot be deprived of activity. To deny activity to it would be to deny it causal efficacy. Being an efficient cause means *acting* as an efficient cause.

Arguing in this way, we reach a primary activity. The primary activity is identified with an efficient cause, counter to Aristotle.[34] But the crucial question remains, what is the One the cause of? What is the proper effect of its causal activity? This question brings us face to face with the rather vague notion of emanation as an interpretation of Neo-Platonic metaphysics generally, and Plotinus' metaphysics in particular.

There are several texts in the *Enneads* which employ noun and verb forms of "flow" (ῥέω) to describe the activity of the One in relation to complex entities. For example,

> For the soul now knows that these things must be, but longs to answer the question repeatedly discussed also by the ancient philosophers, how from the One, if it is such as we say it is, anything else, whether a multiplicity or a dyad or a number, came into existence, and why it did not on the contrary remain by itself, but such a great multiplicity flowed (ἐξερρύη) from it as that which is seen to exist in beings, but which we think it right to refer back to the One. (V.1.6.2–8)

This, we may say, is the first act of generation: the One, perfect because it seeks nothing, has nothing, and needs nothing, overflows (ὑπερερρύη), as it were, and its superabundance makes something other than itself. (V.2.1.7–9)

The first remark I wish to make about these passages is the obvious one that to think of emanating or flowing in contrast to creating is to make a sort of category mistake. I am not here suggesting that the metaphor of emanating in Plotinus is to be dismissed as unimportant. Nevertheless, metaphors are not properly contrasted with technical terminology.[35] If one wants convincing on this point, we need only recall that Thomas Aquinas sometimes uses the same metaphor on behalf of an explanation of creation, not in contrast to it.[36] Conceding this, there is still the reasonable suspicion that *some* fundamental difference remains between Plotinus' metaphysics and a creation metaphysics such as that of Aquinas. Perhaps the reason for this suspicion is that Plotinus is supposed to be the faithful inheritor of the Parmenidean legacy which lays down the axiom that *ex nihilo nihil fit*. Aquinas, however, understands creation as *ex nihilo*. So it would seem just incorrect to construe the metaphors of emanation in a manner which would make Plotinus contradict that axiom.

This reasoning seems less cogent when we begin to explicate the term *ex nihilo*. One thing that *creatio ex nihilo* does not imply in Aquinas is temporal origin. That God is the creator of all Aquinas believes he can demonstrate; that the world did not always exist is held by faith alone (*Summa Theologiae* I. q.46. a.2, respondeo). Thus, the philosophical core of the notion of creation is causal dependence of being: *Deus est causa universalis totius esse*. The proper effect of God's causal activity is the being of everything.[37] Let us compare this with a text of Plotinus:

But how is that One the principle of all things? Is it because as principle it keeps them in being, making each one of them to be (εἶναι)? Yes, and because it caused them to be (ὑπέστησεν αὐτά). (V.3.15.27–9; see also II.4.5.25–6; III.8.10.1–2; IV.8.6.1–6; V.3.17.10–14; V.5.5.5–7; VI.7.42.11; VI.9.1.1–2)[38]

A good question for proponents of emanationism in Plotinus to ask themselves at this point is how this passage and similar ones express a non-creationist metaphysics.[39]

I suspect that the attraction of emanationism as an interpretation of Plotinus' metaphysics derives in part from supposing that this is the best way to explain the derivation of multiplicity from unity or complexity from simplicity. In order to remove this attraction, we need only recall that the ἀρχή of all is known *only* by its effects, which are all cases of complexity. Accordingly, there could be no derivation of multiplicity from unity in the sense of a strict demonstration. If there could be such, then we could know something about the One independently of its effects as the basis for the demonstration.[40]

One proposal sometimes made in order to differentiate a non-creationist from a creationist metaphysics is that in the former creatures exist of necessity whereas in the latter they do not. Indeed, Plotinus does say that what exists does so necessarily and not as a result of the discursive reasoning (λογισμός) of the ἀρχή of all (see III.2.3.1–5; IV.3.13.17–20; IV.3.18.1–13; IV.4.10.6–29; VI.2.21.33–4; VI.7.1.28–9; VI.8.14.30–1; VI.8.17.4).[41] By contrast, Aquinas says in many places that *Deus produxit creaturas, non ex necessitate, sed per intellectum et voluntatem* (see *Summa Theologiae* I. q.19.a.4; q.25.a.5; q.28.a.1, ad. 3; etc.). But of course Aquinas also says that God's knowledge is not discursive, and one of the reasons for this is that discursive knowing implies imperfection (*Summa Contra Gentiles* I.57, amplius). Plotinus too says that the One is perfect and that it acts according to its will (βούλησις) (VI.8.13.7–8, 52–3). So, whereas Aquinas contrasts the alternatives of acting by necessity and acting by will (and intellect), Plotinus contrasts acting by necessity and acting on the basis of discursive reasoning. This should lead us to conclude that the "necessity" as attributed to creation by Plotinus and "necessity" as denied of God's acting by Aquinas do not mean the same thing.[42]

In fact, there are at least two reasons why the necessary existence of things does not entail that the One acts by necessity. First, the term "necessity" (ἀνάγκη) in Plotinus implies constraint from outside. But there is nothing outside the One and it is constrained by nothing. Second, the putative necessity by which the One acts cannot be really distinct from the One or indeed from its will, for this would negate its simplicity. So, to say that the One acts by necessity could mean nothing else but that it acts according to its will. Another albeit esoteric facet of this second reason is that if the One acted by a necessity really distinct from it, then this would set up, counter to Plotinus' express argument, a real relation between the One and what it produces.[43] This would be so because if there is something really distinct from the One, then the One is limited in relation to it. And what prevents the One from being really related to anything is that it is unqualifiedly unlimited. So, it seems that if "necessity" is understood as constraint *ab extra*, then the One does not act of necessity. Since Aquinas' God does not act by this kind of necessity either, we can hardly use it to contrast Plotinus' metaphysics with Thomistic creation metaphysics.

It is sometimes supposed that what distinguishes an emanationist metaphysics is an account of production by the first principle whereby this principle is emptied of all that is in it.[44] Alternatively, one may think of Russian dolls or a telescoped antenna where what is somehow contained within the whole is separated out from it. There are certainly many texts in which Plotinus says that everything is contained within the One (see V.5.9; VI.4.2; VI.5.1.25–6). But none of these texts, or indeed no other that I know of, claims that anything is ever "outside" the One or separated off from it.[45] Thus, the relation between the One and everything else cannot be construed according to the above metaphors, where what is suggested is a two-phase process: first, everything is in the One, and second, everything is *not* in the One, but emptied out of or unfolded from it (III.8.8.46; III.8.10.6–7; V.1.3.9–12; V.5.5.1f.; VI.5.3.5; VI.9.5.37; VI.9.9.3).[46] Furthermore, a metaphor like that of the Russian dolls ignores a crucial disanalogy in the cases of containment. That is, though it is true that body is contained in Soul, Soul is contained in Intellect, and Intellect is contained in the One, the mode of containment is different in each case. The mode of containment is determined by the sense in which each "container" is an ἀρχή.

A somewhat more serious and complex suggestion for characterizing an emanationist metaphysics is to construe its account of causal dependence according to the model of a *per accidens* series. In a *per accidens* causal series as opposed to a *per se* causal series, A is the cause of B, B is the cause of C, and so on. In a *per se* causal series, A would be the cause of C and B would be an instrument of A's causal activity. For example, the tree of Jesse is a *per accidens* causal series: Jesse begat David, who begat Solomon, and so on. A man causing a traffic accident with his car is an example of a *per se* causally ordered series. The popular claim that "people kill people, not guns" is an attempt to make a political point by expressing a social problem in terms of a *per se* as opposed to a *per accidens* series. Applying this distinction to Plotinus' claims about the causal activity of the One, we might interpret him to mean that the causality is according to a *per accidens* ordered series. Thus, the One would cause Intellect to be, Intellect would cause Soul to be, and Soul would presumably cause nature to be (see especially V.1.6.41–6; V.3.12.39ff.; V.4.1.1–5).[47]

We need to distinguish two different questions here. The first question is whether Plotinus' account of metaphysical causality is *per accidens* or *per se*, assuming that these alternatives are exhaustive. The second question is whether the selected alternative does indeed distinguish an emanationist from a creationist metaphysics. Regarding this question, Aquinas is at least clear that God's creative activity does not operate instrumentally.[48] So, were we to opt for a *per accidens* causal series, we should not therefore conclude that a *per se* ordered series is a differentia of a creation metaphysics. Let us turn now to the evidence pertaining to an answer to the first question.

The main text supporting the interpretation of metaphysical causality as a *per accidens* ordered series is a continuation of the text cited above in which the term "emanating" appears:

> This [Intellect], when it has come into being, turns back upon the One and is filled, and becomes Intellect by looking towards it. Its halt and turning towards the One constitutes being, its gaze upon the One, Intellect. Since it halts and turns towards the One that it may see, it becomes at once Intellect and being. Resembling the One thus, Intellect produces likenesses (τὰ ὅμοια ποιεῖ), pouring forth a multiple power –

29

this is an image (εἶδος) of it – just as that which was before it poured it forth. This activity springing from the essence of Intellect is Soul, which comes to be this while Intellect abides unchanged: for Intellect too comes into being while that which is before it abides unchanged. But Soul does not abide unchanged when it produces: it is moved and so brings forth an image. (V.2.1.9–19. See also IV.8.6; VI.7.42.17–20)

If we employ the concept of a *per accidens* ordered causal series to interpret this passage, the causal activity of the One is then taken to be limited to the production of Intellect. We could still say that without this first production nothing else would be produced, but the existence of the One would no longer be a necessary condition for the production of Soul any more than the existence of the grandfather is a necessary condition for the production of the grandson at the time of production. Even if we insist that the One exists necessarily, this existence is irrelevant to the causality of the existence of Soul, which, in the putative *per accidens* series, is attributed solely to Intellect.

The obvious impediments to the endorsement of this interpretation are the many texts where Plotinus says that the One preserves all things in existence. It might be thought that the interpretation can be retained if this preservation is construed as a counterfactual.[49] Thus, that the One preserves everything in existence would mean that if *per impossibile* the One were to cease existing, then everything else would cease existing as well. We can imagine if we like an Atlas holding the earth aloft, an Atlas who is no part of earthly production, but who could not simply disappear without his burden crashing down. Or we could imagine the counterfactual where the first member of a *per accidens* causal series did not exist. The problem with this construal is that it imports an unacceptable self-limitation into the One's activity. It makes the One's direct causal role stop with the production of Intellect. It defines the One's activity as "Intellect-production," thereby implying a limitation in it which is completely unsupported by the texts.

There is another argument against construing the One's causality according to a *per accidens* series. The ἀρχή Intellect is the ultimate explanation or cause of whatever has thinking, life, and essence (see VI.7.13.28–42).[50] It is sufficient at this point to note that it is obviously not the ἀρχή of that which it receives from the One, the ἀρχή above it. Now if the One is the ἀρχή of the existence of Intellect, then in no case is Intellect the ἀρχή of the existence of anything else. If Soul, for example, receives not only life, thinking, and οὐσία from Intellect but existence as well, then Intellect performs for Soul the identical function that the One performs for Intellect. And then the uniqueness of the ἀρχή of existence, to say nothing of its primacy, would be destroyed. I take it that any interpretation that leads to this result is to be firmly rejected.

Is not the interpretation I have rejected, however, supported by the text I have just quoted? The critical phrase is "produces likenesses" (τὰ ὅμοια ποιεῖ), referring to Intellect. On the basis of the other texts I have adduced and the above arguments I think it is a mistake to understand the Greek phrase adverbially, as if it meant "produces in the same manner." This is the way Armstrong understands the phrase in his English translation. Rather, as the next line indicates, Intellect is similar to the One in that it is a producer; it produces images of itself. But the way in which the images of Intellect are images must be different from the way that Intellect itself is an image of the One. This is so simply because the One is not a Form. The images of Intellect stand to Intellect *analogously* to the way the images of the One stand to it. And this analogy does not in itself warrant an inference to a *per accidens* series.

If it is possible for there to be two different causes of existence, then the two must at least be numerically distinct. If they are so, there must be something in each making them different from each other. Whatever this is must be really distinct from its existence. So the two putative causes of existence must be composites – composites which exist. For each of these to be the cause of the existence of something else, they must be efficient causes, that is, they must have their actuality outside themselves. But something cannot give the actuality of existence to something else that it does not possess. The only actual existence that the putative cause possesses is its own. It could not be the cause of the existence of something else except by giving up its own existence to this something else, like a moth and a caterpillar. It cannot give what it does not have. But if it gave up its existence for the existence of its effect, it would not exist when the effect existed, or else it would just be the effect. But it is the existence of the effect that needs to be explained, and on this hypothesis it would seem that the search for such an efficient cause as described would be hopeless, for it could not exist. Hence, only that which is simple in the way the One is simple could be the cause of the existence of everything.[51] And the One is unique.

The falsity of emanationism understood as *per accidens* causality does not gainsay hierarchy or gradation in the causal series.[52] If the One is the cause of the existence of everything else, still things are in some sense closer or farther from their ultimate source or ἀρχή.[53] Participation is the converse of the activity which has been falsely identified as emanation. However, an additional principle will be required to account for diversity and gradations among the products of the One.

If, owing to these objections against an interpretation of the metaphysical causality in Plotinus in terms of a *per accidens* series, we opt for a *per se* ordered series, then the One is the sole cause of the existence of everything else and the role of the other principles is at most instrumental. Actually, we need to express this more precisely. The One is the primary cause of the existence of everything else there is, and Intellect is the instrumental cause of the being of everything else, where "being" roughly means existence plus essence.[54] Accordingly, Intellect is the primary cause of the essence of everything else. As we shall see, the third ἀρχή, Soul, will function instrumentally for Intellect, analogously to the instrumental function of Intellect for the One.[55] Furthermore, though this is a mere corollary and not of central importance, Soul will function as a secondary instrument of the special causal activity of the One.

If instrumental causality is repugnant to creation, then Plotinus' metaphysics is not creationist. To call it emanationist, however, if this is understood at least to include the notion of a *per accidens* causal series, is incorrect. If my interpretation is sound, Plotinus has taken up a subtle middle position. The One is indeed the sole and direct cause of the existence of every complex entity. It is even the cause of its own existence (VI.8.14.41: αἴτιον ἑαυτοῦ. See also VI.8.7.53–4; VI.8.16.29).[56] But in everything beside the One, existence is really distinct from essence. The One does not give essence to anything, including Intellect, the locus of eternal essence, for essence as such needs no cause outside itself, just as the One needs no cause outside itself. Whatever has essence has it from Intellect which is identical with οὐσία, analogously to the way everything that has existence has it from the One. Intellect does not have essence predicatively, but identitatively. But the existence of essence and of everything participating in essence is owing to the One.

Where a creation metaphysics such as that of Aquinas differs from Plotinian metaphysics is in its claim that the ἀρχή of all is the sole cause not of the existence but of the being of everything else, hence, of existence *and* essence. Accordingly, Aquinas must say that God is not just virtually all things but eminently all things as well. That is, every predicate that belongs to complexes belongs to their simple cause in a higher mode of being.[57] In short, οὐσία cannot be a real ἀρχή for him. Were it so, this would compromise the omnipotence of God. By contrast, Plotinus is less concerned with preserving omnipotence than he is with preserving the unqualified simplicity of the first ἀρχή. One way to express the differences between the two in the matter of omnipotence is to say that although they agree that the ἀρχή of all cannot do what is logically impossible, Plotinus would say that the structure of logical possibility is grounded in the second ἀρχή, Intellect, whereas Aquinas will want to say that logical possibility and impossibility are ultimately to be accounted for by the first principle, God.

Further, by refusing to accept that virtuality in being entails eminence in being, Plotinus' negative theology constrains itself in a way that Aquinas' negative theology does not. Plotinus cannot just infer that the One is eminently whatever its effects are in an inferior way. To do so would compromise the simplicity of the One. Aquinas, however, arguing that *esse* is an actualization of essence and that God is *ipsum esse*, is free to pursue the *via eminentiae*. Plotinus must limit himself to deducing the attributes of the perfectly simple, for example, eternality, and the first cause, for example, activity.

As we have seen, however, Plotinus does actually say that the One has all Forms in it indistinctly (μὴ διακεκριμένα) (V.3.15.31. See also V.2.1.1; V.4.2.17; VI.7.32.14; VI.8.21.24–5). In fact, the reason given for the One's having the ability to give existence to everything is just that it has everything in it "beforehand." This would seem to suggest eminence. But this claim must be balanced by another sort, according to which "there is no necessity for something to have what it gives" and "the form is in that which is shaped [Intellect], but the shaper was shapeless" (VI.7.17.3–4, 17–18).

If the indistinctness of the Forms in the One were intended to represent a state prior to a temporal creation, then Plotinus would, I think, have to say that the One is eminently as well as virtually all the Forms, in which case his position would not be substantially different from that of Aquinas. But since Intellect is eternally caused to be by the One, its having the Forms "indistinctly" should not be understood in this way.[58] Rather, as Plotinus tells us, to say that the One is none of the Forms means that they are later (ὕστερα) than it, but to say that the One is all of them means that they come from it (ἐξ αὐτοῦ) (VI.7.32.13–14. See also V.5.12.41). There is of course no temporal implication in the use of "later." The Forms are later in the sense that they are an effect of which the One is the cause, though *what* they are is uncaused.[59] The phrase "come from it" is difficult, but as was argued above, it cannot indicate a process of emptying where the result is that something is *outside* the One, for there is no such thing. If I may anticipate once again the discussion to follow in the next chapter, the phrase "come from it" indicates the result of Intellect's contemplation of the One under the aspect of the Good. That is, Intellect achieves its good by contemplating all the Forms.[60] So, the indistinct existence of Forms in the One does not indicate another mode of being for Forms, much less a superior mode of being.[61] It indicates that the eternal achievement of goodness for Intellect requires that it go beyond itself to the Good itself, but that this amounts to identification with all the Forms in contemplating.[62]

An objection may occur to some. Does not the instrumental activity of Intellect place some constraint or limitation on the One, counter to its purported unlimitedness as explained above? This is an important objection, one which strikes a vital nerve. It is precisely owing to a suspected denial of omnipotence in Christian creation metaphysics born of the Plotinian tradition that Aquinas refuses to join instrumentality with creation. I think that the correct answer to this objection is an admission that it does place a constraint upon the One, but also a denial that it is the sort of constraint that Plotinus means to deny in saying that it is unlimited.

In endowing things with existence, the One is unlimited. It does not run out of power or goodness. There is nothing that could exist that does not or will not at some time.[63] Yet *what* could exist is not the One's business. That birds and bees can and do exist, that griffins could exist, but do not now, and that square circles cannot exist is attributable to facts about essence, to put it crudely. When the One produces existents, it uses the template of essence. Its causal power is a pure stream, flowing out and over whatever it is that can receive it according to its own nature.

One important reason for the difficulty in grasping the meaning of the doctrine of two activities is that within the Aristotelian framework, the actualization of one thing in another implies a relation between agent and patient. Plotinus, however, cannot express the One's activity as resting on a relation between two things, because the One is not a thing at all. It is not possessed of the compositeness that thinghood requires. So, it cannot be a term of a relation among or between things. This would seem to follow directly from its necessary uniqueness. To have a real relation to something it is necessary to be sufficiently complex to be distinct from that in virtue of which there is a relation. To stand in a relation to something requires being *something*, which the One is not. Nevertheless, this does not prevent things from being related to the One. They can be related to it because they are sufficiently complex to possess relational properties, for example, being dependent.[64] Or things can be graded according to their degree of unity and so closer to or farther away from the One. But the One is not thereby closer to or farther away from complexes.

Since the One is related to nothing, its secondary activity does not result in a relation being erected between the One and its products. Its activity is not in another, because this would imply exactly such a relation. Its second activity *is* the existence of other things. As Plotinus puts it, "to say that it [the One] is the cause is not to predicate something accidental to it but of us, because we have something from it while that One is in itself" (VI.9.3.49–51).

It might be thought that an impediment to my interpretation of the doctrine of two activities is that of overlap.[65] The ἐνέργεια ἐκ τῆς οὐσίας of Intellect is seemingly identical with that of the One, but for one member, Intellect itself. Thus, Soul is the ἐνέργεια ἐκ τῆς οὐσίας of both the One and Intellect. This would seem to make practically identical the ἐνέργεια ἐκ τῆς οὐσίας of Intellect and that of the One. But the difference that results from the fact that one series has *n* members and the other series has those same members except for Intellect is enormous, for the One and Intellect are each an ἀρχή of what is "below" Intellect in different ways: Intellect is the ἀρχή of essence and the One is the ἀρχή of the existence of whatever has essence.

The reason the ἐνέργεια ἐκ τῆς οὐσίας of the One is an *ordered* series is that for there to be things with essence, a necessary condition is that there be that which is paradigmatically or primarily essence, and that is Intellect itself.[66] If the One's products were not hierarchically ordered, then the One itself would have to be not just the ἀρχή of the existence of everything else, but the ἀρχή of the essence of everything else as well. It would have no instrument for producing the "whatness" of existents. But then the simplicity of the One would be compromised, for the One would have to be eminently as well as virtually everything it produces. Everything that the One produces

34

except Intellect it produces with the instrumentality of Intellect. And in a way, Intellect is the instrument of its own production, for it is *what* it is owing to itself.[67] That the ἀρχή of existence cannot be identical with the ἀρχή of essence is the central feature of a metaphysics aptly termed "subordinationist" or "instrumentalist."

It is now time to compensate for the exclusive emphasis I have placed on the activity of the One. It is no doubt disconcerting to hear for the first time that Plotinus balances his assertions of the activity of the One with the remarkable claim that the One is also the power (δύναμις) of all things (V.3.15.33. See also III.8.10.1; V.1.7.9–10; V.3.16.2; V.4.1.24–5, 36; V.4.2.38; V.5.12.38–9; VI.7.32.31; VI.7.40.13–14; VI.8.9.45; VI.9.5.36–7). A plausible initial response to Plotinus' claim is to recall Plato's description of the Form of the Good in the *Republic* as "transcending οὐσία by exceeding it in seniority and power" (δυναμέι) (509b9–10). Obviously, the correct translation of δύναμις in this passage is "power."[68] But surely there is more to the matter than this if only because the meaning of the phrase "power of all things" is anything but perspicuous. Even more importantly, Plato never calls the Form of the Good activity, not surprisingly, since the distinction between activity and power is Aristotle's own.

When Plotinus himself refers to the One as activity, he is employing Aristotle's terminology. Furthermore, Plotinus rejects Aristotle's claim that Intellect is primary activity precisely because Intellect cannot be unqualifiedly actual. By contrast, the first principle of all must be absolutely perfect, without potency in any sense. Hence, to interpret Plotinus' phrase "δύναμις of all" as indicating merely unlimited power in the One is much more difficult from within the Aristotelian framework. Unless "power" is, against all plausibility, simply taken as a synonym for "activity," then it is hard to see how some potency is not insinuated into the One by referring to it as "δύναμις of all."

Plotinus certainly emphasizes the idea of supreme power in his characterizations of the One. What precisely is this power supposed to be? How is power to be analyzed? First, as the text in V.3.15.33–6 indicates, Plotinus takes over Aristotle's distinction between a passive and an active power, identifying the latter with the One (see *Metaphysics* 9.1.1046a19ff.).[69] Second, the power of the One is indicated by its result, namely, the existence of everything that can exist. But since the existence of everything that exists is not identical with the One, the One's power is evidently that in virtue of which everything else exists. But this power is in no way really distinguishable from anything else in the One, else its perfect simplicity would be destroyed. The One is virtually everything else, including Intellect.[70] Since, however, the One does not confer existence on a waiting recipient (since the recipient would then *already* exist), the power of the One is not the power to bring about a substantial change like generation. It is something even more radical than this. It is the power to cause to exist everything that can exist, including eternal Intellect and Forms.[71] Without the causal power of the One even eternal truths would not exist.

If we interpret the power of the One in the way I have suggested, we are better placed to understand why Plotinus insists that the One contains all things. That this is not Stoic or Spinozistic monism is evident merely from the need to argue for the uniqueness of the One. If the One were identical with everything, it would just be a logical truth that the One is unique.[72] That everything is contained within the One seems to mean two things. First, it means that the One is virtually everything, in the technical sense of "virtually" I have employed. Thus, everything is dependent on the One for existence and so the One has the power to make everything exist. Second, it means that understanding what anything is or does must include a reference to the Good at which it aims (V.5.9.36–8). Relation to the first principle of all must be included in an account of its products.

That Plotinus believes that the One is not a whole of parts is evident alone from his allusion to Plato's *Parmenides* and his comparison of the One with the Forms there which, at least according to Plotinus' interpretation, are not wholes which are divided up into parts constituting the Forms' instances (V.5.9.24–8. See also III.8.9.44–54). In general, Plotinus frequently has recourse to the Platonic vocabulary of participation.[73] But it must be stressed that the relation of everything to the One is only analogous to the relation of instances of Forms to the Forms themselves *within Plotinus' own system*. The analogy is not a straightforward proportionality a:b::c:d because the relation, or whatever we might call it, of participation is only properly present between Form and instance, and not between the One and *its* participants.

A simple way of stating the difference is to point out that no participant in the One is an instance of it. Anything that is one, that is to say, anything at all, is an instance of the Form of Unity. Instances of this Form are not instances of the One because the uniqueness of the One prevents it from endowing anything with its nature. Whatever exists does so by having its nature perfected or actualized or brought into existence. Furthermore, "exists" is not univocally predicable of whatever exists in the way that a Form's nature is univocally predicable of its instances. Finally, the Forms are not, as the One is, efficient causes of their images or participants. Still, the analogy does indicate that the existence of the One's products is causally derivative. This derivation implies neither emanationism nor monism.

The uniqueness of the One coupled with the denial of monism would seem also to eliminate pantheism as a description of Plotinus' system. Pantheism *would* follow from the premises that the One is everywhere and that there exists a plurality of really distinct entities, if the ubiquity of the One were taken literally.[74] But the presence of the One is not the presence of the cause; it is the presence of the effects of the cause. Whatever exists has as an addition to its nature what the One is by nature. But it does not have it as an individual or species possesses a generic nature, for the One is not that. It possesses the One according to its own nature, and this is always as what is really distinct from it. So, the One is as intimately present to something as its own existence, but this presence is an effect of the One's activity, not the One itself.

The second most important of the One's operational attributes is will or rational desire (βούλησις). Since the One has a life and is engaged in activity, it seems perfectly natural to Plotinus to raise the question of whether or not the One has a will and whether it exercises it freely. In fact, he devotes one entire lengthy treatise, VI.8, to this question. The way he sets up the problem is most instructive. Previous argument has established that the One is omnipotent (πάντα δύνασθαι). "Omnipotence" here means, I believe, that the One has the power to endow with existence every possibility. It is able to cause the existence of whatever can exist. This still leaves the question of whether what the One does is in its power (ἐφ' αὐτῷ), a question which is particularly pointed if the One never withholds its production.

In order to answer *this* question Plotinus embarks on a lengthy discussion of the psychology of human action drawn largely from the third book of Aristotle's *Nicomachean Ethics* (VI.8.1–6). The legitimacy of applying to the One the conclusions about human psychology is entirely analogical. Following Aristotle, Plotinus argues that the term "voluntary" (ἑκούσιον) refers to human actions which are not done through violence from outside the person and which are done consciously or knowingly. The phrase "within our power" (ἐφ' ἡμῖν) refers primarily to voluntary actions which we have the capacity for performing (VI.8.1.34). Although the definitions of "voluntary" and "within our power" are different, they generally refer to the same actions. Exceptions would be actions which we would not perform if we were not ignorant of the correct description of the action. Such actions would be within our power but not voluntary. Actions voluntary and within our power are to be explained by the will (VI.8.3.2–3). The will in turn is referred to reasoning or λόγος and more particularly to right reasoning or ὀρθός λόγος. Will is something like the state of an agent immediately following successful deliberation regarding the means to achieving an end. Unlike the One, human action is born of desire. Will seems to be a specification of desire. But deliberation and desire originate in beings which lack something. The One lacks nothing. So what need has it for deliberation, and how can it have a resultant will?

Plotinus identifies the will of the One with its "essence" and activity (see VI.8.13.1–8, 53; VI.8.16.38–9; VI.8.21.12–15). Elsewhere, Plotinus insists that will in the One is not the result of its desire for any good since it is the source of goodness for everything else (V.5.9.36; VI.9.6.41). Nor does the One deliberate (see III.2.1 and V.8.7). Positively, attributing will to the One means that it is the paradigm of action. There is a perfect "fit" or better, coincidence, between what the One does and what it wants to do. We must distinguish what the One wants to do from desire which occasions deliberation. Its "wanting" is perfectly and immediately identified with its activity. This same point can be more easily understood if we express it negatively. Neither is the One constrained in its activity from outside itself nor is there any hesitation or error as typically results in us when desire, deliberation, or will are corrupted. If will were not identical with "essence" in the One, then the former would be constrained by the latter.[75] By implication, wherever essence is in composition with another principle, that is, everywhere but in the One, essence is a principle of limitation.

Since the One, lacking nothing, desires nothing, its activity, which is in perfect conformity to its will, is not to be understood in terms of its own good. The One is goodness itself and its activity the paradigm of goodness. Following Plato, Plotinus wants to make a metaphysical connection between the desire for good wherever it occurs and an activity which goes out from the agent. The connection is precisely that the desire for good, when successfully fulfilled, produces goodness.

From the point of view of all of the effects of the One's activity, the will of the One is the explanation for the existence of anything at all. The answer to the question, "why does so and so exist?" is always, finally, that the One willed it to be so. In claiming this, however, no real distinction is implied in reference to the One. Its will is really the same as its simple, perfect activity conceived of in one aspect.

Plotinus sees no conflict in saying both that will in the One is limited in no way and that the One cannot do otherwise than it does (see VI.8.13.24–40; VI.8.15.18–26; VI.8.18.38–41; VI.8.20.17–19, 28–39; VI.8.21.1–19, 30–3).[76] What this means is that perfect activity has by definition no defect and "doing otherwise" for the One would mean doing something imperfect. But it also means that the One does not refrain from doing anything, where refraining would not necessarily be a defect but simply indicate an unselected possibility. If the One refrained from acting either because of impotence or grudging, defects would be indicated in it. The One is perfectly free in its operation because it is identical with goodness (VI.8.13.38).[77] As we shall see in chapter 7, the freedom of the One thus becomes the paradigm according to which degrees of human freedom are to be judged.

Traditionally, one of the principal operational attributes of the divine or primary ἀρχή of the universe is providence (πρόνοια). Plotinus harshly criticizes Epicurus' eccentricity in this respect (II.9.15.8–17). Providence, among those who recognized the applicability of the concept, is essentially beneficent management. But Plotinus also recognizes that providence as traditionally conceived is in tension with the claim that the universe is everlasting and that its maker is eternal. As he puts it:

> If, then, we said that after a certain time the universe, which did not previously exist, came into being, we should in our discussion lay down that providence in the All was the same as we said it was in partial

38

things, a foreseeing (προόρασίν) and calculation (λογισμὸν) of god about how this All might come into existence, and how things might be as good as possible. But since we affirm that this universe is everlasting and has never not existed, we should be correct and consistent in saying that providence for the All is its being according to Intellect, and that Intellect is before it, not in the sense that it is prior in time but because the universe comes from Intellect and Intellect is prior in nature, and the cause of the universe as a kind of archetype and model, the universe being an image of it and existing by means of it and everlastingly coming into existence, in this way. (III.2.1.15–16)

Plotinus interprets universal προ-νοῦν as κατὰ νοῦν, given the fact that there was no time before which the universe existed. Providence is the functioning of the world according to the truths contained within Intellect. Indeed, Plotinus elsewhere identifies providence as a relation between "the higher and the lower" (III.3.7.8).[78] But this leaves the embarrassment that since the primary ἀρχή of all is related to nothing outside itself, providence stops at the second ἀρχή. If what is beyond the level of providence is without providence for what is below, then the very wellspring of reality may be a creator, but it can hardly be said to be a beneficent manager.

The way Plotinus deals with this problem is remarkable. First, he makes the claim that "it is enough for providence that he exists from whom all things come" (VI.7.39.26–7. See also VI.7.37.29–31). The existence of the One guarantees providence evidently because providence is a property of dependent existence. Second, while affirming that all things happen as the One wishes (οἷον θέλει), he insists that it is not related to anything outside it, but rather is entirely related to itself alone (VI.8.17.14–25, 26–7). This seems to mean that the effect of the divine will is present in all existents without this producing a real relation between the One and everything else.

Viewed from the perspective of composite being, whatever happens in the world happens as the first principle wills it to happen. And since this first principle is goodness itself, whatever it wills is good. Hence, benevolent management is preserved.[79] Providence is identified with the second activity of the One. But whatever happens is not to be identified as the actualization by an efficient cause outside itself, for then a real relation between agent and patient would be erected. Yet in so far as events exemplify, say, laws of nature, there must be *some* relation obtaining between these events and their eternal foundation.[80] This is presumably why Plotinus distinguishes πρόνοια proper and that which is in charge of providence (τὸν τῆς προνοίας κύριον), where the former refers to Intellect and the latter to the One (II.9.15.11–12).[81] The first principle has an authoritative position because the explanations for the happenings in the world that derive from Intellect are themselves always in principle susceptible to another explanation which is just that that was the way the One willed it to be.[82]

The operation of divine providence is held by Plotinus to be reconcilable with freedom and hence with evil and to be distinguishable from fate (εἰμαρμένη). The former question will occupy us in due course. Regarding fate, Plotinus seems to identify it with necessity, particularly as this is understood by Plato in the *Timaeus* (see III.1.3.8; III.1.4.4–5; III.3.5.14–16).[83] "Necessity" has a general technical meaning for both Plato and Plotinus, referring to whatever happens outside the control of νοῦς or intellect. Whatever it is that does so operate has in some sense a nature, according to which what it does and what can happen to it are necessary. How within the creationist metaphysical framework produced by Plotinus there can be such things is a very difficult question.

If the One is provident, must it be omniscient? The appropriate Plotinian reply seems to be to say that it is in a way (οἶον) omniscient. The literal locus of omniscience is Intellect. What the One must know in a manner of speaking, however, is that it is the goal of everything that exists and that everything that could exist does exist, for it knows itself as activity that is boundless. That everything happens as the One wills it follows from the One's infinite power. But does this entail that everything happens *because* the One willed it to be so? The One certainly does not will the "daring" of souls which initiates their downward descent. Nor does it will the evil that exists in the world, since its will is by definition oriented exclusively to the Good, with which it is identified. Yet if the One has infinite power and is omnibenevolent, then how can anything happen counter to its will?

I think that there is little doubt that on the basis of what has already been said about the One's creative activity and nature, its providence, omniscience, and power must be qualified.[84] Since the One creates instrumentally, limitations or defects in what is created can always be ascribed to the instruments, rather than to the One.[85] That everything happens as the One wills it then means that there exist things (both eternally and in time) which are *what* they are owing not to the One but to Intellect. That the things that exist owing to the activity of the One operate according to their natures is owing to Intellect, not the One. If what results from the instrumentality of Intellect is owing to what Intellect is in itself, then the One's knowledge of and power over this is veiled. The One cannot know how the overflow of goodness in it will turn out. It can only know (in a way) that whatever does exist is good in so far as it exists.

As for the One's knowledge of and responsibility for the existence of evil, this of course depends on how evil is construed. One observation can be made here in anticipation of the discussion in chapter 9. Since evil is privation, the One cannot produce evil itself. The One's product is just the existence of everything else, whereas a privation is a relation of one thing to another. To explain evil we have to go to that which has it and its relation to what it ought to be and is not. The only way the One could be said to be responsible for this evil would be if it were better that some things did not exist at all rather than exist and be inclined to evil. But since the One is goodness itself, this would mean that some things achieved goodness by not achieving goodness, that is, by not existing. So, the only thing the One is responsible for is the necessary condition for the goodness of anything being achieved. If things are handicapped in their pursuit of goodness, then this can be said to be so owing only to the necessary instrument of the One's activity, namely, Intellect.

III

Intellect and Soul

1 Intellect: The Realm of Essence and Life

Plotinus does not regard as serious the question of whether or not intellect in general exists. The phenomenon of thinking or of intellection is regarded by him as evident, and intellect is just that in virtue of which this phenomenon occurs.

> It is perhaps ridiculous to enquire whether there is intellect in the world; though there are, it may be, people who would dispute even this. But it is more disputable if it is such as we say it is, and if it is something separate, and if it is the real beings and if the nature of the Forms is there. (V.9.3.4–8)

The question of whether intellect exists separately, however, is far more contentious, as Plotinus knew from his reading of Plato and Aristotle and their commentators.[1] For Plotinus, this question amounts to the question of whether there is an ἀρχή Intellect, paradigmatically what individual intellects are by participation. Two further questions arise immediately. If separate intellect exists, is it a particular intellect or something else? Second, if separate intellect exists, how are particular intellects related to this, if these themselves are separate or separable?

Plotinus says many obscure things in the course of his reflection on these questions. For example, "Intellect is not the intellect of one individual, but is universal; and being universal, is the Intellect of all things"(III.8.8.41–2).[2] And speaking about Intellect in relation to particular intellects (νοῖ or νόες), he says, "For when it [Intellect] is active in itself, the products of its activity are the other intellects" (VI.2.22.26–7).[3] We seem to have in these passages a distinction between "universal" Intellect and particular intellects.

Plotinus' problems are better understood when we recognize that his account of intellect is at the convergence of two complicated lines of investigation in ancient Greek philosophy, one epistemological and one cosmological. First, and less problematic, is the almost universal recognition of a distinct cognitive activity, normally called "intellection" (νόησις), along with the presumption (usually unargued for) that the existence of such activity implies the existence of a "faculty" called intellect. A principal feature of this activity is that it is or results in an intentional state whose contents are universal truths.[4] This description immediately invites the question of whether other, inferior cognitive states such as believing or opining or imagining could have as their contents the same universal truths. Despite various answers to this question, ancient epistemology is generally much more willing to take this question seriously than is modern epistemology, where what distinguishes optimal cognition from other forms is not a difference in content. Thus, the criterion that turns believing p into knowing p assumes that p remains the same when the criterion is met.

The presumption that the activity of intellection implies intellect is part of the "faculty" psychology that is largely unopposed within Greek philosophy even where it falls into disuse. There are of course many variations on this basic psychological interpretation. The underlying problem, evident in both Plato and Aristotle, but never, I think, satisfactorily solved by them, is the unity of the subject of various forms of cognition, including intellection. The problem becomes particularly acute if it is held that the subject of "higher" cognitive activity is separate or separable from the subject of cognitive activity that is not at least separable. For example, Plato is manifestly puzzled by the identity of a discarnate thinker with an incarnate subject of cognitive activities requiring a body. Aristotle, in his notoriously obscure remarks on the agent intellect, is more or less seized with the same difficulty, even though he wants to reject the Platonic baggage of the doctrine of the immortality of the soul. It is hardly surprising that Plotinus, who so often uses Aristotle first to understand Plato and then to confute Plato's most acute critic in his own terms, does not have available an obvious passage to an authentically Platonic resolution of the difficulty.

The second line of investigation leading to Plotinus' account is equally venerable. Greek philosophical speculation regarding a first principle or ἀρχή of all possibly goes back to the Ionian philosopher Anaximander. The idea of an ἀρχή of all is that of an explanatory entity whose description is such that it itself is not in need of the same sort of explanation which it provides. Indeed, in a strong sense it is crafted to be self-explanatory.

The or at least a fundamental datum of Pre-Socratic philosophy is that the world is a κόσμος, an orderly arrangement of parts perspicuous to an intellect. The claim that the first principle of all should be νοῦς or a mind rests both upon a design argument and a shrewd guess that underlying the κόσμος is motion and that the explanation of all motion must be the sort of thing that moves without itself being moved. In the first instance, there is the claim that if the world is more or less transparent to our intellects, that is because it was made so by another intellect. In the second instance, on the apparent analogy of our own bodily motion caused by a mind which does not move, the hypothesis that the ἀρχή of all is an intellect is not very surprising.

43

What is more surprising is the fidelity of the Greek philosophical tradition to this hypothesis. Plato, Aristotle, and the Stoics all made intellect an ἀρχή of sorts.

Plotinus' role in this tradition is complex. First, he is disposed to align himself with Plato's position in the tradition as he understands that.[5] This means (1) an identification of Intellect with the demiurge in the *Timaeus* and the "divine νοῦς" mentioned elsewhere by Plato, (2) an identification of the Forms as intelligibles (νοητά) for the demiurge, and from (1) and (2), (3) a subordination of Intellect and intelligibles to the ἀρχή of all.[6] Although Plotinus is apparently confident that he grasps Plato's meaning in these matters, it is equally evident to Plotinus and to everyone else that Plato is less than forthcoming about his reasons for saying what he does. Certainly, Plato is not explicit on the relation between the demiurge and individual intellects. This is where Plotinus' treatment of Aristotle's account of intellect as an ἀρχή of all enters into the picture.

Likening the individual intellect contemplating Forms eternally to the Aristotelian agent intellect, Plotinus has a device for interpreting Plato. That is, he can show from the nature of intellect in general that the individual intellect and the demiurge are engaged in the same activity, namely, cognitive identification with all the Forms. Interpreting the agent intellect thus and also assimilating the intellect of the unmoved mover to Plato's demiurge, Plotinus is engaging in a remarkable act of syncretism. We shall have to look closely at his arguments.

Plotinus rejects the unqualified metaphysical primacy of intellect in the *Metaphysics* of Aristotle.[7] Given what has already been said about Plotinus' first principle, the rejection will amount to the demonstration that intellect cannot be absolutely incomposite. Plotinus not only rejects the primacy of intellect as argued for by Aristotle, but rejects his description of intellect as well. These two points are closely connected. For Aristotle, we arrive at the existence of intellect as the necessary cause of everlasting motion. Such a cause must be pure actuality. Hence, we cannot even distinguish between intellect and intellection within it.[8] Since, for Plotinus, only the One is unqualified actuality, an Aristotelian line of argument to unqualified actuality must bypass intellect in favor of the One, thereby leaving the existence of intellect undemonstrated. When Plotinus does address arguments for the existence of Intellect, he does so starting from premises different from those of Aristotle, and not surprisingly the description of Intellect which results is also different. Above all, the "demotion" of Intellect from the role of primary ἀρχή enables its assimilation to the demiurge as described by Plato, with certain important qualifications.

One of the principal descriptions of Intellect is as "one-many" (ἓν πολλά) (see IV.8.3.10; V.1.8.26; V.3.15.11, 22; VI.2.2.2; VI.2.10.11; VI.2.15.14; VI.2.21.7, 46–7; VI.2.22.10; VI.5.6.1–2; VI.6.8.22; VI.6.13.52–3; VI.7.8. 17–18; VI.7.14.11–12; VI.7.39.11–14). As Plotinus tells us, he believes he is following Plato's description of the subject of the second hypothesis in the second part of the *Parmenides* (144e5; 145a2).[9] Despite the fact that Plato does use the words ἓν πολλά to describe this subject, it is sufficiently clear that an understanding of Plotinus' concept of Intellect is not going to be furthered by investigation in this direction. For example, Plotinus holds that Intellect is eternal, whereas the subject of the second hypothesis is in time (V.9.10.9; 155d2–3). Plotinus' Intellect is not in place; the subject of the second hypothesis apparently is (V.9.10.10; 148d–149d with 145bff.). That Plotinus is drawing on a conception of intellect found widely in the dialogues but not actually in the *Parmenides* seems clear enough.

A deduction of Intellect from a premise stating that the One exists would seem to be impossible, since of course from the absolutely simple nothing in particular follows.[10] Nevertheless, Plotinus gives us a kind of logical analysis of the eternal production of Intellect.

> This, we may say, is the first act of generation: the One, perfect because it seeks nothing, has nothing, and needs nothing, overflows, as it were, and its superabundance makes something other than itself. This, when it has come into being, turns back upon the One and is filled, and becomes Intellect by looking towards it. Its halt and turning towards the One constitutes being (τὸ ὄν), its gaze upon the One, Intellect. (V.2.1.7–11. See also III.8.9.29–32; V.1.5.18–19; V.1.7.5–35; V.3.10.40–4; V.3.11. 4–12; V.4.2.4–7; V.5.5.15; VI.7.17.14–16, 21; VI.7.35.19–23)[11]

This analysis resembles a mathematical construction more than it does an historical account. Its central points are: (1) the One is essentially productive; (2) what it produces is necessarily other than it; (3) a product of the One is essentially oriented towards its producer.[12] What does this orientation consist in? In the most general sense, it is a desire to be united with the One in some way. Only on a false literal interpretation of the generation of Intellect is this desire taken to be a desire for something like the *status quo ante*, a desire for the annihilation that would necessarily follow from the elimination of otherness altogether. I shall return to this important matter in the last chapter. For now, we need to ask why the primary orientation towards the One should be that of Intellect.

The explicit answer Plotinus gives to this question is that since Intellect is "closest to the One," it is what the One naturally produces "first" (V.4.2.1–3). The phrase "closest to the One" must mean at least "as simple as possible without being identical with the One." But this hardly explains why it is Intellect that is the most simple or unified product of the One. In the present passage, Plotinus carries the analysis further, saying that Intellect is in itself unlimited, like sight, until it is defined by intelligibles, that is, the Forms.[13] The logical priority of intelligibles to intellection is here crucial.[14] Intellect is complex both because there is a real distinction between it and intelligibles and because the intelligibles themselves constitute a many. It is, however, the least complex thing there is (other than the One) because it is also cognitively identical with Forms eternally. Among complex activities, its activity is the least complex because it acts on Forms which are distinct from its thinking but still identical with it.

Intellect's activity is closest to the paradigm of activity, that of the One, because it acts on or towards nothing outside itself. It is "self-contained" activity. The One's activity is self-contained in the sense that there is nothing outside the One for it to act on. The self-contained activity of Intellect is an image of the One's activity. Since Intellect is identical with all the Forms, it is also the entity least limited by essence. There is nothing which it is not owing to its being something else.

It is a logical fiction to speak about the first phase of the production of Intellect and of the priority of Forms to Intellect. The eternal product of the One is just Intellect, which is cognitively identical with all intelligibles and thereby eternally achieves the most perfect possible union with the One for something other than it.[15] The logical fiction, however, usefully reveals the complexity of the relation of Intellect to the first principle.[16] The priority of intelligibles to cognition is sufficient to guarantee the complexity of Intellect. This priority also indicates that the understanding of cognition that we seek here below begins with οὐσία or the real as a principle. Finally, the priority of intelligibles to intellection indicates the instrumentality of Intellect in its own production. Intellect as the locus of Forms is the instrument of the One in causing the existence of Intellect as cognizer.

In so far as there may be said to be a puzzle about how multiplicity can be generated from unity, the puzzle is solved or rather dissolved by positing the eternal existential dependence of Intellect upon the One. The second ἀρχή does not arise magically or mysteriously from the first. It is co-eternal with the first, but subordinate. It is only as an heuristic device that multiplicity can be said to arise from the One. Intellect is generated from the One roughly as a plane figure is generated from a point.

For Plotinus, the One and Intellect are governing principles. And just as two points determine a line in a plane, so the One and Intellect determine a hierarchy. Intellect is the first product of the One. Therefore, the closer something is to Intellect, the closer it is to the One, and the farther away from Intellect, the farther away from the One. Hierarchy does not by itself imply continuity. Continuity is implied only if we add the proposition that the One is fecund without reserve. The One does not fail to produce anything it can produce, which is to say that it does not fail at all. If it failed to produce something which it could produce, then this would introduce potency illicitly into it. Hierarchy and continuity do not therefore imply infinite gradation, if this is taken to mean that between any two "levels" of the hierarchy there is possibly another. Continuity without infinite gradability implies "gaps" which may be considerable both for the understanding and in reality.

The criterion for judging proximity to the One is degrees of being.[17] I take this to mean degrees of finite being, that is, the composition of essence and existence in everything besides the One. For these beings, it is owing to the One that whatever each thing is exists and is therefore one.[18] Whence the gradation of finite beings?

Plotinus sometimes seems to speak as if unity itself is gradable independently of being (see VI.9.1.14).[19] For example, a chorus, a continuous body, and a soul are said to be ordered in increasing proximity to the One. We might suppose that a soul is more of a unity than a continuous body because it is immaterial and so unlike the chorus it has no actual parts and so unlike the body it does not even have potential parts (see IV.1.1.61–4). This, however, would seem to make the Form of Unity the criterion and not the One itself. And it would make, say, a worm more of a unity than an incarnate human. The appearance of inconsistency fades when we realize that the chorus is first of all something that does not exist by nature (see VI.2.11), whereas the continuous body does. And what exists by nature is an image of Soul. Soul receives images of Forms from Intellect; it transmits images of these images to the things that exist by nature. What does not exist by nature is as such beyond the reach of the ἀρχή Intellect. A continuous body is farther from the One than a soul because it is a body; a chorus is even farther from the One than a body because it is not even an image of a Form. Essence limits existence in Intellect, but materiality and temporality limit the images or instances of essence here below.

Returning to the "generation" of Intellect, what makes this account elusive is that Plotinus is not really arguing for the existence of Intellect but for its properties of eternality and immutability (see I.1.8.4–6; III.7.3.36–8; III.7.5.25–8).[20] The starting-point for the argument for the eternality of Intellect is Plato's theory of Forms. Because Forms exist, eternal Intellect must exist. One reason for believing that Forms exist is that knowledge exists and therefore truth exists. Truth is eternal. But eternal truth could not exist if Forms did not exist. Forms are somehow supposed to explain why, for example, mathematical truths are eternal. And Forms could not exist if eternal Intellect did not exist.[21] Another reason for believing that Forms exist is that the possibility of identity in difference is explicable only if eternal entities exist. For example, the possibility that "large" is univocally predicable of many things is explicable solely if an entity whose proper name is the nature of largeness exists eternally. In general, for any attribute f, if it is possible that f should be predicable of numerically distinct subjects, then a Form F-ness exists.[22]

Predication of universals is of course the common stock of non- or even anti-Platonic realists as well as Platonists. What separates Plato and his disciple Plotinus from their realist opponents, including Aristotle, is that the possibility of universal predication depends on the *priority* of the Form's existence.[23] What separates Plotinus from Plato himself, or at least one

47

common interpretation of Plato, is the insistence that the priority of eternal Forms entails the coexistence of eternal Intellect.

Understanding instantiation in ontological rather than in epistemological terms is peculiarly Platonic. For example, Socrates may be a case of what my concept of man is intended to refer to, but he is first of all an instance of the Form of Man. Concepts do not explain the fact of identity in difference if there be such. Furthermore, the simultaneous coming to be of instances and that of which they are instances is thus precluded as an alternative. Having distinguished an instance and what it is an instance of, it is evident that we imply nothing about the coming into being of the latter when the former comes to be. On the contrary, if the coming into being of an instance is evidence of its prior possibility, then the condition for this possibility must be distinct from the instance itself. Eternally so, a Platonist would hold. To say that what the instance is an instance of comes to be only when the instance comes to be is just to deny ontological priority to the former and thus to deny eternal possibilities or eternal truths.[24]

We thus have a premise: Forms exist, and a conclusion: Intellect exists. What additional premises are employed to connect these two propositions? The additional premises are: if Forms exist, eternal truth exists. But truth is being for or in relation to an Intellect.[25] Hence, eternal truth entails an eternal Intellect. The assumed definition of truth as being in relation to an intellect has its origin in Plato, who in at least two places defines "true" and "false" as attributes of propositions or statements which do or do not "correspond" with reality (*Cratylus* 385b7–9 and *Sophist* 263b4–7). Aristotle is essentially in agreement with Plato's view (*Metaphysics* 4.7.1011b25–9; *De Interpretatione* 19a23). But elsewhere he adds the important qualification that a proposition is a complex judgment and that such judgments exist not in things but only in the mind (ἐν διανοίᾳ) (*Metaphysics* 6.4.1027b29–31).[26] But even if we grant Aristotle's claim, why should we allow the inference from the eternity of Forms to the eternity of truth? Nothing in Aristotle's explication of truth seems to require the unconditional existence of truth, and hence of Intellect, whose eternal existence is thought to follow from the existence of such truth.

In Plotinus' main discussion of these issues, V.5, "That the Intelligibles are not Outside the Intellect and on the Good," there is a suggestion of the line of argument he is following. He seems to want to argue not only that eternal Forms exist, but that these are somehow connected eternally. This is so presumably because it is owing precisely to such eternal connections that instances of Forms are necessarily connected. Thus, if x is f entails that x is g, this is because of the necessary connectedness of F-ness and G-ness.[27] And here we must add that the eternal connection is ontologically on a par with the eternity of each Form in the connection, that is, the condition for the possibility of x being f is no more eternal than the condition for the possibility that if x is f, x must be g. At this point, Plotinus seems to be arguing that the eternal "link" between eternal, immaterial entities must be one thing which is capable of simultaneously being identified with both F-ness and G-ness so that the partial identity of these is grounded in reality (see V.5.1.41–5). This one thing is what Intellect is supposed to be. Intellect must be eternal because any judgment made by an individual mind depends for its truth on eternal reality, including eternal interconnectedness of Forms, hence eternal Intellect which grounds the interconnectedness.

Consider the following example. All fathers are males. But not all males are fathers. So, "father" and "male" are not identical in meaning even if necessarily all fathers are males. The Platonic explanation of this necessary truth, if it be such, is that the Form of Father and the Form of Male are necessarily connected in some way.[28] That is, a *de re* necessity underlies "all fathers are male." Plotinus' claim is that this can be so only if there is some partial identity of these Forms so that the presence of a father guarantees the presence of a male. This Platonic reasoning is analogous to and illuminated by an idea found in Leibniz. Leibniz argued that the predicate of a true proposition is contained within the subject.[29] He believes that the predicate is contained within the subject because the attributes of an individual are each part of what that individual is. But since Leibniz's doctrine is about individuals, he does not believe that there is a difference between accidental and essential predication. Thus, the color of someone's hair is as much a part of his identity as whatever it is that makes him a member of a distinct species. Plotinus, on the other hand, is not arguing for a necessary connection among all predicates and their subjects, based on an account of individuality. He does, however, wish to claim that where there is necessary predication, this is owing to some eternal fact and that partial identity is the key to understanding such facts.

The operative concept here is that of partial identity. A and B are partially identical if A is a part of what B is or B is a part of what A is. In the most general sense, there are two assumptions that make the idea of partial identity applicable to the real world. First, identity is not fundamentally atomic, that is, being does not entail indivisibility. Second, identity is not adventitious, that is, complexity is not artificial. In other words, the parts are real parts. The only reason I can fathom for rejecting physical complexity is the denial of essentialism, the doctrine that things have an essential identity. One could not claim that A was a part of B (except arbitrarily) unless B had an essential identity. As we shall see in the next chapter, Plotinus is in fact attracted to the position that the identities of sensible composites are adventitious precisely because he is led to reject essentialism.

It is otherwise for Intellect, which is in some way identical with Forms. The problem of non-physical or immaterial complex identity is of a quite different sort. Consider the example of a circle and an arc. If it is an analytic truth that a circle contains arcs, one account of the analyticity is that somehow the subject contains the predicate. It is only on the basis of a highly dubious metaphor of concepts as pictures that this view is plausible. If it is true that circles have arcs and not angles, this has nothing to do with anyone's concept, but rather with what a circle is. Concepts may be thought to have parts only if concepts are taken to be pictures, which they are not. Plotinus wants to account for necessary truths like "circles have arcs" and also the distinct explanatory roles of the Form of Circle and the Form of Arc. Each is, as he says, a "separate" paradigm.[30]

The possibility of partial identity among Forms probably derives from Plato's *Sophist*.[31] A circle is partially identical with an arc of the circle. It is in one sense the sum of all the arcs on the circle. A line is partially identical with any point on the line, if a line is a locus of points (see IV.3.2.23–4). But the partial identity of Forms cannot be explained by the containment of Forms within Forms alone. Let part of what Form F is be Form G. Then part of what Form F is is not Form G. If the presence of Form G brings with it the presence of Form F, then how can part of F not be G? If the presence of Form G brings with it only part of Form F, then that part is *wholly* identical with Form G, and the connection between Form G and the part of Form F left which is not wholly identical with Form G is left unexplained.

How is Intellect supposed to provide a solution to this dilemma? If each Form is a separate actuality, nevertheless the cognitive identity of Intellect with each and every Form is a further actuality.

> Intellect possesses them [the Forms] as in thought, but not the discursive kind of thought; but nothing is left out of all the things of which there are intelligible forming principles (λόγοι), but Intellect is like one great complete intelligible principle embracing them all, and it goes through them starting from its own first principles, or rather it has always gone through them, so that it is never true that it is going through them. For in general everywhere, whatever one might apprehend by reasoning as being in nature one will find existing without reasoning in Intellect. (VI.2.21.27–34. See also VI.2.20.25–6; VI.4.4.40–2)

Following the Aristotelian conception, Intellect is in potency to the activity which is being identical with these Forms. Since Intellect is eternally cognitively identical with Forms, there is merely a logical distinction between the actuality that is the separate Form and the actuality that is the cognitive identification with it. According to the former, each Form is a one-over-many or essential cause of its images in the sensible world. According to the latter, all the Forms are aspects of the complex activity of Intellect. Thus, there are different ways of imitating Intellect and Forms, as indicated by the intelligible differences among predicates here below. Since, however, the separate Forms are really identical with the activity of Intellect, that activity is complex.[32] Therefore, that which Intellect cognizes is essentially complex (see V.3.5.1–25; V.3.13.33; V.4.2.39; V.9.10.10–14).[33]

This fact perhaps makes it even more difficult to see how participation in one Form, say, Threeness, guarantees participation in another Form, say, Oddness. It seems that the answer requires that direct participation in Forms by sensibles be rejected and that a mediating role for Intellect (and Soul, as we shall see) must be posited. This is so because the (partial) identity of Forms is grounded in Intellect. Form F and Form G are partially identical because they are different facets of one entity, Intellect. Intellect is cognitively identical with all the Forms, but not in complex judgments. Thus Intellect does not think "three is odd"; it non-propositionally intuits what it is that makes "three is odd" a true proposition, roughly in the way we might imagine one can think of a "simple" object alone. A similar explanation can be given for all eternal truths.

Consider the example of discovering theorems about the circle. These theorems reveal complex truths about Circularity, which is nevertheless one Form. Intellect intuits all these truths "at once," and in a similar way it intuits the complex truths about the Form of Circularity and, say, the Form of Arc and the Forms of Numbers. The complexity of the noetic world is intensive, not extensive, as in the case of magnitudes, where there are parts outside parts.[34] Without Intellect, the complexity would only be in potency and the requisite ontological priority of paradigm to copy would be unexplained. With Intellect, the intensive complexity of essence is eternally actualized.

If three things here below are necessarily odd, it is so because they are somehow imaging or copying what Intellect is when it is cognitively identical with what explains the truth that three is odd. Forms do not contain each other as proper parts, but each one is "transparent" to all the rest because in Intellect they are identical with a single activity. All eternally true propositions are like one proposition grasped as a "unit." Without eternal Intellect, and without participation construed as imitation of Intellect, Plotinus has no way of accounting for eternal truths other than those which state that individual Forms exist. Thus, if we think or observe that "three is odd" is a necessary truth, we should understand this not as founded on the eternal connectedness of two separate Forms, Threeness and Oddness, but as a discovery of a facet of Intellect or οὐσία.[35] The Forms are not really distinct entities, but really distinct aspects of Intellect.

The account of the activity of Intellect as eternally identical with all Forms can be usefully supplemented by a consideration of Plotinus' use of Aristotle's *De Anima*. In particular, Aristotle identifies as a function of intellect the "unifying" or "synthesizing" of concepts in judgments (3.6.430b5–6). For example, in the judgment that the diagonal of a square is incommensurable with a side, it is intellect that, as Aristotle says, "makes [the concepts] one." We need only insert at this point the premise that complex eternal truth exists to arrive at the conclusion that Intellect is eternally unifying all Forms. The unification of the concepts of diagonal and incommensurability by a particular intellect is only a representation of an eternal truth for Plotinus. There just would be no eternal truth if the Forms of Diagonal and Incommensurability were not unified by Intellect.[36] That is why it is not enough to posit Forms to account for eternal truth and temporalized intellects to cognize them.

Plotinus is firm in holding that the activity in which Intellect is engaged is not conceptualization. The argument for this claim is a general reductio ad absurdum of representationalism. If the intentional object of intellection is other than the Forms themselves, then Intellect will have to be able to compare the representation of the Forms with the Forms themselves in order to know that they are accurate. If it can compare them, it does not need the representation in the first place. If it cannot, then eternal truth is not guaranteed. The eternal cognitive act in Intellect will have as object something other than eternal being (see V.5.1.19–21).[37] The necessary complexity of eternal being would not be accounted for. Plotinus is here supposing that eternal truth is not something possessed, where possession is understood as a representational state. So long as truth is agreed to be being in relation to intellect, the only alternative to representationalism of any sort is identity (see III.5.7.50–3; III.9.1.6–10; V.3.5.21–8; 13.12–14; V.4.2.44–6; V.5.1.19–23; V.9.5.7–8; VI.6.7.8–10; VI.7.41.12–13).[38] This identity, because it is a *cognitive* identity, does not result in the conflation of Forms. The complexity of immaterial being is actualized intensively in Intellect.

Aristotle, as we have seen, can go some way with this approach. He claims both that intellect has a unifying function and that in the case of immaterial objects, that which thinks and that which is thought are the same.[39] Where Aristotle demurs is at the point where it is claimed that eternal truth exists and that this is grounded in eternal being. This may seem surprising. I mean that Aristotle rejects the existence of Plato's Forms, that Aristotle's god or intellect is perfectly self-absorbed thinking and so not the locus of eternal complex truths, and that Aristotle makes no clear distinction between the eternal and the everlasting. He does indeed believe that the natures of organic substances are everlasting because species are everlasting. But the truths about these natures, such as those contained within a completed Aristotelian science, are not eternal truths. There is of course Aristotle's agent intellect, which evidently is actually cognitively identical with all forms. If the agent intellect of each person were unqualifiedly separate, Aristotle's doctrine would be virtually identical to Plotinus', for the forms with which the agent intellect would be cognitively identical would seem to differ not at all from Plato's Forms.[40]

It is now time to recall the questions raised by the putative distinction between universal intellect and particular intellects. Is the eternal Intellect that is the guarantor of eternal truth the demiurge? Is it in fact just what "universal intellect" names? How are particular intellects related to the intellect of the demiurge and universal intellect? If each particular intellect is separate and eternal, as Plotinus will want to claim, does the demiurge then become superfluous as guarantor of eternal truth? Would not the intellect of any one of us do as well? And in that case, would universal intellect not then become more like the universal nature that all particular intellects possess? In order to answer these questions we need to look more closely at the activity of the ἀρχή Intellect.

Intellect is the ἀρχή of essence and of life. That is, its activity, intellection of all Forms, is the paradigm of life.[41] It is *per se* essence and life, whereas everything else that has essence and life is so *per aliud*. The ἀρχή of essence will concern us in subsequent chapters as we consider in more detail eternal truth and the participation of sensibles in Forms. For now, let us focus on the second feature, intellection, as the essence of life. Plotinus explains it in this way:

> For in general intellecting (τὸ νοεῖν) seems to be an intimate conscious-ness (συναίσθησις) of the whole when many parts come together in the same thing; [this is so] when a thing has intellection of itself, which is intellecting in the proper sense: each single part is just itself and seeks nothing; but if the process of intellecting is of what is outside, the intellecting will be deficient, and not intellecting in the proper sense. (V.3.13.12–16)[42]

In a purely formal sense, if Intellect is identical with all Forms when it is engaged in thinking or intellecting or knowing, then in knowing, a thing knows itself.[43] This seems to be exactly what Aristotle has said in *De Anima* when he claims that "in the case of objects without matter, that which thinks and that which is being thought are the same" (3.4.430a3–4). The matter is complicated, however, by the fact that Plotinus wants to draw together conceptually particular intellects and the intellect of the demiurge, even if the latter is construed as "universal intellect." But since Plotinus thinks that Aristotle's god is a version of the demiurge, he feels he can draw freely upon Aristotle's characterization of god in order to understand intellect, especially intellect in the highest or most perfect degree. Thus, in the *Metaphysics* Aristotle will say,

> Now thinking according to itself is of the best according to itself, and thinking in the highest degree is of that which is best in the highest degree. Thus, in partaking of the intelligible, it is of himself that the intellect is thinking, for by apprehending and thinking it is he himself who becomes intelligible, and so the intellect and its intelligible object are the same. (12.12.7.1072b18–21)[44]

Clearly, it makes a world of difference what the intelligible object is when intellect knows itself. For Aristotle, god thinks himself, but certainly not by thinking Platonic Forms. For Plotinus, thinking is essentially self-thinking or, equivalently, thinking the Forms, where in effect the agent intellect's activity is conflated with the activity of the unmoved mover, which in turn is treated as the activity of the demiurge thinking the Forms.

If this is in fact what Plotinus is doing, he is not perversely misinterpreting Aristotle for several reasons. First, since Aristotle's god is supposed to be the primary referent of being, if primary being is thinking, then what is said about god's thinking should be the basis for understanding thinking in general. Second, the assimilation to god of the agent intellect, which is naturally inferred to be cognitively identical with all forms, is not unreasonable, as Alexander of Aphrodisias and others amply testify. Third, and most importantly, Plotinus rejects the primacy of Aristotle's god precisely because thinking essentially involves a duality of subject and object.[45] If thinking is self-thinking, then the thinker as subject and the thinker as object must contain this duality, that is, they must be distinguished yet identical. The claim that "knowing itself is knowing in the proper sense" could have been a friendly gloss on Aristotle's characterization of the activity of god but for Plotinus' insistence that thinking is not perfect activity.

This brings us to the crux of the issue. Eternal truth is supposed to entail the existence of eternal Intellect. The entailment is supposed to hold because eternal truth is complex, whereas the One is simple, and the complexity of eternal truth cannot be grounded in a mere multitude of unconnected beings or Forms. Thus, eternal truth is being *for* an intellect. But this is construed, on Aristotelian grounds, as the being *of* an intellect. To have Intellect "looking in" at Forms "from the outside" would be to concede that Intellect is irrelevant to the existence of eternal truth. It is not enough, though, to "internalize" the Forms in Intellect. Plotinus cannot allow that knowing is different parts of a complex whole related to each other (see V.3.5.17–23; V.5.1).[46] What would be in the knowing part would be different from what the other part is, and there would be no identification of knower and known. Thus, the requirement that eternal Intellect exist in order to ground eternal truth leads to the requirement of a particular conception of intellection or knowing. According to this, self-knowing is knowing in the proper sense.

How is this self-knowing then to be understood as knowing Forms? It is to be understood, I would suggest, as the claim that there is no real distinction between knowing and knowing that one is knowing.[47] Thus, sKp and sKsKp are mutually implicative, where "s" is Intellect or an intellect, "K" is the activity of intellecting ($\nu o \epsilon \hat{\iota} \nu$), and "p" is not a proposition but $o \dot{\upsilon} \sigma \acute{\iota} \alpha$ or the complex whole containing all the Forms. One difficulty here would seem to be that if in sKp "p" is not to be construed as a proposition, in sKsKp "sKp" must be so construed. That this is not so follows from the fact that if "sKp" is different in content from "p," then self-knowing is regressive rather than reflexive as it must be if knowing (Forms) is self-knowing. If sKp entails sKsKp but p is an intentional object different from sKp, then knowing p is different from knowing sKp, and the identity of subject and object of knowing would involve a vicious expansion of the object of knowing.

Many philosophers from widely different backgrounds believe that sKp and sKsKp are mutually implicative. Many fewer interpret this implication as a characterization of self-evidence such that for s, sKsKp is sufficient evidence for p. Thus, knowing would entail infallibility. Knowing requires sufficient evidence. The only sufficient evidence for p that s could adduce without initiating an endless regress would be the claim that sKsKp. S knows p if and only if p is self-evident to s. Plotinus is among the philosophers who hold that knowing thus implies infallibility.[48] But even fewer philosophers accept the further implication that the self-reflexivity of self-evidence is possible only if intellect is an immaterial entity.[49] For Plotinus, we might say that since Intellect is immaterial, it naturally follows that knowing is essentially self-knowing. Knowing implies infallibility and infallibility can only obtain when there is self-reflexivity. More precisely, there is infallibility about what is known non-inferentially only when there is self-reflexivity.

It would seem that owing to the condition that knowing is not representational but an identification of knower and known, knowing cannot be essentially inferential. Inference requires a representational element of a logical connective and a judgment that A is so because of B. So, if the intellect is immaterial and if knowing in the primary sense is non-representational and non-inferential and infallible, these conditions are accurately albeit elliptically contained in the claim that knowing is self-knowing. I think it is important to mention here in passing a point that we shall return to later. Plotinus' characterization of Intellect does not depend on an appeal to our own experience, for we are not aware of the activity of separate intellect, either our own or that of the demiurge. He is not arguing that, say, infallible judgments about our own sense-experience indicate the immateriality of intellect or self-reflexivity as its essential property. Sense-experience is not an activity of intellect. And yet all forms of cognition inferior to intellection are potentially illuminated by their paradigm.[50]

From the identity of Intellect and Forms and the mutual implication of sKp and sKsKp Plotinus draws a conclusion that is unfortunately easy to misunderstand. He says that Forms themselves possess life.[51] This has been taken to mean that each Form, for example, the Form of Beauty, is itself an intellect. So Armstrong translates Plotinus' words καὶ ὅλος μὲν ὁ νοῦς τὰ πάντα εἴδη, ἕκαστον δὲ εἶδος νοῦς ἕκαστος, "And Intellect as a whole is all the Forms, and each individual Form is an individual intellect."[52] This translation is inaccurate. The last clause is better rendered "and each Form is each intellect." This text thus rendered only affirms the cognitive identity of each intellect with all Forms. It does not obliterate the distinction between intellect and Forms or that between the activity of intellection and its intentional objects. The supposed interpretation of the above text is not supported by the identity of intellect, intellection, and the intelligible (V.3.5.44–5). For as Plotinus says elsewhere, it is false to say that Forms are "acts of intellection", if this is taken to mean that Forms are not prior to intellection of them or to mean that the Form is just the intellection.[53] On the contrary, we only need to take Plotinus as affirming Aristotle's point that intellect is intelligible in the sense that it is identical with intelligibles cognitively, from which it follows that what is intelligible, i.e., each Form, is identical with every intellect.[54]

Still, it must be said that Plotinus is not attracted to a sort of atomistic picture of a multitude of intellects identical with Forms and cut off from each other:

> Each there has everything in itself and sees all things in every other, so that all are everywhere and each and every one is all and the glory is unbounded; for each of them is great, because even the small is great; and the sun there is all the stars, and each star is the sun and all the others. A different kind of being stands out in each, but in each all are manifest. (V.8.4.6–11. See also IV.3.2; IV.9.5)

Understanding this passage fully will require a treatment of the vexed topic of Forms of individuals, which I deal with in the next chapter. For now, if we may assume that there are Forms at least for each individual that has an intellect, then what Plotinus seems to be saying is that among intellects identification with the Forms will include identification with every other intellect qua Form. And one would suppose, though Plotinus does not say this, that for an intellect, cognitive identification with all Forms includes identification with the Form of itself, though once again this does not entail the breakdown of the distinction between subject and intentional object. Accordingly, the intellect of Socrates would be cognitively identical with, among other Forms, the Form of Man, the Form of Plato, and the Form of Socrates. The self-knowing that the intellect of Socrates has is not, however, to be identified with knowing the Form of Socrates, for every other intellect knows that Form, whereas self-knowing is self-reflexive. The self-knowing of each intellect is numerically distinct. It would seem, then, that interawareness of this choir of angels or community of spirits must consist in each knowing the other as Form or intelligible object, not in some more intimate penetration of the subjective.[55]

We are at last in a position to address the questions regarding the demiurge, universal intellect, and individual intellects. It is *prima facie* implausible that Plotinus should have "demythologized" the demiurge into universal intellect, which is just the nature that all individual intellects share. Yet, if the central argument for the existence of eternal Intellect is as guarantor of eternal truth, then the demiurge truly is a vestigial organ in the body of Platonic thought. Even if the demiurge is supposed to be a kind of *primus inter pares* in the realm of intellect, it is difficult to infer its existence as we can infer the existence of an intellect for each embodied agent of imperfect cognitive activity.

This suggests that we might arrive at the demiurge as the intellect of the soul of the universe. That soul, as we shall see presently, is not identical with any other particular souls. It has a life of its own, the life of the animated universe. But then of course the argument for the demiurge becomes only as strong as an argument for a universal soul. As I suggested, Plotinus is unlikely to have considered the radical surgery to Platonism involved in removing the demiurge. Undoubtedly, he was encouraged in his steadfastness by Aristotle's argument for the existence of god which then goes on to identify god with intellect. It is fairly evident, though, that this argument is undermined by Plotinus' account of the insufficiency of Intellect as first principle of all.

What then of the relation of the demiurge and the individual intellect to universal intellect? Plotinus seems to say inconsistent things in this regard. He holds that "universal intellect" exists on its own and directs particular intellects and is even their cause in some sense but that particular intellects contain universal intellect in the way a particular body of knowledge contains knowledge (VI.2.20). This puzzling description actually follows the lengthy derivation of the μέγιστα γένη or Forms of Being, Sameness, Difference, Motion, and Rest according to Plotinus' understanding of their derivation by Plato in the *Sophist*. For Plotinus, the μέγιστα γένη or greatest kinds are the most general properties of essence or intelligible reality, which, as we have seen, is identical with Intellect. It seems reasonable to conclude that universal intellect is just what these Forms have in common. It is in a sense their *summum genus*, or better, the composite of them.[56] It exists in itself (καθ' αὑτὸν) as much as does any Form. However, as Plotinus says, it is "not active about anything in particular," meaning presumably that it is not a thinking subject whose intentional objects are Forms. The demiurge and particular intellects share in universal intellect in a twofold manner: they are cognitively identical with all the Forms whose *summum genus* is universal intellect and they are engaged in an activity, intellection, whose Form is also universal intellect.

It would also seem reasonable to conclude that universal intellect most closely resembles the hypostasis Intellect. As an ἀρχή, it stands apart from and is not an instance of what it is an ἀρχή of, namely, all noetic activities, including those of the demiurge and other particular intellects. But also as ἀρχή it is the starting-point for explaining all cognitive activity, which imperfectly represents the activity of Intellect. Recall that as an instrument of the One's causal activity, the ἀρχή Intellect is an essential cause. As such, it does not have to be a particular intellect. What I am suggesting is that the ἀρχή or hypostasis Intellect is·what all particular intellects, including that of the soul of the universe, have in common. It is the essential cause of these. It is a principle analogous to the manner in which form, matter, and privation are principles of change for Aristotle. These principles are non-specific. That is, they themselves are never found in things; it is always a particular case of each that accounts for a change. So it is with Intellect, on my interpretation.

The guarantee of eternal truth that Intellect is supposed to provide is accordingly to be understood as non-specific. That is, since eternal truth exists, there must be at least one intellect eternally cognitively identical with all Forms "unifying" them in a sort of judgment, although no one intellect in particular is the guarantor. The access of any incarnate individual to eternal truth, however, depends on *its* own intellect being eternally united with Forms.

2 Soul: The Restless Principle

Intellect is the ἀρχή of essence and life. Because the paradigm of living is the activity of intellection, Intellect is also the ἀρχή of all forms of cognitive activity, which variously partake of intellection. It is *per se* what everything it is the ἀρχή of is *per aliud*. The primary representation of Intellect is Soul. The ἀρχή Soul stands to Intellect analogously to the manner Intellect stands to the One.[57] Just as the secondary activity of the One is an ordered series of existents whose first members are whatever possess intellect, so the secondary activity of Intellect is an ordered series of lives. Since the One, as we have seen, is not really related to anything, the parallel here cannot be exact. Still, it can be carried some way.

An obvious and immediate problem with this is that Intellect as previously characterized does not seem to be able to have a secondary activity, whether that be Soul or anything else.[58] On the contrary, the activity of Intellect may be characterized either as self-contained or as directed to the One as the Good rather than being directed "downward" in any sense. Nevertheless, the arguments of the last two chapters provide us with the material for understanding how Intellect is indeed a principle of that which is below. The ἀρχή Intellect is first of all the paradigm of essence and life for whatever possesses it, and that is primarily whatever possesses soul. So, Intellect is the essential cause of whatever has essence, life, or cognitive activity.

These points, however, sidestep the main problem, which is the presumed association of secondary activity with external efficient causality. But if the secondary activity of the One is the existence of everything else, there is no need for anything besides the One to fulfill this role. Intellect is needed only as an instrument of the efficient causal activity of the One. In the case of Soul, its existence is accounted for by the One; its being is accounted for when we add to its existence the effect of the instrumentality of Intellect as paradigm of essence and life. To say, as Plotinus does, that Soul is "sort of" a secondary activity of Intellect is then to speak analogously. The efficient cause of existence stands to what exists analogously to the way essential cause stands to what possesses essence or intelligible nature. And just as the sharpness of an axe is a cause of the wood's being cut, though the axe is an instrument and would not cut by itself, so the activity of Intellect goes "outside itself" as instrument of the efficient causality of the One. In this way I believe Plotinus replies to Aristotle's objection that Forms are not efficient causes (see *Metaphysics* 12.3.1070a26–8; 6.1071b14–16). They are, but only instrumentally.[59]

The first activity of Intellect is "closest" to the One because it represents the most perfect type of simplicity possible for that which is in fact not perfectly simple, as only the One can be. Similarly, the activity of Soul is "closest" to Intellect because it represents the most perfect type of possession of essence and life for that which is in fact not perfectly or paradigmatically essence and life, as is Intellect. The life that the activity of Intellect is is self-reflexive intellection in which an agent is cognitively identical with all the Forms, thereby eternally attaining its good so far as it is able (V.3.13.12–14 with III.8.8.26–30).[60] The primary activity of Soul is that of a βίος or way of life.[61] As we shall see, this means basically life that is temporal (as opposed to eternal) and such that there is a "gap" between desire and achievement of goals.

Soul is the ἀρχή of anything with a βίος. An unqualifiedly perfect βίος would in fact be eternal, and in it desire and achievement of goals would coincide. This occurs only in the life that is absorbed in intellection. That is why the primary activity of Intellect is also the ἀρχή of things with soul.[62] All ways of living for anything with a soul imperfectly represent the perfect life of Intellect, that is, of any and all eternal intellects.

The reason why the primary representations of essence are in Soul is parallel. The images of essence or Forms in a soul, namely, the concepts or ideas in the soul employed in discursive reasoning, are the most perfect sort of images.[63] The reason why these are more perfect than the images of essence which are instantiations of Forms in the sensible world is that the latter are *mediated* by Soul. As Plotinus would put it, my concept of a circle is a more perfect representation of the Form of Circularity than is the circle I draw, though it is of course distinct from and derived from the Form of Circularity which is in Intellect. Only the images in the mind or concepts are unmediated representations of Forms.

Owing to the "nesting" of ἀρχαί discussed in the second chapter, Soul is an instrument both of Intellect and of the One. Thus, the organic activities of things with soul – all that living things do in so far as they are living – are referred first to Soul as the ἀρχή of these activities, then to Intellect as the ἀρχή of their cognitive activities and their possession of images of Forms, and then to the One as the ἀρχή of their existence.[64] We can state the relation between the ἀρχή Intellect and the ἀρχή Soul somewhat more precisely. Soul is the ἀρχή of the organic aspect of cognitive activities, such as their occurrence in time and in things with bodies; Intellect is their ἀρχή in so far as these activities are cognitive, that is, representative of a state of identification with eternal truth. Proceeding in reverse, the One employs Intellect and Soul instrumentally in causing the existence of things with cognitive powers and with life. And Intellect "employs" Soul in endowing things with images of itself.

The mediating, instrumental role of the ἀρχή Soul, both for Intellect and for the One, is crucial. Under this aspect it is the mediator of Forms to the sensible world.[65] This mediating function is not in the order of essential causality.[66] That is, the causality of Soul does not turn participation from a two-term into a three-term relation. Soul's function is rather "demiurgic," operating as a kind of efficient cause. It is not responsible for the existence of bodies or nature in general but for the presence in it of images of the Forms. As mediator, Plotinus evidently has the soul of the universe in mind more than the souls of individuals. Or rather he is thinking of the manifestation of the ἀρχή Soul which is the soul of the universe. The ἀρχή Intellect is unqualified for this role because it does not trade in images at all. And for Intellect to break out of eternity into the temporalized world would be for it to cease being Intellect or to usurp the function of the One according to which it endows things with existence.

Nor is the intelligibility of the sensible world accounted for by the One with the instrumentality of Intellect alone. In that case we would have failed to account for the feature of ἔφεσις or desire in animated bodies, including the body of the universe. Even the elements, says Plotinus, desire their natural places. To instantiate Forms without Soul would result in a static representation of nature, like a tableau, rather than nature itself. Thus, an instantiation of a Platonic Form becomes for Plotinus a dynamic expression of that Form.[67] Further, it comes to be similar to nature in the Aristotelian sense, in which "nature" means the forms of sensibles that exist by nature (see III.8.2.29; IV.4.13.1–7; IV.6.3.5–7).[68] Accordingly, nature is just the secondary activity of Soul. Its ἀρχή is just the activity of Soul.[69]

Another way of describing the kind of ἀρχή that Soul is is to say that it is the ἀρχή of transitive motion (III.1.8.8; III.6.3.13–15, 24–6).[70] I use the term "transitive" to distinguish the motion of which Soul is the ἀρχή from the kind of "intransitive" motion that can be attributed to Intellect and is synonymous with its activity (II.9.1.28). The motion of Intellect, in contrast to the motion of Soul, is without change (μεταβολῆς) (see IV.7.9.15). Soul is the ἀρχή of motion towards a goal that is external to itself, whereas the motion of Intellect is essentially just activity that "looks inward," rather like the unmoved mover of Aristotle.[71] The designation of Soul as an ἀρχή of motion towards that which is external seems to make Soul an ἀρχή of the motions of embodied souls. Motion towards "externals" is most naturally understood as the motion of bodies towards things outside themselves. This of course raises the problem of what then a soul without a body would be. And this in turn is allied to the problem of distinguishing Soul as an ἀρχή from particular souls, including the soul of the universe.

There is a tangle of issues here both historical and philosophical. Plotinus learned from Aristotle some of the problems in articulating a Platonic account of soul.[72] Plotinus unquestionably regards himself as following Plato in setting Intellect as an ἀρχή above the ἀρχή of Soul. There are certainly texts of Plato which can be interpreted in this way.[73] But Aristotle's own doctrines are an indispensable supplement for appreciating what Plotinus does with the

Platonic sources. One evident and unflagged amendment by Plotinus that is owing to Aristotle is to interpret Plato's phrase κίνησις νοῦ as ἐνέργεια νοῦ, thereby leaving κίνησις (understood in an Aristotelian manner as implying imperfection) as explained solely by Soul.[74]

Further, it is Aristotle who most clearly distinguishes life (ζωή) and soul by saying that in god the activity of intellect is life, whereas in organic beings soul is the first actuality (ἐντελέχεια) of an organic body having life potentially within it (*Metaphysics* 12.7.1072b26–7; *De Anima* 2.1.412a27–8). "Life" is thus a broader term than "soul." It is identified paradigmatically with the activity of intellect. But Aristotle complicates the picture by speaking in *De Anima* of intellect as part of the soul. Indeed, as he goes on to say, it is the only part that could be separable and eternal (see *De Anima* 3.4.429a22; 3.5.430a23).

The general account of the relation of Soul to Intellect developed by Plotinus is as follows. Soul is the ἀρχή of motion in embodied, living things. This includes both individual animals and the universe itself, which is animated by the universal soul. The "part" of the soul that does not animate the body and remains separate in eternity is just intellect (IV.8.8).[75] This of course produces the problem of how what is eternal and what is not are identified, so that I can say now that *my* intellect is eternally contemplating Forms. This problem will have to be set aside until later. More generally, it seems that if intellect is the highest part of soul, then the latter is not an ἀρχή at all.

How can the highest part of soul be another ἀρχή? The organic activities of incarnate or embodied individuals are explained by Soul. The cognitive activities of individuals including the single activity of a disembodied individual are explained by the ἀρχή Intellect. The former are images of the latter and can only properly be understood as such. This includes the faculty of incarnate cognition, discursive reasoning, which is also, alas, sometimes called "intellect" by Plotinus (V.1.3.13). But in this schema Soul does not become superfluous, because the motions of embodied individuals need an ἀρχή distinct from Intellect, which does not explain transitive motion or goal-directed behavior where there is a "gap" between desire and goal. A disembodied intellect is eternally in possession of what it desires; an embodied soul is ever desirous of attaining goals which are outside it. The ἀρχή Intellect explains images of Forms and images of intellection, but it does not explain embodied, goal-directed activities. Various types of cognition are of course implicated in goal-directed behavior, such as reasoning as an instrument of action. But Intellect is not the ἀρχή which explains the having and acting on behalf of external goals. It explains only the cognitive dimension of such acting.

Soul is an ἀρχή of embodied action in a fairly straightforward sense. For example, if we seek to explain why humans desire one kind of food and other animals desire another, finally the explanation will reduce to a statement of what each is, and this is equivalent to an appeal to the kind of soul each has. For embodied individuals putatively identifiable with a disembodied intellect, however, the ultimacy of the explanation of action by Soul is compromised. Intellect explains no such action. That we seek things, like food, which it makes no sense for us who are intellects to seek is a kind of paradox for Plotinus rooted in his subtle account of the twofold nature of human existence.

Just as intellection is the activity of Intellect, so desire is the activity of Soul (IV.4.16.26–7. See also I.7.1.13; III.5.9.40–1). There are two closely related senses, however, in which desire is attributable to Intellect. First, in the logical derivation of Intellect from the One, Intellect is said to desire its good and then to attain it (V.3.11.11; V.6.5.9–10). Second, Intellect is said always to desire its good and always to attain it (III.8.11.23–4). The term ἔφεσις is applied to Intellect because achievement of good through contemplation of Forms does not obliterate a distinction between Intellect and the One. Since the goal of Intellect is other than it, desire in one sense describes this otherness. The use of the term ἔφεσις for Soul and for Intellect is only analogous. Desires that fail to be achieved or to satisfy when achieved are only imitations of a desire that is eternally satisfied.[76]

It is apt that Plotinus uses ἔφεσις for everything besides the One in relation to it under the aspect of the Good. But whereas intellects are directly and eternally related to the Good, everything else seeks the good in something other than the One itself. Hence, its distinctive analogous use for Soul. Every embodied soul as such seeks goods which are necessarily different from the ἀρχή of all. To desire food or sex or friendship or even empirical knowledge is to be oriented in a manner essentially different from the way that Intellect is oriented to the Good. For the goods that the embodied soul seeks are obviously other than the unique Good which is the One. I do not think it is even possible for an embodied soul to desire the One unqualifiedly, as does Intellect. For desiring it as Intellect does would, it seems, mean just being an intellect. What an embodied soul can have, however, is a desire to have the desire that Intellect has, though this be a desire for the relatively unknown. As we shall see, awakening this second-order desire is the main feature of the ascent of the embodied soul to the One.

Parallel to the problem of distinguishing the ἀρχή Intellect, universal intellect, the intellect of the demiurge, and particular intellects is the problem of distinguishing the ἀρχή Soul, universal soul, the soul of the all, and individual souls.[77]

We can start disentangling these by noting first that the soul of each individual and the soul of the universe are in one sense on a par. They are "sisters" derived from prior principles (IV.3.6.13; II.9.18.16).[78] They are each themselves instantiations of the principle that explains embodied motion. But the universal soul is also prior to individual souls because it "prepares the way" for them by producing nature which includes the organic bodies that individual souls inhabit (IV.3.6.10–15; II.9.18.14–17). Hence, there is a kind of overlap in that the bodies of individuals are also parts of the body of the universe. It must have seemed to Plotinus obvious that our bodies are governed conjointly by the laws of nature and by our own souls (IV.4.32.4–9).[79] Further, the soul of the universe looks to universal intellect, whereas individual souls look to their own partial intellects (IV.3.6.15–17). I take it that this means that the soul of the universe has direct access to its own separated intellect, whereas individuals have only indirect access to their own through their discursive intellects.[80]

Next, it would seem most natural to infer that the soul of the universe is the demiurge's soul. Plotinus does not actually say this, but to the extent that the distinction between universal intellect and the intellect of the demiurge is sound, there seems nothing against such an inference (see II.3.18.15; II.9.8.2–5; III.9.1.2; IV.4.10.2–3; IV.8.1.43–4; V.1.8.6–7; V.8.2.4).[81] The relation between the intellect of the demiurge and its soul will be the relation of the intellect of an individual and its soul writ large with the important difference that a faculty of discursive reasoning is absent from the former.[82]

This leaves the problem of the identity of the ἀρχή Soul and universal soul. Given that the soul of the universe and the soul of individuals are the same in form (ὁμοειδής), it should follow that there is an εἶδος of soul in virtue of which they are the same (see I.1.2.6–7; II.9.6.35; IV.3.2.9). On this interpretation, the ἀρχή Soul and universal soul would just be the Form of Soul. This is so because the account of what anything is must be referred to essence. If this were not so, then the distinctive nature of soul would not be available for knowing by intellect. As an ἀρχή, Soul is paradigmatically what all things possessing soul participate in, including the soul of the universe.[83] If this is correct, then the clear priority of intellect to soul is its priority to individual souls. The ἀρχή Soul is eternal just as the ἀρχή Intellect is. It is in the soul of the universe that time originates.

Plotinus devotes a treatise, IV.9, to the question, are all souls one? Our understanding of this cryptic doctrine must be framed by two explicit and clear propositions expressed elsewhere. First, the unity of soul does not eliminate a plurality of souls (VI.4.4.34–5; IV.9.2; IV.9.3.6–9). Second, the unity and plurality of souls is a fact prior to incarnation (VI.4.4.39–40). Plotinus asks, "how then can one essence be present in many?" Indeed, he says, it is the very same thing in the many souls (IV.9.5.1, 7–8).[84] I find it most plausible to understand this in a straightforwardly Platonic manner. The single Form of Soul is present in all souls. The unity of souls is the unity of a kind. Thus, soul is one and many, because there is one Form and many embodied individuals with different lives (IV.9.2.27. See also IV.2.1.53–7). How then can souls be many even prior to incarnation? The obvious answer is that they are many intellects, which is their highest part.[85] The point can be stated in another way. Since there is a multiplicity of intellects which correspond one-to-one to souls (of humans, anyway), the individuation of souls prior to incarnation needs no further explaining.[86]

There are several remarks of Plotinus that have led some to think that he means more than this. For example, he points to sympathy (συμπαθεῖν) among persons and their ability to share pain with others as evidence of the unity of soul (IV.9.3.1–4).[87] And their unity is stressed when he says, "each of them [souls] is not marked off by boundaries; and for this reason it is one" (VI.4.14.7–8). The affinity of souls for each other owing to their similar composition is a relatively unproblematic Stoic doctrine with Platonic roots. I see no reason to infer from the fact of sympathy more than a specific identity among incarnated souls. The absence of boundaries between souls is accounted for by the immateriality of distinct intellects which are separate yet united in the manner explained in the previous section.[88]

IV

Truth and the Forms

1 Where and What is Eternal Truth?

I have argued that Plotinus' account of eternal truth has a central role to play in his metaphysics. Intellect must be held to exist eternally because eternal truth exists. The possibility that eternal truth can be explained by the One itself, thereby rendering Intellect superfluous, is rejected because of the complexity of eternal truth and the simplicity of the One. In this chapter we need to look closer at the basis for the claim that eternal truth must be subordinated to the first principle of all. We shall then turn to what is evidently an innovation of Plotinus, the positing of Forms of individuals.

Plotinus attempts to maintain a delicate balance in the priority of the One to Intellect. On the one hand, Intellect is *what* it is owing to itself.[1] As a principle, nothing outside it explains its nature. On the other hand, Intellect depends on the One for its existence, as we have seen. This dependence is total. That is, Intellect does not have an existence on its own prior to or apart from that which is provided by the One.[2] This of course invites the question of why the One therefore does not make Intellect superfluous. Why should we not say, for example, that the One is the locus of eternal truth? And we might add, conceding Plotinus' argument that truth is being for an intellect, that the One is virtually cognizing the Forms which are virtually within it. After all, Plotinus does in fact agree that cognitive language is analogously applicable to the One.

There are two facile responses to this objection. The first is that the concept of intellect is a bit of historical baggage which Plotinus was simply unwilling to jettison. This will not do because it is irrelevant to the philosophical consideration of the arguments Plotinus actually does provide. The second is to say that virtual eternal truth is not eternal truth and that it is the latter whose explanation Intellect provides. This is unsatisfactory because it is obviously question-begging.

There are two claims Plotinus seems to make in reply to this objection. First, timeless or eternal truth is essentially complex and therefore it cannot be identified with the unqualifiedly simple and primary ἀρχή. Second, he can reply that there is no eternal truth without there being a relation between being and intellect and that this relation is essentially complex. The latter reply is suggested by Plotinus' rejection of Aristotle's god as complex, even if its knowledge is perfectly reflexive self-knowledge. The former reply is suggested by arriving at the proposition that eternal truth exists via Platonic premises. That is, the locus of eternal truth is Platonic Forms.

If "5 is odd" and "4 is even" represent distinct eternal truths because of the necessary connections among distinct Platonic Forms, then the stringency of the criterion of absolute simplicity applied to the One would seem to exclude these truths as being really distinct within that first principle. Virtual eternal truth means nothing unless the secondary activity of the One is coextensive with eternal truth. If we bypassed Intellect and tried to explain eternal truth simply by the One, then we could not say that 5 is odd and 3 is even because of the natures of 5 and 3 and odd and even. We would have to say that 5 is odd and 3 is even because of exactly the same reason, viz., that the One is. Of course, the effects of the causal activity of the One are different and so the explanation of different things ultimately recurs to the One. But the explanations pass through Intellect. In other words, Intellect is an indispensable adjunct to the explanatory role of the One.[3] The One is an explanatory entity of sorts, described in such a way that it cannot explain eternal truth alone. It explains only the existence of eternal truth and that which participates in Forms, its locus. Without the causal activity of the One, eternal truth would not exist. But the nature of eternal truth is not identifiable with the nature of the One.

Perhaps this can be stated differently. An eternal truth needs a formal cause as explanation. The number 5 is odd because of the nature of 5. The One cannot be the formal cause of anything, because the One is not univocally predicable of anything and if the One were the formal cause of anything *and* an efficient cause, the simplicity of the One would be compromised. Hence, the simplicity of the One, deduced from the nature of an ἀρχή of all, limits the One to being an efficient cause of existence, but thereby requiring a formal cause of eternal truth distinct from the One. Further, if the One were the locus of eternal truth, it would stand in a real relation to instantiations of eternal truth. But then its simplicity would also be undermined. If the One were the locus of eternal truths, the One could not be infinite and self-caused. It could not be infinite, because being identical with the nature of 5 would entail some limitation with regard to every other nature. It could not be self-caused, because its existence would be extrinsic to its nature.

The reason for denying that the One is the locus of eternal truth is actually the same as the reason for positing Intellect, namely, the complexity of eternal truth. This complexity also entails the insufficiency of Intellect in explaining its own existence. The complexity entails the real distinction of existence and essence in it. To put this crudely, its essence is a many but its existence is one. So, they must be really distinct. The reason why eternal truth or Intellect do not cause their own existence is that in themselves they can only be essential causes. And an essential cause cannot be the cause of the existence of anything, because it does not exist in itself.

The account Plotinus is providing is best appreciated when viewed alongside what Plato and Aristotle say about the same matters. Plato has a Form of the Good which provides "being and knowability" to the other Forms. What this being is supposed to indicate is far from obvious. Nevertheless, the unqualifiedly superordinate Form of the Good does not seem to usurp the role of the other Forms as essential causes. The ἀρχή of all for Plato is an ἀρχή of all in certain ill-defined respects. It is not an ἀρχή unqualifiedly. Yet, Plato seems to recognize clearly enough that finite being, οὐσία, is in need of a cause of its existence, even though it be eternal and immutable.

Aristotle's problem is somewhat similar. His unmoved mover or god is supposed to be the ἀρχή of all. Even assuming that it is unique, serious problems remain. God's thinking about thinking is, on the most plausible inference from Aristotle's statement of his program for a science of being qua being, held to be the nature of being itself. So far, so good. But the content of god's thinking is not necessarily connected with eternal truth. And once we discard the doctrine of the everlastingness of substance and species, there is no justification within the Aristotelian system for recognizing or explaining eternal truth at all. Aristotle's god is not even an efficient cause. But even if it were, it would not be the ultimate explanans of truth, eternal or otherwise.

That the One is virtually what everything else is because the One produced everything else is a sophisticated response to inadequacies in the accounts of Plato and Aristotle, but it is a response along the same lines. The postulation of Intellect as an eternal principle subordinate to the One, really distinct from it, involves Plotinus in serious problems which have ramifications throughout the system, as we shall see. If eternal Intellect were eliminated, then either eternal truth would have to be rejected, or else it would have to be identified with the One. But then the simplicity of the One could only be retained if eternal truth were reconstructed on a non-Platonic model. For example, it could be maintained that eternal truth when known by us is known not as it exists in the One. Still, it is eternal truth that we know and still it is that truth that resides eternally in the unqualifiedly simple One. As bold and original a thinker as I regard Plotinus to be was yet too devoted to the teachings of his master to think these thoughts.

Aristotle's metaphysics posits intellect alone as first principle. The inadequacy of this position is for Plotinus based upon the complexity of intellect and the premise that the first principle must be non-complex. Assent to the inadequacy of Aristotle's metaphysics in this regard suggests an alternative wherein a simple first principle is posited and Intellect as second principle is eliminated. Many versions of theistic metaphysics might be characterized in this way, for example, St Augustine's. In Plato, the elements of Plotinian metaphysics are surely present – Forms, a divine mind, and a first principle above these called "Good" or perhaps even "One." It must be confessed, however, that these elements are not well integrated in the dialogues. Particularly, a connection between the first principle and everything else besides the divine mind and Forms is nowhere made. Even if one argues that such a connection is implicit because everything desires the good, there is no doubt that the first principle is *not* said to be related to everything else in the way it is related to the Forms, as the cause of their being.

Because Plotinus is inspired by Plato and in many respects does indeed follow him, attacks on Platonism, particularly the theory of Forms, are assumed to apply to and in fact overwhelm Plotinian metaphysics as well. In this section I am going to be concerned exclusively with attacks on Platonism originating from the second type of metaphysical system mentioned above, theistic metaphysics. What I aim to show is the distinctiveness of Plotinian metaphysics, particularly the irreducibility of the first two principles to each other and the indispensability of both. This is most effectively shown when Plotinian metaphysics is confronted with arguments which seek to eliminate Forms and thereby a subordinate Intellect, while at the same time retaining a first principle which is supposed to be a unique metaphysical explanans.

James Ross in a number of powerful and subtle articles has attacked Platonism from a theistic perspective.[4] This attack is very differently situated from one which proceeds from non-theistic principles. Ross denies that there exist eternal Forms, but he affirms that eternal truth does exist. This eternal truth is identical with God, who contains "the one sufficing likeness" for all things created. God is the exemplar of all things. He is and knows them virtually and eminently.[5] It will perhaps be useful to consider Ross's attack on Platonism as a kind of rejoinder to Plotinus' attack on Aristotle.

Let us begin by stressing the parallel between God and the One. As "one sufficing likeness" and as virtually all created things, Plotinus' first principle is in some respects similar to God as described in the metaphysics Ross intends to defend. The difference arises precisely when Ross moves from virtuality to eminence and concludes that if God is not just the creator of all things but is identified with all things in a "higher" sense, then Platonic Forms are not necessary to account for anything. Ross's attack is actually two-pronged. He attempts to show both that the (or a) theory of Forms is inconsistent and that what that theory attempts to account for is in fact satisfactorily accounted for only by a creator who is virtually and eminently all that is created.

It is Ross's contention that the central concept of Platonism is exemplification, a putative relation between Forms and their instances. It is claimed that exemplifiction is unable to explain the being, the whatness or essence, and the individuality of instances.[6] Basically, Ross argues that in exemplification the being of instances is not accounted for because Forms are not causes of being. They are not creators. The Plotinian answer to this charge is that the One is posited as cause of existence with the instrumentality of Intellect.

Second, it is argued that Forms do not account for the essence of anything exemplifying Forms. As Ross puts it, "No modern Platonist (or theistic neoplatonist that I know of) thinks the exemplars *are* the realities of which concrete things are weak copies." This argument *assumes* a version of an Aristotelian essentialist position according to which there is no subject which can exemplify or fail to exemplify an essence. For example, Socrates cannot be the subject of his humanity in such a way that he could lose it. If he were to lose his humanity, he would not exist. I think it is in fact the position of both Plato and Plotinus that Aristotelian essentialism is false, and from this it follows that subjects do gain and lose exemplifications of Forms. The elements that comprise Socrates, for example, might well someday exemplify cathood rather than humanity. Ross is correct to tie the theory of Forms to a denial of essentialism. But he offers no arguments in behalf of the claim that the theory of Forms is thereby unduly encumbered.

Finally, it is argued that exemplification does not account for the individuality of that which is exemplified. This argument is related to both the first and the second. Ross believes that individuality is functionally related to being and essence. A thing is one because it is an existent of a certain sort. So, since Forms explain neither being nor essence, they do not explain individuality. The answer to this argument, like the first, is begun by positing the One as cause of existence with the instrumentality of Intellect. Stated more precisely, the One is the direct and sole cause of existence or, what amounts to the same thing, the cause of being with the instrumentality of Intellect.

Curiously, Ross rejects out of hand what he calls a "retreat to *dependent* necessary beings, to divine idea neoplatonism." He identifies this position as being defended by Alvin Plantinga.[7] The criticism he makes of this position is that

> if the dependent beings are *other* than God, the simplicity and independence of God are compromised. God would not be "creator of all things visible and invisible." If they are "parts" of God, simplicity is denied too. Furthermore, creation is without content because the natures, kinds, and even objects are determined a priori by God's nature. God fills abstracta with being ("actuality") like a boy filling molds with lead to make soldiers.[8]

It is true that Plantinga does not see simplicity as a crucial attribute of God or the ἀρχή of all. But this is certainly not Plotinus' view of the matter.

It is very difficult to see why the simplicity of the first principle is denied if what Ross calls divine ideas are dependent beings. After all, Ross defends a simple creator upon whom all created things are dependent. Evidently, what Ross sees as compromising the simplicity of God is *eternal* dependence.

Either that or he just runs together the positions of Plantinga and Plotinus. It is incumbent on Ross to explain why eternal dependence compromises God's simplicity any more than does temporal dependence. It is also difficult to see why Ross seems to take dependence as a reciprocal relation. He seems to be saying that if natures are eternally dependent upon God, then God is somehow eternally dependent upon these natures. But the dependence of natures upon God is unqualified, whereas the dependence of God upon the natures is hypothetical. So, the relation is not reciprocal. Nor is it a real relation. Only if God wants to make something with, say, the nature of iron is God constrained by that nature. Why should this not be so, and why should this be a constraint upon the divine nature any more than the way that non-contradiction is a constraint upon it? Finally, in reply to the last criticism implicit in the passage quoted from Ross, Plotinus' position is precisely that Forms are not "abstracta" waiting to be filled with being by the One. Rather, Intellect is identical with the Forms and described as the secondary activity of the One. And since the dependence of Intellect upon the One is eternal, there are indeed no "abstracta" waiting to be actualized. There are only paradigms waiting to be copied.

The arguments offered by Ross are perhaps well aimed against possible world theory and the ontology presumed in quantified modal logic. They are even perhaps effective against at least one reasonable interpretation of the theory of Forms in Plato. These arguments do strongly suggest what is lacking in these theories. My claim is that in these respects Plotinus has supplied what is lacking, more or less anticipating Ross's criticisms. But there is more.

Ross wishes to defend a theistic metaphysics according to which "iron rusts" is a necessary truth owing to the nature of iron. But iron does not necessarily exist. He would say that there exists something which necessarily rusts is owing to God's will or wisdom. The nature of iron was created by God, but only through the creation of instances of iron. For Plotinus, this gets things backwards.

> But supposing [Intellect][9] discovered the thought of horse in order that a horse (or some other animal) might come into being here below? Yet how would it be possible for him when he wanted to make a horse to think a horse? For it is already clear that the thought of horse existed if he wanted to make a horse; so that it is not possible for him to think it in order to make it, but the horse which did not come into being must exist before that which was to be afterwards. (VI.7.8.3–8)

If God thought it fitting that there be a world with iron things in it, was it not because he thought it fitting that something with this nature exist? What does "this nature" refer to? Ross says that it refers either to nothing or to the divine nature which is virtually and eminently iron and water and so on. So, when God contemplates creation, he thinks that his nature should be instantiated thus and so. Plotinus would say that, having resolved not to compromise the simplicity of the first principle, he must posit a complex eternal intelligible array in order to make sense of the creation of anything with a nature. The complexity must be removed from the first principle, but it must not be removed from eternity altogether. The instances are instances of distinct natures.[10] It is true that the instances must be instances of what is eminently those natures. But what is eminently those natures, Intellect, is not virtually those natures. It is an instrument of the One, which is virtually all that it causes to be. Iron is not an instance of God; it is an instance of the nature of iron, which is what the Form of Iron is identitatively.[11]

If one *assumes* that creation must be temporal, that eternal truth exists, and that the first principle is absolutely simple, then Ross's position would seem to follow.[12] But there is no *philosophical* reason for assuming this. On the other hand, if one is just resolved to retain the unqualified simplicity of the first principle and is also prepared to concede that "iron rusts" is a necessary truth owing to the nature of iron, whereas "water is wet" is a necessary truth owing to the nature of water, then this seems to be so because of distinct natures. And it seems better (retaining divine simplicity) to posit eternally distinct natures or essences in the Plotinian manner. The dispute between Plotinus and Ross may be summarily expressed in the following way: (1) Plotinus says that the first principle creates a nature or essence and then uses the nature to create individuals which possess it; (2) Ross says that the first principle creates the nature by creating the individuals which possess it. Obviously, if we follow (2), then there are no natures uninstantiated, no eternal intelligible possibilities. What *this* means is that there is no way to talk about divine creation except in terms of the divine will. We cannot intelligibly say, for example, that God wanted things one way *rather* than another, for the words "rather than another" indicate an unactualized eternal possibility.

It must be granted at once that this is hardly a decisive argument on behalf of Plotinus' position. But it should be stressed that for Plotinus the locus of eternal truth is a mind, as it is for the defender of a theistic metaphysics which makes God omniscient. If divine simplicity is nevertheless insisted upon, either eternal truth is complex, in which case it must be subordinated to the first principle, or it is simple, in which case it must be unqualifiedly identical with the mind of the first principle. So Ross agrees with Plotinus in holding that there is some eternal truth in virtue of which iron rusts. He differs from Plotinus in holding, say, that the eternal truth in virtue of which water is wet is exactly the same truth in virtue of which iron rusts.

Further, both Plotinus and Ross believe that the natures or essences have a cause of their being.[13] But Plotinus distinguishes their eternal causality from the temporal causality of the things with these natures, whereas Ross collapses the causality of natures with the causality of things with natures. In so doing, Ross, unlike Plotinus, rejects absolutely any explanatory function for the natures themselves. The *only* explanation allowed is God's will or wisdom. In the proposition "God willed that there be things of such and such a nature," the explanatory role for the intelligible content in each nature is usurped by God's will. Thus, there can be no explanation of why a nature is not instantiated, not even that God willed it that one "part" of what God is virtually not be instantiated.

As I have suggested, Ross's position assumes creation in time as well as divine simplicity. The issue of divine independence is something of a red herring. Ross's first principle is no less constrained hypothetically than is Plotinus' first principle. If God wants a world in which iron rusts, then *that* fact presumably constrains God in other respects.[14] More important, I think, is that Ross's position gets some of its dialectical force from the fact that things like iron and water are of course not eternal. The dialectical force is somewhat blunted in the case of mathematical natures and transcategorical natures such as, say, difference or unity. According to Ross, in the one eternal truth that is the divine mind, difference and sameness are only conceptually distinct. But if God contemplated making anything at all, then God contemplated making something different from Himself, not the same as Himself. If God is different from His creation, then that is because what difference is is not what God is. Again, if the number of things created by God is odd, then oddness is something God instantiated, but oddness is not identical with the simple divine nature.[15] Some *tertium quid* is needed to explain the connection between the absolutely simple and the temporally complex.

It does not seem to me adequate to say with Ross and Aquinas that divine simplicity and a multiplicity of eternal forms coexist so long as we understand this to mean just that the divine nature is imitable in a multitude of ways. It is eternally so imitable and hence a multiplicity will be insinuated into God. The only way to avoid this would seem to be to posit an eternally subordinate second principle, namely, Intellect.

2 Forms of Individuals

Plotinus' use of the Platonic material in his attacks on the Stoics and on Aristotle has many peculiar features, none more so than his apparent claim that Forms of individuals exist. An interpretation of Plato's theory of Forms which countenances Forms of individuals is indeed exceedingly odd. According to the most reasonable understanding of that theory, Forms may themselves be individuals, but they are not of individuals. Forms are postulated to account for identity in difference. They are the "ones over and above the many," where "many" stands for some *repeatable* intelligible content. In so far as an individual is understood as precisely what is not repeatable, the whole point of Forms seems to be lost if Forms of these are postulated. Nowhere in the dialogues does Plato even hint that Forms of individuals make the slightest bit of sense.

72

The testimony of Aristotle, however, indicates that he at least thought that Forms of individuals were implied by one of the arguments the Platonists used to prove the existence of Forms. The argument is briefly alluded to in the *Metaphysics* and set out more explicitly in *On Ideas* (1.9.990b14–15; Alexander of Aphrodisias, *In Meta*. 81.25–82.7). I quote from the latter:

> The argument that tries to establish that there are Ideas from thinking (τοῦ νοεῖν) is as follows. If whenever we think of man or footed or animal, we are thinking of something that is both among the things that exist yet is not one of the particulars (τῶν καθ' ἕκαστον) (for when the latter have perished the same thought [ἔννοια] remains), clearly there is something besides particulars and perceptibles, which we think of whether the latter exist or not; for we are certainly not then thinking of something non-existent. And this is the Form and an Idea. Now he [Aristotle] says that this argument also establishes Ideas of things that are perishing and have perished, and in general of things that are both particulars and perishable – e.g., of Socrates, of Plato; for we think of these men and preserve some image of them even when they no longer exist. And indeed we also think of things that do not exist at all, like a hippocentaur, a chimaera; consequently neither does this argument show that there are Ideas.

In this argument Aristotle is reported as drawing an implication of the argument from thinking that is presumably undesired by the Platonists. Finding that Forms of particulars, and even Forms of imaginary creatures, would be demanded by their argument, the Platonists should want to give up that argument, presumably because they do not accept such Forms.

One obvious difficulty with Aristotle's argument is the apparent equivocation on the meaning of νοεῖν. Thinking about man or footed or animal need not be the same sort of thing as thinking about Socrates when he is no longer present. Indeed, if the argument from thinking is to be an argument for Forms at all, the point must be that there is a kind of thinking which is distinct from thinking about particulars and that it is this kind of thinking which entails Forms. Man, footed, and animal are supposed to have an intelligible content apart from individual men who are two-footed animals. We can know what they are even when the individuals disappear, so, the argument goes, they must exist. It is Aristotle, not Plato, who contends that this is the same type of thinking that occurs when Socrates departs and we think about him. Plato, it seems, need not accept this, even given the version of the argument from thinking that Aristotle uses. When we are thinking about man, footed, and animal we are not thinking about a particular man, even when the particular man is present. This is certainly not the case for our thinking about Socrates, as is even suggested by Aristotle's use of the word φαντασία. The image of Socrates is necessarily connected to him whether he is there or not, as the contents man, footed, and animal are not.[16]

Plotinus certainly knew of this argument as it appears in the *Metaphysics* and quite possibly knew of the longer version as it appears in Alexander of Aphrodisias' commentary on the *Metaphysics*. The most straightforward explanation of Plotinus' apparent assertion of the existence of Forms of particulars is that he accepted the argument from thinking and also the implication that Aristotle drew from this argument.

There is, however, another reason independent of historical considerations which is likely to have inspired Plotinus to consider Forms of particulars. As we have seen, the One is the cause of the existence of everything that exists. Furthermore, Intellect is instrumental in each act of sustaining the existence of anything. Thus, a question naturally arises of how sustaining existence operates for, say, each member of a species. The One always operates in the same way: it operates through Intellect, which invests each thing with intelligible content. If the identity of each individual falls below the threshold of intelligibility, then there is no need to posit an intelligible content in Intellect to account for that identity. If, however, there is intelligible content in the individual as such, then this would seem to need accounting for by Intellect. And for Intellect to account for something is basically for there to be a Form of that thing.

Aristotle had denied that an individual as such is definable, which is equivalent to denying it any intelligible content (see *Metaphysics* 7.15.1040a5–7). He can thus account for individuality with matter, which is in itself unintelligible. By contrast, Plotinus' first principle, through the instrumentality of Intellect, reaches down to the existence of every individual. To deny all intelligible content to the individual as such would seem to block the creative activity of the One. The One's causal activity would seem to outstrip its instrument in this case. To hold that it is the *same* intelligible content in each individual member of a species would yield an identical result. Hence, on Plotinus' general principles, there would seem to be some reason for taking seriously the possibility that there is a distinct intelligible content for each individual and that this content resides eternally in Intellect.[17]

Plotinus devoted an entire treatise to the question of whether or not there are Forms of particulars. The passage in which he explicitly accepts Forms of particulars is at the beginning of the treatise.

> Is there an Idea of each particular thing? Yes, if I and each one of us have a way of ascent and return to the intelligible, the principle of each of us is there (see IV.3.12.3–4). If Socrates, that is the soul of Socrates, always exists, there will be an absolute Socrates (Αὐτοσωκράτης) in the way that an individual soul is said to exist there, that is [eternally].[18] But if Socrates does not always exist, but the soul which was formerly Socrates becomes different people at different times, like Pythagoras or someone else, then there will not be this particular person Socrates

also in the intelligible world. But if the soul of each individual possesses the rational forming principles (τοὺς λόγους) of all the individuals which it animates in succession, then again on this assumption all will exist there; and we do say that each soul possesses all the forming principles in the universe. If then the universe possesses the forming principles, not only of man but of all individual animals, so does the soul; there will therefore be an infinity of forming principles, unless the universe returns on itself in regular periods; this will put a limit to the infinity of forming principles, because the same things in this case recur. Well, then, if the things which come into being in all the periods together are more numerous than the models, why should there have to be forming principles and models of all the things which come into being in one period? One man as model would do for all men, just as souls limited in number produce an infinity of men. No, there cannot be the same forming principle for different individuals, and one man will not serve as a model for several men differing from each other not only by reason of their matter but with a vast number of special differences of form. Men are not related to their Form as portraits of Socrates are to their original, but their different structures must result from different forming principles. The whole revolution of the universe contains all the forming principles, and when it repeats itself it produces the same things again according to the same forming principles. We ought not to be afraid of the infinity which this introduces into the intelligible world: for it is all in an indivisible unity and, we may say, comes forth when it acts. (V.7.1)

At the beginning of the passage, Plotinus of course means to affirm the antecedent of the conditional "if I and each one of us have a way of ascent and return to the intelligible, the principle of each of us is there." This proposition does not assert that there is a different principle for each one of us. By itself, it could simply be taken to mean that there is one principle, say the Form of Man, for all. The next line, however, introduces the notion of "absolute Socrates," and leaves little doubt that he means to affirm a different principle for each individual. But the reason given for affirming this is most puzzling. Why should the immortality of Socrates be relevant to the question of whether or not there is a Form of Socrates? In Plato, no such reason is ever given for generating Forms. The direct answer to the question leaps off the page. "Absolute Socrates" refers to the intellect of Socrates, which eternally resides in the community of intellects. The intellect of Socrates is a Form because Socrates uniquely instantiates a single disembodied intellect.[19] What Socrates is eternally or ideally is an intellect cognitively identical with all Forms. The physical thiswordly Socrates is presumably the unique instance of that intellect.

If this is Plotinus' meaning, then the postulation of Forms of individuals is greatly qualified. It does not refer to individuals without intellect, like a particular rose. More importantly, the reason for postulating Forms of individuals with intellects does not conflict with the general Platonic one-over-many argument for Forms, when we couple this with the relevant reductionism. For example, there is no Form of a particular artifact, say, my house, because there is no Form of artifact at all. There is no Form of a particular movement, say, a particular locomotion now, for all the intelligibility in it is accounted for by the kind movement alone. A similar situation obtains for particular instances of all the subordinate Forms.

Several problems remain. First, there is the matter of reincarnation and transmigration of souls, alluded to in this passage, and elsewhere strongly affirmed by Plotinus (see III.2.13.15; III.4.2.2–4; IV.3.8; IV.7.4.8–14; IV.8.1; VI.7.6–7).[20] In our passage he seems to be saying that if, contrary to fact, the soul of Socrates transmigrates into the soul of Pythagoras, then the particular Socrates will not be present in the intelligible world. He then adds, however, that if the soul of, say, Socrates, possesses the λόγοι of all the individuals it will eventually animate, then all of these will exist in the intelligible world. And the soul of Socrates does do this.

It is not easy to see what is and what is not being asserted here. The two positive claims – that Socrates is present in the intelligible world and that he possesses all the λόγοι of the souls he will or might eventually be identical with – are seemingly set off against a denial that Socrates can turn into Pythagoras and an assertion, at least by implication, that he can. Underlying the palpable ambivalence here seems to be some doubt in Plotinus' mind about the identity of an embodied individual compared with the identity of the discarnate intellect. If the discarnate Socrates is identical with the incarnate Socrates, and the discarnate Socrates is everlasting, it is to say the least difficult to see how he could ever become the incarnate Pythagoras, when the latter is presumably identical with the discarnate Pythagoras, and hence distinct from the discarnate Socrates. A similar problem arises for a putative transmigration into the body of an individual animal, and for Plotinus' claim that Forms of these exist as well (V.7.3.19–20).

The most reasonable interpretation of Plotinus' meaning is that the Form of an individual, the αὐτο-X, stands in a one–many relation to a class of incarnations, including perhaps Socrates, Pythagoras, and some lowly animal. All these no doubt differ from the Form owing to countless material accretions.[21] We call the Form "Socrates" because Socrates happens to be the incarnation of it here and now. But the same Form of Socrates is, at another time and place, aptly identified as the Form of Pythagoras. What this interpretation does exclude is that two individuals existing simultaneously should have the same Form.[22] This interpretation can also explain the initially puzzling claim that there are Forms of individual animals, which should rest upon the same argument from eternal Intellect that the argument for individual Forms of humans does. At the end of the treatise, there is the clear implication that the λόγοι of every individual animal is contained in Intellect. This does not mean that animals as such have intellects. It means, it seems, that intellect transcends biological specification, which occurs below Intellect, from nature and from matter. Even if the puppy in the litter is not the reincarnation of Socrates, it belongs to a family of incarnations which could, and perhaps eventually will, include a man.[23] A Form of Dog and a Form of Socrates would suffice for the reincarnation of Socrates as a dog. There would be no need for an additional Form of Fido.

There is an important principle implicit in the claim that no more than one individual can instantiate the Form of Socrates at the same time. What Socrates instantiates is a unique and eternal activity, that of his own intellect. Unlike the Forms that are its intentional objects and that are multiply instantiable simultaneously, Socrates' intellect uniquely cognizes these. Since, as we have seen, the highest form of cognition is essentially self-reflexive, Socrates can only benefit from his own intellect's activity. How he does so in incarnate cognition will concern us later. The point here is that Socrates and someone else could not simultaneously instantiate one intellect because incarnate cognition does not instantiate a *kind* of activity, but a particular activity of one individual. One does not just use intellect, but one's own intellect.

All of this admittedly highly speculative attempt to combine a version of the theory of Forms with adherence to reincarnation or transmigration must be set over against another treatise in which Plotinus appears to deny Forms of individuals. Actually there is one passage which has been taken to contain an explicit denial of Forms of individuals:

> But if the Form of Man is there [in the intelligible world], and of rational and artistic man, and the arts which are products of Intellect, then one must say that the Forms of universals are there, not of Socrates but of Man. But we must enquire about man whether the Form of the individual is also there;[24] there is individuality, because the same [individual feature] is different in different people: for instance, because one man has a snub nose and the other an aquiline nose, one must assume aquilinity and snubness to be specific differences in the Form of Man, just as there are different species of animal; but one must also assume that the fact that one man has one kind of aquiline nose and one another comes from their matter. And some differences of color are contained in the formative principle but others are produced by matter and by different places of abode. (V.9.12.1–11)

I think that this passsage is actually rather weak evidence for the claim that Plotinus is here contradicting what he says in V.7.[25] First, the explicit denial of a Form of Socrates precedes the words "but we must enquire about man whether the Form of an individual is there," strongly suggesting that the denial is dialectical in nature. Second, as Igal has shown, the apparent denial of a Form of Socrates belongs in the consequent of a conditional proposition.[26] This does not mean that the affirmation of a Form of Socrates requires a denial of the antecedent. It means only that the affirmation of the antecedent does not itself require accepting a Form of Socrates. The question of whether or not there is a Form of Socrates has to be addressed independently. Finally, the reason Plotinus gives for denying Forms of individuals, namely, that individuality is accounted for in part by matter and place, does not conflict with the reason given in V.7 for affirming Forms of individuals. For that reason, as we recall, was the uniqueness of an individual's intellect and its eternal residence in the ἀρχή Intellect, where it is cognitively identical with Forms. The features of composite individuals, such as the aquiline or snub nose, need only be accounted for universally, within the theory of Forms. I conclude that the passage from V.9.12 does not give us any reason to revise our understanding of V.7.

There are several passages which have been taken as contradicting what Plotinus says about Forms of individuals. In the first, he says that it would be absurd to introduce many Ideas of Fire. On the contrary, one Idea of Fire is sufficient to account for whatever it is that an Idea is supposed to account for (VI.5.8.39–41).[27] In arguing for the uniqueness of the Form of Fire and in general for the uniqueness of Forms throughout this treatise, Plotinus actually follows closely the logic of Plato's ἕν ἐπὶ πολλοῖς principle and separation of Forms (see VI.5.6.2–4; VI.5.8.22–3). If, however, I am correct in arguing that Plotinus only believes in Forms of individuals with intellect, then there is no contradiction in his holding generally to the Platonic rationale for generating Forms, namely, the presence of identity in difference.[28]

The other texts speak unequivocally of a Form of Man which accounts for the humanity of individual men (see VI.5.6). But it is a non-sequitur to infer a denial of a Form of Socrates from an affirmation of a Form of Man.[29] Socrates is a man by participation in the Form of Man and he is Socrates by participation in the Form of Socrates. The universal Form of Man is not a man and, conversely, Socrates is not a universal. In the intelligible world, however, the individual intellect takes on universality by being cognitively identical with all Forms, including of course the Form of Man. Accordingly, I do not see the supposed contradiction in Plotinus' doctrine. Forms of individuals do not represent a repudiation of the reason for postulating Forms in Plato's dialogues. They represent an extension of that theory which attempts to take seriously the eternal cognitive activity of individual intellects.

V

Categories and the Tradition

1 The Criticism of Stoic Categories

According to Porphyry, the *Enneads* are full of concealed Stoic and Peripatetic doctrines. This suggests an implicit adoption by Plotinus of ideas taken from traditions more or less hostile to Platonism. As we have seen, the matter is not straightforward. Plotinus reinterprets these doctrines in the light of Platonic principles. A good example of this is Aristotle's principle that actuality is prior to potency, which is made to cohere with the claim that the ἀρχή of all is virtually all of its products. Another example to be discussed later on is the Stoic account of virtue, which is integrated into an ethical theory in which the immortality of the soul is central. Regarding category theory or accounts of the basic divisions of reality, Plotinus had available to him Stoic and Peripatetic material that was far richer in detail than anything to be found in Plato. Yet for Plotinus, since the fundamental principles of all reality are rejected by the Stoics and misunderstood by Aristotle, there could be no question of simply appropriating this material as an adjunct to a Platonic system.

Plotinus follows one tradition of understanding categories as kinds of being or existents (γένη τῶν ὄντων) (VI.1.1.15–18). He is thus able to commensurate the account of Plato with those of the Peripatetics and Stoics. Plato spoke of kinds of being in the *Sophist*, although he did not call them "categories," and Aristotle in several places suggests an identification of categories with kinds of being.[1] Plotinus says that the meaning of "kinds of being" is ambiguous, referring either to the classes of intelligible and sensible entities or to some division within the latter.[2] He is probably correct in holding that but for Plato his predecessors were only concerned with category theory in so far as this applied to sensibles.

The reason for this among the Stoics is straightforward – they denied the existence of separate immaterial entites. In Aristotle, the matter is more complex owing to the fact that at some point he came to deny that being is a genus and hence that it is univocally predicable of its species. Plotinus' basic critical strategy, used against both Aristotle and the Stoics, is to show that category theory, understood as somehow a non-arbitrary division among the things that are, must inevitably rest on a metaphysical principle of being. Plotinus thinks that both Aristotle and the Stoics have got this wrong and Plato has basically got it right.

The criticism of Stoic category theory is for Plotinus more straightforward and less portentous than the much longer criticism of Aristotle's. The governing assumption of this criticism is that the Stoics, as materialists, exclude in principle immaterial being, and hence are doomed to failure.[3] Since the Stoics do not account for immaterial being and hence cannot give an accurate account of being in general, nothing they say about material being can be fully acceptable.

The Stoic theory of categories divides the genus "something" (τι) into four species: subjects (ὑποκείμενα), qualities (ποιά), things in a certain state (πῶς ἔχοντα), and things in relation to something (πρός τί πως ἔχοντα) (VI.1.25.1–3). There are basically two criticisms made of this theory.[4] First, if "something" is a genus, then there must be differentia within this genus. Without differentia there are no species, and without species there is no genus. But if the genus "something" is synonymous with a genus of "being," then there are no differentia of it, for there are no differentia of being. Plotinus is, most interestingly, apparently relying on Aristotle's proof in the *Metaphysics* that being is not a genus because there are no differentia of it (3.3.998b22–999a1; 4.2.1003a33–b12).[5] We should note in passing that the proof would be equally cogent against an attempt to divide a genus being into two species, the intelligible and the sensible. The apparent employment of Aristotle's argument in this way also indicates that by "being" Plotinus here at least means something other than a natural kind or a kind in general. If he meant *that*, then the argument would simply fail. The reason why being is not differentiable is that the differentiae would have to have being and so would automatically become species. It is quite literally a category mistake to make being a genus, where being is that which things or natures possess. This use of "being" here will be seen to be in contrast to its use in defense of Plato, who explicitly posits a genus of being in some sense, although it is not a highest genus.

The second criticism reinforces the assumption brought to the first. If "something" is being and a genus, then this genus either exists or it does not (ἢ ὂν ἢ μὴ ὂν ἐστιν). If it exists, then it is one of its own species; if it does not, then being is non-existent. But if it is one of its own species, then it is both genus and species, which is incoherent. It would be like a class that is a member of itself. In short, if we distinguish being from whatever has being, it is hopeless to suppose that being is a genus, for without differentiae there can be no species and without species there can be no genus. If, however, "being" is taken to refer to a kind or nature or essence, even the most general one, then the question remains of how there can be differentia of it which are not also species. The Stoics mean "something" to be identical either with being or with what has being. In either case they are defeated.[6]

The Stoics hold one variety of the view that to be means to be x, where x can stand for whatever you like, say, the value of a variable, a perceptible object, or that which is extended in space and time. The Stoic version, or at least the one Plotinus is familiar with, holds that to be means to be corporeal or material, the distinction between which we may for the moment ignore. If it can be shown, as Plotinus thinks he can show, that being is really distinct from what has being, then any such view obviously fails. Those like the Stoics who would wish to deny such a distinction need to be shown that the alternatives, namely, that being and what has being are only conceptually or verbally distinct, necessarily lead to incoherence in any account of the basic furniture of the world. Of course, one may decline the invitation to offer such an account as, say, the Sceptics certainly would. But Stoicism is constitutionally unable to refrain from pronouncing on the ultimate nature of things. The Stoics may disdain metaphysics, but this only amounts to renaming it physics. And their crypto-metaphysics comes to grief owing to their misunderstanding of the nature of being.

From the middle of *Ennead* VI.1.25 to the end of VI.1 Plotinus assaults the Stoic arguments for the four categories. The arguments are not uniformly cogent or original and in any case the destruction of the genus "something" as being pretty well guarantees that a principle of the division of what has been shown not to exist is also going to be lacking. I limit my discussion to the treatment of the first category "subjects" because it reveals with great clarity some of the metaphysical principles Plotinus is going to employ constructively.

There are five distinct arguments marshalled against the first Stoic category ((1) VI.1.25.12–33; (2) VI.1.26.1–17; (3) VI.1.26.17–37; (4) VI.1.27.1–47; (5) VI.1.28.5–26). The first argument attempts to show that the Stoics are confused in identifying "subjects" and "matter." A subject is prior in being to its attributes, but supposedly "subjects" is one species among other coordinate species within the genus "something." Species within a genus have the genus univocally predicable of them. Hence, a subject should be said to be in exactly the same sense as an attribute or quality, as indeed would be the case if the division of the highest genus were merely a division of its material kinds. Yet a subject is prior in being to what it is a subject of. Presumably, if the Stoics were to reply that the priority of subject to attribute is an unsupported Aristotelian innovation, then Plotinus' justifiable rejoinder would be that "subject" then becomes an arbitrary designation and hence not a species within a division of kinds of being. Further, if the Stoics were to object to the identification of "subjects" and "matter" while still maintaining that "subjects" is a distinct species of "something," then they would certainly have to deny that to be means to be material. But such a denial means giving up the claim that there is merely a conceptual distinction between being and what has being. If the Stoics concede *this* claim, then what are we to make of the genus "something"? Is it just being or what has being?

The second argument against the Stoic category "subjects" assumes that the Stoics will opt for the alternative that matter is identified with the first category. Plotinus' indebtedness to Aristotle here is evident both in the assumption that matter for the Stoics must be potency and in his appropriation of the principle that actuality is prior to potency. Defenders of the Stoic position might reasonably object that by "matter" is meant body (σῶμα) or extensive magnitude. Indeed, Plotinus himself recognizes elsewhere an apparently canonical Stoic definition of matter as "body without quality, or magnitude" (see II.4.1.13–14 and *SVF* II.309, 326). But if *this* is what matter is, then, as the next argument will demonstrate, matter is not a principle, for a magnitude is divisible according to some principle. If, on the other hand, by "matter" is meant an indivisible principle of body, it is difficult to see what else it could refer to but potency.

Assuming, then, that the interpretation of matter as potency is reasonable, still one wants to know why this makes potency prior to actuality. After all, Aristotle holds that matter is a principle *and* that actuality is prior to potency. The answer is simply that matter as first category or subject will then become the ultimate analysans of reality. The ultimate explanations of Stoic physics will be in terms of potency. But as Plotinus elsewhere shows, relying on Aristotelian arguments, potency is logically parasitic on actuality. No potency can be an ultimate explanation because potencies are, as it were, in the interstice between one actuality and another. Potencies are inferred on the basis of actual attributes possessed by bodies, among other things.

Plotinus was likely to have been aware of one standard interpretation of Stoic physics according to which they held two coordinate principles, matter and an active principle, variously called "god" or "pneuma."[7] But as Plotinus is quick to point out in our present argument, if god or the active principle is separate, then it is immaterial and the Stoics deny the existence of separate, immaterial entities. But if god is a body, as they in fact hold, then god himself is a composite and so not a principle at all. So, in this argument Plotinus is not denying that matter is a principle, but rather that it is the only principle; and, if it is a principle, it cannot be the first principle, in so far as it is identified with potency.

Surely, though, the Stoics could simply reject the legitimacy of the concept of potency altogether. But this entails a rejection of a real distinction between potency and actuality. Then, in referring to the present in relation to the future, there is no way to distinguish non-arbitrarily what something has the potency for being from what it does not have the potency for being. Every moment should be a total surprise, because nothing that was a moment ago has any relevance to what is going to be.[8] So, in so far as the Stoics recognize that nature is changeable, there will be no λόγος of nature, counter to a central Stoic tenet. Certainly, Stoic determinism would be unsustainable.

The next three arguments all take up the alternative that matter is identical with the primary category and body and attempts to show that if it is, matter cannot be a principle. Whatever is a body is composite (πολλὰ), that is, it is analyzable into matter and qualities, where "matter" must be understood as the first category "subjects," and "qualities" as including quantity and whatever else can be predicated of the subject apart from state and relation, the remaining two categories. The underlying argument behind the claim that every body is composite has already been explored in the first chapter. If the Stoics understand body as necessarily including three-dimensionality, they are speaking only of the quantitative properties of body; if they include resistance (ἀντιτυπία) along with three-dimensionality, then it is patent that body is not simple and so if matter is body, it is not a principle. Three-dimensionality is not inter-definable with matter. Hence, the unity of the composite body – a unity between really distinct parts – is explained by a prior principle. That is, if you say that any bit of matter is extended and you agree that this is not an identity statement, then there is in principle available an ultimate explanation of this complex state of affairs. If this is so, then matter is not a principle. The "unity" of an extended bit of matter is accidental (κατὰ συμβεβηκὸς), otherwise there would not be a real distinction between matter (body) and three-dimensionality.

The fourth argument is guided by Aristotle's claim that matter is a subject only in potency because it is only a "this something" (τόδε τι) in potency (see *Metaphysics* 8.1.1042a27–8).[9] Obviously, the argument presumes that the Stoics either continue to conflate potency and actuality or recognize their distinction but retain the priority of the former. The basic point of this obscure passage is that if "subject" is understood as something like a canvas upon which nature produces its creations, then matter is not a principle but a condition for the operation of a principle on it. If, on the other hand, matter is identified with nature and nature's operations, that is, if matter is οὐσία, then it will not be what underlies nature.

The fifth and final argument against the first Stoic category takes a different approach. It purports to display the Stoic rationale for identifying the subject as the primary category. The Stoics thought that the way to arrive at first principles was by the use of sense-perception. On the basis of their senses, they decided that bodies constituted reality. But bodies undergo change, and so, presumably to avoid the embarrassment of having things come into and go out of existence, they posited that which persisted through change, the subjects, as what is primarily real. That something must persist (μένει) through change is demonstrable, but the Stoics err in identifying being with persistence instead of asking first what being is and then showing why persistence belongs to it as a property. They are thus led into the absurdity of holding that place persists but that it is not being, because it is not matter. Further, if sense-perception is of bodies or of the attributes of bodies, and if matter is prior to body, how is matter supposed to be perceived? And if matter is just identified with bodies, then how is the persisting subject perceived?

Finally, the Stoics have deceived themselves in thinking that they have arrived at the first principle through sense-perception, for matter as a principle is not available to the senses. What is available to the senses is only an instantiation of a principle. If, however, they allow that they have arrived at this principle through intellect, then they are in the untenable position of placing matter before intellect, indeed, even denying the real being of intellect. Finally, and here Plotinus makes rare use of a Sceptical argument, it is odd that when the Stoics trust intellect to tell them about principles, when intellect does not exist for them. That is, if, as Plotinus thinks, intellect must be immaterial, and the Stoics deny that immaterial entities exist, then their reliance on intellect is empty.

The force of the above arguments depends upon the accuracy of the interpretation of Stoic views they presume. Undoubtedly, alternative interpretations are available which avoid some of the inconsistencies Plotinus thought he detected. I believe the general point – the inadequacy of Stoic metaphysics and hence the inadequacy of Stoic category theory – is sound. More relevant to our purposes is the set of Aristotelian principles revealed as used by Plotinus in his criticisms of the Stoics. The cogency of the criticisms obviously depends upon the acceptability of these principles.[10] That being is not a genus, that actuality is prior to potency, that categorical priority and posteriority are to be explicated causally, and that subject in the sense of matter cannot be primary οὐσία are Aristotelian principles which Plotinus accepts even as he attacks Aristotle's own category theory. It is to this attack that we now turn.

2 The Criticism of Aristotle's Categories

Plotinus' criticism of Aristotle's account of substance and the other categories is based upon the above-mentioned principles and upon Plotinus' understanding of οὐσία as presented in chapter 3. The central feature of that account which underlies the present criticism is that, contrary to Aristotle, οὐσία is not unqualifiedly primary and hence not the focus of primary philosophy. Further, any theory which takes sensible οὐσία or οὐσία belonging to the categories as the focus of an account of being is going to be misguided. In that case, an image would be substituted for that which it images.

There is, however, some reason to doubt that the theory presented in the *Categories* assumes the hypothesis proffered in the *Metaphysics* that being is οὐσία.[11] Aristotle might reasonably be taken to have been developing an account of categories of sensible being in the earlier work and to have eschewed metaphysical questions. To this defense Plotinus will respond that if Aristotle did not there intend to identify being with substance or οὐσία, he still owes us an answer to the question of how being and οὐσία are related or why οὐσία is fundamental in his schema. The only answer to the question in the *corpus* is in fact that being and οὐσία are identical. Hence, Plotinus is justified in assuming that identification by Aristotle as he examines the theory of the categories. Furthermore, Aristotle, unlike the Stoics, recognizes at least the possibility of immaterial entities. Hence, he must hold either that sensible substances and non-sensible substances are two species of οὐσία, or that each is said to be οὐσία equivocally, or that (presumably) sensible substance is not the fundamental category (see VI.1.1.19–VI.1.2.18).[12] That Aristotle avoids answering this question in the *Categories* and, on the basis of the identfication of being and οὐσία in the *Metaphysics*, cannot answer it satifactorily is a central theme woven throughout the criticism.

In the *Categories* Aristotle offers two basic rules of thumb for picking out substances: (1) it is that which is neither said of nor present in a subject and (2) an οὐσία is a τόδε τι, a "this something" ((1) 5.2a11–13 and 3a8–9; (2) 3b10). As for (1), Plotinus makes the reasonable and mild complaint that negative definitions are not very helpful (VI.1.3.17–23). The major focus of his criticism is (2), and it is in fact to this he turns after a discussion of the other categories in Aristotle, and the Stoic and Platonic categories.

Plotinus' strategy is to argue against Aristotle's account of the category of οὐσία on the assumption that sensible οὐσία is not unqualifiedly independent. Plotinus has Aristotelian grounds for denying the unqualified independence of sensible οὐσία. In book 6 of the *Metaphysics* Aristotle says that being separable (χωριστὸν) and being a τόδε τι seem to be preeminent features of οὐσία. On this basis, he seems to conclude that the sensible composite, the τόδε τι, precisely owing to its materiality, is posterior and should be "set aside" (7.3.1029a27–32).[13] What "posterior" means here is a highly contentious matter. The plausible interpretation followed by Plotinus is that posteriority entails dependence of some sort and so a denial of unqualified separableness for the composite.[14] Consequently, the criteria of separableness and "thisness" are torn apart, and if sensible οὐσία fulfills. the latter, it does not fulfill the former. And so whatever Aristotle says about sensible οὐσία that would require fulfillment of both criteria must be rejected.[15]

If sensible οὐσία is not unqualifiedly separate, it is οὐσία only homonymously (ὁμωνύμως) (VI.1.1.25–8; VI.3.2.1–4). If οὐσία were said synonymously of sensible and non-sensible οὐσία, then they would be species of the genus οὐσία, which would itself be neither sensible nor intelligible (VI.1.2.4–8).[16] One reason for holding that sensible οὐσία is not unqualifiedly separate is the Platonic one that the sensible world in general is only an image of the intelligible world and so is to be identified with becoming (γένεσις) and not true being (VI.3.1.21; VI.3.2.9). Behind this traditional Platonic language is an argument for the existence of Platonic Forms and the consequent "demotion" of the sensible world and Plotinus' response to Aristotle's criticism of this argument. We may set these aside for the moment to concentrate on the anti-Aristotelian argument from Aristotelian principles.

How are we to understand the posteriority of the sensible composite οὐσία and the reason for thinking it is not unqualifiedly separate? When Aristotle speaks of this posteriority he strongly suggests that it is owing to the fact that the composite includes matter. This inclusion of matter means that such actuality as the composite has is constituted in part by matter or potency. That means that the composite as such is not unqualifiedly actual. To analyze the composite otherwise would amount to destroying its unity. If, for example, we said that the composite contained two parts, unqualified potency and unqualified actuality, then the actuality would be just the form or else there would be two actualities, the form and, *per impossibile*, the matter. But actuality for a composite is just to be the composite, and that actuality is compromised by matter. This much Aristotle, I think, accepts.[17] What of course he does not accept is the apparent implication that if the individual composite οὐσία is to be understood or defined according to form, then it is something like an imitation of a form that is separate from it.

Yet even here there is evidence that Aristotle at least saw such an implication. In chapter 6 of book 7 of the *Metaphysics* Aristotle raises the question of whether each thing and its essence (τὸ τί ἦν εἶναι) are the same or not. Answering this question, says Aristotle, is useful for the investigation of οὐσία because each thing is thought to be nothing else than its own οὐσία, and this οὐσία is said to be essence (7.6.1031a15–18). The answer given to the question at the end of the chapter is that "of things which are primary and are stated by themselves (καθ᾽ αὑτα λεγομένων), then, it is clear that each of them and its essence are one and the same" (7.6.1032a5–6).

For Plotinus, the obvious puzzle is just what these things "which are primary and are stated by themselves" are supposed to be. A passage a bit further on in chapter 11 supplies the answer:

> And we have stated that in some cases the essence of a thing and the thing are the same, as in first substances; for example, curvature and its essence are the same, if curvature is a first substance. (By "first substance" I mean one which is not stated as being in something else in an underlying subject as in matter.) But things which exist as matter, or which include matter, are not the same as their essence; nor are those things which are one by accident, such as Socrates and the musical, since these are the same by accident. (7.11.1037a33–b7)

It seems plain that "first substance" is equivalent to "things which are primary and are stated by themselves" and equally clear that Aristotle excludes sensible composites from this class. The reason given is that the composite is in an underlying subject, its matter. Thus, in the next book Aristotle says,

For a soul and the essence of a soul are the same, but the essence of a man is not the same as the man, unless also the soul is called "a man"; accordingly, in some cases a thing and its essence are the same, in others this is not so. (8.3.1043b2–4)[18]

The denial that the sensible composite οὐσία is unqualifiedly separate derives in part from the argument that it is not identical with its essence. The individual composite has been shown to be not identical with the essence which is actuality. Hence, its being is not unqualifiedly actual, but contains potency. If it were objected that the composite is an actuality merely different from the actuality that is essence, Plotinus would reply that then the individual and the essence would be two really different things, with the embarrassing (for Aristotle) consequence that sensible composites could not have essences at all. And so the composite is not unqualifiedly separate, because actuality is prior to potency, and what is posterior is dependent to some extent.

Aristotle is presumably not absolutely adverse to the conclusion that sensible substances are not unqualifiedly separate. If god is to be identified with unqualifiedly separate substance, and being is indeed a πρὸς ἕν equivocal, then *some* sort of causal dependence should obtain between sensible οὐσία and the primary referent of being. This is in line with Aristotle's identification of the science of being qua being with theology. But Aristotle most emphatically does not see this result as a concession to Plato's theory of Forms or to anything like a "two-world" theory. Plotinus, on the other hand, sees it as a vindication of Plato's doctrine. When Aristotle implies that in sensible composites οὐσία is not identical with essence but that in things which are primary and are stated by themselves it is, he is not committed to the existence of more than one such primary being, namely, god. He is not, in short, committed to Forms. The denial that say, a Form of Man exists as a separate οὐσία opens the way for explaining how the individual οὐσία Socrates is related to his humanity otherwise than via a Platonic approach and otherwise than by identifying Socrates with the essence of man.

Aristotle claims that if Platonic Forms existed, and these were the essences of sensible substances, then since these Forms are separate, the essence of sensible substances would be separate from them. In that case, sensible substances would no longer be substances, for substances are those things which are identified with their essence. Plotinus simply accepts the implication that the existence of Forms entails the denial of the substantiality of sensibles. He does not, as Aristotle does, take it as a reductio argument against Forms. Plotinus' counterattack consists in pointing out that Aristotle is explicitly unable to identify sensible substance with essence, because sensibles contain matter. Hence, the reason for rejecting Forms as the essence of things, namely, that their separation would entail the non-identity of sensible substance with essence, is, on Aristotle's own terms, unsupported.

Against Aristotle's assertion that "man and what it is to be a man are not identical," Plotinus says "the Form of Man and man are identical," holding that the "what it is to be" of anything is in fact a Platonic Form (VI.3.4.17).[19] Aristotle analyzes "x is f," where x stands for an individual οὐσία and f for the kind of thing it is in terms of act and potency. "Socrates is a man" means that Socrates is an actualization of man. Aristotle can say that "Socrates is a man" is an identitative use of "is" and not predicative without holding that "man and what it is to be a man are identical" just because there is a real minor distinction *within* Socrates between the composite individual and the form of man.

The opening Plotinus sees which he thinks will enable him to refute or rather correct Aristotle and vindicate Plato is the apparent contradiction between saying that the composite is posterior and also that, as actuality, it is prior. We have seen the grounds for saying that the composite is posterior, namely, that the composite is not perfectly actual. If it were perfectly actual, the least of the difficulties that would ensue is that it could not change because it would not have a potency to any new actuality. But Aristotle also wants to say that the composite, Socrates, is prior in being to the form man. If he did not say this, he would either have to deny that form and composite are really distinct or he would have to allow the priority of man to Socrates. The former denial is out of the question; the reason for not accepting the latter amounts, for Plotinus, to nothing more than an unjustified unwillingness to accept Plato's Forms.

The crux of the dispute between Plotinus and Aristotle comes down to this. Grant that "x is f" but that whatever is f's nature is not unqualifiedly identical with x. It would seem that all anti-nominalists, Plato, Aristotle, Plotinus, *et al.* must grant this much. Let us grant further that form and actuality are identical.[20] Then, how is x related to that nature of f in terms of priority and posteriority in reality? For Plotinus, the correct answer is unavoidably Platonic. Somewhat less tendentiously, the position which at once maintains that act is prior to potency, that form is act, and that the composite is posterior to form cannot consistently also maintain that the composite is prior to the form which is not identical with it. As we have also seen, the composite is not unqualifiedly separate in the sense of existing independently. This fact further diminishes the coherence and the plausibility of the Aristotelian analysis.

The above interpretation of Plotinus' criticism of Aristotle's account of sensible οὐσία should enable us to understand some of the more extreme claims that Plotinus makes. It should be emphasized that the argument against the absolute priority of composite οὐσία and the subsequent vindication of Plato do not strictly speaking abolish sensible οὐσία as the primary category in the sensible world.[21] However, the nature of a "this something" which is separate in relation to its attributes but which is not unqualifiedly separate remains to be explored.

Plotinus' analysis of "Socrates is a man" is as follows:

> For when I predicate "man" of Socrates, I mean it not in the sense in which the wood is white, but in the sense that the white thing is white; for in saying that Socrates is a man, I am saying that a particular man is man, predicating man of the man in Socrates; but this is the same as calling Socrates Socrates, and again as predicating "living being" of this rational living being. (VI.3.5.18–23)[22]

It is clear that in this passage Plotinus is interpreting what Aristotle would call the "said of" relation between secondary and primary οὐσία, which is expressed grammatically as "Socrates is a man" in terms of Platonic participation. For Aristotle, "Socrates is a man" is based on an analysis which yields the priority of the individual over the form along with their real minor distinction.

For Plotinus, "Socrates is a man" means that Socrates partakes of the Form of Man. But what is Socrates? A man, of course. There does, however, seem to be a good deal of difference between saying that this man partakes of the Form of Man and that Socrates is Socrates, counter to what Plotinus says. In the former case there is a distinction between the instance of the Form and the Form; in the latter case there is an identity statement. Or perhaps it is not quite so straightforward. It is true that Plotinus wishes to insist on a distinction between an instance of a Form and the Form itself. But he also must insist on their identity, otherwise instantiation would be entirely opaque.[23] So, the man that Socrates is, is and is not identical with the Form of Man.[24] The composite Socrates is and is not identical with the real Socrates, who resides in the realm of Intellect. The paradoxical "is and is not" is to be glossed roughly as "ideal x and empirical x." In Plotinus' view, this is what Aristotle is actually driven to say when he holds that the sensible composite is and is not identical with its essence. It is just that Aristotle does not see that Forms are thereby vindicated.

Thus does Plotinus attempt to defend the two-world ontology of Plato. The sensible world is an image of the world of Forms (VI.3.1.21. See also II.3.18.17; II.9.4.25; VI.2.22.36).[25] More particularly, the sensible instance of a Form is an image of it (V.9.5.17–19). And just as a picture of an individual is to the individual, so the instances of Forms are to Forms (VI.3.15.31–8). Following Plato, Plotinus emphasizes the dependence of an image upon what it is an image of to sustain it in existence. True images, like those in pools, mirrors, and shadows are distinguished from artistic representations, improperly called "images" (VI.4.10.11–15). Whereas an artistic imitation can continue to exist when the original is destroyed, a true image is sustained in existence only so long as the original exists.

Here is an indication of the different sort of dependence that images have on Forms and the One. An image of a Form depends on the Form for being *what* it is; it depends on the One for being one existent. Neither sort of dependence is reducible to the other, nor are the roles of instrument and primary cause for Intellect and the One reversible. The ἀρχή Intellect is an instrument of the efficient causality of the One, giving to images vestiges of intelligibility. For Aristotle, however, such a causal account is otiose because the instances of a nature are not images of it. If they were, the sensible composite would be posterior in reality to that of which it is an instance. It is this posteriority that Plotinus insists on and, from his point of view, Aristotle does not expunge.

Plotinus' criticism thrusts a dilemma upon Aristotle. Granted that a sensible composite is one thing, that one thing's actuality is either the form or the composite. If it is just the form – and this is the natural suggestion given what Aristotle says about form – then the composite, say Socrates, is not the single actuality. But this is impossible, for the actuality is the οὐσία and that is "this man," not "man." Then, the composite is the single actuality, but the composite is, in Aristotle's own words, "posterior." The form of this composite is corrupted or compromised, as, for example, the red in a pink mixture. On this line of reasoning, one then has a choice of saying that the sensible form is diminished only in relation to the notionally perfect or that it is diminished in relation to the really perfect. In either case, it remains true that the form is named univocally along with the perfect, just as in the color example again, where the red in the pink mixture is not equivocally said to be red. Plotinus has a rather easy time demolishing the alternative that the diminished form is diminished only in relation to the notionally perfect, as we have seen. An instance is posterior to what it is an instance of, whereas a concept is posterior to an instance.

Plotinus attacks head-on Aristotle's claim that the individual is prior to what it is an instance of. Speaking of individual instances of categories and their species and genera he writes:

> For literary skill is not posterior to the particular literary skill but rather it is because literary skill exists that that in you exists; since that in you is particular by being in you, but in itself is the same as the universal. And Socrates did not in his own person give being human to the non-human but humanity gave being human to Socrates: the particular human is so by participation in humanity. Since what could Socrates be except "a man of a particular kind" and what could the "of a particular kind" do towards being more of a substance? But if it is because "humanity is only a form" but Socrates is "form in matter," he would be less human in this respect: for the rational form is worse in matter. But if humanity is not in itself form, but in matter, what less will it have than the particular human in matter, when it is itself the rational form of something in a kind of matter? Again, the more general is prior by nature, as species is prior to the individual; but the prior by nature is also simply prior; how then could it be less? But the individual is prior

in relation to us because it is more knowable; but this does not make a difference in actual fact. (VI.3.9.23–40)

There are a number of important points in this passage. First, let us notice that the Form-instance, in this case, literary skill, is, despite the fact that it is an image, said to be identical with the "universal," that is, the nature that is predicated of many instances. It is striking that Plotinus seems to identify the Form with a universal, which is of course Aristotle's way of stating Plato's position, not Plato's. And one of Aristotle's central arguments against the theory of Forms is that if the Form is a universal it cannot also be an individual, which is apparently what Plato wishes to make of it (see *Metaphysics* 3.6.1003a7–13; 4.2.1005a5–13; 7.13.1038b39–1039a3; 7.16.1040b28–30; 11.2.1060b21; 13.9.1086a34).

Is Plotinus here boldly affirming what Aristotle holds to be impossible, namely, that an individual is also a universal? That seems unlikely for two reasons. First, if individual and universal are contradictories, then it is obviously false that an individual is a universal. Second, Plotinus tells us that the "literary skill" in the particular is the same "in itself" as the universal. If what is in the particular is the same as the universal, then "universal" does not simply refer to what is separate from the particular, namely, the Form. Plotinus appears to be distinguishing separate Form, particular instance or image of the Form, and the universal which is the same in each. What the image has in addition to being what the universal is and what makes it an image is attributable to what it is "in." The universal is paradigmatically in the Form; it is derivatively in the image. Thus univocity in the predication of a universal in addition to diminished reality is affirmed by Plotinus. The Form-instance may not be real, in some sense of "real," but it is not an imperfect embodiment of the real in the sense that it is only equivocally what the Form's nature is.[26]

Further, in this passage the causal priority of humanity to the humanity in Socrates is made explicit. One legitimate causal explanation of Socrates' humanity is given by indicating his parents, but this sort of explanation is irrelevant to what is sought here. Socrates is a man because there is manness in him and there could be no manness in him if manness were not prior, that is, did not exist, apart from Socrates and any other possible instance. The reason why Plotinus thinks that such an explanation is demanded is that the instance of the Form of Humanity in Socrates is diminished in reality, it having been shown that there is no unqualifed actuality in the composite. Plotinus' use of Aristotle's analysis of sensible substance in fact gives him a more precise way of saying this than if he had simply relied on Platonic language. The actuality of "this man" is not unqualified actuality because it is mixed with matter. Aristotle of course refuses to answer the question "why is x f?" by saying "because f-ness is in it," since that would be for him to explain an actuality by a potency.[27]

91

Finally, Plotinus contrasts separate Form with the form that is part of the composite. The latter is diminished owing to its presence in matter. The λόγος or definition of Socrates, the form in matter, is worse (χείρων) than the λόγος of the separate Form. Plotinus presumably does not thus intend to gainsay univocity, but rather to indicate that the λόγος of form plus matter is different from the λόγος of Form alone.

Plotinus inverts the Aristotelian hierarchy of actuality by making the species prior to the individual and the genus prior to the species.[28] It is somewhat misleading to use the language of species and genera here, precisely because of the inversion. Species and genera are not for Plotinus concepts or potencies realized only in the mind or in individuals. They are Platonic Forms. The "containment" of the species within the genus is explained by the variegated unity that is Intellect. The justification for saying, for example, that the Form of Horse is contained within the Form of Animal against Aristotle's claim that animal has less being than horse because it is further removed from primary οὐσία is quite straightforward. Since Forms are existentially and causally prior to their instances, the natural necessity that all horses be animals but that an animal need not be a horse can be explained only if "part" of what animal is is horse. Hence, eternal containment. All the Forms are in fact aspects of the complex whole that is οὐσία, just as line and angle are parts of the complex whole that is a plane figure.

Aristotle frequently contrasts οὐσία which is a "this something" with accidental attributes, called "some such" (ποιόν τι) (see *Metaphysics* 7.4.1030b11–12; 8.6.1045b2; 14.2.1089b17–18). He also contrasts the "this something" with secondary οὐσία, also called "some such" (see *Categories* 3b14–16). What accidents and secondary substances have in common is existential dependence on primary οὐσία, the "this something." Plotinus perhaps has both contrasts in mind when he says that the Form of Man is the true "this something," whereas its image in the sensible world is only a "some such" (VI.3.15.24–38).[29]

It is in this context that we should understand Plotinus' claim that the perceptible Socrates contains only an image of man.[30] The point is complicated by the fact that Plotinus follows Plato in identifying the "real man" with the soul, which is imperceptible. His meaning here, however, seems to be more general than the dualism applicable to the particular example of Socrates. Any instance of a Form is manifested by or constructed out of sensible qualities. And this includes the manness in the sensible Socrates. The claim that "x is f but the real f is the Form" amounts to the existential and causal priority of Form to f. Calling the sensible "this something" really a "some such" is not reducing Socrates' humanity or any other thing to an accident of a Form but to an imperfect manifestation of it.

The refutation of Aristotle's account of sensible οὐσία as unqualifiedly primary is the complement of the refutation of his account of non-sensible οὐσία as unqualifiedly primary. If non-sensible οὐσία or god is unqualifiedly primary because it is unqualifiedly being, then sensible οὐσία cannot be unqualifiedly primary. If non-sensible οὐσία is not unqualifiedly primary because it is not unqualifiedly being, then again sensible οὐσία is not unqualifiedly primary because οὐσία is not. The categorial schema of sensible οὐσία and predicamental accidents is not strictly speaking thereby refuted. That Socrates is not the "true man" does not necessarily entail the impossibility of distinguishing identity conditions and accidental predications. Presumably, we could try to distinguish the essence of the image of man from accidental attributes of it. The resulting essentialism, however, would be nothing like Aristotle's doctrine.

3 Aristotelian Essentialism

Aristotelian essentialism posits a distinction between essence and accidents, primarily for substances. In so far as the focus of the doctrine is sensible substance, this distinction is based upon or equivalent to a distinction between substantial change and accidental change. A sensible substance experiences only two substantial changes throughout its existence, in an attenuated sense of "experience." These are its generation and its destruction. Strictly speaking, it does not experience either of these, for it neither precedes its generation nor perdures through its destruction. Between generation and destruction, the only changes it undergoes are accidental.

Aristotle's essentialism depends upon identity conditions for an individual not being logically independent of essence. The identity conditions are functionally related to the essence. This means that a sensible substance remains the same throughout its existence because it remains the same kind of thing. It would be easy enough to construct a version of essentialism without positing natural kinds by making all the essential properties of something individual properties. But this would not be Aristotle's position. On the other hand, it would make no sense to posit natural kinds without these necessitating at least some individual properties. If this could be done, a sensible substance would have undergone only an accidental change even if it turned into *another* sensible substance of the same kind. In fact, detaching natural kind from individuating properties totally would have the bizarre result that any accidental change could be said to result in a new individual of the same kind. But this is incoherent, for an accidental change is functionally dependent upon essential continuity. Thus, if Socrates cuts his beard, he does not just remain a man; rather he remains the same man. So, the essence of the sensible substance must "control" the identity of the substance in some way.

This, however, leaves us with a crucial question. Are individuating properties, such as origin or spatio-temporal location or physical constitution, essential or accidental? Manifestly, they are not all essential, for then there could be no accidental change with respect to them. If, however, Aristotle wished to say that they are all accidental, then we would face the absurdity mentioned above, namely, that essential identity could be retained for an individual that was no more. Presumably, this dilemma is behind many attempts to focus on one or another type of individuating property as essential, discarding all the rest as accidental.

Aristotle of course does distinguish between properties and accidents. "Being risible" is supposed to be a property of the essence of humanity, whereas "being six feet tall" is not. But properties are commensurately universal attributes of essences (see *Posterior Analytics* I.4.73b27ff.). They are what all and only individuals having a certain essence possess necessarily as a consequence of having that essence. So, the problem we are addressing, that of the functional relationship between essence and the identity of the individual sensible substance, is not at all solved by making such a distinction. Individual identity is no more determined by the commensurately universal properties of an essence than it is by the essence itself.

The solution which is in effect supplied by Aristotle is found in his discussion in book 7, chapter 6 of the *Metaphysics*, where he tries to show how an individual substance is and is not identical with its essence. Briefly, the import of the argument is that in the case of an unqualifiedly primary substance, essence and individual are identical. But for anything else, including sensible substance, essence and individual are only qualifiedly identical. It is easy to see that this could not be otherwise. If a sensible individual were unqualifiedly identical with its essence, then another individual could not have the same essence. Yet if a sensible individual were not qualifiedly identical with its essence, then essence would not determine being and hence identity, which is a property of being. According to Aristotle, the severing of essence and individual being is precisely what Plato's theory of Forms entails.

What does it mean for a sensible substance to be qualifiedly identical with its essence? The consequence most relevant to the solution of our problem is that essence in determining substance does not determine individuality. It is not because Socrates is a man that Socrates is not Plato. Individuality, however, is an actualization of substance or, stated otherwise, substance is in potency to its accidents. Essence and accident are neither identical nor unrelated; the latter consists of expressions or manifestations of the former. Thus, Socrates is not essentially a Greek-speaker. His speaking Greek is an accidental attribute of him. But the fact that he can speak any language at all is a function of his being human.

But this only solves a part of the problem. It does give us a way to relate an accident to an essence functionally. It does not answer the question of whether certain attributes, say, that of being born to a particular woman, are accidental or essential. I suspect, though, that borderline or dubious cases such as this are not a particular problem for Aristotle's theory as opposed to an empirical problem which his theory might be supposed to provide a conceptual basis for solving. More importantly, though the theory explains how accidents are functionally related to essence, it does not explain how accidents are related to each other so that a set of them can be said to belong to the same individual rather than just the same essence. Even if all and only men are capable of doing x and all and only men are capable of doing y, how do we know that it is the *same* man who did x at one time and y at another?

The reply must surely be something like this. The substance is what provides continuity, making a set of accidental attributes belong to one individual rather than another. Here is the opening for Plotinus' attack. Aristotle has admitted that only in the case of absolutely separate substance is essence identical with it. As for sensible substances, they are only qualifiedly identical with their essences. But this is the whole point. If the identity of the substance is not absolutely determined by the essence – if the essence does not pick out unambiguously Socrates from Plato – then how is the identity of the substance determined? Surely not by its accidents. And if not by the accidents and not by the essence, then by what?

My reason for thinking that Plotinus' diagnosis of the fundamental problem in Aristotle's account of essence and identity in sensible substance is as I have described it is first that he sees a direct line between Aristotle's rejection of the theory of Forms and that account. In other words, if Aristotle arrives at his account by rejecting Plato's claim that the essences of sensibles are separate from them, then from Plotinus' point of view what is wrong with that account is precisely what it supplies instead, namely, the qualified identity of essence and sensible substance. In this case, he accepts the implied inference that if the essences of sensibles are separate, then Aristotle's essentialism is false.[31]

Let us recall the cryptic claim of Plotinus quoted in the last section that predicating "man" of Socrates is like predicating "white" of a white thing and not like predicating "white" of a piece of wood. Plotinus thus denies that the predication is either accidental or essential.[32] For Aristotle, "Socrates is human" is a paradigm of essential predication and definitely distinct from "Socrates is Socrates" or "this man is man." If "Socrates is Socrates" is not distinct from "Socrates is a man," then the claim that sensible substance and essence are only qualifiedly identical collapses, for Socrates is more than qualifiedly identical with Socrates.

By contrast, Plotinus' analysis of "Socrates is a man" is shaped by the theory of Forms. For example, in the *Phaedo* we read, "If anything else is beautiful besides the beautiful itself, it is beautiful for no reason at all other than that it participates in that beautiful; and the same goes for all of them" (100c4–6). So, if anything is a man besides the Form of Man, then it is so because it participates in that Form.

Participation is first and foremost a denial of Aristotelian essentialism because it posits essences as not even qualifiedly identical with that which instantiates them. Socrates is not the essence of man. With this Aristotle agrees. But he is not essentially a man in the Aristotelian sense either, because the essence of man is not even qualifiedly identical with him. That essence is identical only with the Form and its instances, for example, the humanity in Socrates. This is perhaps the point of the remark a little later on in the *Phaedo* when Socrates says "not only is largeness itself never willing to be large and small at the same time, but also the largeness in us never admits the small"(102d6–8). Identity with an essence belongs only to an essence. So, even if Socrates has humanity in him, he is not identical with it. He is or has an image of the essence. To state this in a slightly different way, the relation between Socrates and the instance of humanity in him is radically different from the relation between that instance and the Form of Man. This is what Aristotle must deny, for he denies that the essence of man is separate from any individual man.

Having accepted separate Forms, Plotinus must reject a functional relation between essence and individual sensible substance. Once this functional relation is rejected, identity as determined by essence is impossible. Plotinus' alternative is to say that the putative sensible substance is a conglomeration (συμφόρησις) of qualities (ποιοτήτων) and matter (VI.3.8.19–20).[33] As Plotinus explains, the sensible Socrates is to the Form of Man as a picture of Socrates is to Socrates. The sensible Socrates is a representation of the true essence. The crucial point of this analogy is Plotinus' conflation of the artificial with the substantial. Aristotle had difficulty in placing artifacts ontologically, but he seemed to settle on the view that artifacts are not substances, probably because the identity of an individual artifact is even more remotely connected with its essence than is the case with an (organic) substance.

Plotinus' rejection of Aristotelian essentialism frees him to treat artifacts and organic individuals as similar in relation to Forms.[34] Thus, the identity of the sensible substance is adventitious or stipulative. Whether a sensible substance is or is not identical through time depends on how we choose to define it. This does not mean that there is not a non-arbitrarily self-identical Socrates or even that there is not a Form of Socrates. It means that Socrates is not identical with a sensible composite and that this sensible composite does not have an essence. This applies generally to what Aristotle calls sensible substances.[35]

4 The Plotinian Categories

The alternative offered by Plotinus to Aristotelian and Stoic categories derives from a reading of Plato's *Sophist*. In that dialogue, briefly, an attempt is made to define the sophist. It is shown that the sophist is a purveyor of verbal and conceptual falsehoods or images of the truth. Images, Plato argues, are a kind of non-being, although not to be identified with absolutely nothing. The heart of the dialogue is an exploration of the justification for saying that non-being somehow exists and so for assigning to the sophist a real *métier*. The strategy Plato employs to this end is to select five greatest kinds (μέγιστα γένη) from among all the Forms and to track down non-being within these.[36] The greatest kinds are: movement (κίνησις), rest (στάσις), being (τὸ ὄν), sameness (τὸ ταὐτὸν), and difference (τὸ θάτερον). Plato first deduces the real distinctiveness of the five and then proceeds to identify non-being with difference. He shows that whatever has difference in relation to something else is not but exists sufficiently to be different. Hence, the sophist's products, false propositions and beliefs, having been shown to be different from truths, are shown to exist after all.

It is fairly obvious that Plato's aim in the *Sophist*, as I have sketched it, is not easily equated with the aims of Aristotle and the Stoics in laying down categories of reality. It has been questioned, for example, whether μέγιστα means "greatest" or just "very great" without the implication that these are ultimate categories or indeed, whether they are categories at all.[37] I think we can grant that Plotinus' own account of the γένη τῶν ὄντων is a questionable interpretative basis for understanding the *Sophist*. But then Plotinus does not claim to interpret individual dialogues within their own contextual limits.

When we take into account what Plato says about being, sameness, and difference in the composition of the world-soul in the *Timaeus* and also what he says about motion in the divine mind in the *Laws*, the situation is altered somewhat. On the assumption, contentious to be sure, that there is something like a general Platonic doctrine only partially revealed in individual dialogues and consisting of the sum of these parts, Plotinus' claim to be recovering that doctrine is not so far-fetched at all. Whether Plotinus' views are finally to be identified with Plato's or not is primarily an historical matter. At any rate, these views are as much a result of the rejection of Aristotle's and the Stoics' views as they are a result of the attempt to carry forward the banner of Platonism.

The first and perhaps most striking feature of Plato's account of the greatest kinds is the fact that being (τὸ ὄν) is just one among other kinds. The oddness of this claim can at least be mitigated with the appropriate Platonic principles. Even if one resists the assumption that the kinds are Forms, still the kind being is, like Forms, predicable of many participants in it. It has or is a nature (φύσις). Hence, it is a universal or a "whatness" and not identical with the existence which is unique or unrepeatable in anything that has it. Further, in the *Republic* Plato hypothesized a Form of the Good, whose special role is to be the ἀρχή of all Forms. It is that which gives τὸ εἶναί τε καὶ τὴν οὐσίαν and knowability to them all even though it is itself ἐπέκεινα τῆς οὐσίας (509b6–9). The relevance of this fact is that Plato distinguishes the Form of the Good, which in *some* sense exists, from the τὸ εἶναί τε καὶ τὴν οὐσίαν of the other Forms. Therefore, the kind being must not be thought to represent what the Form of the Good also has. Still, Plato refers to each of the Forms as οὐσία, leaving us to wonder what a Form of Being is supposed to be (see *Parmenides* 135 and *Sophist* 258).

I believe that the most plausible interpretation of Plato's meaning is the one that in fact Plotinus adopts. A Form is generally the separate entity whose name names the nature potentially present in many instances. It is the paradigm of a certain intelligible content and, as such, it is limited or distinct.[38] The distinctness of an intelligible content does not prevent its location in a hierarchy. Thus, if x is f and f is a specification of the intelligible content g, then x is also g. The kind being represents intelligible content most generally. That is, if f is a specification of g, and g is a specification of h, there is a limit along this line and it is just the kind being, a kind of *summum genus* of whatness.[39]

Several points need to be stressed. First, the higher up in the direction of the ultimate kind being, the more contentful, not the less. Second, if we agree to call this most general kind "essence," still Plato does not seem to think that yet another kind is responsible for the existence of each intelligible content.[40] Existence apparently goes along automatically with the possession of some specification of essence. Thus, the description of a Form as αὐτὸ ὅ ἐστι F evidently has an existential implication. Finally, presumably nothing beside the kind essence has just essence rather than some specification of it.

Turning to Plotinus' account of the greatest kinds, we encounter a puzzle similar to that found in Plato. As we have already seen, Plotinus typically identifies Intellect with οὐσία (see VI.2.8.14; VI.2.19.20; VI.2.21.39–40; VI.7.36.12; VI.7.39.5; VI.8.9.30–1).[41] And Intellect is the locus of all the Forms. But Plotinus also follows Plato in identifying a single kind οὐσία or τὸ ὄν, along with sameness, difference, movement, and rest. What precisely is the distinction between the two uses of οὐσία supposed to be? Recall that Intellect is composite, else it would be identical with the One. The rough and provisional answer to our question is that the kind οὐσία is Intellect in one of its aspects, or, as Plotinus puts it, one of its elements.[42] And so it will turn out for the other four kinds. Intellect is identified with οὐσία, when Plotinus is contrasting the intelligible world with the sensible world, the world of becoming. The kind οὐσία or τὸ ὄν is derived from an analysis of the intelligible world. It is the Form of Essence, that in which anything that participates in any other Form must participate indirectly.

In order to understand more clearly what Plotinus is trying to do, let us begin with the analysis which yields the two kinds οὐσία or being and movement.

> Since we find in soul οὐσία and life together, and οὐσία is common to all soul, and life also common, and life is also in Intellect, if we bring in also Intellect and its life, we shall posit as common to all life a single genus, movement. And we shall posit οὐσία and movement, which is the primary life, as two genera. For even if they are one, [the observer] separates them in thought (τῇ νοήσει), finding the one not one; otherwise it would not have been possible to separate them. But

observe in other things also how movement and life are clearly separated from being (τὸ εἶναι), even if not in the true being, yet in the shadow and that which has the same name as being.[43] For as in the portrait of a man many things are wanting, and especially the decisively important thing, life, so in the things perceived by sense being is a shadow of being, separated from that which is most fully being, which was life in the archetype. But then, this gives us grounds for separating living from being and being from living. Now there are many species of being (ὄντος) and there is a genus of being; but movement is not to be classed under being nor yet over being, but with being; it is found in being not as inhering in a subject; for it is its activity and neither of them is without the other except in our conception (ἐπινοίᾳ) of them, and the two natures are one nature; for being is actual, not potential. And if, none the less, you take either of them separately, movement will appear in being and being in movement, as if in the "one-being" each taken separately had the other, but all the same discursive thought (διάνοια) says that they are separate and that each form is a double one. (VI.2.7.1–24)

No fewer than three times in this passage Plotinus says that the kind movement and the kind οὐσία are the same in reality but separated in thought. The sameness these kinds possess in reality consists in the fact that they are "elements" of one entity, Intellect, which is identical with all Forms. These kinds are properties of Intellect itself (VI.3.2.21–2). Presumably, this means that analyses of images of Intellect would terminate in five irreducible genera, five different ways in which Intellect is instantiated. That there are no higher genera than these is proven from the fact that there are no defining predicates for them (VI.2.8.43–5).

The distinction between the kind οὐσία and the kind movement appears to be a distinction between the intentional object of Intellect and the activity which is its thinking, the κίνησις νοῦ that Plato spoke of in the *Laws*.[44] That intentional object is all the Forms taken together. The kind οὐσία is what all intelligible contents are specifications or parts of. It is Intellect viewed from the perspective of being alone.

The best argument Plotinus has available to him for the irreducibility of the kind movement to the kind οὐσία is an Aristotelian one. Aristotle defines movement as the actuality of the movable (*Physics* 3.3.202a14). Thus, a movement is not an actuality, but the process of actualization or acquisition of a new form. The irreducible difference among images of Intellect for Plotinus is between form and the process of acquisition of form (VI.3.22.3–4). Within Intellect, however, which is eternal activity, the paradigm of movement is Intellect in relation to οὐσία, the eternal actualization of the "process" of the acquisition of form.[45] Just as Intellect is the paradigm of desire because it is eternally in possession of the good, so its activity is the paradigm of movement.[46] This is so because the activity of Intellect, cognitive identification with the Forms, is eternally complete or perfect. By contrast, any movement, including the movement of souls, is incomplete and defined by the actuality that is outside it. In this way, Plotinus takes the Aristotelian contrast between activity and movement and turns it into a Platonic doctrine according to which activity is the paradigm of movement.

The kind rest is derived as the complement of the kind of movement that primary life is (VI.2.7.24–31). Eternal activity implies no potency. The kind rest indicates the activity of Intellect viewed as it were from the aspect of its eternal achievement. This kind is to be distinguished from the "images" of rest, which imply the temporary absence of movement.[47] An instance of rest implies the privation of movement, whereas the paradigm of rest implies the paradigm of movement, the life of Intellect. The kind rest is not just another name for the kind movement. They are for Plotinus irreducible elements of the analysis of anything other than the One. The fundamental contrast of movement towards an end and possession of that end must be retained in the paradigm of all complex being, Intellect. The conflation of movement and rest in the paradigm would gainsay the evident intelligibility of their contrast in everything else. Movement and the culmination of movement in rest here below represent in different ways the activity of Intellect.

Plotinus offers another curious reason for distinguishing a kind rest distinct from the kind οὐσία.

> If we were to bring rest and being into one, saying that there was not in any way any difference between them, and bring being into one with movement in the same way, we shall bring rest and movement into identity through the medium of being, and movement and rest will be one for us. (VI.2.7.41–5)

If there were no difference between rest and being and no difference between movement and being, rest and movement would be identical but there would not obviously be anything untoward in this. It is only if we are seeking an explanation of facts already accepted, like the difference between things that are at rest and things that are in movement, that we formulate distinct concepts for rest and movement. The real distinction between the kinds rest and movement within the composite unity that is Intellect guarantees a non-arbitrary basis for our conceptualization of sensible rest and movement.[48]

The last two kinds, sameness and difference, are derived from the real distinction of the first three and the recognition that, distinct though they be, they belong to the same entity (VI.2.8.27–44).[49] If difference were not a distinct kind, then the distinctions among the other three would not be real. If sameness were not a distinct kind, then the other three would be distinct according to a major real distinction among entities, and the life of Intellect would be eternally severed from truth or truth would not exist, inasmuch as truth is complex.[50]

Plotinus says that difference and movement together constitute the ἀρχή of intelligible matter (II.4.5.29–30).[51] Intelligible matter is equivalent to the Indefinite Dyad, the product of the One which, together with it, produces Intellect.[52] The basic role of intelligible matter in Plotinus' categorical system emerges with a good deal more clarity than one is led to expect given its obscure historical origins. Forms themselves are self-differentiating, or, as we might put it, each is its own principle of individuation. Yet there must be something in virtue of which they comprise a unity (II.4.4.2–5. See also VI.7.16.4–8).[53] This something is intelligible matter. Why must we suppose that the Forms comprise a unity? The primary reason is that all the Forms are interconnected necessarily. This necessity *de re* is exactly what the unity of the Forms consists in. The necessary interconnectedness of Forms, that which grounds necessarily true propositions, signifies a complex unity.

It was argued in the third chapter that it is Intellect that serves the above unifying function. Forms are identified in and by Intellect. The second ἀρχή is thus identified as the actuality of a potency which is intelligible matter (see III.8.11.1–5; V.3.11).[54] It is like the achievement of sight in proportion to the faculty itself. As the activity of this sight occurs, intelligible matter is that which accounts for the sight of all the Forms being "at one glance." The identity of Intellect with its intelligible objects makes Intellect a complex unity. That is, the cognitive identity of Intellect with each Form eternally is identity with the same subject. So, for example, two Forms, F and G, actualize the same matter, retaining their individual identity. A necessary truth about Forms then is analyzable as a kind of material identity statement, like an equation. By contrast, sensible matter stands in a one-to-one relation to sensible form. That is why Plotinus would want to say that *de re* necessity is not to be found in the sensible world. Forms can be necessarily connected in Intellect, but no such connections pertain to sensibles as such.

Compare the properties of an Aristotelian substance. In an individual substance like Socrates, being bipedal and being mortal partially identify Socrates. If they did not, "Socrates" would represent multiple actualities. Being bipedal and being mortal necessarily go together because all bipedal things are animals and all animals are mortal. But they are not themselves unqualifiedly identical, because there are animals that are not bipedal. Against Aristotle, Plotinus would insist that if the genus animal is a mere potency, then the necessary connectedness between bipedality and mortality is not explained. Potencies only have intelligibility borrowed from actualities. And it is not Socrates who explains a necessary truth about animality. Socrates could lose his legs and it would still be true that bipedality and mortality are necessarily connected. If, however, we posit a "dense" genus animal containing bipedality and mortality without Intellect as a *tertium quid*, their partial identity is not explained. Indeed, the concept of partial identity among a multitude of immaterial entities seems to be incoherent.

This can easily be demonstrated. Consider a Venn diagram. Let there be

101

two circles A and B. Now let them overlap into an ellipse, called C. Why cannot we say that A and B, because they share C, are thus partially identical? Simply because the manner of identifying C is the same as the manner of identifying A and B in the first place. That is, C is another Form with its own identity and we have now three Forms, A (minus C), B (minus C), and C, which are not partially identical. Incidentally, this explanation also tells us why when Plotinus says that Intellect is a Form he means that Intellect is cognitively identical with Forms. If Intellect were a Form in exactly the same sense in which its intentional objects are Forms, then Intellect, far from solving the problem of partial identity of immaterial entities, would be part of the problem. And it is only if an intellect is self-reflexive that this explanation has any force at all.

The five greatest kinds are distinct aspects of the complex unity of Intellect.[55] The proof Plotinus offers to show that these are the *only* greatest kinds indicates the gulf between the Plotinian and Aristotelian schemes. There can be no greatest kinds of quantities, qualities, and the other categories because the greatest kinds are aspects of Intellect, which possesses no accidental attributes (VI.2.13–14). Of course, for Aristotle the categories other than substance are not accidents of substance; accidents are individual instances of these categories.

For Plotinus, quantity is posterior because quantity includes both number (ἀριθμός) and continuous magnitude (μέγεθος). But number is posterior to the measure of number, the unit, and continuous magnitude is posterior to number (VI.2.13.7–15). Quality is not a basic kind because it is posterior to οὐσία. What this amounts to, as Plotinus proceeds to note, is that quality is not an essential constituent of οὐσία (VI.2.14.1–11). On this point, Plotinus is confirming what Aristotle says about primary substance in the *Metaphysics* and playing that off against what he says in the *Categories*. Unqualifiedly separate οὐσία is primary in the *Metaphysics* and must be bereft of accidental attributes, otherwise it would be in potency to these and so would not be pure actuality. In the *Categories*, the genera of the categories are notional, not real. Primary substance is the individual "this something," which has inhering in it instances of the accidental categories. Plotinus is not denying that there are Forms of qualities, or species of the greatest kinds. He is, however, arguing that Intellect is not in potency to any modification of it, quantitative or qualitative. Accordingly, any Aristotelian sensible substance, which is necessarily modified by accidents, cannot be unqualifiedly primary substance. This is, for Plotinus, the conclusion that Aristotle's own principles should have led him to affirm.[56]

Insisting that the greatest kinds consist only of the five mentioned, Plotinus must account for other Forms as specifications of the five. But first he wants to reject some putative Forms, such as Forms of artifacts, and reduce them to their natural elements.[57] He seems to have particular difficulty with the Forms of the virtues. These are not obviously reducible to other Forms or subsumable under the five greatest kinds. He describes the kind virtue and its species as activities of Intellect (VI.2.18.15–17). It is not easy to see what these are supposed to be. Sometimes Plotinus will speak explicitly of the activity of Intellect in the plural, referring to the activity of each individual intellect (for example, VI.6.15.16; VI.7.13.3). But he cannot here mean to identify the virtues with individual intellects. It is all the more puzzling given that Plotinus holds that there is no virtue in Intellect, meaning that its activity is not to be characterized as virtuous (I.2.1.46–50). I conjecture that he can only mean that they are subsumable under the kind οὐσία, under which all genuine Forms must be located. Calling them activities is just Plotinus' elliptical way of saying that they are the intentional objects of the activities of intellects, that is, the activities of cognitive identification with Forms (see II.6.3.21–4).[58]

It is clear that in attempting to accommodate canonical Platonic Forms within the schema of the greatest kinds Plotinus has relied heavily on the Aristotelian identification of primary being with an activity. The world of Forms is anything but a static tableau. As Plotinus says, Intellect possesses these Forms "in the manner proper to Intellect" and "as in thinking" (VI.2.21.27–8). It is an eternal life, which we can know only indirectly. "In general everywhere, whatever one might apprehend by reasoning as being in nature one will find existing without reasoning in Intellect" (VI.2.21.33–4).

Thus, the derivation of the greatest kinds, their limitation to five, the reduction of putative Forms to other simpler Forms, and the ordering of other Forms under the greatest kinds are all based on inferences from our experience of nature and our use of discursive reasoning. That there be a Form F follows for Plotinus from our experience of Fness as an intelligible content in the sensible world and an argument that only if an eternal and immutable entity exists can the repeatability of this content be accounted for. How this Form is related to others within an eternal hierarchy is an independent question. It is not at all clear how we could know that we had attained a uniquely satisfying answer to this question. In no case is any answer to be conflated with the knowledge that Intellect has of Forms. We cannot in our incarnate lives know Forms as Intellect knows them.

VI

A Platonic World

1 The Composition of Sensibles

It is time to turn to Plotinus' positive account of the sensible world based on his rejection of the Aristotelian and Stoic alternatives. The account assumes a Platonic theory of Forms and the consequent "demotion" of the sensible world to the status of image, along with supplementary principles drawn from the *Timaeus* regarding matter and time. Opening the way to this account is the deconstruction of Aristotelian sensible substance. The precise point at which the deconstruction occurs is the argument against the claim in the *Metaphysics* that though the sensible substance is not unqualifiedly identical with its essence, it is yet identical in some sense. Otherwise substances would not be identified by their essences, nor would they be the subjects of change. Aristotle actually agrees with Plotinus that if the essences of sensible substances are separated from them as Plato would have it – if the essence of man is separated from this man – then sensible substances are no longer the focus of being and knowability in the sensible world. Shifting the primary reference of οὐσία from sensibles to Intellect is just what leads to the reconstruction of the sensible world as derivative and as image.

If οὐσία belongs primarily in the intelligible world, then the question arises whether οὐσία used of sensibles is used purely equivocally or whether it remains a term with a focal reference. It is important to recognize that this is a question Aristotle cannot avoid. If the perfectly actual unmoved mover is primary οὐσία, then is the sensible composite said to be οὐσία equivocally or πρὸς ἕν? If the former, then the hypothesized science of being qua being cannot be the science of god, as Aristotle says it is. If the latter, then the dependence of the posterior sensible composite on the primary is in no way accounted for in the analysis of its being.

Plotinus' answer to this question is that οὐσία is said homonymously (ὁμωνύμως) of Intellect and sensible bodies (VI.3.2.1–4). Aristotle clearly distinguishes between a term said ὁμωνύμως of two things and a term that is πρὸς ἕν (*Metaphysics* 4.2.1003a33–4; 7.4.1030b1). So, it would seem that Plotinus is denying a πρὸς ἕν connection between οὐσία in Intellect and οὐσία when said of sensibles. On the other hand, he also seems to connect them as "prior" and "posterior," which is not the way that things merely with a name in common are usually described (VI.1.1.25–8). This is in fact to be expected where sensibles are images of Forms.

As we saw in the last chapter, instances of a Form are the "same" as the universal, though "posterior" to the Form. For example, a drawing of a house is, as image, posterior to the real house, though its proportions may be the same as those of the house. Calling a sensible composite οὐσία is like calling the drawing a house. But its proportions are not equivocally those of the house; they are the same, though posterior. Another example would be a film which is homonymously that which it images, but which also contains synonymous images as well, such as the words spoken by the actors. If sensibles were merely homonymous images of Forms, there would be no intelligible content in them. If they were merely synonymous images of Forms, they would possess being in the same way as Forms, that is, eternally.[1] In fact, owing to the uniqueness of each Form, an unqualifiedly synonymous image of it would seem to be impossible.

An individual *subject* as such is an homonymous image. It is never an instance of a Form. This is obviously true when instances of Forms are in subjects. But it is equally true in the case of Forms of natural kinds whose instances might be thought to be the subjects themselves. But if Socrates were the instance of humanity rather than the subject in which the instance of humanity is manifested, then since Socrates is a composite of forms and matter, that composite would stand to the Form not as the picture stands to the original but as the proportions stand to those of the original. That must be false. The *composite* is never the same as the universal, which is immaterial. This is generally true for all sensible subjects.[2] Thus, Socrates is not an instance of the Form of Humanity, but the bearer of that instance. He is homonymously a man. The humanity in him is a synonymous image of the Form. A reference to the humanity in Socrates is a reference to a synonymous image; a reference to this man in all his particularity is a reference to an homonymous image.

The sensible world is ὁμώνυμον and an image of the intelligible world basically because its subjects are made according their original models (VI.3.1.21; III.7.11.27–9. See also I.2.2; II.3.18.17; II.8.5.6; II.9.8.19–26; III.2.1.25; III.2.14.26; III.6.13; III.8.11.29; IV.4.36.7ff.; V.3.7.33; V.3.16.8ff.; V.8.12.11ff.; V.9.13.10; VI.2.7.11; VI.2.22.38; VI.3.1.20–1; VI.3.8.32; VI.6.15.4; VI.7.6.6; VI.7.7.21; VI.7.12.2).[3] These images are identified by Plotinus in the traditional Platonic way as the world of becoming (VI.3.2.4).[4] The universal soul is the instrument of Intellect in the production of these images. By contrast, the images *in* souls that are concepts are of a different sort.[5] The former are identified with the secondary activity of Soul or nature or sensible form; the latter are the direct product of Intellect itself.[6]

Soul is an instrumental efficient cause as Intellect is an instrumental formal cause for the One's production of existents in the sensible world.[7] One might well suppose that the distribution of causal roles to the three distinct primary principles is what Plotinus relies on for resisting the substantial unity of sensible composites. Neither Soul nor Intellect nor even the One can alone make a sensible substance in the Aristotelian mode. Because Soul's secondary activity is nature, the operation of nature is only at the level of sensible form. For example, parents deliver to their offspring the sensible form that they already possess. The parents are not the cause of the being of the children, because their procreative activity is only itself an image of psychic activity. And psychic activity as such causes no substance to be.

In general, all natural processes or activities are representations of their ἀρχή, Soul, which is the paradigm of "transitive" motion, that is, motion towards an external goal. Thus, for example, the growth process of a plant is transitive motion. But it is only an image of the paradigm of psychic activity because the cognitive powers which make consciousness of a goal possible are missing.[8] And consciousness of a goal is a requisite of the highest psychic activity because Soul is an image of Intellect, whose activity is identified as self-conscious.

The activity of soul in the sensible world produces not an Aristotelian substance but a "conglomeration" (συμφόρησις) of qualities and matter, or bodies (VI.3.8.20).[9] The qualities are just the instances of Forms, or what Aristotle would call sensible forms. Since the only plausible substrate or subject in these conglomerations is matter itself, Aristotle's claim that essence is what a thing is in virtue of itself is rejected (*Metaphysics* 7.4.1029b13–14). Thus, Socrates is not essentially a man. He is the actual composite of qualities in matter. These qualities in matter, like the visible qualities "tall" and "white," are images of Forms. These images bear their names univocally with Forms. But their λόγοι necessarily include matter. Thus the tallness in Socrates is self-identically tallness, like the Form. But the tallness in Socrates is necessarily the particular tallness of a body. So, the composite Socrates, who is just these qualities in matter, is like the drawing of the original and not the proportions in relation to the original (VI.3.15.31–8).

It might be objected, however, that if qualities A, B, and C together in matter represent the Form of Man, then the essence of man is in the individual man just if the essential qualities are present. The presence of the essence is just the presence of the representation of the Form. But unless the essence identifies Socrates, then Socrates is not essentially a man any more than he is essentially any other quality that he may have. In one sense, Socrates is indeed identified by all his qualities. Plotinus is not denying this. But the essentialist needs a special identifying sense for the essential qualities. And so long as Socrates is not identified with these, he is no more essentially a man than he is essentially seated at any one moment or essentially bearded. So, we have to say that Socrates is a man if there is manness in him, but he is not essentially a man.[10]

Should we then allow that Socrates could become, say, a sparrow? One might suppose judging from what Plotinus says about reincarnation that the answer is yes. I think that answer should not be given too hastily. The Socrates now at issue is the sensible composite, and it is false that the sensible composite is reincarnated as anything. It is the soul of Socrates that may enter the body of another animal. This suggests that the identity of Socrates is not the identity of a sensible composite but that of a soul which exists apart from the body. As we have seen, that is what Aristotle denies. The identity of the individual sensible composite, severed from essence, is not determinable non-arbitrarily.

The abandonment of Aristotelian sensible substance is complete in Plotinus' embrace of what Aristotle regards as an absurdity: that we make substances out of non-substances.[11] Plotinus here of course means putative sensible substances. They are constructed out of qualities and matter. This apparently means both that we designate various "conglomerates" as substance and that the elements of these conglomerates are matter and qualities. This naturally invites the question of whether matter then becomes substance, a result that Aristotle declares is impossible (*Metaphysics* 7.3.1029a26–7). It does not become so for Plotinus any more than for Aristotle, because matter is not a "this something" (see II.6.2.14; VI.1.2.11–12). The identity of any bit of matter is not determined by essence.

Owing to the fact that qualities or instances of Forms are univocally bearers of the Forms' natures, pragmatic categorizations of sensible composites are possible.

But what species of it (sensible substance) should one posit, and how should one divide them? Now the whole must be classed as body, and of bodies some are matterish and some organic; the matterish are fire, earth, water, air; the organic the bodies of plants and animals, which have their differences according to their shapes (μορφάς). Then one should take the species of earth and of the other elements, and in the case of organic bodies one should divide the plants, and the bodies of animals, according to their shapes; or by the fact that some are on and in the earth, and, element by element [one should class separately], the bodies in each; or [one could class them on the ground that] some are light, some are heavy, and some in between, and that some stand in the middle, some surround them above, and some are in between; and in each of these the bodies are already differentiated by their outlines, so as to be some of them bodies of celestial living beings and others appropriate to the other elements; or one should divide the four according to their species and afterwards proceed in another way to weave them together by blending their differences according to places and shapes and mixtures, classing them as fiery or earthly, called so according to the largest and predominant element [in the mixture]. (VI.3.9.2–18. See also VI.3.17.4; VI.3.18.9–11)

It is important to grasp what is and what is not being suggested here. Plotinus wants to maintain that, say, the Form of Humanity, or more precisely, the nature that the Form of Humanity's name names, is present in the sensible composite that is called "Socrates." The Form of Humanity is eternally self-identical and distinct from the Form of Horse. But since so-called sensible substances are not identical with the natures of Forms, the classifications of these composites must occur through perception (VI.3.8.2–3. See also VI.3.10.10–12). Knowing what the Form of Humanity is does not provide the criterion for classifying a conglomeration of qualities and matter. We can call one organic composite a man and one a horse owing to their shapes (a quality plus a mass of extended matter), but this does not imply that things with these shapes are essentially human or horse.

It is appropriate in this context to recall Plato's argument that Forms are manifested in sensible instances via material that can also instantiate opposite Forms. Thus in the first book of the *Republic* returning someone's possession can be an instance of justice, but it can also be an instance of injustice. And in the *Symposium*, Beauty can be manifested in a body, but bodily qualities are not essential to the manifestation of Beauty, for Beauty can be manifested in non-bodily souls.

A classification of conglomerates is a classification of homonymous images. Take a drawing of a conical shape. Is it a teepee or an ice-cream cone? The answer is purely contextual or pragmatic because what the drawing is of is not entailed by the shape.[12] The conical shape, however, is or contains a synonymous image of the Form. The classification of homonymous images, like sensible composites, in terms of synonymous images, like the instances of Forms, is interdicted because sensible composites are bodies that contain matter. There is no more of a necessary connection between these two types of images than there is between the proportions of a drawing and the medium in which the drawing is rendered.

An artifact for Aristotle is not a substance. It does not exist by nature. The relation between the form and matter of an artifact is therefore less intimate than it is for a substance. For example, an artifact, like a ball, that is defined in part by its shape, can lose the shape without the nature of its matter being altered. A lifeless hand may not be a hand, but a flattened ball can still be a ball. As I suggested in the last chapter, it is perhaps possible to construe Plotinus' account of non-substantial sensible things as if they are akin to Aristotelian artifacts.[13] This would after all not be surprising if we take the sensible world or physical nature as merely an image of true nature, the world of Forms.

2 Matter

Plotinus is generally thought to hold an excessively gloomy view of the material world. The relevance of his account of matter to his moral teaching will concern us in a later chapter. For the present, I shall limit my discussion to Plotinus' attempt to construct an account of matter based on his understanding of Platonic and Aristotelian texts.[14] Such an account naturally comes under suspicion of being a confused syncretism, for it will be fairly said that whatever Plato means by the word ὕλη in those very few places in which he uses it, it is not what Aristotle means. In fact, in the case of matter, as in so much else, Plotinus understands Plato through Aristotle's own interpretation. He actually accepts Aristotle's interpretation of the receptacle of becoming in the *Timaeus* as matter (see II.4.1.1–2; III.6.13.12–18; III.6.14.29–32; III.6.19.15–18).[15] According to Aristotle, Plato implicitly identified matter and space (χώρα) because the participant (μεταληπτικὸν) and space are said by Plato to be the same (*Physics* 4.2.209b11–13).[16] Plato does suggest that the receptacle (ὑποδοχή) is a participant in some way and say that the receptacle is space (see *Timaeus* 51a8–b1, 52a8–b5).

It is because Aristotle is so confident that the description of the participant is a description of matter that he has no hesitation in claiming that Plato identifies matter and space. For example, Plato says of the receptacle that it is formless (ἄμορφον) (see *Timaeus* 50d7, e4, 51a3, 7). He variously compares it to a "base" for qualities like the odorless base for perfume oils, wax that is ready to receive any shape, and the invisible underlying recipient of the elements earth, air, fire, and water. It is pointless, though, to press the comparison much further, principally because in Aristotle matter is a principle of sensible substance. But since in the *Timaeus* the complexes resulting from the demiurge's imposition of forms and numbers on the receptacle are not sensible substances, the receptacle may resemble Aristotle's matter in certain important respects, even though they cannot, finally, be identified.

Plotinus does not take a critical, historical position in regard to Aristotle's interpretation of Plato. His view is best understood as the use of Aristotelian distinctions on behalf of a reinvigorated Platonic metaphysics. When Aristotle attributes a concept or distinction to Plato and then leaves it to the reader to infer the internal contradictions that thereby arise in the Platonic system, Plotinus leaps to the challenge and tries to show that the Platonic conclusion is not just defensible, but superior to the Aristotelian alternative. In the present case, we might say that he tries to make a case for Aristotelian matter without Aristotelian substance.

To begin, Plotinus embraces Aristotle's distinction between matter in general as a principle and the designated matter of some particular thing, like the bronze of a statue.[17] This distinction in Aristotle has almost universally been taken as a distinction between prime and proximate matter, as a distinction between a principle of substantial change and accidental change. The textual basis for this assumption is somewhat less firm than is often supposed. In any case, although Plotinus does follow Aristotle in using the phrase πρώτη ὕλη to refer to the matter underlying the elements, he does not mean to distinguish matter underlying substantial change from matter underlying accidental change for the simple reason that he does not accept such a distinction among changes.[18]

Generally, when Plotinus is speaking about matter he is referring to unqualified or undesignated matter, not to a particular kind of matter which is a component of a particular kind of thing, such as corporeal matter (see III.5.6.36; V.9.6.17). Unqualified matter is said to be without magnitude (μέγεθος) (III.6.16.27), bodiless (ἀσώματος) (II.4.8.2; II.4.9.5; II.4.12.35), invisible (ἀόρατος) (II.4.12.23; III.6.7.14), without quality (ἄποιος) (II.4.8.2), or affections (ἀπαθές) (III.6.7.3; III.6.9.36–9; III.6.11.45), unalterable (μὴ ἀλλοιοῦσθαι) (III.6.10.20), and indestructible (ἀνώλεθρον) (II.5.5.34),[19] unlimited (ἀόριστος) (II.4.10.4), and indefinite (ἄπειρον) (II.4.15.11, 19). It has no mass (ὄγκος) (II.4.11.25–7). Nevertheless, it does have a nature, even though it has no form of its own (I.8.10.5, 16).[20] It is an underlying substrate (ὑποκείμενον) (II.4.1.2; II.4.6.3; II.4.12.23; III.6.7.1; VI.3.4.24–8).

Designated matter is also an underlying substrate and is identified with that which exists in potency (δυνάμει) in relation to the composite in actuality (ἐνεργείᾳ) (II.5.2.27–8). By implication, unqualified matter might seem to be unqualified potency. It is not evident, however, that a concept of unqualified potency makes any sense without a concept of substantial change. Matter is also said to be a necessary condition for the existence of sensibles, but it is in no way an efficient cause of them (VI.3.7.1–12; III.6.14.1).[21] It never exists apart from form or shape (οὐδέποτε ἄνευ μορφῆς) (II.4.5.3).[22] But unlike the receptacle in Plato's *Timaeus*, with which Aristotle and Plotinus apparently identify matter, matter is generated, although not in time. Its generation means that it is dependent or contingent (see II.5.5.12–13; II.9.3.15).[23]

Thus far Plotinus follows Aristotle rather closely. But he begins to diverge on his own path when he identifies matter with privation (στέρησις), holding that privation is not destroyed by the arrival of that of which it is a privation (II.4.16.3–8).[24] This explicitly contradicts Aristotle's claim that, whereas matter is indestructible, privation is destroyed when what the privation is a privation of comes to be (*Physics* 1.9.192a27ff.).[25] Plotinus' reason for holding that privation is not destroyed is just that it is the same thing as matter and unlimitedness and as such its nature is impervious to information. Matter or privation or unlimitedness name an indestructible and irremovable feature of sensibles.[26]

What Plotinus appears to be doing is conflating the concepts of matter as a principle and matter as an element. If he followed Aristotle strictly in making matter a principle distinct from the elements that comprise an individual substance, the integrity and primacy of individual substance would be more difficult to deny. In Aristotle, the concept of matter, along with the concepts of form and privation, are introduced as principles of change in changeable things. These are principles in the sense of starting-points for understanding change. The integrity of the things undergoing change is assumed. Each one is an actual substance. But if Plotinus insists that matter is an element so that the sensible composite is a compound of two elements, form and matter, it does not seem that matter can be said to be pure potency or a principle of pure potency. Matter would seem to be an *actual* element. In that case, there is not just one composite actuality as there is for Aristotle.

When Aristotle transports the concept of matter into his science of being qua being, the issue becomes not the analysis of change in changeables, but the analysis of being, with changeable things as conveniently accessible experimental data. On the hypothesis that being is substance – an hypothesis, it will be recalled, that Plotinus rejects – Aristotle has to give a metaphysical analysis of the substantiality of just what it is that corresponds to the principle of change in changeables, namely, matter. Aristotle concludes that matter is not substance because it does not meet the criteria of being separable and a "this something" (*Metaphysics* 7.3.1029a27–8). He adds, however, that the form and the composite would seem to be substance to a higher degree (μᾶλλον) than matter.[27] So, matter is not primary substance, but it is, metaphysically speaking, not nothing either. What is it? The answer that emerges is that matter is potency. And potency is to be understood as a function of the composites that possess it. It is not an element, because it is posterior to the composite. The composite is that which is actual. Therefore, the being of matter is not in need of an account separate from the being of the composite. Composite being should yield to a thorough metaphysical analysis which will include all there is to say about matter.

Plotinus' rejection of the hypothesis that being is substance means that Aristotle's metaphysical approach to matter is unsatisfactory. The being of matter is not accounted for by the being of the composite, because the composite substance is not primary being. Rather, the composite becomes a complex of two "elements," form or quality and matter, and the account of the former is, so to speak, discontinuous with *any* putative account of the latter. Recall that we are speaking now not of designated matter, which is metaphysically irrelevant. Bronze, organic bodies, water, and so on are not metaphysical concepts either for Plotinus or Aristotle. They belong to the spheres of the special sciences. So, Plotinus' insistence on giving a meta- physical meaning to the concept of matter is a result of his argument that a substance metaphysics is false and so is unable to provide such an account. The necessity for such an account follows from the affirmation of the reality of that which is other than and not reducible to the intelligible.

There are a number of passages in which Plotinus offers programmatic principles of his revised metaphysics of the sensible world. For example, he says that "being is different for matter and form," by which he means that the being within a given composite is different for each.[28] The composite is derived from these, so they are not to be understood in terms of it, as if sensible composites were metaphysical subjects. The unity that the composite has, as we have learned, is extrinsic. This claim alone marks a significant difference between his doctrine and Aristotle's. For Aristotle, the being of the composite is one being. For Plotinus, too, matter can never exist on its own. But since the distinction between essential and accidental being has broken down, this allows him to speak of sensible substance as a "conglomeration" of qualities and matter, more like Aristotelian artifacts or "heaps" than Aristotelian substances. Accordingly, form is neither the "possession" of matter nor its actualization, but merely an external limit imposed on it or received in it (VI.3.2.22–7. See also II.5.2.8–10; VI.3.4.16).[29] Matter, therefore, cannot be pure potency. There is no need for a principle of pure potency in a metaphysics that rejects substantial change because it rejects substances.

Plotinus rejects Aristotle's analysis of change according to which matter is actualized in a change (see II.4.6.2–8; III.6.9–10). When a green leaf turns red, Aristotle accounts for this by the actualization of a potency in the leaf for acquiring a contrary. By contrast, Plotinus wants to say that "there is a change from one form into another," with a concurrent impassibility of matter. Accounting for change as a succession of forms is of a piece with the denial of a distinction between prime matter and proximate matter and the rejection of the real unity of a sensible substance. It also follows from treating what Aristotle calls "nature" as having no intrinsic intelligibility. A succession of forms is understood as a succession of images. It is as if the natural world were a film. One image on a movie screen is not in potency to the next image. Nor are any images actualizations of the screen itself. The succession of images can of course be intelligible but this is owing to a cause outside them.

The insistence on the distinct, albeit diminished and inseparable, being of matter is undoubtedly due in part to fidelity to Plato. In addition to identifying matter with the receptacle and the "seat" or "base" of becoming, Plotinus frequently employs the metaphor of a mirror, the main point being that like a mirror matter is unaffected by that which is reflected in it (III.6.7.25–6; III.6.9.16ff.; III.6.13.43ff.; III.6.14.1ff.). Following the *Timaeus*, he identifies the mode of cognition appropriate to matter not as perception, but as a kind of "spurious reasoning" (52b; II.4.10.10–12; II.4.12.28–30).[30] He seems to go beyond Plato, however, in claiming that matter is "truly non-being; it is a ghostly image of bulk, a tendency towards existence" (ὑποστάσεως ἔφεσις) (III.6.7.12–13).[31] Transforming the receptacle into matter, and starting from the critique of Aristotelian sensible substance, he arrives at an account of the relative non-being that Plato speaks about rather more vaguely and imprecisely, both in the middle and later dialogues.

I think that the best description of matter in Plotinus is that it is the unintelligible element in nature. It is that which accounts for the diminished reality of the sensible world. I have already discussed Plotinus' account of intelligible matter, which refers to Intellect in relation to the Forms with which it is in cognitive union (II.5.3.13–14. See also II.4.3.10–17; II.4.4.7–21;

II.4.5.12–39; II.4.16.25–7). I also leave aside designated matter, which is apparently understood by Plotinus in an unremarkable Aristotelian manner.

Unqualified matter, however, the "shadow" of λόγος, does have a distinctive role in Plotinian metaphysics (VI.3.7.8). First, his reformulation of the Aristotelian concept of matter entails a reinterpretation of sensible substance. The sensible substance is more like an artifact or an adventitious heap than it is like a fundamental constituent of reality. This is in line with the location of true being in the unqualifiedly intelligible realm. All that is intelligible in the sensible composite is a synonymous image of a Form.

The sensible composite as such is a composite of matter and form. All that is intelligible in the composite is in the form. But the matter is a necessary condition for the existence of the composite, not in the way that an atmosphere is a necessary condition for the existence of animals but in the way that a reflecting surface is a necessary condition for the existence of an image. A description of the composite which left out the matter would revert to a description of some portion of the intelligible world, just as a description of the perceptual contents of a visual image which left out the fact that it was an image would be indistinguishable from a description of what it is an image of. For example, a description of a picture of an animal which left out its pictorial qualities would be indistinguishable from a description of the animal itself. Adding the element of matter to a description is like adding the pictorial qualities that identify the picture as being other than a real animal. Thus, the nature of beauty is truly in Helen, but she is beautiful in a specific way. The description of *how* she instantiates the Form of Beauty necessarily incorporates that which could be part of the description of the instantiation of the opposite Form in another context, say, flesh and bones. Helen could not be beautiful except in an ontologically compromising manner.

One might object, however, that flesh and bones are designated matter, not unqualified matter. Indeed, they are not. But Helen's beauty is not the arrangement of flesh and bones. These are included in the account of the way she instantiates Beauty. And the description of her flesh and bones is compromised in the same way as is the description of her beauty. It could not be otherwise for a physical representation of the immaterial Form. The problem here is not with definitions, which are of Forms or of the natures that Forms' names name, but with the conditions for the application of definitions to individuals. The individual composite cannot exist and hence is not identifiable apart from an unintelligible element. Treating designated matter and hence the composites which include designated matter as intrinsically intelligible must therefore involve a kind of pretense.

Even if matter is absolutely deprived of form and has a tenuous hold on being, it is not nothing, and so it is not deprived entirely of the One.[32] This is only puzzling if the One is misconceived of as a Form of Unity or Goodness. The fact that matter is not nothing even though it has no form or principle of limit in it reveals quite clearly the distinction between the causal activities of the One and its instruments, Intellect and Soul. It also poses a problem for Plotinus' metaphysics. Why should matter exist at all? How can the ἀρχή of all intelligible existence be the cause of existence of the formless?

One suggestion Plotinus makes is that matter is actually a sort of ultimate form (εἶδος τι ἔσχατον), thereby making the production of matter in principle no different from anything else (V.8.7.22–3. See also I.8.3.3–6). But this hardly accounts adequately for the strongly antithetical character of matter in relation to form and strikes us as a trivial verbalism. Two rather more serious arguments, however, are supplied. First, he says that matter is a necessary condition for the existence of the contraries which necessarily belong to the sensible universe. Second, he reasons that if anything besides the One is going to exist, then there must be a conclusion of the process of going out from it. The end of the process, after which there is nothing else, is matter or that which is identified with matter, namely, evil. In effect, if there is a first, then there must be a last (I.8.7.1–4, 17–23).[33] These two arguments are of course closely related. After the coming to be of Soul, the secondary activity of Intellect, a secondary activity for Soul turns out to be what is called nature. So, the two arguments amount to the same claim that the ultimate result of the One's creative activity is the physical universe, which must contain matter as a necessary condition for the existence of anything with contraries. Thus, the beginning of evil is identified with the first act of separation from the One, whether we explain this by the One's will or by the fundamental daring (τόλμα) of Intellect (see V.1.1.3–5).

The explanation of the origin of matter is worth considering further. The One is infinite activity, limited only hypothetically in its causality by Intellect. In producing with the instrumentality of Intellect, the only things that can be produced are images of Intellect, that is, everything below Intellect. If images of Intellect were not producible, this would be more than an hypothetical limitation on the One. It would be an absolute limitation. But nothing in Intellect itself prevents its being copied in images, so long as the condition for imagery is available. This is the so-called receptacle or matter or space. It is a condition roughly in the sense that Aristotle speaks of matter as an hypothetical condition for some end being achieved (see *Physics* 2.9.200a13–15). That for Plotinus this condition must itself be completely bereft of intelligibility follows logically. Let matter have an intelligible element. Then that element will either be identical with Intellect, in which case it will not be an image of Intellect, or it will itself be an image. But that image, which has only derivative being, needs a condition for imagery other than it. This cannot be Intellect itself, which is the principle of intelligibility, not of imagery. Therefore, even if matter had an intelligible element, we would still need to posit a condition for the qualified intelligibility of images. And *that* would be matter.

The analysis of the metaphysical concept of an image yields form and matter as principles. Homonymous and synonymous imagery are two aspects of the diminished or qualified intelligibility of the sensible world. Matter is the principle of privation in the sensible world. "Privation" means absence of essence, which belongs only to Intellect. Any image of Intellect under the aspect of οὐσία must contain an instantiation of the principle of matter, by definition. When Plotinus says that matter has a nature even though it does not have a form, I think he means to indicate the specific role that matter plays. Distinguishing nature and form in this way is really the outcome of the distinction between essence and existence that we began with in the intelligible world. Matter, let alone the composites of matter and form, ultimately depends on the One for existence. In being made responsible for the existence of matter, the One is only constrained hypothetically. That is, the One cannot make images unless matter exists. Matter is the necessary element in image-making or creation below the level of Intellect.

The previous discussion of Forms of individuals seems most relevant here. What distinguishes the "true" Socrates in the intelligible realm from the Socrates here below is, finally, nothing but matter. If we were to engage in the analysis of the sensible composite in the manner of abstraction (ἀφαίρεσις) recommended by Plotinus, always distinguishing a formal and material element as we proceed, it would turn out that matter is very little indeed compared to form. Successive analyses into form and matter always add to the formal and never leave an absolute residue of matter until the end. Let $S = f_1 + m_1$. Then the analysis of $m_1 = f_2 + m_2$. The analysis of $m_2 = f_3 + m_3$. We keep adding to the formal elements, without leaving any material elements permanently until we get to the end. The form of the individual is everything but this material element or at least everything except what could not exist without it.

Matter as evil looms so large in Plotinus' thinking because it is an impediment removable only indirectly, by separation from the body or designated matter. Matter is the element of evil for beings who have a destiny in Intellect. Only for such beings is the status of image not a necessary one. For beings that do not have such a destiny, matter is just a necessary condition for nature's operation. And this is nature conceived as image and artifact, not nature in the Aristotelian conception of it. Plotinus says that there is an escape from evil for those capable of it, meaning to distinguish these from men who are corrupt beyond repair (I.8.5.29–30. See also I.8.7.12–14). For things that have no place in the intelligible world the conceptual distinction between matter and evil is erased.

3 Time and Eternity

The *Ennead* III.7, "On Eternity and Time," and Aristotle's *Physics* IV.10–14 contain the two main discussions of this topic extant from antiquity. Plotinus' treatise is inspired by *Timaeus* 37d–38b and contains an attack on Aristotle's position, which Plotinus typically sees as the main alternative to his own Platonic one. As Armstrong notes in the introduction to his translation of the treatise, Plotinus' treatment of the subject became paradigmatic not for later Neo-Platonists but rather for the Christian tradition. The strong distinction Plotinus makes between eternity and time, repeated almost word for word by Boethius, is a window between Christian and Plotinian creation metaphysics.

In the *Timaeus* passage referred to above, Plato gives his famous definition of time as a "moving image of eternity (αἰῶνος)." He seems to use αἰώνιος as synonymous with ἀίδιος, a word which is also apt for meaning "everlasting," that is, having no beginning and no end. The distinction in Plato between that to which no temporal predicate applies, that is, eternity, and that which is "in" time is clear. There is no clear distinction between eternal and everlasting where temporal predicates could apply but where there is no beginning and no end. Such a distinction would not be surprising in the *Timaeus* and elsewhere for the following reason.

Plato does believe that things in the sensible world, which are in time, do have a beginning and an end, whereas the demiurge or divine intellect does not. Since the latter, however, has a life and movement in some sense, it might not seem inappropriate to attribute to it temporal predicates, at least something like "duration." Further, human souls and heaven itself have a beginning but no end. Plato might have distinguished a category for these, either "everlastingness once begun" or sempiternity, indicating the difference between the eternal on the one hand and what is generated and destroyed on the other. As I say, Plato might have reasonably made such a distinction, although he does not explicitly do so. Whatever the status of the divine intellect, heaven, and human souls, the distinction between the eternal and the temporal is obviously prior to a further distinction within the temporal between that which does and that which does not have a beginning or end. Whatever is everlasting is defined in negative terms as not having a particular temporal predicate, although other temporal predicates apply to it. Of course, eternity may be defined negatively as well. But eternity is the contradictory of temporality, whereas everlastingness is a contrary temporal predicate of that which is in time.

Plotinus essentially follows Plato in refraining from attributing αἰώνιον and ἀίδιον to different things. He does make a slight technical distinction between αἰώνιον and ἀίδιον as applied to Intellect, but he does not make much of it and it can be safely ignored.[34] The central distinction for Plotinus is between that which is outside of time altogether and that to which temporal predicates are attached, whatever these may be.[35]

The definition of αἰών is our starting-point. "The life, then, which belongs to that which exists and is in being, all together and full, completely without extension or interval, is that which we are looking for, eternity" (III.7.5.12–18. See also III.7.3.23–4). The life to which Plotinus is referring is the life of Intellect. It is life that is eternally complete. That life is immeasurable, if measurability is assumed to be a property only of magnitudes or of that with parts outside parts. By contrast, a life that is in time is "spread out" with a past that is no longer, a future that is not yet, and an ever-shifting present. Since time is posterior to the life of Intellect, it of course follows that eternity applies (analogously) to the One, although he does not say this explicitly. The One is "beyond" eternity just as it is beyond being and life.

The attribution of αἰών to the life of a divine Intellect is well established in the tradition by Aristotle as much as by Plato. Aristotle also calls this divine intellect ἀΐδιος. But Aristotle also uses the term ἀΐδιος for the first heaven, which is in motion and hence has temporal predicates (cf. *Metaphysics* 12.7.1072a23 and 1072b28–30). So, it is far from certain that Aristotle actually makes a distinction between that which is and is not in time and that he attributes the latter to divine intellect.[36] It is reasonable to assume that Plotinus' definition of eternity and application of that definition to Intellect is intended as much as a refutation of Aristotle as it is as an exposition of Plato.[37]

The notion of a life literally outside time altogether is a most striking one, only indirectly inferable from anything in Plato.[38] The basic idea is evidently of life abstracted from all its timebound features, for example, change, expectation, memory, and so on.[39] Such a life is nothing but the primary activity of Intellect, cognitive identification with the totality of intelligible reality. The denial of temporal predicates to that life, that is, the denial of the claim that it is just an everlasting life with no beginning and no end, depends on the key concepts of completeness and partlessness (see III.7.3.18, 38; III.7.4.14–15, 37–8). The activity of Intellect is to be conceived of so that that activity does not have a beginning, a middle, and an end. To say that it is complete at every *moment* is of course to beg the question against eternity.

Aristotle would admit that any activity is complete at every moment, especially that of the ἀρχή of all, but as we have seen, he does not seem to think of that activity as completely without temporality. Why should we? Why not say, for example, that before and after, infinite before and after, if we like, can be attributed to this activity, so that Intellect literally was always, is now, and will always be engaged in contemplation of Forms? The reason why we and Aristotle might be inclined to speak this way and Plotinus certainly is not turns on a dispute regarding the creation of time. If the temporal or time is posterior in being to something else, then it is possible and perhaps even necessary to speak of what is prior to it without employing temporal predicates. If, on the other hand, time is posterior in being to nothing, then there is nothing that cannot be measured by time, if only to the extent that it can be said to be everlasting.[40]

That time is created follows from the uniqueness of the uncreated first principle of all. If time were uncreated, it could only be indistinct from the One. But if time is at all complex, this is impossible. Even if time were simple, attributing temporal predicates to the One would introduce an illicit complexity into it. More difficult to understand is why Plotinus will want to claim that the creation of time accompanies the creation of universal soul and what it means to attribute timeless life to Intellect (see III.7.11.43–56; IV.4.15.2–4). Let us consider the second difficulty first.

We have already seen the mediating role played by Soul between the intelligible and sensible realms. Just as Intellect is a kind of instrument of the One in bestowing existence on all creatures, so Soul is a kind of instrument of Intellect in bestowing intelligibility on the natural world. Eternity is a mode of being in Intellect, and becoming is a mode of being of sensibles. Soul seems to be in some sense a link between the eternal and the temporal because it possesses characteristics of both being and becoming.[41] However, the attempt to "derive" the temporal from the eternal with or without the mediation of Soul is as misguided as the attempt to "derive" the many from the One. Given that the existence of matter is hypothetically necessary for the existence of images of Intellect, we need to ask why these images must be *moving* images, that is, images in time.

Plotinus says that we must place sameness in eternity and difference in time (IV.4.15.7–9).[42] Sameness characterizes the activity of Intellect. The contemplation of intelligible reality by Intellect is "all together" and without succession. The difficulty of imagining atemporal activity is more psychological than logical. We tend to think of activity on the model of human activity, which is measurable by time that is independent of it. We can think about one thing for, say, five seconds, because time marches on apart from us. There is potentially a many–one correspondence between units of time and cognitive states, which is just to say that time is independent, if only in definition. Alternatively, imagine that you think about something as the stopwatch is set at 0 and the stopwatch does not advance until you think about something else. So, you could think about the same thing without time advancing. No doubt this is in some sense conceivable, but it will be replied that nevertheless there is a celestial stopwatch that ticks away and that is beyond our control. This celestial stopwatch is independent of everything here below, so *any* activity or state, no matter how monotonous, is measurable by it. Time measures its duration.

I think that Plotinus is not unsympathetic to at least the first part of this thought experiment. Where he would object is at the claim that the celestial stopwatch is absolutely independent, for if, like everything else but the One, time is created, it is dependent in the most crucial respect. The celestial stopwatch does not stand outside what is prior to it in being, namely, Intellect and the One. Their activities are not measurable by time because what is ontologically posterior cannot be predicated of what is ontologically prior.[43] Time is not absolute because it is not independent.

Following this line of reasoning, we may still ask why Plotinus does not hold that time is created along with Intellect in such a way that *its* activity is measurable by time. The answer is that time is no part of intelligible reality because change does not belong to it. Time is not "outside" intelligible reality as a measure of it because there is nothing outside Intellect besides the One. Time is neither a Form nor the activity of cognitive identification with all the Forms. If all that existed were the One and unchanging Intellect, then time would not exist. Eternal life is unchanging life. What gives this claim point is that time is not an uncreated measure of this such that we could say that Intellect has been engaged in its activity forever or that it continues to engage in it. We can of course say that Intellect was contemplating Forms yesterday, but this is not to predicate time of Intellect but of us.[44] Distinguishing yesterday from today depends on a difference in that to which the terms are applied. There can be no such differences in Intellect (see III.7.12.11–15; IV.4.1.12–13).

If this is true, however, one might then conjecture that like the One, Intellect is not really related to anything else. If it were, then changes in what Intellect is related to would be changes in Intellect. For example, if one person were to awaken to the life of the mind, it would be true to say of Intellect today what was false yesterday, namely, that it is loved by so and so. In general, it might seem that if A and B are really related, and A is susceptible to temporal predication, then so is B because any change in A such that it is susceptible to such predication is a change in B in some way. But is this really so? Is Plotinus faced with the dilemma of either denying that Intellect is really related to anything else or denying that it is eternal?

Plotinus seems to be aware of this dilemma when he says that we have a share in eternity but then asks how this is possible if we are in time.[45] Let us recall that the reason the One is not really related to anything is that it is not an entity, and so cannot be a term of a real relation. This is not the case for Intellect or for intellects. If Intellect were not really related to sensible composites, then at least it would be incoherent to claim that right now my intellect is eternally contemplating Forms or that sometime in the future I shall be reunited with that contemplator. But implicating Intellect in real relations does not require that we implicate it in time. As we have already seen, Forms are really related to their instances. But as we have also seen, the argument for postulating Forms in the first place entails their eternality.

The problem we are dealing with is not quite the same as the traditional theological problem of reconciling the concept of an eternal God with the efficacy of petitionary prayer, knowledge of future contingents, and so on. Intellect is absorbed exclusively in the contemplation of Forms. Even the providence of Intellect is so general in content that it need not involve incursions into temporally contingent events. It is rather the problem of whether or not union by temporal beings with Intellect requires us to ascribe temporal predicates to it. On reflection, however, both sorts of problems have the same solution. The history of beings in time, even including their relations to the eternal, is *their* history, not the history of Intellect. If it is true that I shall be reunited with my intellect in the future, this is so because it is my intellect now. "Now" of course is not a predicate of Intellect, but of me. Nothing that I do or shall do can change what Intellect is, for the life of Intellect is unqualifiedly complete.

The cogency of the claim that I am now associated with the eternal depends upon showing that the temporal is an image of the eternal. The claim does not depend upon the construction of parallel, existentially independent universes, one eternal and one temporal. In this Plotinus is following Plato, but with more precision (III.7.13.24–5. See also III.7.11.46–7). Time is an homonymous image of eternity.[46] It is a representation of the life of Intellect. That is why Plotinus so easily identifies it with the life of the universal soul. There is no simultaneity between the temporal aspect of the life of the universal soul and the eternal aspect of the life of Intellect because there is no synonymy between the homonymous image of time and that which it images, eternity. Thus, to examine temporality in order to understand eternity is as inappropriate as examining the merely symbolic representations or homonymous images of things in order to understand the things themselves.

The life of the universal soul, upon analysis, turns out to be an image of perfect life. Desires for what is external and future imperfectly represent a desire that is perfectly satisfied. And this excludes even the notion of continued satisfaction in the future. It is of course one thing to construe something as an homonymous image of the notionally perfect. It is another thing to hold, as Plotinus does, that the perfect is real. As we have seen, the bridge from the notional to the real in this case is the argument that eternal truth exists but that it could not exist unless there were an eternal intellect contemplating it.

Against the Stoics, Plotinus argues that time cannot be identified with movement, for movement is in time (III.7.8.2–6, 56–8).[47] Further, whereas movement can be interrupted or stopped, time cannot. Even if time were identified with the uninterrupted movement of the universe, that movement too would be in time. Finally, it is possible for something to be at rest for the same interval in which something else is in movement (III.7.8.65–7).[48] In this case, again, time cannot simply be identified with movement.

Against Aristotle (*Physics* 4.11.219b1–2; 4.12.220b32–221a1), Plotinus argues that time is not the number or measure of movement (III.7.9). Even granting that time could measure both regular and irregular movements, to say that time is a measure does not tell us what the nature of the measure is itself. If time is a number, it will have to have a specific magnitude, say, 10. Then how will it differ from an eternal number? If time is a (continuous) measure, it will also have to have a specific magnitude. Then where shall we locate time, in the measured movement or in the measuring magnitude? If the former, there will be a need for another measuring magnitude to measure it. And then *this*, the measuring magnitude, will be time. In any case, the concept of time is prior to the concept of a certain amount of time by which we measure a movement. So it would seem that time is different from the measure of movement. Further, time seems to belong to movement apart from its measure, like magnitudes which belong to bodies apart from their being measured by us. The soul might use magnitudes to measure time, but this does not explain time itself.[49]

Against Epicurus, Plotinus argues that time is not an attribute (παρα-κολούθημα) of movement (III.7.10).[50] The argument seems to be that things that are not in motion are also in time, so that on Epicurus' account, time will be an attribute of movement in time. In any case, there is not in Epicurus even a pretense of explaining the nature of time as opposed to suggestions for measuring time by the movements of bodies.

The common thread in the criticism of the Stoics, Aristotle, and Epicurus is the claim that they have all failed to distinguish time from that which is in time or measured by time. Plotinus' alternative is to identify time with the life of soul. "Time is the life (ζωὴν) of soul in a movement of passage from one way of life (βίον) to another" (III.7.11.43–5).[51] Just as eternity is life at rest in contemplation of Forms, so the image of that life will be the characteristic successiveness and incompleteness of soul's activity (III.7.11.45ff.).

Two features of this definition merit emphasis. First, time is not like other homonymous images. A picture of a house has a kind of intelligibility on its own because it also contains synonymous images, for example, its shape. But time is, so to speak, a pure homonymous image. It can be grasped only indirectly via the life of soul and the synonymous images of Intellect in it. Like matter, it possesses only a kind of quasi-intelligibility. One must start with Intellect and its self-reflexive cognition and fulfilled desire and then, in order to understand its images, separate thinker from the thought and desirer from the object of desire. For instance, the future is to be understood in relation to present desires. And the past is to be understood as something like a representation of the present in relation to the future. Such distinctions make no sense for Intellect, for there is no incompleteness in its life. Since Intellect's life is complete, it has no future, and because it has no future, it has no past (see III.7.12.11–13).

Second, time is not a really distinct attribute of soul's life, but that life itself considered in its successiveness or disparateness. Time is only conceptually distinct from life. If time itself were an attribute, it would have an independent source of intelligibility, namely, the Form which it instantiated (see III.7.11.58–61). One does not understand independently of life. The generation of time by soul is just the generation of its activity or the activity itself.[52] To say that something is "in time" is to place it in relation to this activity, namely, the life of the universe. For example, we can take the periodic movement of heavenly bodies as a measure of other movements and speak of the time in which the latter occurred in relation to the former (III.7.12.33–6). That periodic movement is itself in time in the sense that it is a portion of the life of the whole universe in movement (III.7.13.1).

It seems clear enough from the definition of time that the primary locus of time is the life of the soul of the universe (III.7.12.22–3).[53] By so defining time, Plotinus can preserve time's unity (III.7.13.45–7).[54] The objective measure of all relative time-frames is the life of the universe. Since there is no time apart from soul, it is unintelligible to say that there was a time when soul was not. There was no time when soul (and time) were created.[55] That is why the attempt to derive time from eternity is misguided. The creation of soul and time is just their dependence on the One with the instrumentality of Intellect. Does this mean that we can give no sense to the notion of a first movement of soul? If a first movement means a movement *before* which there was none, then it does not seem that we can speak of a first. But a putatively first movement can be distinguished from all others by simply noticing that it is at least logically possible for every movement but one to have a predecessor. In short, the Plotinian account of time does not in itself entail a position on whether the universe had a temporal beginning or not.

The distinction between the life of soul and movements which are measured according to this life is sometimes represented as a distinction between "psychical" and "physical" time.[56] I do not think this is quite right, for it suggests a division between soul and nature which for Plotinus is misleading. But there is good reason to emphasize the priority of the psychical to the non-psychical. It is certainly easy enough to challenge Plotinus in this regard and say that the non-psychical is prior. Can we not imagine movements in a universe bereft of life and with them a form of time? In reply, Plotinus would no doubt wish to say that then the question regarding the nature of time arises once again. And if it is neither the postulated movement itself nor a measure of it, then an alternative account is required. Non-psychical time might seem prior to or at least independent of psychical time if it is not recognized that time is an homonymous image of the paradigm of life, the eternal activity of Intellect. So, the real issue is whether time is prior or posterior to eternity in conception.

Plotinus' arguments against the accounts of his predecessors constitute the basis for his claim that it is posterior. The positive reason for identifying time as an image is the general argument for the posteriority of becoming to being.[57] The posteriority of becoming to being in intelligibility is analogous to the posteriority of potency to actuality. A potency is intelligible only in terms of an actuality in relation to another actuality. For example, the concept of breakability is parasitic upon the concepts of unbrokenness or intactness and being broken, whereas the reverse is not true. Similarly, the concept of becoming is parasitic upon the concepts of the termini of the process of becoming. The realization of a process of becoming, however, is qualified. If, say, X becomes f at t_2, it is not yet f at t_1. And if X's being in time means that it is essentially time-bound, as all Plotinus' opponents agree, then to say merely that X has become f is to take a restricted perspective. The term of becoming has always to be given with a temporal predicate. Without the temporal predicate, the description is essentially incomplete. Since any temporal predicate for that which is becoming refers either to the non-existent future or to the specious present, becoming f is only an imitation of being f. Understanding a temporally bound individual as being f requires an imaginative application of the concept of really being f, which is being f unqualifiedly or eternally.[58]

Once the priority of eternal being to temporal becoming is established, we need only recur to the argument that eternal being is the life of an eternal mind. It would then follow that the primary imitation of this life is temporally bound life, of which Soul is the ἀρχή. A temporally bound life is prior in conception to a temporally bound inanimate object because Soul is ontologically prior to physical nature. Even without a universal soul, however, the temporal would remain posterior to the eternal.

The heuristic device for representing the relation of the temporal to the eternal is contained in a powerful passage which is worth quoting in full.

> But since there was a restlessly active nature [i.e., soul] which wanted to control itself and be on its own, and chose to seek for more than its present state, this moved, and time moved with it; and so, always moving on to the "next" and the "after," and what is not the same, but one thing after another, we made a long stretch of our journey and constructed time as an image of eternity. For because soul had an unquiet power, which wanted to keep on transferring what it saw there to something else, it did not want the whole to be present to it all together; and, as from a quiet seed the formative principle (λόγος), unfolding itself, advances, as it thinks, to largeness, but does away with the largeness by division and, instead of keeping its unity in itself, squanders it outside itself and so goes forward to a weaker extension; in the same way soul, making the world of sense in imitation of that other world, moving with a motion which is not that which exists there, but like it, and intending to be an image of it, first of all put itself into time, which it made instead of eternity, and then handed over that which came into being as a slave to time, by making the whole of it exist in time and encompassing all its ways with time. For since the world of sense moves in soul – there is no other place of it (this universe) than soul – it moves also in the time of soul. (III.7.11.15–35)[59]

In this passage time is generated by discontent. But the notion of discontent within Intellect is unthinkable. It suggests the gap between desire and object of desire that is time itself and insinuates it into eternity. But an image as such is distinct in being from that of which it is an image. I do not think that this passage can possibly mean that soul is supposed to have suddenly become discontented with noetic activity, at which time it longed for goals which inevitably drew it "downward." What we have here is language similar to that used in temporalizing the derivation of Intellect from the One. Discontent is of the essence of anything with a soul or of anything in time and aware of itself in time. The striking phrase "put itself into time" as applied to soul should not be taken literally. It does not mean that soul caused itself to be. As we have seen, Plotinus is explicit that the One alone is self-caused. The derivation of the temporal from the eternal in this passage is a kind of dramatization of the eternal activity of the One and Intellect. The temporal is contained within the eternal in only one sense, namely, that in which an image is contained within what it is an image of, hypothetically.

We can thus explain why images of Intellect are moving images or in time. Just as matter is hypothetically necessary for the existence of images of Forms, so time is hypothetically necessary for the existence of souls, which are images of Intellect. Time is just the life that imitates the paradigm of life viewed with respect to its successiveness. Souls are identified at least in part by their desires. Desires are either eternally fulfilled or temporally situated or eternally unfulfillable. The horror of the last-mentioned possibility ought to be excluded by the nature of the activity of the ἀρχή of all, the One. As an instance of a Form is diminished in reality owing to matter, so an incarnate soul is diminished in life owing to the fact that what it aims at is always beyond it or in the future. This includes the desire for the continued possession of what it has already attained. Unlike inanimate objects, however, souls can aim not just at future temporal states but also at the eternal reality that they imitate.

In the remaining chapters of this book I turn to the discussion of Plotinus' remarkable account of human beings as incarnate souls living in this Platonic world.

Part II

VII

Human Psychology

1 A Refined Dualism

Plotinus can be described as a post-Aristotelian Platonic dualist. His dualism is shaped by a confrontation with Aristotle's hylomorphic account of the individual organic composite, especially in *De Anima*. Platonic dualism holds that soul and body are two really distinct entities. But this is plainly inadequate, for it does not answer the question whether the person or self is to be identified with either or both of these entities. If we are told that the real distinction between soul and body enables us to show that the soul can exist when the body no longer exists, it does not follow that *we* can exist when our bodies do not. Only if we are identical with that soul does the putative proof of its separate existence have more than theoretical interest.

Plotinus' version of Platonic dualism is devoted in part to the exploration and proof of the separate entitative character of the soul. As we have already seen, Plotinus argues that the true identity of each individual is as an intellect contemplating Forms eternally. The connection between these two claims then consists in showing that the separated soul is the true person and that this is nothing but an intellect. This approach opens up new questions. For example, if the true person only exists discarnately and eternally, in what sense is the true Socrates identical with the incarnated, temporal individual? Is it not gratuitous so to identify the two when there is evidently no *psychological* continuity between them? When Socrates died would he notice the difference if he inadvertently slipped into the persona of the discarnate Plato? And if he noticed the difference would it matter to him at all, since on Plotinus' account he would in any case be engaged in the same kind of activity? The answers to these questions will find Plotinus appropriating an Aristotelian account for a Platonic end.

The simple concept of soul in ancient Greek philosophy is ambiguous. At its vaguest it refers to whatever it might be that differentiates the living from the dead and the non-living. Accordingly, one might suppose that it refers to a property that a body possesses and then loses at death, like self-motion. A problem with this arises immediately when we consider the different kinds of self-motion that exist. Is life a simple generic property that plants and animals share, or is it equivocal in reference to different kinds of life? It does not seem to be the former because, for example, there is no basis for saying that a plant is growing *and* that it is alive. Growing is just one of the activities that its life consists in. It is, however, hard to accept the alternative that life is used purely equivocally when attributed to different forms of life. Where is the equivocity in an announcement that men and cattle both lost their lives in the storm?

Plato in the *Phaedo* was the first to present arguments for the claim that soul does not primarily name a property of bodies but an entity with its own properties such that the presence or absence of that entity in a body differentiates the living from the dead. His arguments are taken up by Plotinus, and we shall consider them presently. Let us notice first, though, that Plato's approach yields its own huge problems. First, even if the soul has properties, it does not follow that it itself is not a property. In that case we might only need to posit first- and second-order properties, like color and intensity. Second, if body and soul are two entities, let alone two entities that can exist separately, is the living plant or animal two agents or sources of activity or one? Is it some third entity, perhaps a mixture of the other two?

The fundamental ambiguity running through both Plato's and Plotinus' discussions of the soul and its relation to the body is between soul as agent or source of activity on the one hand and soul as the activities themselves or the entity which the agent somehow employs in acting. In the first case, the agent becomes the entity distinct from the body, distinct from its activities. In the second case, the agent is only a part of the entity distinct from the body, which includes those activities. So, for example, to hold a form of dualism according to which the soul can exist when the body is destroyed can mean either holding that an agent, say, the person or the self, can exist separately or it can mean that an agent along with a range of activities that identifies the incarnate life of that agent can exist separately. In the former case, continuity of the self requires no continuity of activities that are essentially incarnate or discarnate. In the latter case, it would seem to be otherwise. For example, if the self is identified by its memories, and a discarnate self can have no memories, then it is hard to see how an incarnate self could be continuous with a discarnate one. This problem at least would disappear if the identity of the self did not include memory.

We turn now to Plotinus' arguments against those who for one reason or another deny that "soul" names an incorporeal entity and hold instead that it is a body or a property of a body. Plotinus sets out his arguments against opponents of the non-bodily entitative character of the soul in one of his earliest treatises, IV.7, titled by Porphyry "On the Immortality of the Soul." Actually, Plotinus does not say a great deal directly about the immortality of the soul in this lengthy and difficult work. Rather he, and presumably

Porphyry, just assumes that the proof that the soul is a non-bodily entity is tantamount to the proof of its immortality.[1] More of this a bit later.

The opposing views Plotinus attacks are those of Epicurus, the Stoics, and Aristotle. Epicurus is dealt with summarily in a brief but interesting argument:

> But if someone says that it [a formative principle] could not come from anywhere [except from soul] is not so, but that atoms or things without parts make the soul when they come together by unity (ἐνώσει) and community of feeling (ὁμοπαθείᾳ), he could be refuted by their [mere] juxtaposition, and that not a complete one,[2] since nothing which is one and united with itself in community of feeling (συμπαθοῦς) can come from bodies which are without feeling and unable to be united, but soul is united with itself in community of feeling. But no body or magnitude could be produced from partless constituents. (IV.7.3.1–6)

This difficult argument depends on an account of the soul by Epicurus that Plotinus seems to have before him. According to Epicurus, the soul is a

> body [made up of] fine parts distributed throughout the entire aggregate [of atoms] (παρ' ὅλον τὸ ἄθροισμα παρεσπαρμένον), and most closely resembling breath (πνεύματι) with a certain admixture of heat, in one way resembling breath and in another resembling heat. There is also the <third> part, which is much finer than even these [components] and because of this is more closely in harmony (συμπαθὲς) with the rest of the aggregate too. (*Letter to Herodotus* 63)

Plotinus is arguing that συμπάθεια is a property of soul, but that an aggregate of atomic bodies cannot possess this property. This claim certainly seems to beg the question prior to adducing a bit more of the background of the argument.

First, Plotinus is evidently relying on an argument against the Stoics used later in this treatise and elsewhere that the "total interpenetration of bodies" (κρᾶσις δι' ὅλου) is impossible (see IV.7.8[2] and II.7). Thus, the putative Epicurean "soul atoms" can at best be "juxtaposed" with those that make up the rest of the body. Second, the meaning of συμπάθεια must be taken into account. In a later treatise, Plotinus tells us that συμπάθεια in an animal with itself and among its parts depends on its being one thing (IV.5.3.15–18. See also IV.5.8.1–4). Of course, Epicurus in speaking of an animal as an "aggregate" of atoms does not wish to deny an integrity or unity to it. What Plotinus is getting at, I suppose, is that the unity possessed by an aggregate of atoms is not the sort of unity which could result in συμπάθεια. Surely, Plotinus does not wish to deny that, for example, heat could radiate through a body composed of atoms, resulting in the entire body becoming hot. The Epicurean model actually accounts for the migration of qualities through an aggregate of atoms quite well. Why then could not the unity of the animal's life be accounted for by a set of atoms joined by "connectors" which transmit information throughout the network?

Plotinus seems to be thinking of psychic activities which cannot be explained in terms of what we would call feedback mechanisms. The principle of mechanical feedback is a venerable one, evinced splendidly in James Watt's flywheel governor and today as ready to hand as the nearest thermostat. The relevance of this to an ancient dispute over the soul requires a bit of explanation. First of all, Plotinus is following Plato, who in *Theaetetus* 184b–185e argued that the ability to unify in a judgment the objects of different senses cannot be accounted for by a body. Thus, for example, to be able to judge that a sound and a color are different from each other is neither the work of an organ dedicated to one sensible nor the work of an organ dedicated to any sensibles, for difference is not something sensed.

The issue is deeper than this, however, as Plotinus realized. The materialist might easily counter with an hypothesis of second-order material activities somehow monitoring and reporting on the first-order ones. Whereas, say, a color is the object of a first-order material activity, the difference between a color and a sound is the object of a second-order one. Plotinus is here relying on the paradigm of cognitional activity in Intellect, namely, self-reflexivity. In this regard, he was following Aristotle and Alexander of Aphrodisias when he laid great stress upon the fact that what distinguishes cognitive activities from other natural organic activities is self-reflexivity (see *De Anima* 3.4.429b9–430a9; 430b24).[3] For example, Aristotle says that "there is something in us which is aware (τὸ αἰσθανόμενον) that we are in activity, and so we are aware (αἰσθανόμεθα) that we are sensing and we would be thinking that we are thinking" (*Nicomachean Ethics* 10.9.1170a31–3).

It is clear both for Aristotle and Plotinus that this self-awareness cannot be glossed as communication of information between two different things or two different parts of the same thing. By contrast, in feedback mechanisms there is no true self-reflexivity. Rather, information – electrical or chemical or whatever – is passed from one part of the mechanism to a distinct part, which is programmed to react in a particular way.

Whether we call what Aristotle and Plotinus are talking about "self-consciousness" is not now important. What is important is that they both reject the claim that this natural activity could be the property of a body or of an "aggregate" of bodies. Sometimes both Aristotle and Plotinus are content to offer question-begging explanations of this, for example, that organic substances possess potencies for contraries that inorganic natural bodies do not. But the fundamental reason they offer which is *not* question-begging in the slightest is that bodies essentially have parts outside parts, and if awareness and self-awareness are activities of all or some of these parts, these activities must involve *different* parts. For example, let "being cold" be analyzed as a state of a body and let "feeling cold" indicate the awareness of the state. The awareness of the initial state cannot be the state of another body, because the second state's awareness that the first state is cold is not what feeling cold is. It cannot even be another state of the same body, because there would still have to be a division between what is in one state and what is in the other.

In reply, it will be urged that feeling cold for an organism is essentially no different from feeling cold for a thermostat, wherein a sub-system records the state of the whole and therefore the state of itself. Presumably, Plotinus would want to insist that the inference a sub-system makes about itself on the basis of its measuring the state of the whole is not equivalent to the immediacy of self-awareness and that the latter is impossible for a body. A body cannot literally measure itself if there is, as there must be, a physical distinction between measurer and what is measured. A sub-system S follows a rule which states that if system R is cold and S is a part of R, then S is cold. But feeling cold is not known inferentially.

The unity of that which is alone capable of some form of self-reflexive activity is, I take it, the unity that is a necessary condition for συμπάθεια.[4] The soul is the posited non-bodily entity which is the locus of such activity or states. Because Intellect is the paradigm of life and life is identified with self-reflexive activity, all forms of living will be images of the paradigm. That Soul is also a paradigm means that the images of the activity of Intellect in souls will also be instances of the activity that arises from desires for external goals. For example, the introspective awareness of our own psychic states is a prelude to activity intended to continue or alter or eliminate them. Nothing without a soul could desire in this sense. Things with soul but without intellects, like plants, could have desire without self-reflexive cognition.

The only example of that which has self-reflexive awareness but no desire for external goals is a disembodied intellect. I just assume that the sort of empirical introspective evidence that Plotinus would appeal to on behalf of his refutation of the materialist account is to be taken as additional support for a conclusion that could be derived from the nature of Intellect and a premise stating that psychic activity is an image of the activity of Intellect. An Epicurean account of the soul purports to construct self-reflexive activity out of atoms in physical states. Such an approach is difficult to maintain for the reasons given above. A materialist conception of the soul is bound to try to construct an account of psychological activity that will not explain its fundamental feature. Hence, a non-material or non-bodily entity needs to be posited as a means of explanation.[5]

It should be stressed that the phenomenon of self-reflexivity is not to be conflated with privacy. On the basis of Wittgenstein's argument against a private language, it has been claimed that what is fundamentally wrong with Cartesian dualism is that it identifies the self with the private as opposed to the body, which is public. We might observe, however, that for Plotinus ideal, self-reflexive cognition is assimilated to knowledge of eternal truth. Thus, what is strictly speaking private is in this context severely qualified. What it is that the discarnate intellect cognizes is actually identical with what it is that every other discarnate intellect cognizes. Thus, self-discovery is not the discovery of the private. Indeed, it is more accurately characterized as discovery of the universal.[6] The difference between private and public breaks down for a community of eternal cognizers.

It will no doubt have occurred to some readers that a proof of the non-bodily entitative character of the soul based on self-reflexive activity as recognized by Aristotle is deeply suspicious, for Aristotle certainly does not derive this conclusion unambiguously from the premise adopted by Plotinus. In fact, Plotinus will take on the Aristotelian alternative of hylomorphic composition after he has disposed of the arch-materialists, the Stoics. A prior problem is whether in basing his proof of the non-bodily entitative character of the soul on self-reflexive activity Plotinus has proven too much. The souls of plants can be safely set aside in order to be otherwise accounted for, since there is nothing about their activity which requires us to describe it as self-reflexive. But what about the souls of non-human animals? Is Plotinus obliged to admit that in so far as these animals engage in self-reflexive activity they too possess non-bodily souls? And if he is, must he also admit that these souls are immortal? This is a problem rather than merely an embarrassment because Plotinus denies that sense-perception occurs apart from the complex of body and soul (see IV.3.26.1–9; I.1.7). Accordingly, if animal souls exist apart from their bodies, then the activities they engage in are not perceptual, but "higher" ones. The problem is that there is no evidence for such activities in animals. The solution to this problem must await the discussion of the distinction between soul and self.

Let us turn now to the assault on the Stoic account of the soul. This massive attack, consisting of almost a score of arguments, dwarfs the peremptory dismissal of Epicureanism. It reflects the stature of Stoicism in the third century. There is no doubt that the Stoics held a materialist theory of soul.[7] It is composed of πνεῦμα or breath and is alternatively identified with that body which holds together the entire composite or the leading part (τὸ ἡγεμονικόν) of the unifying agent (Sextus Empiricus, *Against the Logicians* 1.234). The arguments Plotinus marshalls against Stoic materialism are of uneven value. They are mainly variations on the theme that only a non-bodily entity could account for certain evident mental phenomena.[8] There are several arguments, however, which deserve a closer look.

The Stoics maintain a distinction between a pain and the perception of a pain, the former located in a part of the body and the latter located in the ἡγεμονικόν (IV.7.7).[9] But if the soul or its leading part is a body, then the perception of the pain will be the result of the transmission (διαδόσει) of the πάθος from one body to another. A succession of bodies will receive and transmit the pain until it arrives at the soul. Then what the soul feels will not be the original pain, but the pain in the bodily part adjacent to it. Evidently, what Plotinus finds unacceptable in this account of "I feel a pain in my toe" is that the pain and the perception of the pain should be in two different bodies. And on the Stoic account, soul is a body different from that which is ensouled.

The difficulty can be brought out if we gloss the above datum as "I perceive my toe-pain," where the "I" is, it seems, implicated in the object as well as in the subject of the sentence. "I perceive my toe-pain" is not like "I perceive my toe." The Stoic account, if it is not merely circular, leans towards making it a matter of degree whether I perceive my pain or yours. By contrast, Plotinus holds, rightly I think, that my perceiving that you have a pain is different in kind from my perceiving my own pain. What Plotinus is really saying is that the distinction between my pain and my perception of my pain is in principle different from the distinction between my perception of your pain and your pain.[10] If soul is a body different from that which is ensouled, this will not be so.

The Stoic might counter with the truly bizarre doctrine of the total interpenetration of bodies. This is the doctrine that there can and do exist certain mixtures of bodies such that each part of the mixture is coextensive with the other. All the parts are present in any part, regardless of how small. The principal point of this doctrine seems to have been to explain the presence of active soul-body or $\pi\nu\epsilon\hat{\upsilon}\mu\alpha$ everywhere in the type of body that is the passive recipient of the active principle (see Alexander of Aphrodisias, *De Mixtione* 216.14–218.6 (*SVF* II.480)).

By rejecting the alternative materialist explanation to juxtaposition, namely, total interpenetration, Plotinus aims to show the hopelessness of any materialistic account of psychic activities in general. His central strategy depends upon foisting an ineluctable dilemma upon the Stoics (IV.7.8.³).[11] Either the mixture of soul-body with the other type of body produces a new product, in which case soul is not actually present in the mixture as such, counter to what the Stoics would presumably allow. Or else, the mixture of soul-body with the other type of body leaves both types of bodies intact, in which case total interpenetration would mean the division of each body into geometrical points. That is, there would be no body or part of body anywhere the other body was not. But the actually infinite division of an extended body into geometrical points is impossible. Therefore, total interpenetration accounts no more adequately than juxtaposition for the relation of soul to body.

One may perhaps reply to this argument that it merely assumes an atomic model of matter which the Stoics in fact repudiate. The interpenetration of bodies should rather be understood according to a non-atomic model, the dynamic continuum model, according to which soul-body and non-soul-body are actually different properties of the same physical body, as, for example, extension and weight are different properties of the same body and everywhere coextensive. This reply, however, accomplishes nothing more than defending the Stoics by making them Peripatetics and translating the doctrine of the interpenetration of bodies into some version of hylomorphism. In a moment we shall turn to Plotinus' attack on this alternative.

One further argument deserves mention. It is an argument which has its roots in Plato but is also endorsed by Aristotle in a qualified way.[12] Accordingly, it is not an argument that depends on essentially Platonic or anti-Platonic principles; it is generically anti-materialist. The argument depends on the premise that there are at least some immaterial objects of thought and that thinking of these could not be the activity of a body (IV.7.8.7–17). The term "immaterial" is of course ambiguous, referring either to (1) that which is independent of space and time or (2) that which is dependent somehow on that which is in space and time.

Underlying Plotinus' argument is the rejection of any representational theory of knowledge, as we have seen. If knowing is interpreted as a kind of dynamic identification of the knower with the object known, no body could be identical with an immaterial object. It could be identical with some representation of that object, but this would not be knowledge, on Plotinus' view. On the basis of the rejection of representationalism and on the basis of the postulation of immaterial objects of knowledge, the conclusion that the knower is an immaterial entity is reached. Whereas Plotinus takes the claim that the objects of knowledge are immaterial in sense (1), Aristotle takes it in sense (2). Accordingly, each reaches a different conclusion regarding the immateriality of the knower.

Having eliminated all the available materialistic conceptions of the soul, Plotinus moves on to try to show that Peripatetic hylomorphism can provide no satisfactory alternative. To this end, he focuses on Aristotle's De Anima, where Aristotle does say things which play right into Plotinus' hands and which make a consistent interpretation of hylomorphic psychology difficult. It is also probably relevant to note that Plotinus is likely to have been especially pleased to take up the defense of Plato's psychology against the explicit attack on it made there. According to Aristotle, "the soul is the first actuality (ἐντελέχεια) of an organic body having life potentially within it" (De Anima 2.1.412a27–8).[13]

The first important point to note about this famous definition is that it is an application of Aristotle's general principles of nature. A naturally occurring sensible substance is analyzable in terms of the inseparable principles of form and matter. Inseparability is to be carefully distinguished from indissolubility, which Aristotle certainly does not wish to affirm for a sub-lunary sensible composite. All it means is that what instantiates the principles of form and matter – in the present case soul and body – could not each exist on its own and continue to be what it is as part of the composite. For example, when the composite animal is destroyed, the result is only a body equivocally.

Plotinus' first objection against the view of soul as ἐντελέχεια of the body is perhaps to be understood as misconstruing this point (IV.7.8⁵.5–9).[14] For Plotinus says that if soul is just one species of form, then when a part of the body is cut off, a part of the soul will be cut off with it. Moreover, if the soul is a form, then it cannot withdraw from the body in sleep. Leaving aside the latter point, which turns upon a dispute over the physiology of sleep, it is not clear to me that Plotinus is misinterpreting Aristotle here as opposed to excluding one impossible interpretation of how soul is related to body, namely, one such that soul is materialized. But why would Plotinus think that this has anything at all to do with Aristotle's doctrine? One reason would be that matter and form are principles of composites whose actuality is nothing but the composite. To deny that absurd interpretation of soul as partially departing with an amputated limb is yet to leave in the dark the unity of diverse principles. In this regard, the Stoic materialists have a much easier case to make than does Aristotle precisely because they reject a diversity of principles in explaining organic life. True, they have an active and a passive principle, and this is quite obscure, but they also insist that the active principle is material. I understand Plotinus to be focusing his attack on an account which insists on an enduring diversity of principles within a unity, that of the hylomorphic composite.

The next brief but portentous argument against Aristotle's hylomorphism is well worth our attention. Plotinus says that if the soul were an ἐντελέχεια, then the opposition between reason and desire would be impossible. That is, there could be "no disagreement in the whole with itself" (οὐ διαφωνοῦν ἑαυτῷ) (IV.7.8⁵.11–14). What Plotinus is referring to here is the phenomenon of incontinence or ἀκρασία, rejected by Plato in the *Protagoras*, affirmed along with a dualistic psychology in the *Republic*, and more or less rejected again by Aristotle in the *Nicomachean Ethics*. To be accurate, Aristotle does agree that there is such a thing as incontinence, but he does so by redescribing it. He concludes his discussion by saying, however, that if incontinence is as Socrates in the *Protagoras* described it, then it is indeed impossible (*Nicomachean Ethics* 7.5.1147b13–17).[15] That description makes of incontinence a matter of literally wanting and not wanting the same thing at the same time. Since Socrates in the *Protagoras* thinks of the human agent as a single ἀρχή of action, such a phenomenon is impossible. This is precisely why Aristotle finds that he must redescribe incontinence in order to accept its possibility. According to his hylomorphic psychology, there is but one ἀρχή of action, the human substance, and what it wants or does not want is determinable precisely and unambiguously by what it inclines towards.

Plotinus accepts the strong description of incontinence, according to which we can want to refrain from doing something but do it anyway because in some sense we want it as well, and whatever it is that wants to refrain is overcome by whatever it is that wants to do it.[16] Incontinence so described is impossible on the hylomorphic model of the soul, as Aristotle himself recognizes. One agent cannot literally want and not want the same thing at the same time. If, however, it turns out that Plotinus' strong description of incontinence is correct, it is not yet clear that his anti-hylomorphic psychology is better able to explain this puzzling phenomenon. All we need note for the present is that Plato explains incontinence only within the context of the tripartition of the immaterial soul (*Republic* 440ab). It is likely, then, that Plotinus believes that the existence of incontinence indicates the truth of dualism or at least of a non-hylomorphic, non-materialist account of the soul.

The major objection against Aristotle's doctrine is that it can account for sense-perception but not for intellection (IV.7.8⁵.14–18). Evidently, Aristotle recognizes something in higher cognitive activity that is not sufficiently accounted for if the soul is simply the ἐντελέχεια of the body. In three passages in *De Anima* Aristotle leaves open the possibility that in the case of rational animals a "part" of the form of the sensible substance can indeed exist separately (*De Anima* 2.1.413a5–9; 2.2.413b24–9; 3.5.430a10–25). It is well known that Aristotle is remarkably reticent about developing the implications of this possibility. I do not propose here to take up the perhaps unanswerable question of whether Aristotle thought that the separate existence of a part of the soul was more than just a possibility. From our perspective, the interesting questions are what are the reasons Aristotle had in mind when he said that it was a possibility at all and whether these reasons recoil upon the basic hylomorphic analysis to its detriment.

It is plausible that what Aristotle is thinking of is the need for an efficient cause of intellection. This efficient cause, the agent intellect, is not identical with the first actuality of the body; indeed it does not appear to be the actualization of any potency (*De Anima* 3.5.430a18). And it is the agent intellect that is undoubtedly the putative separable part of the soul. Plotinus quite reasonably points out that the introduction of "another soul or intellect," by which is meant the agent intellect, must entail that the "reasoning soul" (λογιζομένην ψυχὴν) is an ἐντελέχεια in a different sense (IV.7.8⁵.16–19).[17] It is clear enough that Aristotle cannot have it both ways. Either the primary ἐντελέχεια is a unity, in which case there is no separate actuality apart from the sensible composite, or else there are two *different* actualities needed to account for the life of an intelligent organism.[18] The former alternative is manifestly unsatisfactory according to Aristotle's own words. The latter alternative provides the entrée to the position he set out to repudiate, namely, dualism.

But it is only the entrée. The distinctive form of dualism that is emerging is not a crude dualism of body and soul but a dualism of something like a non-hylomorphic composite and an additional principle, the true self.[19] The composite is a part of nature, the product of the universal soul. The self is an independent principle in a human being, with a separate lineage in Intellect.[20] Yet even if we grant the need to postulate a separate actuality to account for intellection, it remains deeply obscure how this is to be related to the actual composite. This seems to be a problem both for Aristotle and for Plotinus. The latter, however, regards its solution as requiring the abandonment of psychic hylomorphism.

Having rejected Aristotle's account of the soul, Plotinus turns to his own Platonic position. In the course of setting this forth, he offers his central argument for the immortality of the soul.

For soul is the "origin of motion" and is responsible (χορηγοῦσα) for the motion of other things, and it is moved by itself, and gives life to the ensouled body, but has it of itself, and never loses it because it has it of itself. For certainly all things cannot have a borrowed life (ἐπακτῷ ζωῇ): or it [the process of borrowing] will go on to infinity; but there must be some nature which is primarily alive, which must be indestructible and immortal of necessity since it is also the origin of life to the others. (IV.7.9.6–13)[21]

This argument originates in Plato's *Phaedrus*, where it is stated somewhat more perspicuously (254c5ff.):

1. Whatever is always in motion is immortal.
2. Soul is always in motion.
3. Soul is immortal.

The justification for 2 is:

4. Only what moves in virtue of another can cease to be in motion.
5. Soul does not move in virtue of another.
6. Soul cannot cease to be in motion.

The justification for 5 is:

7. The ἀρχή of motion does not move in virtue of another.
8. Soul is the ἀρχή of motion.
9. Soul does not move in virtue of another (i.e., soul is a self-mover).

The justification for 8 is, alas, 9, which is just a repetition of 5.[22]

What is clearly missing in this argument is a proof that there is an ἀρχή of motion and that it is soul. This Plotinus seems to be trying to provide in the passage quoted. He is arguing that the motion of an ensouled or animate body can only be explained by a soul but that the motion of a soul itself needs no explanation outside it. This is so because soul is self-moved. He concludes that since this is so, soul is indestructible and immortal. Why, though, should he believe that soul is self-moved? Presumably, the reason is contained in the claim "all things cannot have a borrowed life: or it will go on to infinity." If soul is not self-moved, then soul, like the ensouled body, will be in need of a causal explanation. If soul is the cause of all motion, then this causal explanation will be another soul, which itself will be in need of a causal explanation for its motion, and so on.

I take it that the reason for supposing that soul is the cause of all motion is that, apart from that which is ensouled (and so explained by soul), the only remaining possible cause of a motion is something inanimate. But inanimate things are, by definition, those things which do not have a cause of motion in themselves. If a soul could be moved by something inanimate, that would only be because it was the instrument of another soul. So, the one question that remains is why souls cannot explain the motion of other souls indefinitely, the way souls explain the motion of ensouled bodies. Again, why is soul a self-mover?

The curious phrase "borrowed life" suggests the answer to this question. An ensouled body has a life borrowed from the soul which governs it. As Plotinus says, the soul is the "primary life." The ensouled body moves because the soul moves. Thus, the motion of the ensouled body is *per aliud*. The term *per aliud* suggests that the motion of the ensouled body is in need of a causal explanation. The only alternative for Plotinus would be to say that the motion of the ensouled body is *per se*, which seems implausible if we realize that things without souls, for example, corpses, do not move at all. If a living body differs from a corpse by its mobility, it is reasonable to assume that the cause of mobility and the cause of being alive are the same.

If, however, we grant that the motion of an ensouled body is *per aliud*, we might still be able to hold that this motion is caused by *another per aliud* motion, that of the soul. Then perhaps we would have no need to claim that the soul is a *per se* mover, because we could adduce *per aliud* motions as explanations indefinitely. So, Plotinus needs to show that the motion of the ensouled body is not caused by another motion, that of the soul, but that there is actually one motion with two components. This is not really such a strange idea at all. When, say, someone draws a figure, this complex motion can be analyzed into two components, the motion of the pen and the motion of the one drawing. But drawing a figure is not two motions, the way drawing a figure and giving the drawing to someone are two motions. It is one motion with a primary and a derivative or instrumental component. Similarly, Plotinus thinks that unless souls are primary or self-movers, then no causal explanation of the motion of ensouled bodies can be given.

The attentive reader will notice a crucial disanalogy in the example of drawing a figure and Plotinus' account of the motion of ensouled bodies. To make the analogy more precise, I should have said that the soul moves the body, not that the soul moves the ensouled body. In that case the claim that the motion of the ensouled body is one motion would have seemed less plausible. A motion of a soul might account for a motion of a body, but surely these are two motions. As we have seen, however, Plotinus is not interested in a soul–body dualism. Souls do not move bodies; persons or selves move their ensouled bodies, the non-hylomorphic composites. Thus, whether or not the argument that that which is self-moving is indestructible is a good one, it should be understood as an argument for the immortality of the person or self. This is after all not surprising given that the destiny of the person is to be found within Intellect, which is prior to Soul.

Let us turn then to consider Plotinus' reasons for distinguishing soul and self.

2 Soul and Self

One of the outstanding pioneers in Neo-Platonic studies, E. R. Dodds, once remarked that Plotinus' greatness as a psychologist lay in, among other things, his distinction between the concepts of soul and ego.[23] I do not think it can be truly maintained that Plotinus was actually the first philosopher to employ such a distinction, but as we shall see, he made more extensive use of it than anyone before him had done.

Part of the problem in identifying the concept of self or ego in Plotinus or in any other Greek philosopher is that there is not a unique, agreed-upon word to represent this concept. Almost universally, when the concept is employed a simple pronoun, αὐτός or ἡμεῖς, is used to stand for the concept, or else, as in Plato, a metaphorical circumlocution, for example, "the man within the man," is used. Furthermore, the concept of the self is a contentious and obscure concept precisely when it is used to indicate something other than the whole, empirical, human being. For example, the Delphic oracle's injunction "know thyself" admits of numerous interpretations, at least some of which do not presuppose any theory which purports to distinguish the biological and social individual from something "deeper" or "more real." The concept of the self only begins to emerge if a philosopher begins to be dissatisfied for one reason or another with the implicit acceptance that a person is more or less just what you see when you look in a mirror. Thus, when Aristotle defines a friend as "another self" (ἕτερον αὐτὸν) (*Nicomachean Ethics* 9.9.1169b6–7), he is obviously intending more than that a friend is another human being.

I should like to make one further preliminary observation in aid of coming to grips with what Plotinus has to say about the self. Every language makes a distinction between "me" and "mine." The mere use of the possessive implies a distinction between possessor and possessed. It is true that there is a persistent grey area within this distinction, referring especially to bodily parts, but also to mental attributes. For example, my hair or any other bodily part is not mine in the same sense in which my house is mine, because on *no* reasonable account of the self would the latter be included, while on some accounts the former would. It is of course possible to trivialize the problem of distinguishing between "me" and "mine" by making the semantics of "I——my——" ontologically exiguous, that is, insisting that there is only a conceptual distinction between possessor and possessed or by stipulating that there is only a conceptual distinction between self and body. At this point we only need note that, assuming the immateriality of the soul, a stipulation that the self is extensionally equivalent with the body is certainly not going to appear very plausible. And with the rejection of Aristotle's hylomorphic alternative, the problem of the identity of the self arises as a search for the reality behind the appearances.

Plotinus tells us that "every man is double, one of him is the sort of composite being and one of him is the self" (ὁ αὐτός) (II.3.9.30–1. See also I.1.2.2–3; I.1.5.1–2; I.1.9.7). The composite is, roughly, the organic, non-hylomorphic composite. Because it is organic or alive, it includes soul in some sense. The self is distinct from the composite, although Plotinus sometimes confusingly identifies it with the soul.[24] Yet, he also explicitly distinguishes the self from the soul in some way: "What is it that has carried out this investigation? Is it 'we' or the soul? It is 'we,' but by the soul. And what do we mean by 'by the soul'? Did 'we' investigate by having soul? No, but in so far as we are soul" (I.1.13.1–3).

To begin to sort out the distinctions being used here, let us notice first that soul is a locus of activities, including the highest, the activity of intellect, which does not require a body, and all the other activities, cognitive, affective, reproductive, vegetative, and so on, which do require a body. The distinction between the self and the composite being is, it seems, a distinction between that highest activity and all the rest. But it is more than that. "Man" or "we" refers not to the activities but to their agent, either the agent of incarnate activities or the agent of the one discarnate activity. In the first quotation above, it is not clear what "self" refers to, although it is evidently somehow related to the agent of incarnate activities. The "we" that investigates in the second quotation clearly refers to this agent. If the "we" and the "self" are the same, then soul is identified with both only in the sense that it is distinct from the composite. The emphatic identification of the self with soul is meant to indicate that the agent of incarnate cognitive activities is not the composite. The composite of body and soul does not think, even if all psychic activities other than the highest form of thinking cannot be done without a body. I take it that this is the fundamental anti-hylomorphic claim.[25]

It seems that Plotinus wants to distinguish between the agent of human activities and the activities themselves. These activities, but for the highest discarnate activity, all require a body. Those elementary activities, such as digestion, that normally occur below the threshold of consciousness, may be said to have as their agent the composite itself. For the rest, especially cognitive activities, the agent is other than the composite, even though these activities may not occur apart from the composite. Thus, for example, I engage in discursive reasoning by using my organic body. The basic reason for distinguishing the "I" from the composite as agent of this activity is that I continue to be active in a discarnate state. The ambiguity of "soul" makes this difficult to see. It seems to refer variously to the powers of an incarnate agent or to the agent itself. In the use of those powers of which we are conscious, "soul" refers both to agent and activity at once. Thus, it is the soul that investigates, to use Plotinus' example, indicating an agent engaged in an incarnate activity. But in so far as the agent exists discarnately, it exists apart from incarnate psychic activities. The immortality of the soul is more accurately designated as the immortality of the self. It is, however, easy enough for Plotinus to fall into speaking about the immortality of the soul, when it is the same self that exists discarnately and incarnately and in the latter state is inseparable from some psychic activities, like discursive reasoning.

It would be tempting to say that what Plotinus means is that there are different kinds of soul. One kind is part of the composite and one kind is not. The latter is identified with the self. The latter uses the former by using the composite. Plotinus does sometimes speak in this way (II.3.9.24–30; 32–3). This manner of speaking, however, produces its own problems. For example, the composite may be the agent of digestion and the self the agent of thinking, but apparently the same self is the agent of countless composite activities. Plotinus has to be able to make sense of a perfectly ordinary claim like "I am tired from all the thinking that I have been doing." Speaking of two kinds of soul might just be a prelude to bifurcating the person into two selves, the thinking self and the tired self. Plotinus does not want to do this.

He does, however, want to make a distinction between what I shall call an "endowed self" and an "ideal self." Psychologists tell us that infants begin to distinguish themselves from others at about six months of age. By the "endowed self" I mean what humans at some point early in their development recognize as the subject of diverse activities and states.[26] Thus I recognize that *I* am hungry and that it is the same *I* that was hungry yesterday. I also recognize that I am the sort of entity that likes certain sorts of food. This certainly need not be and normally is not a very sophisticated kind of recognition; but it is a cognitive ability sufficient, for example, to enable us to think the thought that, while others in the room may not be hungry, *I* am. It is of course possible to go through one's whole life doing no more than noting one's own agency and its apparent continuity through time. It is, however, also possible to reflect critically upon one's own agency, as when one says, for example, "I do not like being the sort of person who habitually desires unhealthy food" or when one says "I would like to be the sort of person who appreciates art, although I am not now that person." The difference is between on the one hand people who just find themselves liking or disliking art and people who reflect on what they like or dislike and make the judgment that they would like that situation to change. A person can thus project an ideal self, which is more or less defined. Ideal selves in general have merely notional existence. Were I to attain such an ideal, this would constitute an alteration from my initial endowment.[27]

Plotinus believes, however, that one's ideal self is eternally real and that it is the same in kind for everyone. That ideal self is the agent of contemplation of Forms. The ideal selves that incarnate selves hold before their minds are gradable according to their proximity to the true ideal. Can a person entertain as an ideal self the true ideal self? One might suppose that the answer to this question is a simple yes, for of all the things I can imagine myself becoming, surely preeminent among these is the self that I really already am. Yet imagining myself, say, liking art is far easier than imagining myself eternally contemplating Forms. In the former case, I am imagining myself acquiring a new property. And of course I am imagining an incarnate self. I do not suppose that the new art-lover will be another person, except perhaps metaphorically. But in the latter case, I cannot imagine that I am contemplating Forms eternally, where "I" stands for anything that I recognize as "I" now. The reason for this is that in eternity I have no past and no future, which seem at least to be categories essential for constructing self-recognition in incarnate persons. If this is so, then at best one could construct an incarnate ideal self that is an approximation of the true ideal self superior to any other. We can recognize what the true ideal self is and then proceed to construct for ourselves an ideal image of it.[28]

The endowed self is partially identified through its agency. In human activities requiring a body, for example, sense-perception, the whole composite is the agent (I.1.7.1–2; IV.3.26.1–9). Presumably, the selves that reflect on such activities are supposed to be distinct from these composites. In other cases, such as discursive reasoning, the soul (in the sense in which it is distinct from the composite) is said to be the agent, although it cannot operate without a prior contribution from the body (see I.1.2.26–7; I.1.7; I.1.9.15–21). The real or true ideal self is just the agent of ideal, that is, discarnate noetic activity. The endowed self is basically the agent of all incarnate psychic activities down to those of which we are unconscious (I.1.7.16–18; V.3.3.34–9). The agent of these latter activities is the composite itself. The self that controls the composite of body and soul is closer to the ideal than is the composite of body and soul because incarnate cognitive activity is a more perfect image of discarnate contemplation than is organic activity. More of this in the next chapter.

The endowed self identifies itself sporadically or episodically (see IV.3.8.13–16). It is that which is capable of recognizing its agency in particular circumstances. For example, we can become conscious of the activities of which we are normally unaware. What makes such acts of identification images of the paradigm case of an intellect's activity is that self-reflexivity is involved. One might say that to be an endowed self is to be self-aware, even if only intermittently. The connections among *tokens* of acts of self-identification seem to be rather adventitious. The persistence or continuity of the endowed self seems, appropriately enough, to be trivialized by the rejection of Aristotelian essentialism. A faulty memory alone would seem to guarantee discontinuity.

One begins to construct an ideal self by fixing a hierarchical or preferential order of *types* of incarnate activity. The identity of this ideal is just the preferential order.[29] This can also be described as a kind of self-definition whereby one ranks activities according to whether they are "me" or "mine."

For example, someone who constructs an ideal self as a philosopher will tend to regard activities of the mere composite and even of the endowed self as those which could be lost without a loss of self-identity. Others, who construct ideal selves that are little or no different from the endowed self, will view their self-identity as including these activities. Someone who viewed the unconscious activities of the composite as constitutive of an ideal self would actually be idealizing the obliteration of his endowed self. Perhaps this is a psychologically impossible limiting case.

Plotinus distinguishes between the real ideal self which is the same in kind for everyone and the result for one who recognizes it as such.

> Other men, we maintain, who have it [a perfect kind of life] potentially, have it as a part, but the man who is well off, who actually is this and has altered in relation to it, *is* this (μεταβέβηκε πρὸς τὸ αὐτό, εἶναι τοῦτο). Everything else is just something he wears; you could not call it part of him because he wears it without wanting to; it would be his if he united it to him by an act of the will. (I.4.4.12–17. See also 1.4.15.17–26)

The fact that there is a real ideal self eternally in Intellect for each person means that there is a standard according to which incarnate ideals can be judged. The act of will referred to in the last sentence of this passage is what determines an ideal for any endowed self.

The endowed self constructs an ideal from a range of potentialities. As Plotinus puts it obscurely, "each one is [that] according to which he is active."[30] What this seems to mean is that from among the range of possible activities a person will identify strongly with one kind or another. Perhaps here the simplest division of these activities is according to the three kinds of lives which both Plato and Aristotle take as fundamental: the rational, the political, and the banausic (*Republic* 581cff.; *Nicomachean Ethics* 1.3.1095b17ff.). But there is nothing against recognizing a more complex list of possibly dominant activities and indeed a rapid succession of identifications by a person with any subset or mixture of these.[31]

The basic point is that a person identifies himself as the subject of these activities in two ways. First, he recognizes that he is the subject of a particular activity. Second, he recognizes himself as the sort of person for whom a particular *kind* of activity is dominant in the sense that it will define a pattern in his life. Activities not engaged in are simply dormant. A person says both "I eat" and "I think," but there is no contradiction and no multiplication of selves in saying both and subordinating one to the other. Any ideal is a pattern of activities or a way of life (βίος).

Plotinus seems to hold that the endowed self is never aware of the activity of the true ideal self and that it never has the self-consciousness of this activity that the ideal self has.[32] What then does it mean for the endowed self to aspire to be finally identified with the true ideal self? Would it then become another self?[33] If the analogy cited in the previous note were relied on, identification with the ideal self would amount to a new awareness of an activity which one immediately recognizes as one's own. It would also presumably involve a recognition of something like the fittingness of this activity. One who had led the appropriate sort of life and approached as nearly as an incarnate individual can to the ideal state would find the activity supremely "comfortable." This last point is, I think, the justification for speaking of the ideal self as in some sense continuous with the endowed one. A person could only find the achievement of the ideal comfortable if it were one's own ideal state.[34] That it be one's own does not, of course, mean that it need be qualitatively different from another's.

Since we are held to be unconscious of the desire that belongs to the true ideal self, it is appropriate to connect the endowed self and this ideal self according to conscious and unconscious desires. It is at least intelligible to say of someone that he does not realize that he desires so and so but that if he were to attain it, he would then recognize that that is what he desired all along. It might be thought in this case that having something "awakens" a desire for it. But in order to make the comparison with Plotinus' account more exact, we have to add that the endowed self may be better or worse prepared to recognize the activity of the ideal self as what the endowed self in fact desires. If we do not do this, then all that Plotinus will say about an ethical and psychological ascent to the Good in this life will be irrelevant. Death would not just be an equalizer, but a redeemer. All persons, no matter how they lived, could be confident that they would gladly embrace the discarnate life of Intellect that was waiting for them. And even if they were not confident, what would it matter in the end?

It is clear that for Plotinus the psychological continuity of the endowed and ideal selves does not depend upon memory. Philosophers have held that memory is essential to self-identity. To lose one's memories irretrievably on this view is to become another person. For Plotinus, memories are not ideally constitutive of the self, even though one may regard them as a basis for the continuity of an endowed self. I am not here suggesting that Plotinus is right or wrong about memories, but rather that his concept of the ideal self is set over against the endowed self and the loosely connected experiences of agency. Apart from the possibility of discarnate existence, another reason that soul and self are distinguished is that different patterns and self-definition are possible in regard to the same set of activities. One can rank activities differently, and this implies a distinction between the activities and the one who ranks them.

There are a number of passages which indicate that Plotinus thought of self-definition in the way suggested above. For example, he says that when the soul "leaves the body it becomes what there was most of in it" (III.4.2.11–12).[35] I take it that the phrase "most of in it" does not refer to quantities of time spent in one kind of activity rather than another but rather to dominant activities, in the sense of those regarded by the person as most important to them, that is, as belonging to their self-definition. This interpretation is, I think, confirmed in the following lines of the text, where Plotinus describes in some detail the different reincarnations likely to result from different types of lives. When he says that "those who guarded the man in them, become men again," he is surely not making a quantitative judgment but a judgment about orientation and self-definition.

Again, when Plotinus exhorts us

> to flee from here and separate ourselves from what has been added to us, and not be the composite thing, the ensouled body in which the nature of body (which has some trace of soul) has the greater power, so that the common life belongs more to the body

he seems to be urging self-definition of a particular sort, not suicide or even mortification of the flesh (II.3.9.19–24).[36]

Further, in a complex discussion of Aristotle's hylomorphic analysis of an organism, Plotinus seems to distinguish two senses of "man": the "rationale" (λόγος) of a rational animal (ζῷον λογικόν) and the composite of soul and body, which is just the rational animal (VI.7.4.29–34).[37] It is clear that the former is prior and separable and in some sense identified with a non-bodily agent.[38] Finally, ideal self-definition is brought out strongly in the following explanation Plotinus gives of the meaning of ἡμεῖς:

> "We ourselves" refers to the dominant and essential part of us; this body is in a different way ours, but ours all the same. So we are concerned with its pains and pleasures, more in proportion as we are weaker and do not separate ourselves, but consider the body the most honorable part of ourselves and the real man, and, so to speak, sink ourselves in it. (IV.4.18.14–19)

As I have noted, Greek does not felicitously distinguish between a substantive self and the possessive pronoun. But it is clear enough that in this passage Plotinus is describing the plight of one who constructs an ideal self which is virtually identical with or in no way superior to the endowed self.[39]

As we shall see, Plotinus has much to say about the conditions for and impediments to optimal self-definition. The concept of self-definition is the key to what is most distinctive about his ethical, religious, and even aesthetic doctrines. It is no doubt prudent for us to separate, as E. R. Dodds would wish to do, Plotinus' frankly introspective psychology from the metaphysical context within which it is imbedded, for these can be evaluated independently. Nevertheless, Plotinus would certainly insist that there is a relationship of what medieval philosophers would call *convenientia* between the two. That is, the more compelling or plausible is the account of the ἀρχαί Intellect and Soul, the more compelling or plausible will be the account of the ideal self, and vice versa.

Plotinus' distinction between soul and self does not entail that disembodied intellectual activity is the ideal. One could presumably argue that even if disembodied activities exist, they are inferior to incarnate ones. In this regard one may compare Aquinas' dictum "I am not my soul" and his conviction that the ideal human condition nevertheless involves some form of embodiment. We need to explore further Plotinus' psychological account of the person which leads him to reject even a non-hylomorphic embodiment as ideal.

3 The Psychology of the Endowed Self

Plotinus rejects hylomorphism for persons or at least Aristotle's account of it as he understands that.[40] He is obliged then to explain the apparent experiences of animate beings. As Plotinus admits, "it is the composite that perceives," and "when a man has an appetite for sexual pleasures, it will be the man that desires, but in another way it will be the desiring part of the soul that desires" (I.1.7.1; I.1.5.29–31).[41] How are soul and self supposed to be related to the body?

> But soul will certainly not be in body as in a substrate, either: for that which is in a substrate is an affection of that in which it is, color and shape, for instance, and soul is something separable. It is certainly not, either, like a part in a whole: for soul is not a part of body. If someone were to suggest that it was like a part in a whole living creature, first of all the same difficulty would remain about how it is in the whole: for it is not, presumably, as the wine is in the jar of wine, or the gallon in the gallon jar, or in the way in which some one thing is in itself. But it is not, either, in body as a whole is in its parts: for it would be absurd to say that the soul is a whole and the body its parts. But it is not, either, present like the form in matter: for the form in matter is inseparable, and it comes afterwards to the matter which is already there. But soul makes the form in matter and is other than the form [which it makes]. (IV.3.20.27–39)

The central claim in this passage is that soul is not the form of a body because it is separable, but it makes the form in the body. This seems to be just an evasion. Either it removes the problem to the relation of soul to form-in-matter or it accommodates hylomorphism without the name.

The distinction between soul and self developed in the last section is here essential. Soul, as we have seen, includes a range of activities, some of which, like digestion, include body in the definition of their essence. All these come under the general heading "nature" and are to be explained according to its principles. One activity alone, that of intellection, can occur without a body.[42] The "link" between incarnate and discarnate activities is the self. In effect, the justification for saying that the same self can exist both discarnately and incarnately is that the incarnated self is distinct from the organic composite that it governs. The evidence for governance is the sort of psychic conflict that Plato recounts in the *Republic* and explains in terms of a tripartite soul.[43] Since I am sometimes aware of resisting the appetites of my (organic) body, I am an agent other than the one which generates the appetite. But of course both Plato and Plotinus realize that these appetites are not like those of another person or another self. They are appetites of an endowed self episodically identified. That is, at one time I recognize myself as the agent having the appetites and also as the agent who resists them.

It was Plato's insight that these two episodes of agency recognition cannot simply be reduced to a case of one agent wanting incompatible things. There are of course many cases where one can suppose that one desires something more or less than something else. But it seems incoherent to claim that the agent that desires something is identical with the agent that desires the opposite. In order to achieve coherence, the second desire would have to be interpreted as being actually a desire for something else. For Plato and Plotinus, however, such an interpretation falsifies the phenomenology of experience. More than that, it obscures an essential feature of endowed self-identity, namely, the *priority* of the rational agent to the agent of any other type of activity.[44]

Suppose that I recognize myself as the agent of an appetitive desire and also as an agent who believes that the desire ought to be resisted. I might then raise the question of why I should "give in" to my rational desire rather than my appetitive desire. Even if on reflection I concluded that I ought not to believe what I believe or that I ought to ignore what I believe, that would be a rational determination of the conflict: I would have decided that I ought to satisfy my appetite. Merely recognizing such a conflict is an act of a rational agent.[45]

The priority of the self as an agent of rational activity to the self as an agent of any other type of incarnate activity is determined by the priority of the true ideal self to the endowed self. This priority provides the basis for the following analogy: true ideal self:endowed self::rational endowed self: composite self. An endowed self which constructed an ideal self in which the desires of the composite dominated would be taking an incoherent path to self-identification. It would be like choosing to abandon rational control with no ulterior (rational) motive. But even if the endowed self were to construct an ideal self in which rational desires dominated, there would still remain a kind of insufficiency in such construction precisely because having desires is less desirable than having desires fulfilled. In other words, if one is capable of recognizing that one's identity is as a rational agent, then one is on the way to recognizing that the true ideal of rational agency for oneself excludes incarnation. It is no doubt disputable whether all would embrace the sort of ideal envisaged by Plotinus. As we shall see, Plotinus devotes a good deal of thought to the problem of how one can be led to correct a misidentification of one's own ideal self.

The agency of the composite is an image of the agency of the rationally endowed self just as the latter is an image of the agency of a discarnate intellect. Thus, Plotinus does not conceive of a soul–body problem as a problem of how different sorts of entities can be causally related but as a problem in the metaphysics of imagery. It is a problem of how the endowed self is an image of the true ideal self or how the agent of incarnate activities can be the same agent as the agent of one discarnate activity and still be an image of it. It is a special case of the general problem of homonymous and synonymous imagery. The oddness of saying that the endowed self is to the true ideal self as an instance of a Form is to a Form is mitigated at least somewhat by insisting that Intellect is the paradigm both of life and of οὐσία. The "return" to the true ideal self is made more plausible by the recognition that the Form's nature really is in the image. Our return depends upon realizing that what we are when we engage in rational activity is an imperfect version of what we really are, eternal cognizers.

Plotinus frequently says that the soul uses the body as a tool (I.1.3.15–16; I.1.4.18–20; I.4.16.21–9; IV.7.1.23–4; VI.7.5.24). The use of this traditional metaphor is not entirely straightforward given what has already been said. Is the tool the composite or living thing and the user the endowed self construed as the agent of composite activity or is the tool the body of the living thing? It certainly appears as if it should be the former. Just as "soul" is sometimes used for "self," so "body" is sometimes used for "composite organism."

> He [the good man] must give to this bodily life as much as it needs and he can, but he is himself other than it and free to abandon it, and he will abandon it in nature's good time, and, besides, has the right to decide about this for himself. So some of his activities will tend towards well-being; others will not be directed to the goal and will really not belong to him but to that which is joined to him, which he will care for and bear with as long as he can use it; if he cannot use it he will change to another, or give up using the lyre and abandon the activities directed to it. Then he will have something else to do which does not need the lyre, and will let it lie unregarded beside him while he sings without an instrument. Yet this instrument was not given to him at the beginning without good reason. He has used it often up till now. (I.4.16.17–29)

The activities of which this passage speaks are those of the endowed self. They are divided according to whether they are directed to well-being or to the care and needs of the composite. Those directed to well-being are of course not discarnate activities. They are activities which bring the endowed self closer to its true ideal. The metaphor of a tool indicates the essential point of the distinction of composite and self. That the tool is the composite which includes agency ("the composite perceives") indicates the fundamental variability of the self as endowed.

. Another striking metaphor employed by Plotinus in this regard is that of the theatre (see III.2.15–18). The central idea here is that of the actor in relation to his role. An endowed self "takes on the role" of embodied agent. Imagine an actor engrossed in a part who says, "I really felt that my adversary in the play was abusing *me*. I suffered *in my role*." But of course the person who takes the role does not necessarily suffer. The ambiguity of "I" is precisely that of the actor in the role. The two extreme limits of identification are on the one hand that of the actor who cannot distinguish his real life from his role or even does not wish to do so and on the other hand that of an actor who refuses to perform in the role or who does so without the least "commitment" to it, "going through the motions," as we might say. However, that which would be a defect in an actor would be for Plotinus a virtue for a person in real life.

We are now in a position to understand one of Plotinus' more puzzling claims, namely, that the soul is impassive (ἀπαθής) while the composite undergoes all sorts of affections or πάθη (see I.1.4.12–18; III.6.5.1–2; IV.4.18–20; IV.4.24.17–21).[46] Plotinus seems to insist on the soul being impassive in the teeth of common sense. Is it not obviously the case that emotions like anger, fear, and grief can change people or indicate changes in people such that we must admit that the soul is affected in some way? Indeed, as Plotinus admits, we typically speak of τὸ παθητικόν, that "part" of the soul in virtue of which we have πάθη.[47] He is evidently not content merely to endorse Aristotle's claim that the agent intellect or the "thinking part" of the soul is impassive, thereby separating it off from the hylomorphic composite and preserving the unity of each (*De Anima* 1.4.408b25; 3.4.429a15).

A πάθος is, very roughly, what happens to something as a result of the action of something else. When applied to animate individuals, πάθος includes a special kind of happening which in some respects corresponds to what we would call "emotion." But it also includes feelings of pleasure and pain.[48] Plotinus follows Aristotle in distinguising sharply between an affection and an activity (see III.6.1.1–2; III.6.2.49–52). He also seems to follow Aristotle in his threefold distinction between affections, powers, and habits (*Nicomachean Ethics* 2.4.1105b20).[49] Although Aristotle calls these "three things in the soul," Plotinus is of course arguing that only the latter two are in the soul. The explanation of how πάθη are related to the soul is this:

> But what about the soul's accepting things as its own or rejecting them as alien? And, surely, feelings of grief and anger, pleasures, desires and fears, are changes and affections present in the soul and moving there. About these, too, one must certainly make a distinction in this way. To deny that alterations in the soul, and intense perceptions of them, do occur is to contradict the obvious facts. But when we accept this we ought to enquire what it is that is changed. For we run the risk, when we say this of the soul, of understanding it in the same sort of way as if we say that the soul blushes or turns pale again, not taking into

account that these affections are brought about by the soul but occur in the other structure [the organic body]. But the shame is in soul, when the idea of something disgraceful arises in it; but the body, which the soul in a way possesses – not to be led astray by words – being subject to the soul and not the same thing as a lifeless body, is changed by way of the blood, which is easy to move. (III.6.3.1–15)[50]

The essential discontinuity of the affective and the cognitive could not be more clearly stated. The idea of shame is in the soul, but the feeling of shame is identified as a bodily state or more correctly as a state of the composite. We need once again to have recourse to the equivocal status of the self. An emotional state must be distinguished from a objective bodily state such as temperature, where agency is irrelevant. In order to maintain the impassiveness of the soul *and* to identify emotions as something that persons actually do experience, the self must be the connecting link across the various activities. The endowed self finds itself as the subject both of states of the composite body, that is, emotional states among others, and of cognitive activities. This subject of emotional states is an image of the true ideal self which, in its disembodied state, is incapable of emotional experiences. The question is whether or not it is doomed to carry the baggage of its embodied emotional experiences.

Plotinus seems to want to make two claims. First, the incommensurability of emotive states and cognitive activities in the same person means that whatever burden the person carries as he moves from being the agent of the former to the latter is not emotional. Second, despite the impassivity of the soul, the fact that there must be a subject of emotional states means that at least some of the soul's faculties must be understood in such a way that what happens *in* the organic body still happens *to* a person.

I shall take up the latter claim first. Plotinus says that the part of the soul which is the subject of emotional states is the form of the body (III.6.4.30–1). We must understand this as the form provided by the soul or self to the body or the composite. What Plotinus is getting at becomes clear a bit further on in the chapter when he explains that the form of the body is an activity and as such it is the cause of the emotional state (III.6.4.41–6).[51] By explicitly identifying the form with an activity, Plotinus implicitly distinguishes it from the agent engaged in that activity (see I.1.6.1–4).[52] The agent can be none other than the endowed self, possessed of a body. The impassivity of the soul, even in relation to the activities requiring a body, is guaranteed by the distinction of cognitive agent and composite agent. Only the agent of the activity could experience the emotion; at that, it experiences it in the body. The endowed self recognizes itself as the agent whose organic body experiences an emotion. It is impassive just in the sense that it can also reflect upon an emotional experience and then identify itself as an agent detached from it. The endowed self can say, for example, that it will refuse to act in response to the anger it feels as a composite. What is impassive is the rational agent, the governor of the endowed self. The difference between someone who realizes this and someone who does not is like the difference between someone who thinks that he is affected directly by an attack on a voodoo doll made in his image and someone who knows that he is not.

Separation from emotional experiences then amounts to disengagement of the self from the experiences and related activities. Does this self bear the scars of its emotional experiences? No, it is marked only to the extent that it identified with the activities which cause such experiences. Plotinus describes the disengagement metaphorically as purification (κάθαρσις) or waking up (ἔγερσις).[53] These metaphors are difficult to interpret precisely. The most plausible interpretation, I think, focuses on the central fact of "waking up from a dream," which is the realization that that which one took to be one's own experience or activity is not really so. The idea of the metaphor is that a dream state is to a real state of the agent as an emotional state is to a cognitive state or activity. Stated thus, Plotinus' claim is not that an emotional state is a dream; rather, it is dreamlike because it is not a state of real life, Platonically speaking. One who "awakened" to that life would say, "I was not really in that emotional state, although in some sense I was the subject of it," much as one would say, "I was not really experiencing what I dreamed I was experiencing, although it was I who was dreaming." Only someone who was attached to those dreams in the way a psychotic believes that he is, say, really hearing otherworldly voices, would be substantially affected by them.[54]

This leads to the first claim, namely, that emotions are non-exportable from incarnate to discarnate states. The person who confused his endowed, embodied self with his true ideal self would, in the extreme case, view cognitive activity as dreamlike. The precise error that such a person is burdened with is of course cognitive, as are all errors. More exactly, it is an error about self-identity.[55] I shall have more to say about the ethical aspect of error in chapter 9. In the present chapter I shall move on to discuss two remaining topics, desire and free will.

4 Desires of the Dispossessed

The topic of desire in Plotinus is laden with terminological complexities. I begin by gratefully endorsing René Arnou's conclusion that "[e]n fait entre tous ces termes ἔρως, ἔφεσις, πόθος, ὄρεξις, ὁρμή, il ne reste chez Plotin que des nuances, qui souvent s'effacent."[56] Some slight qualification to this claim will be necessary in due course. For now, I shall simply use the word "desire" to indicate broadly the organic phenomenon which is the origin of movement towards a goal. It is generally what all things with souls have in common just in so far as they have souls. The terminological obscurity, in Plotinus at any rate, is owing to the fact that there is nothing like a consensus among his predecessors regarding an appropriate vocabulary for speaking about desire and its various forms, in persons and in other animate individuals. Plato himself eschews a consistent vocabulary. Aristotle, when speaking systematically, tends to use the term ὄρεξις generically, and Plotinus certainly does employ this term with some frequency. But it is not a term used by Plato, a fact which probably contributes to Plotinus' diffidence and his sometime preference for the term ἔρως, especially of course when commenting on passages from the *Symposium* and the *Phaedrus*.

Terminological problems aside, the starting-point of Plotinus' account is Plato's tripartitioning of the soul and his strong suggestion that human desire is in itself an undifferentiated and finite force which is directable through one or another of the three parts.[57] This doctrine is in turn supported by an earlier comprehensive claim that all men desire (the terms ἐπιθυμία and βούλησις are both used) the good (see *Meno* 77c; *Gorgias* 468bc). Whatever else this latter claim entails, I take it that it at least means that people do whatever they do because they think that the ultimate result will be a state they will find intrinsically satisfying, i.e., desirable. This is a logical point about the meaning of "good," but it is also a psychological point about the nature of desire. Let us leave aside for now the further portentous claim of both Plato and Plotinus that there is no necessary connection between what people think is desirable and what in fact is satisfying for them when obtained.

I have said that Plotinus is somewhat ambivalent about the tripartitioning of the soul. He does not completely reject it, but he sometimes uses the language of a faculty psychology which is not easily harmonized with the language of tripartition. Aristotle, however, at least follows Plato to the extent of distinguishing three species of ὄρεξις: ἐπιθυμία, θυμός, and βούλησις, the first two of which are actually said to be in the irrational part of the soul and the last-mentioned in the rational part (see *De Anima* 2.3.414b2, 3.9.432b5–6; *Eudemian Ethics* 2.7.1223a27–8; *On the Motion of Animals* 6.700b22).[58] He also follows Plato in designating desire or ὄρεξις as the ἀρχή of animal action (*De Anima* 3.10.433a16–17). Whether we speak of parts or faculties, and whether we speak of ὀρέξεις or use some other term, there is an obvious similarity in the approaches of Plato and Aristotle, a similarity manifested most strikingly in their concurrence in the conception of a basic psychological phenomenon which is differentiated roughly according to the presence or absence of reason.[59] We should not be surprised to discover that the underlying agreement of Plato and Aristotle would be reflected in the basis of Plotinus' own account.

The differentiation of an underlying psychological phenomenon along the lines taken by Plato and Aristotle is strongly hinted at it the *Enneads*, although it is not explicitly stated. For example, Plotinus distinguishes ἐπιθυμία from θυμός and generally the displacement (ἔκστασις) in relation to anything outside itself as a type of ὄρεξις (I.1.5.21–3). In addition, he regularly speaks of βούλησις for the good, which he sometimes explicitly calls a form of ὄρεξις (see I.2.1.14; IV.8.4.1). With these remarks the limit to plain-sailing is pretty well reached.

The first difficulty we face is occasioned by Plotinus' puzzling remark that:

> the division of desires is a division of the desires themselves and not the substance (τῆς οὐσίας) from which they come. That substance is not itself a desire but perhaps it brings to completion the desire by connecting the activity from itself to it. (IV.4.28.70–3)

The context within which this remark is made indicates that the desires spoken of here are exclusively the two belonging to the so-called irrational part and that the substance which is their source is the soul.[60] The division of desire and the undividedness of that which is their source appear to conform to the faculty psychology. What precisely is the "activity" which is said to bring about the fulfillment of such desires?

Plotinus uses forms of the word ὄρεξις in describing rational desire (see I.1.5.27; I.2.1.14; I.6.7.1f.; I.8.15.21; IV.8.4.1f.). But the important distinction is between that which does and that which does not require a body. The former are ἐπιθυμία and θυμός; the latter is βούλησις. Rational desire is unequivocally identified with desire for the good (cf. VI.8.6.37–8).[61] Thus, it would seem that the activity distinguished from irrational desires but the source of their fulfillment is the basic identifying activity of the soul, a desire for the good whether this be real or apparent. This activity is the motive behind action on behalf of any "lower" kind of desire. On this interpretation, the words "brings to completion the desire by connecting the activity from itself to it" indicate the general desire for the good as directed through a composite. When the endowed self endorses the occurrent desires of the composite, it moves to satisfy them. Plotinus is perhaps here thinking of the possibility that one can actually reject these desires or endorse them diffidently. But these are not desires for the real good. They are at best desires for the apparent good.

An endowed self that desired only the real good would have none of the desires of the composite. In Plotinus' eschatology, our happiness does not depend in any way on anything requiring a body. The reason why the activity which is desiring the good and which is the essence of the soul does actually bring incarnate desires to completion (or at least attempts to) is precisely the "descent" of the soul into the body (see IV.7.13).[62] Owing to this descent, endowed selves do not in fact desire only the real good.

Plotinus wants to be able to account for the obvious fact that we do in some sense desire pleasures and the "necessities" of life. Yet these are not even good for us instrumentally speaking. The endowed self intermittently or sporadically identifies with the composite and its "lower" psychic activities. The differentiation of desires between rational and irrational corresponds to the complexity of the endowed self. An endowed self projects an ideal self by creating a hierarchy of desires. The total denial of irrational or rational desires represents the two logical extremes. The best situation that an endowed self could hope to achieve so long as it exists incarnately is that it would view irrational desires with sublime indifference. They would then be no part of its constructed ideal self. Desire for the real good and bodily desires are not therefore desires for alternative commensurable goods. To think otherwise is to make the mistake of viewing some sort of incarnate existence as the true ideal.[63]

Plotinus suggests that perhaps ὀρέξεις should be divided according to whether they follow reason or whether they are "drags" upon one; in the former case they are "doings" (ποιήσεις), whereas in the latter they are "experiencings" (πείσεις) (VI.1.21.16–19).[64] It seems likely enough that the former refers to βούλησις and the latter to θυμός and ἐπιθυμία. The suggested classification of θυμός and ἐπιθυμία as types of πείσεις (= πάθη) should not surprise us if we recall the various definitions and descriptions of πάθη in Plato, Aristotle, and the Stoics. The implication perhaps drawn by Plotinus is that if we recognize βούλησις as an ὄρεξις only equivocally, then ὄρεξις in the main sense and πάθος indicate the same phenomenon or at least closely related phases of the same phenomenon.[65] This phenomenon requires a body for its presence. It is the condition of an ensouled body which moves it to act. If reason is applied at this point, then the action is rational; if it is not, then the action is not.

For example, the feeling of weariness and desire for rest seem to be inseparable.[66] It would be very odd in any case to imagine the presence of the one without the other. Perhaps Plotinus' hesitation and ours in equating the two is nevertheless owing to our not knowing where the affective and connative event ends and the cognitive begins. If it is a constituent of the desire alone, then it will be necessary to resist the identification of the desire with the feeling. This is what Aristotle seems to do when he defines choice as "deliberative desire." But if we look at what Aristotle says more carefully, choice is not a "mixture" of deliberation and desire, but deliberation about a desire which is recognized as present. And deliberating about my feeling of weariness does not seem to be importantly different from deliberating about my desire for rest.

The issue is, however, more complicated for Plotinus owing to his account of the self. Whether desires are assimilated to feelings or not, the subject of both is the self, that is, the endowed self. Plotinus, however, wants to insist on an ideal end-point of human striving in which desire or feeling as a passive state is eliminated.[67] The true ideal self has desire or βούλησις in a very attenuated sense, that according to which it is actually indistinguishable from intelligence (φρόνησις) (IV.4.12.46). The strong impression one gets is that the polar opposite to βούλησις in so far as it is indistinguishable from φρόνησις is that form of desire completely bereft of intelligence. The normal lives of most people contain βούλησις detached from φρόνησις and the lower forms of desire. It is owing to the fact that we have βούλησις at all that we can deliberate regarding our desires. Βούλησις is present in every member of the species, essentially orienting us towards the good. In a person whose ideal self is close to the true ideal, the lower desires will be viewed not as one's own but as those of one's possessions (see I.4.4.25–36; I.4.6.14–24). Such a person may calculate that it is well to satisfy these desires, but not because he views their satisfaction as constitutive of his happiness or because he believes his ideal self is their subject. Alternately, a person may mistake the satisfaction of such desires as essential to his happiness; he may think that what he desires (ἐπιθυμία) is what he rationally wills (βούλησις), disoriented as he is from his true goal.

Severing βούλησις from the other forms of ὄρεξις in this way, and distinguishing the ideal from the endowed self, Plotinus has a more effective way of expressing the doctrine equally adhered to by Plato, namely, the superiority and indeed naturalness of a disembodied existence. An objector – Aristotelian, I suspect – may claim that all forms of desire, including the bodily, are essential to our happiness (I.4.5–6). It is probably relevant to mention that the objector could be a Christian, too, who views the ideal state of a person as requiring bodily resurrection. For Plotinus and Plato, the objection amounts to a claim about the ideal self. For Plotinus, it is a claim more easily countered if tripartition is restricted to incarnation and denied of the soul in its discarnate state. If the soul is tripartite, it seems difficult both to conceive of its ideal state as being something other than this and to conceive of a tripartite discarnate soul.[68] If instead of parts, faculties of the soul are posited, the lower faculties can be apportioned to the incarnate self alone. Indeed, Plato himself perhaps finally came to accept this, thereby modifying his view of triparition (see *Timaeus* 69c8 d1, d5–6; 41cd; 90a). It should be added that Plotinus never proposes to meet the objector in his own, psychological terms. That is, he never questions the implausibility of the claim of discarnate superiority to one whose constructed ideal self affects a personal attachment to bodily desires. Someone who says that he cannot imagine a discarnate existence as the state in which his perfect happiness would be achieved is to be taken at his word. It is only a metaphysical, not a psychological, argument that could convince one that this is just in fact a failure of imagination.

5 Free Will

What Plotinus has to say about free will springs from two sources: first, what he concludes about desire and second, his response to Aristotle's account in the third book of the *Nicomachean Ethics*. Plato does not have a great deal to say about this issue, although undoubtedly Plotinus is convinced that what he, Plotinus, is going to say is in principle in harmony with his master. Stoic doctrine would have been the overwhelmingly dominant immediate background for Plotinus. But curiously Plotinus does not seem to take much account of the Stoics in this matter. At the end of this section, I shall attempt to say why and also how Plotinus' account compares with Stoic compatibilism.

Since that account is so closely connected to Aristotle's analysis of action and choice, we need to begin with the salient features of that analysis. First, Aristotle divides actions into those that are voluntary (ἑκούσιον) and those that are involuntary (ἀκούσιον) (*Nicomachean Ethics* 3.1.1109b30–2). The latter are divided into those done by force, that is, where the moving principle is outside the agent, and those done because of ignorance, that is, cases where the agent would not have acted had he been in possession of relevant knowledge (1109b35–1110a1; 2.1110b18–20).[69] Actions which are voluntary are, by contrast, done with knowledge and are within our power (ἐφ' ἡμῖν) (1110a15–18; 1110b4; 3.1111a23–4). Voluntary actions are divided into those done with and those done without choice (προαίρεσις) (4.1111b6ff.). Since choice is defined by Aristotle as "deliberate desire (βουλευτικὴ ὄρεξις) of things within our power," we may infer that the second type of voluntary action, what is done without choice, refers to those where deliberate desire is not the ἀρχή, presumably because deliberation is missing although desire is present (5.1113a10–11; 4.1111b8–10). According to this definition, choice is not to be identified with rational desire (βούλησις) alone, or with other forms of ὄρεξις, or with the voluntary (see *Eudemian Ethics* 2.6.1223a15ff.). It is also not to be identified with opinion or belief (4.1111b10–12). It is not identified with βούλησις because choice regards things which it is within our power to bring about, whereas βούλησις may regard what is not within our power (5.1112a18ff.).[70] Further, βούλησις is always of an end, whereas choice is of a means to an end (4.1111b19–29).

On the basis of this analysis, the question of whether or not our choices are free is answered decisively. This is so at least if a free action and a voluntary one are the same. Choice is a division within the genus of voluntary action. There could be no such thing as involuntary choice. Choices, of course, may be hard or easy; indeed, they may be so hard that they may be treated by others as practically involuntary actions. But Aristotle is firm that in so far as the action tends to the involuntary, it is not a choice (2.1110a5ff.).

Aristotle's definition of the voluntary as "that whose principle is the agent who knows the particulars on which the action depends" seems to make knowledge and being "within our power" jointly necessary and sufficient conditions of the voluntary (3.1111a22–3). Accordingly, he does not exactly countenance two different types of voluntary action corresponding to the two different types of involuntary action, namely, those done by force and those done because of ignorance. The two types of voluntary action, those done with choice and those done without choice, are not the true counterparts to involuntary actions done by force or because of ignorance because voluntary actions done without choice still require knowledge of particulars and this knowledge is not equivalent to deliberation. It is not equivalent because deliberation requires the ability to formulate a universal proposition as part of a practical syllogism, whereas the knowledge of children and animals does not extend this far.

This point is of considerable importance for the following reason. Problems about human freedom frequently focus upon free will as opposed to free choice. It is envisaged that there are putative cases in which knowledge of particulars is present, and deliberate desire is present, at least hypothetically, but that some constraint, either external or internal, prevents one from acting upon the choice. In such cases, one might want to argue that the will was free, even though it was not within one's power to act on it. Since, however, Aristotle only thinks of volition as a property of a kind of action, he is not concerned with volition apart from action, that is, supposed cases where there is knowledge of particulars but action is not "within our power," or with supposed cases where what is "within our power" is something other than action.

I do not think it will do to say simply that since for Aristotle ethics is a practical science, what counts after all is action. However, Aristotle's account is easily amended to cover the putative cases by broadening the definition of action to include any result of desire, deliberate or otherwise, even if this is just the state of mind of the agent. With this amendment, free choice and free will are generically identical. The result of a deliberate desire is voluntary when there is knowledge of particulars and the action is "within our power," now understanding action to include a state of mind that is achieved. To say that someone's will was free would also be to claim that he had deliberate desire and knowledge of particulars and the action was "within his power," even though it might not involve a motion outside of himself. The proposed amendment is actually warranted by the term προαίρεσις, which I have translated as "choice" but which includes intention, that is, the initial stage in a process leading to the actual motion of the person.

Because Aristotle discusses choice within the context of his narrow definition of action, he takes the question of what is and what is not "within our power" as admitting of a fairly straightforward answer. The only cases of involuntary action are those where external force has been applied and where the agent has acted because of ignorance of particulars. Aristotle is quite explicit that "external" means that the moving cause is outside the person, such as the wind which blows the ship and its crew off course and men who have us in their power (2.1110b16–18. See also 1110a1–8). The only difficult case Aristotle recognizes is the so-called "mixed" action, an action done through fear of a greater evil. Even in this case, such actions are more like voluntary ones than like involuntary ones, precisely because their origin is a choice.

The cases of involuntary action are those in which the ἀρχή of action is thwarted from completing what it started; the cases of voluntary action are those in which the ἀρχή of action is effective in carrying through what it started. The incontinent man still acts voluntarily (7.11.1152a15–16). An action is voluntary only if it is "within our power." The starting-point for determining whether something was in our power is the ἀρχή of the action. Whatever that is, is a given. There is no conceptual space in Aristotle's analysis for questioning whether the ἀρχή itself was "within our power." Now possible defects in the ἀρχή are of two sorts, defects in deliberation and defects in desire. Aristotle of course recognizes defects in both of these, but the determination of whether an action is voluntary or not does not depend on the prior determination of whether or not there was a defect of either sort. Plotinus, however, is prepared to consider defects in the ἀρχή of action as potentially determinative of whether the action was voluntary or involuntary. As a result, the ambit of free choice or will is going to be considerably constricted.

It is well to preface Plotinus' positive account with mention of his uncompromising rejection in *Ennead* III.1 of Stoic and Epicurean positions and the position of those who hold to astrological determinism. First, Plotinus accepts a qualified principle of universal causation for "everything that becomes or which always is but does not always act in the same way" (III.1.1.13–16). It is on the basis of this principle that he summarily rejects Epicurus' account of freedom on the basis of the "swerve" of atoms. Acceptance of the principle of universal causation, however, does not for Plotinus entail determinism or that all things are fated to be as they are. That some things are within our power (ἐφ' ἡμῖν) is a datum evident from introspection that must be accounted for within a universal causal framework (III.1.7).[71] Thus, Plotinus appeals to the apparent opposition of the soul to the body and to apparent choice as inexplicable within a deterministic framework (III.1.3.20–7).[72]

How then are we supposed to reconcile the universal causal principle and the claim that some things are ἐφ' ἡμῖν, which means that in these cases we are the ἀρχή of action? Plotinus rejects as specious a Stoic solution which makes our participation in our actions one necessary link in a universal chain of causes (III.1.7).[73] On such an account, the agent would be no true ἀρχή of his action. The bare bones of Plotinus' solution are contained in the following passage:

> Now when the soul is without a body it is in absolute control of itself (κυριωτάτη) and free (ἐλευθέρα), and outside the causation of the physical universe; but when it is brought into a body it is no longer in all ways in control, as it forms part of an order with other things. Chances direct, for the most part, all the things round it, among which it has fallen when it comes to this middle point, so that it does some things because of these, but sometimes it masters them itself and leads them where it wishes. The better soul has power over more, the worse over less. (III.1.8.9–15)

The first part of this passage looks as if it is taking advantage of the escape clause in the qualified universal principle of causality. The separation of the soul from the body must refer principally to a state in which there is no becoming or change, that is, the activity of a discarnate intellect. Perhaps it refers derivatively to an embodied state in which the agent acts as if he were disembodied. But this is hardly a refutation of the Stoic position if it in fact concedes universal causality for everything embodied. We notice, however, that the discarnate state is one of perfect freedom, whereas embodiment does not eliminate it, but rather merely constricts it.

So the nub of the issue is how we can be in control of or the ἀρχή of embodied actions in any way. In order to appreciate Plotinus' response to this question we shall have to turn to his far more detailed account of freedom in VI.8, where Aristotle's analysis is brought to bear on the issue. We may note, though, that a schematic of the response will have the unqualifiedly free activity of Intellect somehow introduced in an explanatory role in relation to embodied actions (see VI.8.6.36–8). Thus an embodied action will be a kind of synonymous image of the activity of Intellect and also a kind of homonymous image. That is, the intelligible content of the discarnate perfect activity of Intellect will be present in an embodied action, but its manifestation will be compromised by embodiment. On this understanding, the Stoic account would not exactly be wrong; rather, it would be incomplete because it deals only with the material conditions for the manifestation of the image of Intellect, and not with the intelligible content. In effect, it pretends that action can be understood as if it were mere physical motion.

If one proceeds from the third book of Aristotle's *Nicomachean Ethics* to the first six chapters of *Ennead* VI.8, "Free Will and the Will of the One," it will be immediately evident how closely Plotinus is following the analysis of Aristotle. The question governing Plotinus' investigation is whether or not there is anything within our power (VI.8.1.15–16).[74] The Aristotelian answer to this question is, as we have seen, that what is within our power is whatever action is not involuntary, owing either to force or ignorance. Plotinus accedes to the definition of the voluntary as that which is done neither through force nor ignorance (VI.8.1.33–4).[75] But he seems to resist the claim that if an action is voluntary it is necessarily within our power. He notes the oddity of holding that an action was in our power if it was "enslaved" to our βούλησις, that is, if it was necessitated by a rational desire (VI.8.1.30–3).[76] How does the "enslavement" to our desire differ from enslavement to chance or compulsion or passion? For an action to be within our power, it is not enough that it be voluntary. It must also be one over which we have control (VI.8.1.34).[77] Accordingly, an action may be voluntary without being within our power.

Can an action also be one over which we have control without that action being voluntary? The example Plotinus gives of this putative possibility is curious. If someone kills a man not knowing that the man is his own father, he may have control over the action, even though it is not voluntary

(VI.8.1.34–8). Plotinus then wonders if the ignorance in this case undermines control as well. The conceptual confusion Plotinus is here struggling with concerns an ambiguity in the meaning of βούλησις or rational desire. Shall we call a desire "rational" if it depends upon a mistaken belief or only if it depends on knowledge? If we say the latter, we shall be tending towards the conclusion that the only unqualifiedly rational desire is that of an omniscient being. If we recoil from this alternative, then a rational desire would seem not to be one over which we have control, since it is contingent upon defeasible beliefs. In the case of the killer, it is difficult to see how he could be in control and act involuntarily if the absence of volition owing to ignorance undercuts his control.

The question then becomes: How do volition and control contribute to making an action one which is within our power? Mere volition without choice is certainly not enough for an act to be within one's power, for animals, children, madmen, and those under the influence of drugs and adventitious imagination all act voluntarily but are not in control (VI.8.2.5–8).[78] But even when there is volition with choice the action is not within one's power if the calculation accompanying the desire is incorrect, for the incorrect calculation undermines the control of the agent. It is not clear whether this is intended to eliminate Aristotle's other category of voluntary action, choice, or if it is intended to be limited to a type of voluntary action which is not choice because the cognitive element is defective. But the next sentence leaves no doubt that Plotinus is bringing into question even the claim that a choice is within our power, for he wonders whether even if calculation and desire are correct, we are in control if the calculation was the efficient cause of the desire (VI.8.2.9–12).

Presumably, what Plotinus has in mind is that there may be a difference between an initial unfocused desire and the final desire which is part of the ἀρχή of the action and that in the interval calculation operates to shape the final desire. For example, the desire for food may be followed by calculation about a particular food and how to get it, and subsequently, the desire is specified as being for a particular food. In that case, Plotinus suggests, we are not in control and so the action is not within our power because our final desire was not the unqualified ἀρχή of the action; it was preceded by the calculation and, presumably, the original desire.

Plotinus proceeds to ask the general question, "how can we be in control when we are led?," meaning by this, I take it, that only when we are not led is an action within our power. "Being led" must mean that the putative ἀρχή of the action is itself moved by something else. In effect, a dilemma is presented. The ἀρχή of an action is either reason or desire. It cannot be reason (λόγος), because reason alone is not the ἀρχή of any action. If it is desire alone, we are "led" by the desire or state in which we find ourselves. Therefore, the action is not within our power.[79] Recall that for Aristotle, the literal ἀρχή of voluntary action is not a "mixture" of reason and desire, but desire alone (see *De Anima* 3.10.433a20–6). The addition of reason or calculation makes the voluntary action a choice. Plotinus is bringing into question the Aristotelian account which just assumes that a voluntary action is within our power, no matter what the desire may be or what produced it. He is bringing into question the adequacy of this account.

In fact, Plotinus wants to hold that an action is within our power only if it is voluntary in a particular way, that is, if it originates in a rational desire alone, that is, a desire for the true good (VI.8.3.28–31). For this reason, he denies that the actions of bad people are voluntary or within their power (VI.8.3.17–19).[80] Such a characterization is reserved only for those whose actions depend on Intellect and whose actions are unencumbered by affections of the body (i.e., the two types of desire other than βούλησις) (VI.8.3.19–21).[81]

A free action "depends on Intellect" when it originates in a desire produced by thinking.[82] There seem to be two conditions necessary for this to happen. First, the thinking must be of a universal truth. More specifically, it is intellection of a universal premise in a practical syllogism. Second, one must identify the universal truth that such and such is good as a truth about what is good for oneself. Since each person acts on his desire for his own good, one who knows that what is good simply is good for himself will immediately desire to act accordingly. Anyone who performed the same type of action for any reason other than that it was the good thing to do would be acting from tainted motives, that is, irrational desires. Accordingly, his act would not be unqualifiedly free. For these motives or irrational desires would be ones over which he did not exert control. They would be ones which had originated in the composite, not in a constructed ideal self acting in imitation of the true, discarnate ideal self.

One of the very striking features of this account is that it does not seem to leave conceptual space for a rational desire that is corrupted or misguided. If an action originates in a rational desire, it is free; otherwise, it is constrained. There is for Plotinus no such thing as discovering or generating in oneself a rational desire for anything but the good. If the desire is not for the good, it is not rational. Could there not be, however, a sort of untutored desire for the good that does not originate in intellection of universal truths?

The answer to this question depends on what one means by an untutored desire for the good. One might have a sort of unfocused desire to "do the right thing" or to be a good person, but would this prompt any specific action? I doubt it. If, on the other hand, the desire for the good is a desire to initiate specific actions, it is difficult to see how it could be simply untutored. As Plotinus points out, the desire is produced by thinking about a universal premise. In response to the objection that a desire formed by mistaken thinking about universal premises is no less rational for all that, Plotinus would insist that thinking, like perceiving, is never mistaken. Either it occurs or it does not. Someone who acted as a result of a form of cognition other than thinking would not be acting freely because he would not know why what he was doing was good (VI.8.3.4–8). For such a person, not knowing why an action is good suggests an inability to identify the good with one's own good. This is so because one would be cognizing an apparent good, not the true good. The situation then would very likely be one in which reason was put in the service of irrational desire rather than one in which rational desire was the ἀρχή of the action.[83]

There is thus no rational desire for the apparent good. And rational desire is formed by our contact with the universal truths contained within Intellect. We are only in control and therefore free when we identify ourselves as agents of rational desire. Needless to say, for an incarnate individual this is likely to be episodic.

Plotinus actually claims that even virtuous deeds are not within our power because they are compelled by circumstances (VI.8.5.11–13. See also I.4.6.19–21). This does not mean that we ought to refrain from doing virtuous deeds or even that it is a matter of indifference whether we do them or not. What it does mean above all else is that we ought not to suppose that our good or our happiness consists in doing virtuous deeds. In general, a desire to attain anything for which incarnation is a condition is a desire that is more or less compromised.

Plotinus endorses Plato's doctrine that no one does wrong willingly.[84] Persons do wrong owing to the fact that their actions originate in irrational desires. The use of reason in support of the satisfaction of these desires does not turn them into rational ones. In so far as acting willingly means acting on the basis of a rational desire, no one who does wrong acts willingly. Someone who even sporadically thought of himself as an agent of rational desire would not at those times have the slightest motive for wrongdoing. He would not be reasoning with any premises expressing irrational desires. One who doubts this might find it interesting to try to concoct a story about willing wrongdoing by an endowed self thus conceived.

Plotinus' account of free will is innocent of any concern to solve two traditional problems, that of reconciling human freedom with divine providence and that of reconciling human freedom with a doctrine of universal causality. Since both divine providence and universal causality are precisely the grounds for the Stoics' denial of freedom, one might have expected Plotinus' orientation to be other than it is. In fact, it is intensely psychologically introspective, eschewing the temptation to try to show that ordinary actions are unqualifiedly free. The only true free acts for Plotinus are those that originate in a rational desire for the true good.[85] What is ordinarily regarded as voluntary may well be preferable to what is ordinarily regarded as involuntary, but it is as nothing compared with the discipline leading to detachment from the desires originating mundane putatively voluntary actions.

The endowed self and any of its incarnate ideal projections cannot be completely free. Such freedom as an endowed self possesses is not gained without a struggle. It requires the construction of an ideal self in which irrational desires are discounted or trivialized. An ordinary endowed self setting out on such a construction project aims to become the sort of person whose only desires conform to the deliverances of his intellect.

VIII

Some Epistemological Questions

The governing principle for the interpretation of the various modes of cognition of incarnate individuals is that they are all images and inferior versions of the form of cognition that is found in the ἀρχή, Intellect.[1] As we have seen, Plotinus holds that intellection is essentially self-reflexive. It entails an identification of subject and object. Inferior forms of cognition – images of the highest form – involve increasing qualifications of this identification in the direction of the externalization of the object in relation to the subject. Thus, a form of cognition is in proximity to the paradigm according to the extent to which it identifies with its object. This approach seems to be suggested by Aristotle's claim that "in the case of objects without matter, that which thinks and that which is being thought are the same" (*De Anima* 3.4.430a3–4). In cases of cognition where the object is *not* without matter, the identification of thinker and object thought is qualified. The limit of cognition is reached when the subject can in no sense be identified with the object. This would be the case with matter which, though it has a nature, is formless.

1 Perceptual Realism

Plotinus' account of sense-perception (αἴσθησις) has as a touchstone Plato's rejection of the hypothesis that knowledge (ἐπιστήμη) is sense-perception in the *Theaetetus* (184b–186e). Beyond this claim, however, Plato does not have a great deal to say about sense-perception that is not metaphorical or rhetorical. The other main accounts of sense-perception available to Plotinus – Peripatetic, Stoic, and Epicurean – are in principle unacceptable to Plotinus because of their antipathy to dualism and to Forms. Plotinus believes not only that sense-perception is not knowledge, but that such intelligibility as the sensible world possesses is attributable to participation in Intellect and that sense-perception is an image of higher cognition.[2]

Regarding specific principles on the basis of which the account is to be shaped, we can start by recalling Plotinus' insistence on the impassivity of the soul. Given this, if, as Plotinus also wants to hold, there are affections

164

involved somehow in sense-perception and the ensouled individual is also identified as perceiver, then a distinction of something like phases within or parts of sense-perception must be made.[3] Plotinus must distinguish a passive phase from whatever it is the soul does within the composite in sense-perception so that the soul is not affected. The term αἴσθησις, like most Greek abstract nouns with the -σις termination, indicates a process. When, as in the case of αἴσθησις, the process is complex, usage of the term may point to different phases of the one process. In fact, Plotinus does appear to want to distinguish a phase of sense-perception which we might call "sensation" from sense-perception proper, which is said by him to be a discriminative judgment (κρίσις) (see III.6.1.1–7; IV.3.3.22–5; IV.3.26.7–9; IV.4.8.14–16; IV.4.23.36–43; IV.6.2.16–19; VI.4.6.8–19).[4] In order for such judgments to occur there must be a prior event, something like a pure sensory experience, in virtue of which the judgments are made.[5]

This claim is expressed in the following dense passage:

> And soul's power of sense-perception need not be perception of sensibles, but rather it must be receptive (ἀντιληπτικὴν) of the impressions (τύπων) produced by sense-perception on the living being; these are already intelligible entities. So external sense-perception (τὴν αἴσθησιν τὴν ἔξω) is the image of this sense-perception of the soul, which is in its essence truer and is a contemplation of Forms alone without being affected (ἀπαθῶς). From these Forms, from which the soul alone receives its lordship over the living being, come reasonings (διάνοιαι), and opinions and acts of intellection (νοήσεις); and this precisely is where "we" are. (I.1.7.9–17)

Plotinus' analysis is hampered by his use of one term, "sense-perception," for a process that he has come to realize is distinguishable into several phases. If we do not see this, then the first sentence of the above text is nonsense. The second occurrence of "sense-perception" cannot coherently indicate the same activity as the first. The sense-perception that produces impressions cannot be the sense-perception that is receptive of them. Clearly, in the second sentence "external sense-perception" is not the same as the sense-perception of which it is an image. Identifying "productive sense-perception" with "external sense-perception" we arrive minimally at the first phase of a process which latterly consists in a judgment. The affection or πάθος in the process is limited to this initial phase (see III.6.1.1–3; IV.3.3.21–5; IV.3.26.8–9; IV.4.23.20–3; IV.6.2.16–19; VI.4.6.10–11). This affection, productive of impressions, is an image of "sense-perception in the soul." Presumably, this is so because an activity is logically prior to an affection. Thus, in the individual organism, organic activity is prior to the experiences an organism may undergo.

If the affection occurring initially in the process of sense-perception is aptly termed a "sensation," then we need to ask if the judgment made in regard to this implies a mediating role for the former and a denial of direct realism. The above passage along with another has been thought to imply this: "that which is known by sense-perception is an image of the thing, and sense-perception does not apprehend the thing itself: for that remains outside" (V.5.1.17–19). According to one interpretation based upon these texts, Plotinus is committed to some form of indirect rather than direct realism.[6]

This interpretation is based upon a dichotomy – representationalism or non-representationalism – that is too crude to capture Plotinus' meaning. The paradigm of cognition is the activity of Intellect, and this is self-reflexive. But even in the paradigm there is, as we have seen, a distinction of subject and object. All lesser forms of cognition down to sense-perception will increasingly accentuate this distinction without failing to be images of self-reflexivity. In sense-perception, the object is external to the cognizer, not just distinct from it. If direct realism is understood as the view that the cognizer is identical with objects of sense-perception as Intellect is identical with Forms, then of course Plotinus is not a direct realist. But the crude dichotomy has it that if this is so, then Plotinus is an indirect realist, where this evidently means that he holds that the object of sense-perception is something other than the sensible qualities which are themselves images of Forms. This position, however, seems to be explicitly rejected by Plotinus. For example, he denies the consequent of the following conditional:

> if we received impressions of what we see, there will be no possibility of looking at the actual things we see, but we shall look at images and shadows of the objects of sight, so that the objects themselves will be different from the things we see. (IV.6.1.29–32. See also IV.4.23.15–19; IV.5.2.50–3; IV.5.3.10–13; V.3.8.32–3)

But in implying the denial of the antecedent, is not Plotinus contradicting what he said in the passage quoted above?

The problem is with the equivocity of "receiving impressions." In one sense, this is a sub-cognitive process. That is, in sensation impressions can be received independently of sense-perception.[7] This is based on a passive potency. It is an affection. It seems possible that such an affection can occur without the awareness of the perceiver. In another sense, receiving impressions is based on an active potency.[8] The soul or self is capable of the activity of cognizing impressions.[9] As in all forms of cognition, this is a two-term relation, not a three-term relation as the representationalist would have it. Plotinus give us the explanation of how this is possible: these impressions are already intelligible entities.

The reason for distinguishing the two senses of "receiving impressions" and for making only the latter cognitive is that only thus can the difficulties of representationalism be avoided. Obviously, the first sense alone would not suffice, since it is sub-cognitive. The second sense alone would not suffice because it cannot explain how the sensible world is in any sense a cause of my sense-perception. Stated differently, it would not suffice because in that case my having a sense-perception would be absolutely no basis for making inferences about the external world (IV.4.23.19–29). The two senses cannot be merged into something that would be described as a cognitive affection, for we already have before us the paradigm of cognition, intellection, which is an activity and which requires an intentional object. An affection, however, is not an activity, nor is it a term of a relation. Even if it were, the subject would be the sensible, whereas in cognition the subject is the soul or self. It seems fairly clear then that if we understand and distinguish the two senses of "receiving impressions" we have no need to attribute to Plotinus a form of indirect realism.

In effect, taking Plotinus' account of sense-perception as a form of indirect realism means treating sense-perception as if it were a *per accidens* series of events: the sensible object produces an impression in me and then another event occurs which is my cognizing that impression. Just the fact that what I have called "sensation" is said to be an image of sense-perception is sufficient to undermine this construal. In a *per accidens* series AB, BC, CD, and so on, the terms are all coordinate. That is, B is a cause in the same sense in which A is a cause. But sensation is not a cause of sense-perception in the way that the sensible is a cause of sensation. A physical motion can cause an affection if the latter is physical, but an affection cannot thus cause an activity in an immaterial entity. Actually, sense-perception is more like a *per se* series in which sensation is an instrument.[10] Sensation is the instrument whereby the agent perceives the sensible object.

The relation between the cognizer and the subject of affection is not primarily the relation between the immaterial and the material, but the relation between a model and a copy where the model is an activity. The physical process of sensation is an image of the discriminative judgment that is sense-perception. The imagery consists in the manner in which form is found in the physical process and the manner in which it is found in the judgment. The mere presence of an intelligible structure in a sensation is an inferior version of the awareness of intelligible structure in sense-perception. This is so because the latter is closer to the activity of Intellect wherein intelligible structure or Form is found paradigmatically.

Plotinus regularly describes sense-perception in the Aristotelian manner, which is incompatible with representationalism. He says that sense-perception is "the reception of a form or of an affection of a body" (I.1.2.26–7).[11] This manner of speaking is incompatible with representationalism, for according to this position sense-perception is not directly of external objects but of some mediating representational analogue.[12] For Plotinus and for Aristotle, form is not a representational analogue, but rather all that a thing is actually.[13] Hence, the reception of form is what distinguishes Plotinus' account from any non-realist alternative.

The faculty of sensation must itself be somehow a mean between sensible and intelligible, because it receives the one and transmits the other.

> [That which receives the form] must be jointly subject to like affections and of one matter with the sense-object, and it must be this which is affected and the other principle [the soul] which knows; and its affection must be of such a kind that it retains something of that which produced it, but is not the same as it, but as it is between the producer of the affection and the soul, it must have an affection which lies between the sensible and the intelligible, a proportional mean somehow linking the extremes to each other, with the capacity both of receiving and of transmitting information (δεκτικὸν ἅμα καὶ ἀπαγγελτικὸν ὑπάρχον), suitable to be assimilated to each of the extremes. (IV.4.23.21–9)[14]

In this passage there might seem to be a calculated concession to Aristotelian epistemology in despite of Platonic metaphysics. How can sensation as it were bridge between the two worlds of Plato, the sensible and intelligible? The answer is simply that "sensible-intelligible" or "becoming-being" is also a false dichotomy. Forms were adduced originally to *explain* intelligibility in the sensible world. That explanation would be a mockery if it consisted in removing all intelligibility from it. Sensible images of Forms can be synonymous as well as homonymous. The synonymous images are manifested in material capable of manifesting opposite Forms. That is why the images are homonymous as well. Still, the intelligibility is in the image which sensation receives. The intelligibility that is in that same homonymous image ("these are already intelligible entities") is information available for an entity capable of decoding it. The affection in the organic composite is a mean between the intelligible structure in the sensible object and cognitive activity.

Thus, Plotinus can say that the affection actually becomes a form when sense-perception occurs (IV.4.23.29–34). This does not mean that a form as such is generated, for that is impossible. I take it that it means that there is intelligible content in sensation which becomes identified with the perceiver in an act of sense-perception. The intelligible content is the synonymous image of a Form. It is transmitted to the perceiver by means of the sensation.

Such an account fits well with Plotinus' insistence on the unity of sense-perception (IV.7.6.3–10). The differentiation of the sense-organs results in qualitatively distinct affections. Nevertheless, we are able to make perceptual judgments that the yellow thing is bitter, the brown thing is smooth, and so on. This is possible owing to the commensurability of the forms transmitted through the affections. That is, the form of yellow and the form of bitter are both intelligible structures, apt for identification with a unified agent even though the homonymous images of Forms of Yellow and Bitter are not.

We might add that this conclusion supports the account of sense-perception as a *per se* rather than a *per accidens* series. Sense-perception involves identification with forms, but it manifestly also involves experience of different kinds of perceptibles. In a *per se* series, sense-perception is identification with forms using the animate body as an instrument. There is no need for equating the alterations in the instrument with what the agent is doing. Indeed, as Plotinus urges, there is in this case no need for supposing that the agent is affected at all by the alteration in the instrument. If sense-perception were a *per accidens* series, however, then not only would the unity of perceptual judgments remain unaccounted for, but we would still have to make a distinction between affections and judgments by means of these.

If sense-perception is a judgment, we may reasonably ask how it differs from belief (δόξα). Plotinus does appear to distinguish the two.[15] For example, sense-perception is without reasoning (λόγος) (VI.3.18.10). I take it that this means at least that sense-perception excludes inference. Yet sense-perception resembles belief at least to the extent that it is fallible (I.1.9.11–12). Sense-perception seems to be non-inferential judgments about the experiences we have through our five senses.[16] It is obvious that if there are inferential judgments, there must be non-inferential judgments. It is less obvious how non-inferential judgments are susceptible to error. It would seem that it is just here that the distinction between sensation and sense-perception is most relevant. The non-inferential judgments of sense-perception are nevertheless mediated by the affection in the animate body which is an instrument of cognition. For example, if we perceptually judge an oar in water to be bent, it is because we are having a sensation of an appearance which diverges from reality. What is really straight appears bent for physical reasons. I take it that the reason for saying that sense-perception is fallible rather than that sensation is fallible is that the former is cognitive whereas the latter is not. Error is a defect in cognition. Thus, Plotinus *could* say that even reports about the sensation of proper sensibles are fallible judgments, thereby putting him in opposition to both Plato and Aristotle.[17]

Because sense-perception is a mode of cognition, it is to be understood according to its paradigm, whose essential property is self-reflexivity.[18] A perceptual judgment then, whether it be of a proper sensible ("this is green") or of an indirect sensible ("this is a man"), is a kind of awareness (ἀντίληψις, IV.4.23.1–2], which is an image of the perfect self-awareness of intellection. This perfect self-awareness, as we have seen, is eternal cognitive identification with Forms. What is the image of this perfect self-awareness supposed to be?

> When sense-perception, then, sees the form in bodies binding and mastering the nature opposed to it [i.e., matter], which is shapeless, and shape riding gloriously upon other shapes, it gathers into one that which appears dispersed and brings it back and takes it in, now without parts, to the soul's interior and presents it to that which is within as something in tune with it and fitting it and dear to it; just as when a good man sees

a trace of virtue in the young, which is in tune with his own inner truth, the sight delights him. (I.6.3.9–16)[19]

In this passage, the metaphor of harmony or sympathetic vibration substitutes for the metaphor of conceptual classification.[20] The recognition of the harmony of the intelligible form latent in the affection of sensation with the intelligible form already in the soul is the image of self-reflexivity. For example, perceiving that this is a man by comparing the form in sensation with the form in the soul is an imperfect version of the self-reflexive awareness by Intellect of its cognitive identification with the Form of Man. It is imperfect because what is perceived, the man, is other than the perceiver, and even the form of what is perceived is only a copy of the Form with which Intellect is identical. Sense-perception is construed as a judgment that a particular form has affected the sense-organ. But this could not occur without the recognition of what form it is. And the recognition expressed in a claim such as "I see a round shape" is an image of Intellect's awareness that it is cognitively identical with the Form of Circularity.

Further, the identity of conceiver with concept, implied in the claim "I know what a man is and *this* is one," is itself only an image of separate Intellect. Conceptualization itself is presumably closer to intellection than sense-perception because there is a higher degree of identity or unity between conceiver and conceived than there is between perceiver and perceived. This is so because conceptualization requires no instrument whereas sense-perception requires sensation. But that a perceptual judgment could not occur without conceptualization is for Plotinus additional confirmation that a lower form of cognition could not occur without the higher occurring.[21]

2 On Thinking Incarnately

For Plotinus, like Aristotle, the paradigm of thinking is the activity of discarnate Intellect. How are the lower forms of cognition, which require sensation and sense-perception, related to this activity?

The informational content contained in sensation is an impression. When sense-perception occurs, the impression, which is describable naturally or physically, is for the first time employed cognitively. The result of an act of sense-perception is that there is an image in the soul. An image (φάντασμα) requires the impressions left by sensation (IV.4.13.12–15). It is in fact a kind of residue of sense-perception, available as intentional objects of imagination or memory when the extra-mental objects of sense-perception are no longer present (IV.3.29.19–26; IV.4.17.12).[22]

An image is evidently supposed to have the same informational content as an impression. Just as an affection conveys a form when sense-perception is occurring, so it seems that the result of a sense-perception becomes an image when imagination occurs. Informational content is portable from sense-perception to imagination for exactly the same reason that it is portable from sensation to sense-perception, that is, synonymity in the various copies of a Form which are also homonymously present in the sensible object, sensation, sense-perception, imagination, and so on. So, for example, the identical content whose nature the Form of Man is, is variously represented in the individual man, in the sense-perception of that man, and in the image of him. The image of the man is no more the separate Form than is the individual. Because the mental image and the sensible object are synonymous images of an identical intelligible content, the mental image is a synonymous image of the sensible object. That is, it represents the sensible in a non-symbolic manner, unlike a purely homonymous image.

The relation of images to thinking complicates considerably this rather simple account of pictorial imagination. By way of approaching the question of the memories possibly retained by the discarnate individual, Plotinus asks what is the image involved in the memory of a previous thought. His provocative suggestion is that this image is the λόγος the apprehension of which reveals that thinking is occurring or has occurred.

> Perhaps the reception into the image-making power would be of the expression (λόγος) which accompanies the thought (τῷ νοήματι). The thought is without parts and has not, so to speak, come out into the open, but remains unobserved within, but the expression unfolds its content and brings it out of the thought into the image-making power, and so shows the thought as if in a mirror, and this is how there is apprehension and persistence and memory of it. Therefore, even though the soul is always moved to thinking,[23] it is when it comes to be in the image-making power that we apprehend it. The thinking (νόησις) is one thing and the apprehension of it another, and we are always thinking, but do not always apprehend our activity; and this is because that which receives it does not only receive acts of thinking (νοήσεις), but also, on its other side, acts of sense-perception. (IV.3.30.5–16. See also I.4.10)

Two striking features of this passage are the claim that λόγος accompanies thought and the implication that λόγος is an image of thought.[24] Presumably, the simplest λόγος accompanying a thought would be a word standing for the thought. Thus, I remember that yesterday I was thinking about cats by having an image that is the λόγος "cat." A more complex λόγος would be a statement, like the simplest statements Plato mentions in the *Sophist* (261e–262c). That the λόγος "unfolds" the thought in the imaginative faculty indicates that it is probably the latter sort that he has in mind. Plotinus is careful not to say that such a λόγος is necessary for thinking for the obvious reason that the primary example of thinking, the activity of Intellect, requires no images. But even in the case of incarnate thinking, it is not the thinking but rather the apprehension of its occurrence that depends on images.

171

Normally, having something like propositions as intentional objects represents thinking and makes memory of thinking possible.

What does it mean to apprehend that thinking is occurring without actually thinking? Presumably, one way of doing so would be to apprehend an effect of thinking and apply to it an argument from effect to cause. Metaphorically, it is apparently like apprehending an image in a mirror and inferring that which is imaged. In the present case, however, it is difficult to see how a λόγος stands to a thought as a mirror-image stands to that which is imaged even in the case of an absolutely simple λόγος like "cat." Such a λόγος, unlike a mirror-image, is not a synonymous image.

The similarity between the apprehension that thinking is occurring and sense-perception is made explicit in the following passage:

> when that kind of thing in us which mirrors the images (εἰκονίσματα)
> of thought and intellect is undisturbed, we see them and know them in
> a way parallel to sense-perception, along with the prior knowledge that
> it is intellect and thought that are active. (I.4.10.13–16)

What Plotinus seems to want to say is that the awareness that thinking is occurring is occasioned by "projections" of thinking, the "images" in the imaginative faculty. The apprehension of such images indicates the activity of thinking just as sense-perception indicates the causal activity of a perceptible object. The imaginative faculty contains both the images left by sense-perception and the images which indicate that thinking is occurring. The apprehension of images, however, is not what thinking essentially is (I.4.10.20–1).

All of this is rather obscure viewed apart from the Aristotelian context. In *De Anima* 3.5 Aristotle introduces the agent intellect as efficient cause of intellection in an individual. In this highly compressed and contentious text, several points are tolerably clear: (1) the agent intellect is always thinking; (2) when separated from the body the agent intellect is just what it is and it alone is eternal and immortal; (3) we do not remember its activity; (4) without its activity thinking cannot occur. I believe we shall understand Plotinus better if we suppose that he is trying to integrate Aristotle's account of the agent intellect into his own Platonic metaphysics and epistemology.

Plotinus is, as we have seen, hospitable to the notion that we have what can be aptly termed an agent intellect and that its true nature is realized in separation from the body. This separated intellect is just the eternal intellect of each person contemplating Forms in communion with all other intellects. We need not suppose, however, that for Aristotle or Plotinus there is a distinction between the agent intellect "in us" and the agent intellect that is separate.[25] Accordingly, I am going to proceed on the most economical hypothesis, namely, that when Plotinus speaks about intellection or thinking in the highest form in the incarnate individual, he is following Aristotle's brief account of the agent intellect and that this intellection is indistinguishable from the activity that the eternal intellect of each person is engaged in.

What we are aware of then when we are aware that thinking is occurring is the activity of our eternal intellects. This awareness is apparently owing to an inference from the existence of λόγοι in us to their cause. But to be aware that intellection is occurring or has occurred is not the same thing as engaging in it. The endowed self never does that. To imply that this is the case, as I believe Plotinus does, is perhaps to go beyond Aristotle's more limited claim that "we do not remember" the activity of the agent intellect. Nevertheless, Plotinus has good reason for doing so. If endowed selves did what separated intellects do, they would be cognitively identical with all Forms. No one, I take it, is aware of doing *that*. Even if endowed selves could have access to eternal truths, they would not do so in the way that an intellect does, by being identical with all eternal truth at once. At best, they have access to images of eternal truth, among which are λόγοι.[26]

The problem Plotinus appears to be struggling with is one facing any non-empiricist account of knowing. How are we able to do more than record and report our sense-experience? For Plotinus, the problem is precisely how we as incarnate cognizers can make use of our eternal heritage in Intellect. How, to recur to the Aristotelian model, does the agent intellect operate in us in order that we can reason, make judgments, and so on?

An impression is, as we have seen, the informational content in a sensation. Plotinus also seems to use "impression" to indicate some sort of representation of what is in an intellect (see V.3.2.10; V.3.5.18–19).[27] In this sense, it is used synonymously with the term "concept" (ἔννοια).[28] So, there are two types of impressions, originating respectively from sense-perception and from Intellect.[29] The surprising implication of the plain sense of these texts is that concepts do not originate in sense-perception. If this were simply the case, it would be difficult to see the relevance of sense-perception to incarnate higher cognition.[30]

It is clear enough that a concept of a Form must be different from the Form itself. It is not so clear, however, how Plotinus supposes that the latter has a paradigmatic role for the former. For example, he says: "[the soul] did not have the realities themselves but impressions (τύποι) of them: so it must bring the impressions into accord with (ἐφαρμόσαι) the true realities of which they are the impressions" (I.2.4.23–5).[31] What is this "accord" supposed to be? Sometimes, Plotinus uses the term in a fairly precise sense to indicate something like "coincidence," as when two lines coincide because they are the same length (II.7.1.47). Sometimes, however, he uses the term in a looser sense, as when he suggests that we bring the being, motion, and rest in ourselves into accord with the greatest kinds (VI.2.8.28–31). Further, he says, puzzlingly, that the intelligible line or fire or man cannot be brought into accord with the sensible (IV.4.23.9–11). This last passage gives us the important clue that being in accord with is not equivalent to synonymity, for the sensible line, fire, and man do of course contain synonymous images of their Forms.

What would it mean to bring a mental impression or concept into accord with a Form? One possibility is that the accord is a kind of proportionality or analogy. Thus, my impression of Form F, whether this be a verbal or conceptual λόγος, is in accord with Form F if and only if my impression is related to other impressions analogous to the relations among Forms. Thus, if it is true that according to my conceptual system plane figures are inscribable in circles, then my concepts of plane figure and of circle are in harmony with their Forms to that extent. My concept of, say, man is not in harmony with the Form of Man if with this concept I am disposed to believe falsehoods about man. On this interpretation, the reason why sensibles are not in harmony with Forms is that a sensible includes matter and so can manifest opposite Forms. As we have seen, Socrates is a man, but not essentially a man. If so, then though we may suppose that the Form of Man and the Form of Rationality are necessarily connected, Socrates is not necessarily rational even if it is true that necessarily if Socrates is a man, he is rational. There are no necessary connections among sensibles such as there are among Forms and, ideally, among our concepts.

From this it would follow, reasonably enough, that λόγοι are not the locus of eternal truth. For example, the statement "if A is greater than B, and B is greater than C, then A is greater than C" is an impression or image of an eternal truth, not the eternal truth itself. It is not even an impression of a particular Form. Speaking of the Forms of Being and Movement, Plotinus says: "neither of them is without the other except in our conception (ἐπινοίᾳ) of them, and the two natures are one nature" (VI.2.7.19–20). It seems plausible that the concepts involved here are just the impressions spoken of above. That the Forms are each "without the other" in our conception of them just means that we can formulate distinct concepts of these Forms.

I think we can make this more precise. In a material identity statement we make a claim of the form "A = B." If the identity statement is true, it is true, roughly, because "A" and "B" represent or stand for the same thing. Being and Movement are one nature, but if we conceive of and assert the material identity statement "being = movement," we are in accord with true reality. It would be exactly similar for the case of, say, "5 + 3 = 8." Even to talk about the Form of Five is to talk about the impression that we are only representing with the λόγος "five."

This interpretation is intended to take seriously the claim that conceptualization or intelligible speech are only images of the activity of Intellect. Nevertheless, these images are supposed not to be arbitrary symbols. When we think some mathematical equation and it is self-evidently true to us, we want to be able to say that were it not for the activity of Intellect we could not do this but that what we are doing is not that activity. If our concepts are or contain synonymous images of Forms, the absence of independent access to Intellect would perhaps make plausible our claim to know eternal truths, even though we do not know them as Intellect knows them.

It is interesting to ask the following Fregean question: how are the two forms of identity statements, "A = A" and "A = B," related? Are they two species of one genus such that the "=" means the same in each case, or does the "=" mean something radically different in each case, or is there priority and posteriority in its use? It is, I think, evident that Plotinus would regard what we call formal identity as prior and material identity as posterior. But he would do so for reasons very different from those that have led contemporary analytic philosophers to make a similar claim.

The paradigm of identity is the self-identity of the One. Nothing is self-identical in the way the One is (see VI.8.21.32–3). The identity of Intellect and οὐσία is that of two "objects" which are in fact one. Further, on my interpretation eternally true material identity statements represent as multiple what is one, namely, οὐσία, considered in abstraction from its eternal identity with Intellect. Any Form is just one of the multitude of ways that οὐσία is cognized by Intellect. Incarnate modes of cognition represent these true material identity statements, for the concepts which are employed in incarnate cognition are not the Forms themselves. When A = B is necessarily true, it represents or is an image of one facet of the life of Intellect which is eternally identical with all Forms. In reality, what A = B represents is identical with what, say, C = D represents.

Cases of necessarily true predicative statements like "5 is odd" can perhaps be treated similarly. Such a λόγος might be said to represent explicitly what is only implicit in Intellect. This cannot be quite right, because the implicit seems to be logically posterior to the explicit. It is better, though certainly odder, to say that "5 is odd" is an image of true reality. This oddness is mitigated somewhat if we recall that what is being imaged is complex and not simple. We need not hold – as we would if the One were the paradigm – that what "5 is odd" images is exactly the same thing as what "4 is even" images. Rather, both express different aspects of true reality. This would be analogous, say, to various drawings of a house from different angles revealing aspects of it.

We may well ask, however, whether in employing λόγοι or impressions as the elementary objects of incarnate thinking Plotinus has introduced a form of representationalism that was rejected for the paradigmatic case of knowing in Intellect. How can we know that we are with our concepts representing eternal truths? Is Plotinus not himself susceptible to the basic error of representationalism, that of being unable to adduce criteria for judging representations to be adequate? As I noted a short while ago, if the impression originating in Intellect and the impressions originating in sense-perception are unconnected or merely sit side by side in the imaginative faculty, sense-perception would seem to be irrelevant to conceptualization. In addition, the only escape from a lapse into representationalism would be blocked. It is implausible, however, that Plotinus means to trivialize the contribution of sense-perception to the activity that employs concepts. This is particularly so when our concepts are used not for the knowledge of eternal truth but for higher cognition of the sensible world. But there is no reason for Plotinus to trivialize the contribution of sense-perception. After all, even in sensation we are in contact with synonymous images of Forms. Sense-perception is of individuals and thinking is of universals, but sensible individuals are, too, images of Forms which are identical with Intellect.

It is clear enough that Plotinus wants to locate the incarnate thinker somehow "between" Intellect and the agent of sense-perception.

> But we shall not say that it [Intellect] belongs to soul, but we shall say that it is our intellect, being different from the reasoning part and having gone up on high, but all the same ours, even if we should not count it among the parts of the soul, yes, really it is ours and not ours; for this reason we use it and do not use it – but we always use discursive reasoning – it [Intellect] is ours when we use it, but not ours when we do not use it. But what is this "using" it? Is it when we become it and speak like it? No, [when we reason discursively] according to it (κατ' ἐκεῖνον): for we ourselves are not Intellect. We are, then, in accord with it by our rational power which first receives it (τῷ λογιστικῷ πρώτῳ δεχομένῳ). For we perceive through sense-perception, even if it is not we ourselves who are the perceivers: do we then reason like this, and think through Intellect like this?[32] No, it is we ourselves who reason and we ourselves who think thoughts in discursive reasoning; for this is what we ourselves are. The activities of Intellect are from above in the same way that those of sense-perception are from below; we are this, the principal part of the soul, in the middle between two powers, a worse and a better, the worse that of sense-perception, the better that of Intellect. (V.3.3.23–39)

The central claim in this passage is that we use Intellect when we reason discursively. Implied, though not stated directly, is that sense-perception is at least relevant to this use of Intellect. The relevance of sense-perception, however, is explicitly affirmed in the first passage quoted at the beginning of this chapter: from the forms in sensation arise acts of discursive reasoning and acts of intellection. The problem facing Plotinus is, I think, fairly evident. It is how to balance the contributions of Intellect and sense-perception in the account of higher incarnate cognition.

The relation of Intellect to discursive reasoning is interestingly characterized by Plotinus when he says that we reason in accord with Intellect either when we have its writings written in us like laws (νόμοι) or when we are in a way filled with it and perceive it to be present (V.3.4.1–4. See also I.8.2.11). The second possibility should be understood in the same way that we took the claim that we apprehend the operation of intellect without actually performing that operation. The first possibility is probably an allusion to *De Anima* 3.4.430a1, where Aristotle characterizes the passive intellect as the capacity of a tablet with nothing yet written on it. A little later on in the passage Plotinus calls these laws "rules" (κανόνες).

It is difficult to interpret such a vague claim. But it is tempting to make the deliverances of Intellect parallel to the deliverances of sense-perception and to make the agent of discursive reasoning the recipient of two different kinds of information from two different sources. On this interpretation, incarnate thinking would be something like a reconciliation or comparison of the two different types of information. Judgment and inference would at least in part consist in the recognition and classification of the images derived from sense-perception according to the images derived from Intellect.

Something like a reconciliation or comparison of two types of images is the basic feature of this account. Nevertheless, there are difficulties with the claim that one of the types of images comes directly from Intellect. First, what is an image derived directly from Intellect supposed to be? Second, how are the images like "laws" of Intellect written in us and how does the writing occur in the first place? In this regard one must guard against an anachronistic understanding of Plotinus' use of term νόμοι, translated as "laws." Plotinus does use the expression "law of nature" in several places (see IV.8.5.11; IV.8.7.21; VI.4.16.21). He also calls Intellect the "primary lawgiver" and "itself the law of being" (νόμος αὐτὸς τοῦ εἶναι) (V.9.5.28–9). It is not clear, however, that Plotinus therefore conceives of the laws of Intellect written in us as something like a priori categories. It is difficult to see why an image of Intellect would appear in this way in us.

Aristotle seems to face similar problems with the agent intellect. If the actualization of the passive intellect is owing to the efficient causal activity of the agent intellect, it is quite obscure how this is supposed to be done. It does seem clear, however, that there is nothing like independent access to the agent intellect for us or a comparison of the contents of the agent intellect with those of the imagination. It is also abundantly clear that for Aristotle the reason for positing an agent intellect in the first place is connected to the account of cognition beginning with sense-perception. That is, the agent intellect is introduced to supplement what sense-perception alone cannot explain.

It will be recalled that Plotinus has stressed that the impressions derived from sense-perception are already intelligible (νοητὰ). In so far as they are intelligible, they are synonymous images of Forms. These are, I believe, the laws written in us. They differ from sensible forms which are homonymous images as well. We do not in fact need independent access to Forms in order to reason or make judgments. But we do need to have the ability to separate intelligible from sensible form. This we have as a legacy of the One's operation through Intellect and through Soul.[33] The "making" that Aristotle's agent intellect does is transformed by Plotinus into another kind of making by the One with the instrumentality of Intellect. Accordingly, the answer to the first problem is straightforward. What we do when we classify or judge is not compare synonymous and homonymous images. Rather, we employ the synonymous images of Forms acquired through sense-perception and imagination with those encountered in subsequent acts of sense-perception.

But the synonymous images of Forms in us are not the Forms themselves. Consider the following passage:

> We possess this [Intellect] too, as something that transcends us. We have it either as common to all or particular to ourselves, or both common and particular; common because it is without parts and one and everywhere the same, particular to ourselves because each has the whole of it in the primary part of his soul. So we also possess the Forms in two ways, in our soul, in a manner of speaking (οἶον) unfolded and separated, in Intellect all together. (I.1.8.3–8. See also I.8.2.15–21)[34]

I think that some scholars have been misled into supposing that having Forms in the soul "in a manner of speaking unfolded and separated" indicates that what we have are the Forms themselves. In order to see that this is a mistake we need only compare the passage from IV.3.30 quoted above, where it is said that λόγος unfolds the contents of Intellect and brings them into the image-making power. That being the case, the "Form in the soul" can be nothing more than what λόγος represents. What is in the soul is not a Form because what is in the soul is the intelligible structure found in an instance of a Form and derived from sense-perception. One way that Forms are "unfolded and separated" is through the instrumentality of Soul and nature and matter. The representation conceptually of the instances of Forms that we encounter through sense-perception is another way that they are unfolded and separated.[35] The judgments constitutive of discursive reasoning so represent them.

Plotinus distinguishes between discursive intellect and Intellect that makes discursive reasoning possible.[36] The former is characterized as "dividing intellect" or τὸ λογιστικόν and the latter as "undivided Intellect."[37] What is the distinction being aimed at here? On my interpretation, discursive reasoning represents as divided what is in fact united or identical.[38] It is related to undivided Intellect as the latter is related to the One. In Intellect, that which is unqualifiedly simple is represented as a complex unity; in divided intellect the complex unity is typically represented in judgments of material identity with really distinct concepts. For example, dividing intellect judges "the whale is a mammal" and "$9 + 6 = 15$." It represents as divided what are in reality undivided, that is, the Forms, and then makes a judgment that they are materially identical in part or in whole. When discursive intellect identifies the two sides of the equation, $A = B$, it is representing symbolically what is eminently or pardigmatically united in Intellect.

One important indication of the difference between dividing and undivided

Intellect is that in the latter, the simultaneous identity of Intellect with all intelligibles precludes the understanding of its activity as a judgment. This is so because in a judgment what is judged is picked out or isolated from the background. Particularly in judgments of material identity, what is actually one is represented dually and must be designated as such. For example, in the judgment that the morning star is the evening star two different ways of describing the same thing are identified as such. But the descriptions are posterior to what they describe. There is no plausibility in the claim that the primary activity of Intellect involves judgments about the material identity of various descriptions of intelligibles or οὐσία. On the other hand, if there are material identity statements that represent necessary truths, or rather, if there are necessary truths that can be represented as material identity statements, it is because what they represent exists eternally as one.

Dividing intellect which, say, judges that justice is a virtue or that rest is different from movement represents in a kind of material identity statement what is supposed to be eternally one. Material identity statements are images of the variegated identity of Intellect. Eternal οὐσία is a complex whole either grasped as such by Intellect or articulated by dividing intellect in judgments.[39] If this is so, it is not surprising why we are unconscious of our participation in the primary activity of the second ἀρχή.

I am aware that my interpretation of Intellect's "laws" that are written in us as being actually the intelligible content of sense-perception is hard to accept, at least initially. We must keep in mind, however, the constraints that Plotinus' own claims make on any interpretation. First, these laws are impressions. Second, we are in accord with Intellect when we reason according to it, not when we "become it." Third, since Intellect does not change, it does not change in relation to each person throughout a life. On the contrary, growth in conceptual achievement roughly parallels experience of the sensible world, not ever new deliverances of Intellect. For these reasons, I think we should understand Plotinus to hold that in the matter of cognition our endowment from Intellect is a natural cognitive ability and that the intelligible contents upon which this ability is exercised are derived from sense-perception.

We might well wonder at this point whether Plotinus' Aristotelianizing account of incarnate cognition is compromised by Plato's doctrine of recollection (ἀνάμνησις). Actually, Plotinus seems to make little use of this doctrine as it is explained in the *Meno* and the *Phaedo*.[40] In the *Meno*, Socrates accounts for the slave-boy's ability to arrive at a true belief about the answer to a mathematical problem by recollection (85ce). That is, through questioning, the true belief is "stirred up like a dream" in him. In the *Phaedo*, Socrates argues that one's ability to judge sensible equals as somehow deficient with respect to equality depends on our having had prior knowledge of the Form of Equality (73cff.). In both passages recollection plays an active role in judgments made about sensible particulars. Strictly speaking, the issue for Plotinus is not prior knowledge. In an attenuated sense of "prior" we certainly have prior knowledge of Forms, because we, as ideal selves, have that knowledge eternally. Rather, the issue is how we here below make use of that knowledge. In particular, can we have recourse to it in making judgments upon the deliverances of sense-perception?

Plato holds that in recollection we are led to recover the knowledge we had in a discarnate state. For Plotinus, the only discarnate state we have is that of our intellects or ideal selves. But these do not descend. Therefore, the recovery of knowledge, if there be such, has to be differently construed. In the light of this problem, one can see why an agent intellect, actively contributing to the acquisition of knowledge, is desirable. Aristotle does not, however, tell us how exactly the agent intellect works. It does not seem that it can work in the way that a Plotinian intellect works. For the latter is identified with the undivided totality of Forms. And conceptualization is not the same sort of thing as the instantiation of Forms by the activity of souls.

There is one passage in the *Enneads* which seems to imply the independent access to Forms that I have been denying Plotinus holds:

> As for the things which come to it [the soul] from Intellect, it observes what one might call their impressions (οἷον τοὺς τύπους), and has the same power also in dealing with these; and it continues to acquire understanding as if by recognizing the new and recently arrived impressions and fitting them to those which have long been within it: this process is what we should call the "recollections" of the soul. (V.3.2.9–14)[41]

This passage describes the comparison of new and old impressions. It is of course true that *all* impressions, new as well as old, ultimately come from the second ἀρχή, Intellect. This passage does not tell us, however, that the old impressions are independently accessed from Intellect itself. On the contrary, presumably since new impressions will in time become old impressions, and new impressions come through sense-perception, one may infer that the old impressions arrived this way as well. But these old impressions are being considered now in their relation to Forms, not the sensible individuals in which they originated. We do not have to suppose a special kind of conceptual image of Forms.[42]

Nevertheless, recollection is evidently more than the comparison of just any old and new impressions. It is more than memory (μνήμη). So, it would be natural to take the old impressions as those belonging to a previous incarnation rather than to a previous experience of the same incarnate individual. This relatively straightforward position is, alas, complicated by Plotinus' apparent willingness to countenance the possibility of memory in discarnate individuals. No doubt, this has encouraged the view that memory or recollection could be of the activity of a discarnate intellect.

Let us briefly consider the question of memory and personal identity.

Memory, says Plotinus, is acquired along with individuality and a desire to be different.[43] Memory only begins when the soul has left the higher region of Intellect (IV.4.5.11–13).[44] It only occurs in time (see IV.3.25.13–15; IV.4.6.1–3). Thus, the pure activity of intellection is not something we do as incarnate individuals. We, as ideal selves, can participate in this activity, but only at a loss of our endowed individuality and memory, though not at a loss of consciousness in some sense (IV.4.2.30–2).[45] Memory seems to be viewed here as a necessary condition for individuality, so long as individuality is identified with the endowed self. This being so, the aprioristic element in cognitive activity up to intellection is very severely restricted. That is, the concepts or images we employ in the judgments that are acts of sense-perception and the concepts we employ in other judgments are not remnants retained from our discarnate lives. On the contrary, as we have seen, in discursive reasoning, the images derived from sense-perception are combined and divided. Nor is the activity of Intellect available to us on behalf of making such judgments. We cannot, as it were, retire momentarily into the chamber of Intellect, snatch a bit of a priori knowledge, and return with it ready to pronounce on some necessity in nature.[46]

Ordinary memories of past sense-perceptions are distinguished from memories of previous psychic events including desires and thoughts (IV.3.26.34–6; IV.3.30). Since sense-perception, unlike the highest form of desire and thought, requires an animate body as agent, the question arises whether there are different memories and even different imaginative faculties for the agent of sense-perception and for the agent of thought (IV.3.30.1–5). Plotinus seems to recognize that there is no empirical basis for postulating different memories as if they were the memories of two different persons. Empirically, our identifications of the subject of each type of memory coincide (IV.3.27.4–6). Nevertheless, he also seems to want at least to consider the possibility that the discarnate individual should have memories of its incarnate existence, memories which would at least in part be grounded in bodily experience. Presumably, the memories of such experiences should be understood along the lines of the metaphor of an actor and his roles, that is, memories by the actor of what happened to the character in his role. How much and for how long the soul separated from the body would remember is purely speculative, as Plotinus recognizes. But even if the memories of incarnate existence are retained for some period of time after death and even if these memories are reconstituted for the reincarnated individual, they will not be memories of life in Intellect. Rather, they will be memories of a previous incarnation.

When finally forced to address the question of what memories the discarnate soul might retain of its incarnate life, Plotinus is loath to conclude that there is nothing. He is evidently uneasy with the idea that an ideal state for *us* here below should be discontinuous in memory with the lives we have lived. Certainly, some memories are not worthy of retention.

But as for the memories of friends, children, wives, and country, remembering these would not be out of place, although Plotinus cannot resist adding that a good man will attach no emotion to them (IV.3.32.1–6). In this bit of revealing and unsupported speculation Plotinus comes as close as he ever does to confessing dissatisfaction with the spirit of Platonism. For in admitting that it is fitting that we retain such memories after separation from the body, even if only for a short time, he is dramatically qualifying his account of the ideal self.[47] The memory of ennobling experiences is somehow admitted into that ideal, even if these experiences bear the unmistakable marks of temporality. But one who has undergone the descent from Intellect has to be judged according to a somewhat different ideal. If the soul is to remain unaffected, as Plotinus says, the descended self is yet differently constituted, at least to the extent that some personal memories may be thought to belong to it.[48]

There is another respect in which Plotinus' account of intellect is usefully compared with Plato's. One might surmise from *Republic* 608c–621a that Plato believed that the highest part of the tripartite soul was alone immortal. This is the rational part, responsible for cognition generally. The *Timaeus* (41cd, 69c8–d1, d5–6, 90a) seems to take this approach unambiguously. The immortality of the highest part of the soul is the immortality of the self, the self which is punished for incarnate sins by reincarnation or finally released from incarnation altogether to live everlastingly with the Forms. There seem to be no grounds in either dialogue for distinguishing the highest part of the soul from that which Plotinus' undescended intellect is and does. Plato can thus account more easily than Plotinus for the identity of incarnate and discarnate individuals. Plotinus in effect forgoes this Platonic advantage owing to his account of intellect. He is thereby led to diverge further from Plato in his account of incarnate cognition.

We can better grasp the parts of the puzzle if we recur to Plotinus' analysis of Forms and his postulation of Intellect as necessarily eternally identical with οὐσία. Without an undescended self that is an intellect, it is difficult to see how the incarnate individual had access to a priori knowledge. With an undescended self with which we are united as image to model, we can be understood to be as it were structurally apt for higher cognition. This account, however, is purchased at the price of diminishing the identity of a discarnate and an incarnate self. Plato, in the *Phaedrus*, for example, stresses the identity by making the discarnate self somehow tripartite. On this basis, punishment in the after-life for sins committed here below is readily comprehensible. We can see how the same self is punished. And his doctrine of recollection is supposed to explain how what we learned in a discarnate state is actually accessible to us incarnately.

Plotinus' undescended true self is different. It is different because its eternal activity is so different from incarnate cognition. His speculations about discarnate memory are, I believe, an effort to fix a psychological problem that arises when the consequences of his metaphysical innovations are realized.[49]

As soon as Plotinus opens a window on the desirability of the idiosyncratic consciousness, however, he slams it shut. Evidently, personal memories are retainable only for some unspᴄcified period of time prior to reconnection with Intellect.

> The more it [the higher soul] presses on towards the heights the more it will forget, unless perhaps all its life, even here below, has been such that its memories are only of higher things; since here below too it is best to be detached from human concerns (ἀνθρωπείων σπουδασμάτων), and so necessarily from human memories.(IV.3.32.12–17)

This soul will not even remember that it engaged in philosophy and even that here it contemplated. It will remember neither intellectual nor sense-related activity. It is not possible, when engaged unqualifiedly in intellection, to remember anything (IV.4.1.4–11).[50] The ultimate destiny of the ideal self is as a subject eternally contemplating, bereft of memories altogether. It is united with Intellect substantially, although it has an awareness of itself being so united.[51]

The personal identity determined by memory is insinuated into the generally non-idiosyncratic state of the soul in the intelligible realm in two specific ways. First, a soul can leave the intelligible realm and recover its memories (IV.4.4.14–20).[52] This is misleading. One who leaves the intelligible realm has not left it completely; he still has a true ideal self that is undescended. Perhaps "leaving the intelligible realm" amounts to nothing more than incarnation. If this is so, then when Plotinus says that intellect has the memories in potency even while contemplating and that contemplating just occludes these, he means merely to assert an identity among reincarnated versions of a person and an eternal intellect. This continuity of memories is presumably what makes the identification of an incarnated individual with a previously incarnated individual non-arbitrarily describable as reincarnation. Second, and less clearly, the soul in the intelligible realm sees the Good or the One (IV.4.4.1. See also I.7.2.2–3; 6–8; I.8.2.23–5). Since a soul which descends into reincarnation is said not to be able to bear unity (οὐκ ἀνασχομένη τὸ ἕν) (IV.4.3.1), presumably this is at least in part owing to its previous memories and the effect they have had on the soul. There seems to be room therefore to distinguish degrees of intensity of devotion to the first principle of all among contemplators based upon their various degrees of attachment to incarnate existence, which is describable in part by a set of memories.

The tension between Plotinus' psychology and metaphysics is evident in his epistemology. It is not obvious that an undescended intellect eternally united with Forms is helpful in explaining my higher cognition or my personal destiny. Perhaps some of the problems we have encountered in this chapter are among those which led Porphyry to resist the doctrine that the objects of thought do not exist outside the intellect (see *Life of Plotinus* 18.10ff.). For if they did, an undescended intellect might not have seemed necessary. It will be recalled that the reason for holding that the Forms do not exist outside Intellect is to guarantee eternal truth. It is therefore somewhat ironic that the guarantee seems to entail that incarnate cognizers possess only λόγοι of eternal truth.

IX

Conquering Virtue

In the first book of the *Nicomachean Ethics* Aristotle attacks Plato's notion of a Form of the Good. It is reasonable for him to have supposed that arguments against what is apparently the first principle of a system of ethics would undermine the entire account. I believe that this strategy can legitimately be brought into question especially if we approach Plato's ethics through his psychology rather than his metaphysics. This is not, however, Plotinus' view of the matter. As has already been noted, Plotinus' Plato is a Plato without Socrates. This is hardly surprising given Plotinus' propensity to follow Aristotle's interpretations of Plato. Accordingly, in ethics as in much else Plotinus wants to defend Platonism by responding to Aristotle's attacks, based of course on Aristotle's interpretations.

One seldom-noticed consequence of Plotinus' Aristotelian reading of Plato concerns the relation of ethics and politics. Whereas Aristotle believes that ethics just is political science, he does not recognize this as so for Plato.[1] His criticism in the *Politics* of the political side of the *Republic* is completely independent of his criticism of the ethical side in the *Nicomachean Ethics*. Following the Plato that Aristotle presents to him, it apparently does not even occur to Plotinus to judge ethical claims according to political criteria. There is another reason for this, I think. The ideal state of an individual is for Plotinus a discarnate one. And the community of discarnate contemplators is decidedly not political. Hence, political philosophy, if not exactly irrelevant, is definitely subordinate to ethics. I suppose that this is in fact true for Plato as well, but it is not so explicit in his writings.

1 The Good Life

Aristotle defines virtue in the *Nicomachean Ethics* as "a habit concerned with choice, residing in a mean relative to us, defined by reason, and in the way that the prudent man would define it" (2.6.1106b36–1107a2). And he defines happiness as "a certain type of activity of the soul according to virtue" (1.10.1099b26). Three claims here need concern us above all: the distinction between virtue and happiness, the identification of happiness with an activity,

185

and the identification of happiness with a goal that is in some sense ultimate (see 1.7.1097a30). In expressing an association between virtue and happiness, Aristotle is of course making a claim that is not exclusively Peripatetic. Indeed, apart from some of Socrates' less reputable interlocutors, such as Callicles in the *Gorgias*, it would be difficult to point to anyone actually holding the irrelevance of virtue to happiness. Perhaps Epicurus is the sole exception to this, although it is not clear that he meant that it was irrelevant rather than unnecessary.

Naturally, among all those who associate virtue and happiness there are diverse conceptions of virtue. And with diverse conceptions of virtue, diverse conceptions of happiness follow. But the diversity in the latter is a material diversity, not a formal one. Aristotle's claim that happiness is an ultimate good is a deeply ingrained common Greek conception. Although other philosophers may conceive the contents of a happy life differently – for example, laying greater or lesser stress on political activity or external goods – all would agree with him that it is something self-sufficient and so not serving any further purpose.

Plotinus is very far from wishing to reject the three Aristotelian claims listed above, and to that extent he testifies to an impressively long tradition of consensus. Nevertheless, he firmly believes that metaphysics is not irrelevant to ethics. Far from it. As Plotinus puts it, "everything depends on the One." This includes all the facts about the world on the basis of which an ethical doctrine ought to be constructed. So, a distinctive metaphysics yields, not surprisingly, a distinctive ethics.[2]

Proximity to the One, under the aspect of the Good, is the objective criterion of moral evaluation. In so far as actions, persons, and things are susceptible to moral evaluation, they are judged to be good or bad, right or wrong, relative to each other depending on how close they are to the One. Whatever supports and produces advancement towards the first principle is positively evaluated; whatever does the opposite is negatively evaluated. Everything other than the One can be judged according to whether it is made to be more of a unity and whether its activity advances it towards unity (see I.7.1.11–13). Specifically, whatever is not soul is brought closer to the One by the imposition of form; whatever possesses soul approaches the One to the extent that it identifies with Intellect, that is, the self-reflexive life of Intellect. Furthermore, since form reaches the inanimate through soul, Plotinus can say that soulless things are directed to the first principle by being directed to soul, whereas soul itself is directed to the Good through Intellect (I.7.2.1–3).

The fact that the One is the Good and the fact that everything that exists participates in the One would seem to imply that everything that exists participates in the Good. This is not the case. Matter is unqualifiedly evil, as we shall see later in this chapter, and so cannot partake in the Good. Plotinus does not believe that everything is good just in so far as it exists, even though everything that exists is one. How is this possible? Since "the Good" is a name for the ἀρχή of all under the aspect of end or goal, something is good only in so far as it can be related to that goal. Matter alone is incapable of contributing to anyone's return to the One because it is bereft of form, or the instrumental causality of Intellect. But matter exists and so participates in the One because it is a necessary condition for the actualization of all the possibilities that are just individual images of Intellect and Soul.[3]

The ἀρχή of all is the end or goal of all, and as such "the Good" is the proper way to describe it. Apart from a gratifying neatness or simplicity, why is this so? Why should the most desirable goal for anything be a return to its source? Far from being obvious, it seems absurd that in general a creature's goal is ever to be reabsorbed into the creator. Its goal may be installed by the creator, but if this goal were reabsorption, it would seem that it negates the creation itself. It would be like writing a book only then to erase every line. In fact, Plotinus does not conceive of achieving one's own good as reabsorption into the One. The ultimate goal for the individual is achieving its good by participation in Intellect, and this must involve some residual distinction between individual and the Good. Therefore, return to the source does not mean reabsorption unqualifiedly into it. Attaining one's own good does not mean becoming "the Good."[4]

The reason why proximity to the source is the measure of goodness is something like the following. All striving or desire aims at achieving an intrinsically satisfying condition not already present or the continuation of such a condition. That is self-evident. Achieving what is not already possessed indicates a lack of some sort. That is also self-evident. The reason why the One is the measure of goodness is that it provides the way to measure achievement, that is, the coincidence of desire and result. The perfect coincidence of desire and achievement is attributed to Intellect. In so far as individuals attain to identification with the activity of Intellect, they have the Good in the only way it can be "had." This means that "good" is equivocal, referring either to the ideal state achieved by the individual or to the One, which is really the principle of goodness. But since achieving the good means the closest possible contact with the first principle, these two meanings are very close.

In chapter 4 of book 1 of the *Nicomachean Ethics* Aristotle raises many objections to Plato's positing a Form of the Good. Of course, his general objections to Forms are intended to apply to a Form of the Good. We may leave these aside to concentrate on his objections against making goodness a Form. Plotinus was unquestionably aware of these criticisms, although curiously enough he does not seem interested in addressing them. They are worth our attention because, though they are addressed to Plato, they help illuminate Plotinus' doctrine as well. The four objections to making a Form out of goodness are: (1) Goodness is found in all categories and so is equivocal. There can be no Form owing to which "good" is univocally predicable in all categories; (2) The term "good" is equivocal precisely in the way "being" is equivocal; (3) If there were a single Form of the Good, there would be a single science of goodness. But there are in fact many sciences of many different types of goodness having nothing to do with each other; (4) There are many things, such as thinking, seeing, pleasure, and honor, which are unqualifiedly good and many other things which are instrumental goods. Considering the prior type of good, if the Form of the Good were the only thing unqualifiedly good, the rest would not be so. If they are unqualifiedly good as well, then the definition of goodness should apply to them equally. But their definitions are distinct, and they differ in their goodness. That is, for instance, the goodness of thinking has to be defined by what thinking is, and the goodness of pleasure by what pleasure is, and these differ.

I think that there are two replies Plotinus can make to these objections on the basis of the above brief account. First, he need not deny categorical priority and posteriority in general and so he need not deny that the so-called substances, that is, composites of quality and matter, do not have goodness in the way that attributes have it. Nor need he deny in general that among things other than the One, goodness is variously manifested. Whatever exists is good because it participates in the One, even though the goodness is as various as the kinds of things that exist (see I.8.3.1–3). This is so attributable to the fact that being includes existence and essence. Plotinus is in no way committed to holding that, say, the goodness of a good horse is the same thing as the goodness of a good father.

Second, Plotinus can agree to the distinction between instrumental and unqualified good yet deny the claim that anything but a kind of union with the Good is unqualifiedly good. But he can do so only on the basis of his distinction between the incarnate individual and the real self (see I.4.14.13–14). Plotinus can claim that Aristotle is running together two ideas, that of the unqualifiedly good and that of intrinsic satisfaction. That which is claimed to be intrinsically satisfying or good is precisely not unqualifiedly good if the claim is defeasible in the light of a reconsideration of what the self is that is making the claim. In other words, what appears to be intrinsically satisfying to the composite individual may not truly be so for the ideal self.

People do of course claim to find all sorts of experiences intrinsically desirable in the sense that they do not claim to want these for the sake of anything else. Plotinus is not inclined to dispute the psychological accuracy of such claims. Indeed, he takes so seriously the identification of goodness with a goal of intrinsically satisfying experiences that he sees nothing logically untoward in saying that plants and animals are happy if they attain their natural states (see I.4.1.10–15).[5] The correct response in Plotinus' view is that no one *should* be content with anything less than union with the One, so long as he is capable of it. Or stated slightly differently, no one really is content with anything else, despite what they think or say. Plants and animals can be "content" with less because they are not capable of more.

The tension in Plotinus' response arises from two competing claims. On the one hand, he wants to hold that the end for man is as a discarnate self in union with the Good. And whether or not this is achieved is an objective matter. As Plotinus puts it, just as the question of whether a particular man is handsome or healthy does not depend on his opinion of the matter, so too whether someone is happy or not does not depend on what he thinks (I.4.9.10ff.). He does not even have to be conscious of the fact that he is engaging in the activity that is the perfect life in order to do so. On the other hand, the concept of a goal of human action connotes intrinsic satisfaction of a desire. And how can one find something intrinsically satisfying when he is unaware of it? The composite individual is surely never intrinsically satisfied with the life of its true ideal self. The analogies of health and beauty belie the irreducibility of ethical to metaphysical discourse, at least in so far as ethics is thought to include reference to desires and ends and the awareness of these.

We recall that Plotinus holds that identification with Intellect includes reflexive awareness of this activity. This awareness must include ultimate satisfaction.[6] So, Plotinus can say that the tension described above is really nothing more than a tension caused by ambiguity about personal identity. It is true that the endowed or projected ideal self of most persons conceives of intrinsic satisfaction as belonging to states which are either bodily or require a body. To say that none of these are intrinsically satisfying for the person identified with the true ideal self is not to deny anything about the logic of action. It is instead to distinguish the type of desire, βούλησις, motivating the ideal self from any other (I.4.6.17–21. See also I.4.4.17). He who identifies himself more or less exclusively as a subject of βούλησις is psychologically discontinuous with the subject of other types of desire. He is the one most likely to desire to have the sort of desire that the discarnate self possesses exclusively.

If these ideas are indeed what underlie Plotinus' account, then we can begin to understand the remarkable extremism of his ethics, an extremism so alien to Aristotle and surpassing even that of Plato in his darkest moments. Plotinus does not admit that the things that ordinary people find intrinsically satisfying are such even to a minimal degree. Nor are these things even contributions to happiness.[7] For example, the presence of pain or absence of pleasure does not make the life of one good man any better than that of another (I.4.15).[8] Bad fortune will not affect the good man.[9] He desires "externals" not at all (I.4.11.3–12). All of this is implausible in the extreme unless the good man has become virtually identified with the true ideal self and Plotinus is denying that ordinarily desirable things or states are the objects of his βούλησις.

Plotinus does appear to hedge a bit. He says that the happy man will desire (ἐθέλει) necessities not because they are instrumental to happiness, but because they are instrumental to his existence (τὸ εἶναι) (I.4.7.1–3). Obviously, Plotinus is referring to the existence of the composite, because necessities have nothing to do with the existence of the discarnate individual. Still, why should the happy man care about the existence of the animate body which he governs? He does not really care about it at all. However, active or passive participation in its dissolution indicate an emotional defect such as grief or anger. It also indicates an arrogant preemption of providence. Finally, it ends the possibility for moral improvement (I.9.1.17–19).[10]

It is the last-mentioned reason that seems to be uppermost in Plotinus' mind when he says that the animate body was given to the man as a possession "not in vain" (οὐ μάτην) (I.4.16.27). Caring for this possession in the proper way is useful for creating the conditions under which moral progress can be made. But moral progress concerns the self and not one's possessions. The Good alone is the cause of goodness in him.[11] Nothing that happens to the animate body is a cause of progress towards the Good. The claim that incarnation provides the opportunity for moral progress supports my interpretation of identification with the ideal self as an achievement, not an automatic result of separation from the body. Moral progress cannot mean just managing to die. It must be achieving a state such that when one does die, the true ideal self is recognized as one's own. It must also be a state in which the desire to attain that state is fulfilled.

Another important qualification of Plotinus' austere self-regarding account of morality is his claim that (ordinary) virtue is a sort of spontaneous result of the recognition that our rational desire is for the Good:

> For anyone who feels affection for anything at all shows kindness to all
> that is akin to the object of his affection, and to the children of the father
> he loves. But every soul is a child of That Father. (II.9.16.7–9)[12]

This fine insight is formulated in subtly different ways by both Plato and Aristotle.[13] But in no case do these philosophers descend to the bathetic justification for virtue based on the confused notion of the "intrinsic value of other persons" or the obscurantist and arbitrary "categorical imperative." For Plotinus a *universal* principle of benevolent action towards others, as opposed to an instrumentalist approach on particular occasions ("I was nice to him because he was or will be nice to me"), has to be built on something more solid than human life. Plotinus thinks it rather obvious that once one realizes what he really wants, which is nothing other than the Good itself, he cannot but be favorably disposed to its products. That is just what lovers do.[14] I do not think that Plotinus would even understand, much less grant, the following criticism: If you do not act virtuously towards others for their own sake, then you are not acting virtuously at all. One acts virtuously towards others as a consequence of one's love of the Good.

It is noteworthy that a description of a desirable state of indifference to the fortunes of one's own body is only barely graspable by means of a

comparison with pathological psychological states of disassociation or extraordinary accounts of out-of-body near-death experiences. But it is enough if
such states are imaginable to pass on to the more important question of
whether or not they are conceivably desirable. Unfortunately, if this question
is put by one who has not already renounced this world, there can be no
reasoned definite answer. It is just question-begging to say that one would
not care to live a life indifferent to physical pleasure, when it is the ordinary
endowed self one is referring to. The life Plotinus recommends and the life
he disdains are discontinuous in the sense that the former is not an enhancement or qualitative improvement over the latter. The idea of renouncing one
life and embracing another, where the other is in principle unknown, is a
profoundly difficult one. It is the essence of conversion – philosophical or
religious – and we shall see how Plotinus deals with it in the next chapter.
For now it is enough to suggest that if we find incredible the austere life
idealized by Plotinus, this is hardly to the point.

It will occur to some readers, as indeed it occurred to Plotinus, that his
account is redolent of certain Stoic themes (I.4.2).[15] Nevertheless, he sees an
important difference. The Stoics say that happiness consists in a rational life.
Either this means that reason is required as an instrument for achieving the
primary natural things (τὰ πρῶτα κατὰ φύσις) like health and bodily goods,
or else reason is valuable in itself. If the former, then animals who achieve
their needs without reason will be happy, and reason by itself will not be
worth having. If the latter, the Stoics can give no account of the desirability
of non-instrumental reason, that is, theoretical rational activity.

This criticism is particularly interesting because it shows that Plotinus, who
feels an obvious affinity for the Stoic approach in ethics, thinks that they are
not able to explain adequately the correct attitude one ought to take towards
externals and the sensible world in general.[16] Perhaps there is some irony in
Plotinus' suspicion that Stoics view externals too favorably. For Plotinus, the
paradigm of the rational life is the life of Intellect. This is the life of our true
ideal selves, and we are not conscious of it. It is a life that the Stoics are
unable to endorse because they reject discarnate existence. In practice, the
ideal Stoic life would perhaps not differ greatly from the ideal (incarnate)
Plotinian life. Both lives disdain externals. But Plotinus, unlike the Stoics,
can hold that the ideal life of an endowed self is at best still an inferior version
of the true ideal life. Fidelity to that life means that "living according to
nature" or "living virtuously" literally adds nothing to true happiness, nor
is it constitutive of happiness. If this is so, however, then how does a good
incarnate life differ from an evil one? To this question we must now turn.

2 Evil

We have already encountered briefly Plotinus' identification of matter with
evil (τὸ κακόν). Such an identification, along with the identification of

goodness with the first principle of all, gives coordinates as it were by which to judge moral progress and decline. These can be described alternatively as approaching one terminus and distancing the other. Just as approaching the Good means incremental identification with noetic activity, so declining towards evil means incremental identification with things contaminated with evil.[17] The latter notion is quite obscure. Understanding this rather notorious facet of Plotinus' thought requires some excavating beneath the surface.

The major innovation in Plotinus' account of matter is his notorious equation of it with evil (see VI.7.28.12; I.8.5.8–12; I.8.8.10–11; I.8.10.1–5; I.8.11.1–6).[18] That "evil" and "matter" refer to the same thing means that they are merely conceptually distinct. Furthermore, we should not be surprised to discover that if evil is equated with matter, then particular or relative evils are to be equated with particulars that include matter.[19] The conceptual distinctiveness of evil is that it is matter viewed in relation to Form and the Good, its ἀρχή (I.8.1.17–19; I.8.11).[20] It is a nature (φύσις) considered in its absolute privation of both (see I.8.10.5, 16). Relative evil, whether it be physical or moral, is to be understood as privation with respect to a particular form. Thus, for example, Plotinus can say that the body is relatively evil in the soul–body composite because it is the defective element in that composite. Forms when instantiated are corrupted by matter, which is evil for that reason.

Matter or evil does not exist on its own (I.8.11.4).[21] Primary or pure evil is described as ἀμετρία or unmeasuredness (I.8.3.25).[22] What this seems to mean is that in composite beings other than Intellect and Soul analysis yields a conglomerate of qualities and another principle of formlessness, that which is essentially opaque to cognition.[23] Matter or evil is what is left when in thought we separate out whatever is thinkable in the thing. Furthermore, the composition is not made of two principles where each is unaffected by the other. It is not like a material suspension. But it is not like an Aristotelian substance either, where there is one actuality. The forms in matter are not the same (οὐ ταὐτά), as those same forms would be separated from matter (I.8.8.13–16).[24] That is why they are homonymous images. Forms in matter, what Plotinus calls λόγοι ἔνυλοι, are corrupted by their presence in matter and infected with its nature. It is, for example, presence in matter that differentiates ordinary fire from the Form of Fire. Similarly, the soul in the animate individual is bound to be corrupted by its presence in a body.

Plotinus' account of matter or evil belongs, therefore, to that family of accounts which makes evil an unintended but inevitable side-effect of something else. These accounts range from the crude and mundane – "you can't make an omelet without breaking eggs" – to the highly sophisticated attempts to make the problem one of logic. But they are of a piece because the necessity is in every case hypothetical. Whether it is omelets you want or a universe of free creatures, there are certain constraints inevitably encountered. It is true that Plotinus sometimes seems excessively anxious about these constraints, but perhaps that is owing as much to temperament as to anything else.[25] Creatures moving along the upward path will naturally conceive of the impediments to the successful conclusion of their journey in material terms.

Underlying this analysis by Plotinus is an ambiguity we have already noticed between unqualified and relative or designated matter. If body is, for example, matter for the soul, it is not matter as described above, namely, opaque to the intellect and utterly without form of its own. This is evident from the fact that matter has no qualities, although it has a nature (I.8.10.1–5), and that it is perfectly deficient (παντελῶς ἐλλείπῃ) (I.8.5.8). So, this seems to make matter just unqualified unintelligibility distinct from the matter of any sensible composite.

This interpretation is supported by Plotinus' distinction between evil and kinds of evil (I.8.5.14–17). The distinction is explained by the further identification of evil with privation (στέρησις), that is, the privation of a form that ought to be present.[26] A kind of evil is then the privation of a form that ought to be present. But what is this supposed to mean? If a form is not present, what does it mean to say that it is supposed to be present as opposed to being simply absent? Clearly, Plotinus is not speaking of a substantial form, for if he were, this would amount to saying that an individual member of one type of substance is evil just because it is not another. Rather he is referring to an additional form, whose presence is required by a nature in the composite and whose absence is truly a privation (see I.8.12). This is what he means when he says that illness, ugliness, and poverty are evils, not for the man who is ideally identified with Intellect, but for the animated individual (see I.8.5.19–26). Illness is failure of the body to preserve order and measure; ugliness is matter (i.e., relative or designated matter) not mastered by form; poverty is privation of things needed by the animate individual for its preservation. Types of evil are the result of matter combined with λόγοι ἔνυλοι. The definitions of types of evil indicate the particular corruption experienced by the form owing to its immersion in an alien milieu.[27]

I think the correct way to state this doctrine is to say that because a soul acquires a body the occasion for evil arises, rather than to say that bodies are evil. And just as acquisition of a body is the occasion for evil, so the way to escape evil is to escape from the body (I.8.7.12–13; I.8.8.27–9). Stated thus, Plotinus can hold that the visible gods, i.e., the heavenly bodies, do not have evil, because their souls are sufficiently vigorous and pure to enable them to resist corruption. Neither apparently do certain men who are virtuous (I.8.5.30–5).[28] Having a body then does not unqualifiedly necessitate the presence or at least the realization of evil. It would seem that only the sort of soul that is susceptible to corruption already is likely to experience it when incarnated. A person experiences evil just to the extent that he identifies with the animate body.

If human souls are susceptible to evil, then it is owing to something in them distinct from their bodies. Matter is *not* evil for a soul impervious to it for one reason or another. In the case of the visible gods, they are impervious to evil presumably because their natural destiny is incarnation; there is no "higher" state to which they need aspire or from which they have declined. The soul of the universe is also exempt from evil, principally because it is not susceptible to influence from its body (see II.9.7.7–18; IV.8.5.1–10).[29] For human souls this is of course not the case. But this leaves us with the possible inference that there is a type of evil that is not to be identified with matter, namely, the privation or defect in a soul which makes it susceptible to corruption when incarnated.

Plotinus distinguishes between vice (ἡ κακία) and evil (τὸ κακὸν), saying that the former is the special defect of the soul leading to the latter (I.8.13.5).[30] Vice is basically the "downward" trajectory of the soul; virtue the opposite. But it is not at all clear that vice belongs to soul prior and apart from its incarnation. Plotinus seems to endorse an interpretation of Plato according to which the discarnate soul is perfect.[31] His claim that the weakness (ἀσθένεια) of soul "must be in the souls which have fallen, those which are not pure and have not been purified" is ambiguous as to when the weakness occurs. Plotinus goes on to say in the same passage that matter seduces soul. But of course this could reasonably be said to be successful only if the soul were antecedently so disposed. Finally, he seems to settle on matter as the cause of weakness and vice.[32] And that seems to be his opinion.

There are at least two considerations, however, which should make us hesitate to accept this conclusion at face value. First, soul is instrumental in the production of matter and in general the effect is contained within the cause (see I.8.14.49–54; III.9.3.7–16).[33] So, in some sense soul is implicated in the cause of evil even if evil is alien to and infects the individual soul. Second, in an earlier passage in the treatise on evil Plotinus distinguishes between the perfect soul, which is inclined towards Intellect, and the imperfect soul, which goes out from it, owing to its own deficiency (τῷ ἐλλείμματι) (I.8.4.25–32).[34] This deficiency seems to have nothing to do with matter. On the contrary, it is prior to and evidently responsible for the soul's wishing to consort with matter. This deficiency is, predictably enough, identified with the irrational part of the soul (I.8.4.8–9).[35] However, Plotinus is emphatic that by "irrational part of the soul" he means the soul that is "fused" with the body, that is, the soul of the animate organism. How the irrational part of the soul is to be related to the imperfect soul which is prior to the body is obscure. There are obviously forces pulling Plotinus in different directions.

Evil is unmeasuredness. There is qualified evil in the soul of the animate organism just as there is qualified evil in the body. If we recall that Plotinus' dualism rests on a distinction between animate organism or sensible composite and self, we can easily infer that both sorts of evil can be set on one side over against what is independent altogether of matter. The seeming incoherence in Plotinus' account of evil in the soul is traceable to the fact that one person is equivocally identified with two principles, the endowed self and the ideal self, the former being the agent of the activity of the animate organism and the latter being the putative cohort of Intellect. But "person" is an abstraction, only realized in one or another type of activity, that of eternally contemplating and that of organic living. Only in a peculiar sense can it be true to say that the form of the animate organism imported evil to it from outside. The perfect soul mentioned above refers to the eternal noetic activity of which we are not aware until we identify with it. This does not descend and there is no vice in it (or any virtue, as we shall see presently).

The problem is in identifying the origin of the person. That is, does a person, identified with the true ideal self, fall owing to a defect which it brings to the soul of the body, or does the person come into being with the generation of the animate organism? The latter alternative is of course neater since it avoids having to account for discarnate vice. It would make of vice a sort of original sin inevitably associated with generation because it is in generation that a person becomes associated with matter. The latter alternative, however, conflicts with reincarnation which, as we have seen, is a principle from which Plotinus does not waver. Nevertheless, the former alternative does not entail that the vice is discarnate. Rather, it can be attributed to the soul in a previous incarnated state, and so indirectly to the person identified with that soul, the same person who lives discarnately. It is of course true that if we deny discarnate vice as such except in the sense in which the person bears it as a scar from incarnation, then we shall have to say either that the origin of the person was the first incarnation or that at least the person did not start out in a discarnate state.[36]

I think it is Plotinus' view that if, *per impossibile*, a person were to come into being as the subject of contemplative activity, that person would be perfect and would never "fall." It seems, though, that human nature is such that incarnation inevitably occasions vice, which is in effect the tendency to construct an ideal self that includes a body.[37] My contention is that vice is exclusively an attribute of an incarnate person or endowed self. It is false that either matter or the ideal self is a cause of vice. It is false in the first case, because matter or evil is no more of a cause of the downward trajectory of the soul than an asymptote is the cause of a curve's approaching it. It is false in the latter case because Intellect is an ἀρχή of οὐσία and life. It can no more explain vice than the multiplication table can explain errors in calculation. But an incarnate individual necessarily consorts with (relative) matter and retains an ideal identity in Intellect. So both matter and Intellect conjointly explain the conditions for the cause of vice operating, namely, incarnation of a person.

Further, we only know incarnated persons, which are either new persons (not Plotinus' view) or persons who are veterans of previous incarnations.

They bring no vice to the body that is not a carryover from a previous incarnation.[38] It is essential here to keep in mind that, although the incarnate individual is in one sense identical with something discarnate, this discarnate or ideal self does not descend. So, in the relevant sense the incarnate individual is a new person (reincarnation aside). We have no grounds for positing a discarnate self distinct from the true ideal self, longing for the joys of incarnation, and then suffering the dolorous consequences.

The operation of nature according to which individuals are incarnated is viewed by Plotinus as necessary and hence he is prepared to argue that evil necessarily exists. But all that he is committed to is hypothetical necessity. Clearly, one motive for saying that evil is necessary is fidelity to Plato. In the *Theaetetus* Plato affirms the necessity of the existence of evil as the contrary of good (176a). In the *Timaeus* and *Statesman* he posits a principle of becoming outside the control of the divine mind (see *Timaeus* 47e5–48a1; 53b1–5; *Statesman* 273b5). It is a reasonable, though by no means inevitable, inference that this principle is to be identified with evil as mentioned in the *Theaetetus*. When he says that this principle exists of necessity, he means primarily just this, although Plato would probably have added that since this principle is outside rational control its dissolution is an unintelligible notion. If god could dissolve it, it would then, counter to what it is, be within divine control. If it could dissolve on its own, this could only be because it is generable. But for Plato everything generable is caused (*Timaeus* 27c). Plato means "has a cause outside itself." But the only principle outside the non-intelligible principle of becoming is mind, and so once again what was posited as outside divine control would be within divine control. So, this principle is not generable and not destructible. We should add that, by contrast, the universe which is the product of necessity and mind is also indestructible, but the reason for this is the divine will (41ab).

This is the relevant background to Plotinus' argument that evil exists of necessity. But there are several subtle differences in his account. First, he probably has a more rigorous notion of unmeasuredness or absence of form than does Plato, owing, I believe, to his reading of Aristotle. For Plato, the physical universe prior to the imposition of divine order is describable and so in some sense intelligible. For Plotinus, on the other hand, it is important that matter be limited to the principle of unintelligibility, utterly beyond direct cognitive access. This makes it, as we have seen, more like Aristotle's prime matter.

Second, even though matter is bereft of form, it exists, both for Plato and Plotinus.[39] For Plato, this is an unaccounted for feature of his ontology. The Form of the Good is the cause of the being of the other Forms, but neither it nor anything else is said to be the cause of the being of what becomes, much less the principle of becoming. For Plotinus, however, the One is the cause of the being of absolutely everything. Absence of form does not entail absence of being. So, Plotinus has at least in part a more coherent account than Plato, for the unity of the universe is retained by making the One reach down all the way to the edge of nothing. Nevertheless, there is obviously a serious impediment to coherence in another respect. If matter or evil exists owing to the One, then it would seem that the One is somehow implicated in its creation.[40]

Let us look at the two reasons Plotinus actually gives for the necessity of evil in order to see whether this putative incoherence can be removed. First, he says that matter is necessary for the existence of the all (τὸ πᾶν), meaning the ensouled universe (I.8.7.2–4). Second, he argues that there must be an end to the process of going out (ἐκβάσις) from the Good. So, since the first must exist, the last must exist. And this is matter, which possesses nothing of the Good (I.8.7.12–22).[41]

These two reasons are not unconnected. We recall that matter, though it exists, does not exist by itself independently of form. It is hypothetically necessary for the existence of nature, the secondary activity of Soul. Nature could not exist without matter, but nature necessarily exists as a manifestation of life and the locus of the images of Intellect. The claim that matter is hypothetically necessary for the existence of nature does not of course mean that matter is prior in existence to nature. What it means is that from the initial decline from the One, not just an order unfolds, but an order with a definite "negative" limit. The very idea of secondary activity, along with the principle of the unicity of the One, guarantees that the last member of the series should be not just inferior to the first, but unqualifiedly inferior. So, it is the logical conclusion of production from the One that matter exists. It is a hypothetical necessity based upon an unqualified natural necessity. Thus, given that the One acts with the instrumentality of Intellect, its products are going to be images of the One by being images of that instrument. The making of such images requires matter.

The result of decline cannot be to be cast beyond the reach of the One. That would be a logical impossibility. The end product of the decline is itself without form, though not without a nature (I.8.10.5). Plotinus must say this if whatever exists is to be distinct from its existence and that which makes it exist. I suggest that when he says that evil has nothing of the Good, what he means is that matter in itself has no form, which is the only way that anything can participate in the Good. We should then understand "good in so far as it exists" as limited to whatever has form, the means by which goodness is received. Thus "matter (evil) exists" is true, but "matter (evil) has intelligible existence" and "matter (evil) is good because it exists" are false.

I have argued that it is appropriate to speak of matter or evil as an element in bodies. If we think of it as a principle we shall be inclined to identify its instantiations with body, and I have argued that this is not correct. The body is not evil; but the way that one approaches evil is by attachment to a body. Conceiving of evil as an element present in anything lower than soul seems decidedly less misleading. It is what is left over after everything intelligible in something has been separated. If there were no such residue, there would be no difference between the eternal world of Forms and the world of becoming. Evil is not body, but the way that something embodied escapes evil is by separation from that body.

There is one more argument for the necessity of evil worth mentioning. Plotinus says that one who denies the necessity of evil must also abolish the Good (I.8.15). This argument is different from the above, for it rests not upon the necessity of development from the Good down to the last stage of being, but rather upon the nature of activity between the first and last principle. It is clear from the argument that Plotinus is not saying that, logically speaking, the One or the Good could not exist if evil did not exist. If this means that the One alone is unqualifiedly independent, Plotinus certainly does in fact hold this. Rather, he is claiming that if evil did not exist, the Good would be abolished in so far as this concerned anything in the sensible world, including an endowed self. As Plotinus puts it, "he would have no object to aim at." This is surely a very odd claim unless Plotinus means that without evil an endowed self could not exist. The desires of an endowed self are either in the direction of evil or in the direction of its opposite. Incarnate existence entails a separation from the Good. If there were no evil, the separation would be eliminated. The One under the aspect of the Good is just the goal of endowed selves confronted with evil as a necessary alternative goal.

It is important to stress that evil is not a thing possessing some intelligible content. Since all nature and all psychic activity bear the mark of intelligible being, albeit ever so slightly, whatever happens by nature or according to the activity of soul cannot be evil itself. There can, however, be a persistent tendency towards evil. Since Soul is the ἀρχή of transitive activity, an incarnated soul has a tendency to go downward to evil to the extent that it acts to fulfill the body's needs.[42] Unqualified instantiation of evil for a soul would be, *per impossibile*, its transformation into a different nature. But the fundamental feature of the essence of the soul is desire, and desire is for the Good.

Plotinus does raise the possibility of a soul so totally inured to vice that it actually approaches a kind of metamorphosis into another nature (I.8.13.12–26). In this circumstance, the soul "dies" and so changes its nature, but only until such time as "it raises itself and somehow manages to look away from the mud." That the dying is not unconditional and so obviously metaphorical is decisive evidence that evil belongs primarily to the metaphysical order and not to the ethical order.[43] That is, evil must be understood as necessitated by principles of being and creation and only then itself employed for understanding the activities of individual creatures. For Plotinus, the world in which we live is not a neutral background for ethical discourse. Conclusions regarding its nature are therefore elementary principles of ethics.

3 Virtue

Aristotle says that virtue is a habit (ἕξις). We come into this world not exactly with a blank slate, for our bodily constitutions are morally relevant, but strictly speaking a newborn is neither virtuous nor vicious. Plotinus, however, believes that the newborn is an inheritor of the condition of previous incarnations. Even if he did not believe this, or even if the inheritance were morally exiguous, the newborn individual suffers from infection by evil just because it is embodied. Accordingly, virtue is not the positive habituation of the life of the composite, but rather something more radical, namely, separation from it. Plotinus does in one passage call virtue a ἕξις, but it is an odd habit indeed, one which in a way intellectualizes the soul (οἷον νοωθῆναι τὴν ψυχὴν ποιοῦσα) (VI.8.5.35–6). This habit is discontinuous with previous states, and not the perfection of them. It is most readily understandable as that which aids in the transformation of a person into the sort of entity capable of recognizing a discarnate contemplator as his true ideal self.

More typically, Plotinus calls virtue a purifying process (κάθαρσις) (I.2.4. See also I.6.6.1–3; I.7.3.21–2; III.6.5.13–29; V.1.10.24–6).[44] As a process, it aims at something beyond the process itself. By comparison, the Aristotelian habit that is virtue is intrinsically desirable. Even if we add that activity according to the habit is superior to the habit itself and its aim, the habit is not purely instrumental. Plotinus' dualism is manifested nowhere more powerfully than in his denial of this. Like Epicurus, who holds that τὸ καλόν is of purely instrumental value only in so far as it produces pleasure, Plotinus makes virtue the means to achieving a state which transcends virtue altogether.[45] The task set for the incarnate person is not to make himself comfortable or successful in this life, however comfort and success may be understood, but to escape to an entirely different life. As Plotinus puts it, there is no virtue in Intellect, and it is in association with Intellect that our ideal destiny resides (I.2.1.46–53; I.2.3.24–6; I.2.6.16–17).

Plotinus' account of the virtues is formed essentially by his reading of Plato's *Republic*. In book 4 of the *Republic* Plato defines the four virtues, wisdom, courage, temperance, and justice, in the state and then tries to show that these virtues are identical in the tripartite soul (427e–434d). The general account of virtue as psychic health enables Socrates to answer the question posed at the beginning of the second book, namely, whether virtue, specifically, justice, is intrinsically desirable. But the second question posed there, whether virtue is desirable for its consequences, is not answered until the end of book 9. There is at least some reason to believe that between the beginning of book 5 and the end of book 9 a different account of virtue is being advanced. It is at the beginning of book 5 that the description of the philosopher as opposed to the philodoxer begins to unfold. And the description of the virtuous man at the end of book 9, called the "aristocratic man," is identical with that of the philosopher. There is in fact no reason to identify the virtues defined at the end of book 4 with those of the philosopher. Plotinus simply assumes that they are different and that the virtues of the philosopher are in fact those described in *Theaetetus* 176ab as being part of the assimilation to god (ὁμοίωσις θεῷ).[46]

Plotinus therefore makes a distinction between the "lower" and "higher" virtues, the former essentially identical with those of book 4 of the *Republic* (I.2.1.16–21).[47] The latter are defined in two ways, negatively and positively (I.2.3.15–19; I.2.6.23–7). The negative definitions indicate disassociation with the body or indifference to its attractions. This of course must be understood as pertaining to the animate composite. The positive definitions indicate association with or affinity to Intellect.

Plotinus seems to be grudgingly prepared to grant to the lower virtues some instrumental role in attaining the Good (see I.2.1.23–7; I.2.2.13–18).[48] They do make a contribution to the removal of unmeasuredness in the soul.[49] But precisely because these virtues pertain to the organization and control of the organic individual (Plotinus' diffidence about tripartition is evident here), they are rather beside the point. If the goal is escape from the body, then attention to its albeit subordinate role is more or less time-wasting.

Why then are the lower virtues instrumental at all? Surely it is not because practicing them leads to intrinsically satisfying states. Rather, they constitute a kind of elementary ascetic practice whereby the person can become gradually detached from the animate body. The interesting question is whether they are an indispensable form of training. Would a pathological state of indifference to one's own physical well-being plus chronic misanthropy do as well as virtue in making us long for the ideal as conceived by Plotinus? Perhaps psychologically it can. I suspect that Plotinus would wish to say that it is the disposition to practice the lower virtues that is effective in contributing to the goal. In that case, then, it is appropriate to ask if the hypothetical morbid hermit is so disposed or not. If so, then he is no counterexample. If not, then he would seem to be acting in violation of the principle that one who loves the Good also loves its products.[50]

There are two features of Plato's account of virtue retained by Plotinus but transposed owing to the distinction between the higher and lower virtues. First, Plato shows a strong tendency to identify virtue with knowledge. This is more evident in the early and middle dialogues prior to his tripartitioning of the soul and the consequent recognition of the possibility of incontinence than it is in the later dialogues. Nevertheless, whether or not it was Plato's settled view that knowledge is necessary and sufficient for virtue, it seems fairly clear that virtue is essentially a kind of knowledge. The second and related feature is that Plato is strongly attracted to the notion of the unity of the virtues, that is, their mutual implication. Indeed, it is only if virtue is a type of knowledge of a very general sort that this latter claim is at all plausible. The particular virtues would then be names for various areas of human life in which this type of knowledge would be applied.

Plotinus seems to accept some version of both of these claims regarding both the lower and higher virtues. All of the higher virtues are specifications or facets of the process of orientation towards Intellect (I.8.6.21–8).[51] They indicate the activity of self-identification with the subject of contemplation or the recovery of knowledge. This would make virtue a matter of degree, something like degrees of self-knowledge or degrees of identification with rational desire. As the individual person came to know more and more clearly who his ideal self is, he would be closer and closer to identification with members of the family of eternal contemplators. Yet it is essential to stress that possession of higher virtue approaches asymptotically the state of perfect identification with Intellect, which is beyond virtue. Someone with higher virtue will manifest indifference to himself and others only relatively speaking (see I.4.7.1ff.; I.4.15.21–5).[52]

This indifference is nicely revealed in an example Plotinus himself provides:

> If some boys, who have kept their bodies in good training, but are inferior in soul to their bodily condition because of lack of education, win a wrestle with others who are trained neither in body nor soul and grab their food and their dainty clothes, would the affair be anything but a joke? Or would it not be right for even the lawgiver to allow them to suffer this as a penalty for their laziness and luxury, these bodies, who, though they were assigned training-grounds, because of laziness and soft and slack living allowed themselves to become fattened lambs, the prey of wolves? (III.2.8.16–26)

As Plotinus goes on to point out, providence will punish the malefactors anyway. They will bear the burden of living the lives of wolves, and when they die, "the rational and natural consequences follow," presumably, their reincarnation in inferior states. Thus providence or the natural necessity of Intellect is represented as providing the model of the sort of attitude the philosopher seeks to acquire. By refraining from intervening, he manifests an attachment to what is "higher" than virtue. We might note in passing, however, that if Plotinus seriously intended this ethical insight to translate into law, it is a very good thing that he was denied his dream of setting up a separate Platonic state.

The mutual implication of the higher virtues follows in part from the fact that virtue is a single path towards a single goal (I.8.7.1–13).[53] But this is clearly not enough. Every virtue could conceivably advance one along the path to goodness independently, so that having one or a few virtues would be desirable but not as efficacious as having all. What must be added is that having one without the others would actually make the one ineffective. Thus does Plotinus come close to the Stoic doctrine that if one is not virtuous, then one is vicious. That is, there is no middle ground. If one is not in the process of removing the impediments to self-identification with Intellect, then one is

201

ensnared in the opposite process of attachment to these.[54] Practically speaking, and without introducing pointless trivial counter-examples, this position is psychologically insightful, and probably necessary on the basis of Plotinus' principles. The idea of neutral temporizing or of activity without moral import is at least alien to a moral philosophy such as that of Plotinus. Simply to carry on with the banalities of incarnate existence is not, on this view, to mark time but rather to bind oneself increasingly to the bodily. The psychological insight is in the fact that people become comfortable with what they do repeatedly. To fail to advance towards the ideal is to retreat in the opposite direction.

Someone who possesses the higher virtues necessarily possesses the lower, at least potentially. But the opposite is alas not true (I.2.7.10–12).[55] It is easy enough to understand why the latter is the case, for an image of order is not order itself, and someone who practices ordinary decency and civility is very far from the detached ideal contemplator. Possessing the higher virtues entails possessing the potency for the lower for the reason given above, namely, love, or at least respect for the products of the Good. I take the qualification "potentially" to indicate something a good deal less than enthusiasm for virtuous practice. It seems to be equivalent in meaning to "hypothetically." In so far as this man is required to don the role of incarnate moral agent he will, so to speak, recreate an image of true virtue. But his disassociation from this life is such that he does not unqualifiedly desire to perform such acts, nor does he desire the occasion for their performance or even any particular outcome.[56] Plotinus assumes a radical discontinuity in a man before and after a conversion experience.[57] He says that the man possessing higher virtue will no longer live the life of a good man, that is, he will no longer live according to "political virtue" (I.2.7.23–7).[58] He will separate himself from his lower nature and live the life of the gods.

What of the individual who is incapable of attaining such a lofty state? Can it be said in regard to him, as Aristotle would have it, that the life of political virtue is a "second prize"? This question is somewhat analogous to the tendentious question one might pose to a Catholic theologian. If contraception is wrong according to natural law and illicit sexual intercourse is wrong as well, is it better to use contraception than not if one is determined to engage in this kind of sex? It does not seem to me to strain the logic of either position to accept the hypothetical while at the same time rejecting without qualification the desirability of the antecedent. Political virtue is better than vice for one who constructs an ideal self rooted in incarnate existence.

X

Philosophy of Religion

1 Religion as Return to Self

Little is known of Plotinus' view of the prevailing civic religion of his time. The best guess is that he felt for it polite indifference bordering on disdain.[1] If Plotinus did indeed have a low opinion of "organized" Roman religion, this would contrast sharply with his personal devotional practices. It is also likely that he viewed with contempt the newest religion of the day, Christianity. His most faithful disciple, Porphyry, certainly did. When I use the term "religion" in reference to Plotinus' thought, I refer to those activities or practices he endorses as leading to higher virtue and beyond, ultimately to association with Intellect and through it to union with the One. However, I use the term with some hesitation. I recognize the force of the claim that religion has an essentially social or interpersonal element, and this is quite foreign to what Plotinus is recommending.[2]

The central notion of Plotinus' philosophy of religion is that of return (ἐπιστροφή).[3] All creation is disposed by nature to return to the source whence it came, in so far as it is able. It is on this basis, first of all, that Plotinus can make a distinction between phenomenal and real desire. Appearances notwithstanding, what all things really desire is to be united or reunited with the source of their being. Second, given that the universe is an ordered hierarchy, the stages of return are fixed. Short-cuts are not allowed. The reason for this is that the ascent or return to the One must involve a refolding of what was unfolded.[4] To attempt a short-cut would then amount to nothing less than a spurious ascent. This is the source of Plotinus' deep antipathy to any form of Gnosticism (see II.9).[5] Gnosticism disdains the notion that religion is hard work governed by objective rules. It invites one to practice bogus religion.

There is a more important reason, though, for Plotinus' insistence on an orderly ascent "from external to internal, from lower to higher." The ascent does not end with acceptance of conclusions of arguments about the existence of Intellect or the One. The ascent, if it is to be successful, must consist in the construction of an ideal self in the incarnate individual which includes a kind of synonymous image of the true ideal self. One must become the person who naturally acts like that ideal self. So, the ascent must include what can only be called a conversion experience. And this means recapitulating the metaphysical order – One, Intellect, Soul, nature – in reverse. For example, Plotinus does not envision a vicious man as bypassing lower virtue and ascending directly to higher virtue or even to the construction of an ideal self beyond virtue. A conversion from vice is a conversion to what vice is a corruption of, namely, the lower virtues.

The notion of return to one's home needs to be distinguished both from a notion of approaching a goal which is a new, emerging vista and from the notion of a goal which is new for the aspirant, but antecedently ordained for him. In the first instance, I have in mind something like process theology. According to one of its distinguished proponents, Charles Hartshorne, all creation along with the creator has as a goal limitless self-surpassing creativity.[6] In the nature of the case, creativity aims at something which does not already exist. Creator and creature become collaborators in a never-ending project. According to such a view, an eternally existent true ideal self can have no meaning. In the second instance, I have in mind all religions which posit some ideal state, incarnate or discarnate, prepared for humans by the divine. Since on this view human life has a beginning but no end, the achievement of the ideal state is not understood as a return. Humans are ordained to this state, and the aim of religion is seen both as bringing one to comprehend this and as preparing one to be suitable for it.

In the case of these religions, there is, I think, an illuminating comparison to be made between Plotinus' and their concepts of the ideal self. In both cases, the ideal is something of which we have no direct experience. But for Plotinus, the idea of return is intended to make commitment to the ideal more plausible psychologically. It is after all our own true selves to which we are returning. And yet one might argue that, say, the Christian ideal of a resurrected embodied state is more psychologically compelling because it is at least imaginable as being something like what endowed selves already experience, only infinitely better.

It is obvious what Plotinus would say in reply to such a claim. The Christian has incorrectly subordinated metaphysics to psychology. To posit an ideal self based on what we as endowed selves view as ideal is to pretend that incarnate states of desire which are necessarily imperfect are in fact perfectible. The Christian will reply that revealed theology trumps metaphysics. Plotinus would, I think, respond that an ideal self possessing any kind of body is in fact even less psychologically accessible than is an ideal self as discarnate contemplator. We can certainly imagine ourselves with indestructible bodies. But we cannot so easily imagine the desires of incarnate agents perfectly and instantly satisfied. That, however, is just what the putative ideal self would have to have.

It is therefore essential to distinguish sharply between the notion of return in Plotinus and his doctrine of reincarnation. The return is not to a previous incarnate state. The path of the return is, so to speak, in a different plane from the path produced by a history of repeated reincarnations. What enables Plotinus to speak of a return which has nothing to do with a previous incarnation is the distinction between the endowed and the true ideal self. This is evident in one of the most eloquent texts in the *Enneads*:

What is it, then, which has made the souls forget their father, god, and be ignorant of themselves and him, even though they are parts which come from his higher world and altogether belong to it? The beginning (ἀρχή) of evil for them was audacity (τόλμα) and coming to birth (γένεσις) and the first otherness (πρώτη ἑτερότης) and the wishing to belong to themselves. Since they were clearly delighted with their own independence, and made great use of self-movement, running the opposite course and getting as far away as possible, they were ignorant even that they themselves came from that world; just as children who are immediately torn from their parents and brought up far away do not know who they themselves or their parents are. Since they do not any more see their father or themselves, they despise themselves through ignorance of their birth and honor other things, admiring everything rather than themselves, and, astonished and delighted by and dependent on these [earthly] things, they have broken themselves loose as far as they could in contempt of that from which they turned away; so that their honor for these things here, and their contempt for themselves is the cause of their utter ignorance of god. For what pursues and admires something else admits at the same time its own inferiority; but by making itself inferior to things which come into being and perish and considering itself the most contemptible and the most liable to death of all the things which it admires it could not possibly have any idea of the nature and power of god. One must therefore speak in two ways to men who are in this state of mind, if one is going to turn them round to what lies in the opposite direction and is primary, and to lead them up to that which is highest, one, and first. What, then, are these two ways? One shows how contemptible are the things now honored by the soul, and this we shall develop more amply elsewhere, but the other teaches and reminds the soul how high its birth and value are, and this is prior to the other one and when it is clarified will also make the other obvious. (V.1.1)[7]

There are many features of this passage deserving our attention. First, there is the ambiguity of the use of the term ἀρχή, meaning "beginning" as well as "principle." Both meanings can be applied to beings in time. The former meaning can be applied to that which is eternal only metaphorically.

Next, let us note that Plotinus describes the ἀρχή of evil in four ways: audacity,[8] coming to birth, first otherness, and wishing to belong to themselves. The focus of this passage is clearly individual souls. But individual souls have undescended intellects. One might suppose then that the beginnings or principles of evil have to be understood differently for each. For the undescended intellects, the story about the beginning of evil for them would be part of the larger story of their generation, elaborated no doubt for heuristic purposes.

The notion of metaphorical evil is, however, obscure. It is not, I think, equivalent to intelligible matter. The obscurity arises from the fact that evil is a principle of unintelligibility. How could it then be present in the intelligible realm? Some scholars have held that behind the metaphorical representation of evil in Intellect must be some literal meaning. In that case, a discarnate intellect would want to overcome its otherness and repent of its audacity, and so on. But that would mean that the true ideal self for an endowed self is not an ideal after all. I shall argue in the last section of this chapter that this view is mistaken. For the moment I shall only refer to the ambiguity of the term ἀρχή and note that an ἀρχή as principle stands apart from that of which it is a principle. Therefore, if, for example, "first otherness" in Intellect is an ἀρχή of evil in one sense, that does not mean that there is evil in the lives of undescended intellects.

I have already argued that there is no evil in Intellect or in the intelligible realm generally. Thus, to say that the ἀρχή of evil for souls was "first otherness" need only mean that it is owing to Intellect and the Forms internal to it that endowed selves are enmeshed in matter. We can trace evil back to the hypothetical necessity entailed by the nature of imagery. The One's creative activity works through the instrumentality of Intellect to produce images of Intellect which must contain matter. Intellect becomes the ἀρχή of evil for incarnate individuals precisely because such images are multiply deficient. They must have bodies which include matter and they must have souls which are the sources of desire, irrational as well as rational. Vice is the downward trajectory towards evil of a soul that is malleable in its imitation of Intellect.

We notice that after the description of the ἀρχή of evil for souls, the remainder of the passage deals exclusively with these souls, that is, with incarnate individuals. They, not the undescended intellect of each, have literally forgotten their origin. Evil is what they are drawn towards as a consequence of incarnation. But this does not make incarnation vicious or culpable unless we deliberately connect it with punishment for sins in a previous incarnation. As I have argued, even if Plotinus affirmed this rather than just considered it speculatively, it is not equivalent to making an initial incarnation a sin committed in the discarnate state. There is no vice (or virtue) in Intellect, and the realm of Intellect is the only location for a discarnate soul.[9]

Still, one might want to argue that at the time of writing an early treatise such as V.1 Plotinus would have believed that a putative initial incarnation had better not have taken place at all. This is how E. R. Dodds understands our passage. He argues that it indicates a certain pessimism in Plotinus which is to be accounted for by the influence of Numenius and his still friendly association with Gnostics.[10] Dodds claims that after Plotinus' break with Gnosticism, he came to view the descent of the soul in a more favorable light, considering it as rather more spontaneous and natural than sinful. I do not see this discontinuity of thought in the treatises. On the one hand, I think that Plotinus was fairly pessimistic about the fate of most incarnate individuals throughout his life. On the other hand, I think he also consistently believed that incarnation itself is part of the orderly operation of nature and that to despise it is, finally, to assume a self-defeating position in relation to the One.[11]

In this way Plotinus actually undercuts the legitimacy of the question, what is the point of an initial incarnation if the goal of life is just to return to an eternal discarnate state which is not in the slightest improved by one's sojourn here below? The "point" of all creation is the limitless activity of the One. Then if we ask why does the One produce limitlessly, the answer for Plotinus is, appropriately enough, a recapitulation of the argument for the existence and nature of an ἀρχή of all.

Further, the goal of life is to identify eternally with Intellect which is related to the Good through contemplation. This is what our discarnate intellects are doing eternally. Given that an endowed self comes to be, in whatever manner, it is better for it that it be united with its true ideal self than that it not be so united. It is certainly not better for *me*, endowed self that I am, that I had not existed. It also seems incoherent to hold that it would have been better had the Good not operated as it does in producing, among other things, a multitude of endowed selves.

The impediments to return to the Good – forgetting the father and ignorance of self – are in fact the same. For removing the impediment of ignorance of self amounts to recognition of the ideal self as contemplator, that which attains the Good through association with Intellect.[12] The return to the One is perfect identification with the One's secondary activity. I take it that this is the main point of the metaphor of father in this passage. Return to Intellect is identifying with that with which we are genetically related. The claim then that there is true religion is based on the claim that the ideal self is objectively determined. Identification with it is the goal of rational desire. Authentic religious practices are those which abet this goal. False religious practices are those which only appear to do so.

At the end of the passage Plotinus indicates that the principal technique for promoting true religion is to remind people of their exalted parentage. It is clear enough in the text that hearing and understanding the reminder is not equivalent to religion itself, much less to having its aim. The problem here is what it would mean to acknowledge that one's true ideal self is what it is said to be without actually identifying with it. I believe that the putative gap here revealed indicates a shrewd psychological insight by Plotinus. There is a great difference among persons, one of whom says that he has no interest in being a person of a certain kind, another one of whom says that he wants to be such a person but is not and perhaps does not know how to be, and yet another, who is or is becoming that person.

I believe that in this passage Plotinus is thinking about the second case, the person who can be made to desire to be what Plotinus regards the true ideal self as being. What reason has he for believing that such a desire should be capable of being elicited? The only answer can be that there is a sufficient amount of the true ideal self in the endowed self that one can recognize the proposed ideal as authentically one's own. But how is one supposed to recognize as authentically oneself that which, by hypothesis, is only available to one via a description of its activities? In other words, to recommend a self to someone is to recommend a way of living, an activity or spectrum of activities which someone, being the self he is right now, can appreciate as personally desirable. But this is as much as to recommend the true ideal life to the endowed incarnate self, a recommendation which might reasonably enough seem quite unattractive.

In speaking about the ascent to the One as a return to and remembering of the father and in identifying this with self-knowledge, Plotinus is relying on the Platonic doctrine that the relation between the endowed and the true ideal selves is a relation of image to model. So, the recommendation of the ideal life may be supposed to appeal to the self because the endowed self contains a synonymous image of the ideal self and therefore bears a structural similarity to it. Specifically, the activity of self-knowledge in the endowed self is a synonymous image of the activity of self-knowledge in Intellect. What self-knowledge means for the endowed self is knowledge that its identity is that of a rational agent. The ideal and endowed selves then cannot be viewed as if they were like two different endowed selves. Hence, it is supposed that the aspirant who acquires self-knowledge will gradually realize that what he at first did not want at all is what he really wanted all along. In coming to desire a way of life, he comes to desire identification with the true ideal self.[13] It is not supposed that he is being asked to do what is probably psychologically impossible, namely, to desire to become another self altogether.

The other technique alluded to by Plotinus for promoting true religion is to produce dishonor (ἀτιμίαν) for the things now honored by the soul. One must here avoid an incautious over-interpretation of Plotinus' meaning. What he means at least (and perhaps no more) is that an appropriate device for eliciting recognition of one's true ideal self is detachment from the things and activities whereby one is inclined to constitute a self as other than that true ideal. If one regards, say, luxurious living as an ideal for oneself, then one is facing a formidable impediment to the recognition of the true ideal. But to dishonor luxurious living is only to reject it as contributing essentially to the ideal life. The response elicited by such dishonor need not be anything so extreme as revulsion. Dishonoring luxurious living as irrelevant to the ideal life may even be compatible with honoring its elements, like beauty, at the same time (II.9.16).

The decline of the soul may, without further qualification, imply either a previous incarnate state or a discarnate one. I have argued that decline from a discarnate state has no meaning for Plotinus. This is not to say, however, that reincarnation is an essential part of his eschatology. Nevertheless, the evidence strongly suggests that Plotinus did in fact believe in reincarnation. It is just that his description of the burdens of incarnation and the remedy for these does not seem to require that we employ the concept of reincarnation. The concept does seem relevant, however, if like Plotinus we wish to give sense to the notion of failure to achieve the ideal or to the notion of punishment for a badly conducted life. If, for example, death resulted in the automatic reuniting of the endowed self with its true ideal counterpart, a good life strategy might be to devote oneself wholeheartedly to the satisfaction of the desires of the incarnate individual so long as one was able to do so. For Plotinus, such a strategy is more than flawed; it is pathetic. But this can only be because there are unavoidable bad consequences for so constructing one's ideal self.

The problem here is not so much with proposing reincarnation as the bad consequence, as it is with identifying the judge who imposes the punishment. We might suppose that the punishment is self-imposed in the sense that the wicked, newly discarnate agent simply cannot bear life as a contemplator. So, he throws himself back into the only milieu in which he finds comfort and satisfaction. As we saw at the end of chapter 8, this is why Plotinus posits a temporary discarnate state for self-judging. It is remarkable that the acid test is memory. One who has constructed an ideal life which is synonymous with the true ideal can see the rejection of memorial identity as the last step of progress. One who clings to this form of identity must face reincarnation. He is unwilling to refer to an eternal intellect and say "that is me."

Thus return is also discovery. Paradoxically, the idea is of a return to what we are, not a return to what we were.[14] The latter would be intelligible for Plotinus only in relation to a previous incarnate state. There is indeed a decline, viewing the matter ontologically: one state is inferior to the other even though there is an identity between the subject of both states. And just as an instance of a Form, when abstracted from its material manifestations, is nothing but the nature of the Form itself, so an endowed self when divested of all attachment to the animate body is nothing but an eternal intellect.

Consider Adam. After the Fall, he finds himself in a state of decline. It is not just his circumstances that have changed, of course. *He* has changed as well. There is little difficulty in understanding what it would mean to say that he desires to return to his pre-fallen state and to his pre-fallen self. From Plotinus' perspective, however, that pre-fallen state would just be the state of another endowed self.[15] If it were truly the state of an ideal self, then there

209

would be no possibility of his having fallen from it. As incarnate individuals, we are separated from our ideal state. To speak of this separation as a decline is to indicate that the ideal state is a state that we did possess. Now eliminate the implied temporal element and substitute an analogue of the Platonic idea of the relation between model and copy for the subject of the ideal state and the subject of the declined state. The idea is to recover oneself, but this is not a recovery of the endowed self. It is a recovery of what in one sense we (the endowed self) never were and yet in another sense what we (the ideal self) eternally are. We (the endowed self) are not necessarily guilty or responsible for the state we are in, although it most definitely is our problem. If we diligently practice true religion, we can reverse the decline.[16]

The solution to the problem raised earlier regarding a man's reincarnation into an animal is solved by the rejection of Aristotelian essentialism, the distinction of soul and self, and the use of the concept of activity in explaining the complexity of the soul. A human who was reincarnated as an animal engages in a subset of activities from among all the activities that make up soul. Another subset, those involving reason, are dormant, presumably somehow capable of being reactivated sometime after death.[17] Perhaps we should add as a possibility that reincarnation in a particular kind of body makes the activation of rational powers impossible, though we should insist that the soul of a man is the same kind of thing as the soul of an animal.[18]

If decline is just embodiment, it would be a mistake to try to explain the corrupt state as being independent of embodiment and then to fix embodiment as the punishment.[19] Plotinus is speaking about the endowed self. The corrupt state of the self, which must be properly diagnosed before a strategy for its elimination can be prescribed, is an embodied one. The descriptive phrases, especially "wishing to belong to themselves," need to be glossed by the remainder of the passage. They suggest a fundamental misconception about personal identity. Why is this the mistake uniquely characteristic of the embodied self? Because someone who thinks that his ideal self is an embodied self will inevitably end up subordinating himself to something other than his true self, namely, some reputedly ideal state of that organic body.

This is an extraordinary claim. I interpret Plotinus to mean that the endowed self is at least inclined to identify itself as the subject of desire for bodily possessions and for bodily states. To desire something is to subordinate oneself to it in the sense of one's incompleteness or imperfection relative to the object of desire or relative to the state in which the object of desired is attained. For example, to take the case of luxurious living once again, if one desires this, one claims that to be a luxurious liver is to be superior to what one is at present. But all the states of the endowed self belong to the class of "things which come into being and perish." If I desire to be in a certain state, it is clear enough that there is a real distinction between "I" and that state even though that state is one in which I will be the subject. That is, we need not foist upon Plotinus the inherently dubious interpretation according to which he imagines that I subordinate myself to some thing in the sense that I would be content to be obliterated so long as that thing or "possession" were to survive or to be realized. If I am right in understanding the corruption as essentially a function of embodiment, then it would seem correct to say that endowed selves naturally or spontaneously desire future states of endowed selves, states which are transitory.

I think we must interpret Plotinus this way if we are to account for his decidedly lukewarm endorsement of "political virtue." The politically virtuous man, though he would presumably discriminate among possible future states on the basis of some vague attachment to non-transitory principles, nevertheless pursues a life according to a spurious conception of the ideal self. This is the only plausible explanation of why Plotinus could hold the apparently repugnant position that the detached contemplator, utterly indifferent to his surroundings, is superior to an altruistically or civic-minded individual who sees himself *ideally* as a beneficent contributor to a community of endowed selves. The misconception of the ideal self attained by the practice of ordinary virtue is, as we have seen, not entirely without value. And Plotinus is correct on these grounds to see such virtue as a mark of progress in true religion, although only to the extent that it is recognized as being removed from the true goal.

When Plotinus condemns individuals for failing to honor themselves, he obviously means their true ideal selves. This is apparently a striking departure from the import of one of the most remarkable speeches in all of Plato's writings. In *Laws* 731d6–732b4 Plato has the Athenian Stranger declare that the greatest evil for men is excessive self-love. By contrast, a man who aims for greatness must care neither for his self nor for his possessions, but for justice, whether practiced by himself or by someone else. It seems evident that this justice is part of what Plotinus would call ordinary or lower virtue. Plato does not in his speech give any inkling that justice is inferior to a "higher" self-love. Of course, we can soften the sharp contrast between what Plato says and what Plotinus says by holding that Plotinus' conception of the highest virtue and true religion is not properly called self-love at all, but love of the Good. I grant that there is something in this and that the context of the *Laws* is perhaps not the appropriate place to expect to find promotion of the contemplative life. Still, Plato seems to have a higher regard for ordinary virtue and its potential selflessness than does Plotinus.

In sum, Plotinus' religion can be defined as those practices which "teach and remind the soul how high its birth and value are" and secondarily, "show how contemptible are the things now honored by the soul." In this regard Plotinus asks what is the method (μέθοδος) or practice (ἐπιτήδευσις) which leads us up to the One. He answers that the demonstrations of the existence of the One are themselves a kind of ascent to the One (I.3.1.1–5).[20] He is not saying that the demonstrations result in true religion or even in subsequent conversion. These demonstrations are themselves part of the process (see

VI.9.10).[21] He evidently means the activity of working through such demonstrations, which presumably has the effect of producing recognition in the self of its true nature and parentage.

It is quite startling to see philosophical theology proposed as a means of self-analysis. The Stoics alone among Plotinus' predecessors would be likely to have warmed to such a notion. But that is because the Stoics are pantheists and so self-knowledge is identical with knowledge of the divine. It is fair to say that not everyone has a taste for philosophical theology and that even if they do, they would not necessarily approach it in the spirit in which Plotinus thinks most useful. He is open to other methods of ascent (I.3.1.11–12). The principal alternative for him is appreciation of beauty.

2 Beauty

The ἀρχή of all, the One, is, as object of desire, the Good itself. As object of a desire that has been satisfied, the One is Beauty.

> The man who has not seen it may desire it [the One] as good, but he who has seen it glories in its beauty and is full of wonder and delight, enduring a shock which causes no hurt, loving with true passion and piercing longing. (I.6.7.14–18)

Strictly speaking, of course, "Beauty" is an improper way of naming the ἀρχή of all, as are "Good" and "One." The proper referent of the beautiful is the intelligible realm, and "beauty" is used of the first cause by analogy (I.6.9.40–3).[22] Thus, just as the desire for good is the desire to be associated with Intellect in contemplating Forms, so beauty is that aspect of intelligible reality that produces delight in the contemplator when contemplation is occurring.[23] This delight is the eternal endowment of an intellect. It is what aspirants here below can only have intimations of. One who has such intimations presumably needs no religious conversion. His need for Plotinian religion would seem to be limited to those practices, particularly higher virtue, which will remove any residual attachments to incarnate existence.

Because beauty is a property of Forms as contemplated, images of Forms possess images of that property. Images of beauty are found in bodies, and generally in objects of sight; objects of other senses; ways of life; actions; characters; and virtue (I.6.1). Formally, it is participation in a Form that makes bodies beautiful; soul is the instrumental efficient cause of that participation (I.6.2.13; see also V.9.2.19–20). The beauty in soul comes from Intellect; the beauty in everything else comes from souls (I.6.6.27–9). Forms in nature are produced by the soul of the universe; artistic forms and the lower virtues are produced by incarnate individuals.

Beauty in the soul, that is, virtue, is true beauty compared with the beauty produced by soul (I.6.4.12–15). The superiority of the immaterial beauty of soul to the sensible beauty produced by soul is owing to their relative proximity to the paradigm of beauty, Intellect. Souls become beautiful by being in love with Intellect. And the inculcation of love for a beautiful soul is the beginning of love for that which made the soul beautiful. First, one loves the image. Second, one recognizes it to be an image, and transfers the love to the real thing.

Perhaps surprisingly, in a much later treatise Plotinus also claims that artistic beauty is superior to natural beauty, counter to what Plato says in book 10 of the *Republic*. That is, the beauty produced by incarnate individuals is better even than that produced by the soul of the universe (V.8.1). Plotinus asks us to compare two stones, one untouched by human hands and the other sculpted into an image of some man or god. The latter is superior, that is, more beautiful, just because it imitates Intellect doubly, as stone and as art. Perhaps another implicit reason for the superiority in beauty is that the product of conscious imitation is closer to the activity of Intellect than is the product of non-conscious imitation. One is more keenly aware of a soul at work when regarding works of art than when regarding works of nature. The former delights us more than the latter because it is closer to the paradigm of delight, self-reflexive awareness of Forms.

Plotinus understands the account of beauty that he is developing as being in opposition to the widely accepted identification of beauty with good proportion or symmetry plus good color (I.6.1.20ff.). The objections to this view are basically two: it does not account for the beauty of simple objects and it does not account for immaterial beauty. Both objections are seemingly straightforward.[24] The second one depends on the Platonic principle that a Form is univocally present in all its instances. So, if the definition of beauty in bodies cannot be applied to beauty in souls, then the definition is defective. It cannot be so applied to souls, because though the soul has parts in some sense, there is no obvious formula for their putative proportion that could equally be applied to bodies.

On reflection, however, the refusal to identify beauty, even bodily beauty, with symmetry is somewhat puzzling. As we have seen, matter is unmeasuredness or absence of symmetry and form is a kind of symmetry. And Plotinus seems to treat bodily beauty as precisely owing to the participation in form (see I.6.2.13–14). Indeed, he goes on to say that beauty in a body results when the parts are brought into a unity, presumably the complex unity that is naturally understood as symmetry. And ugliness is just the absence of domination of matter by form (I.6.2.16–18. See also I.6.3.17–19).

Plotinus is only slightly more forthcoming in a later treatise when he identifies beauty as "what illuminates symmetry rather than the symmetry itself, and this is what is lovable" (VI.7.22.24–6). As his subsequent examples show, what illuminates symmetry is soul. This is in line with the account above, where all beauty is in soul or produced by soul. Beauty, however, cannot then be "illuminated" symmetry, for as we have seen, the definition of beauty as symmetry is rejected because there are beautiful things

213

in which symmetry plays no part. Rather, it seems that beauty is just the illuminating or operation of soul whether it produces symmetry or not. It is this that produces delight. It does so, as Plotinus says in the same passage, because it is "somehow colored by the light of the Good."[25] The implication of the operation of soul in the beautiful would explain why artistic beauty surpasses natural beauty. In the former case, the operation of soul is more evident. It would explain the previous characterization of beauty and ugliness as domination and absence of domination of matter by form. The domination of matter by form is actually the domination of matter by soul with the instrument of form. It will be recalled that "nature," the product of Soul, refers in one sense to form (III.8.2.29; IV.4.13.1–7; IV.6.3.5–7). Domination and illumination are two metaphors indicating the same activity.

Most importantly, the above account would explain why souls do in fact delight in bodily beauty and not just in psychic beauty. Such beauty evokes a response of recognition in the soul. The soul recognizes what is akin (συγγενὲς) to it, namely, an active soul, and delights in the recognition (I.6.2.7–11. See also III.5.1.16–19). The recognition is delightful because it produces a sort of resonance in the soul.[26] And this resonance is pleasurable. Even the recognition of bodily beauty that inspires the desires of the organic composite can be so explained, though their satisfaction has nothing to do with beauty.

The distinction between apparent and real beauty, hence the distinction between a spurious and a true delight, depends on making precise what domination of matter by soul through form means.[27] Apparent beauty must be ugliness, not an image of beauty, for either form dominates matter or it does not. This domination must be something like the successful production of a synonymous image of a Form. Purely homonymous images, like symbolic representations of Forms, are neither beautiful nor ugly on this account. But the activities of soul which produce them can be recognized as such. According to this distinction, one who takes delight in a body where form incompletely dominates matter is experiencing a false pleasure. The recognition is spurious. It is just a false belief if one supposes that the ugly has actually resonated with one's soul.

Plotinus curiously remarks that some lovers "fall into ugliness and they too do so because of beauty" (III.5.1.63). And he adds, "for in fact the desire for good often involves the fall into evil." Someone who "falls into ugliness" may have begun with an attachment to bodily beauty but later comes to take delight in the ugly. But why is this "because of beauty"? Plotinus does not say why, but the answer may be connected to his discussion of another kind of error earlier in the chapter. It is the error of someone who mistakes bodily beauty for true beauty.[28] Such a person errs in taking an image for what it is an image of. In so doing, he misdirects his desire for the Good. Perhaps then the fall into ugliness is the natural result of mistaking an image of beauty, bodily beauty, for true immaterial beauty.

214

The root of the error of the person who thus begins a downward slide is not in holding a false belief about a beautiful body, but in failing to contextualize his true belief. He is even beyond reproach if he holds that that which he has rightly judged to be beautiful is good. His mistake is in thinking that in delighting in something that is good, he is delighting in goodness itself. But this is false. The satisfaction and delight in that which is good are only an image of its paradigm. The descent into ugliness begins when delight in bodily beauty does not produce the desired satisfaction. That could only be produced by our identification with that which is higher than soul. Only in Intellect is the desire of the endowed self perfectly satisfied. That someone who begins by mistaking an image for its paradigm eventually falls into ugliness shows that there is but one road in which the Good and its opposite are termini. If one is not advancing towards the one, then one is advancing towards the other.[29]

When Plotinus speaks about "the error of falling into sexual intercourse" we must understand this along the lines of the error of falling into ugliness (III.5.1.38). If, on the one hand, sexual intercourse is ugly, then the logic of Plotinus' argument requires that he renounce it unqualifiedly. On the other hand, however, he also praises sex which is inspired by a love of beauty (III.5.1.55–62). The right interpretation then seems to be that all depends on whether the delight in sex is correctly viewed as an image or mistakenly viewed as the paradigm itself. Sexual intercourse is not unqualifiedly condemned by Plotinus. In this respect, his view should be distinguished from that of the more extreme ascetics. His relatively moderate view is that the desirability of sexual intercourse can only be properly evaluated according to whether it abets or inhibits ascent to the Good. Perhaps even if it does not abet the ascent, it is acceptable so long as it does not inhibit it. Unfortunately, this is often something not easy to determine except after the fact.

We can explain in the same way Plotinus' striking belief that intelligible beauty can distract us from the Good (V.5.12.36–7). Certainly, no discarnate intellect experiences such a distraction. It is those endowed selves who have intimations of intellectual beauty through the work of their own intellects who are susceptible if they do not at the same time recognize the subordination of Intellect to the Good. I suppose Plotinus would have thought that Aristotle was a stellar example of someone so misled. In general, it would seem that any example of beauty can be instrumental in the ascent to the Good or it can be an impediment depending on whether that beauty's proper place in the hierarchy of reality is understood or not.

The description of the goal of the ascent as a vision of Beauty is given in a dramatic passage:

> Here the greatest, the ultimate contest is set before our souls; all our toil and trouble is for this, not to be left without a share in the best of visions. The man who attains this is blessed in seeing that "blessed

sight," and he who fails to attain it has failed utterly. A man has not failed if he fails to win beauty of colors or bodies, or power or office or kingship even, but if he fails to win this and only this. For this he should give up the attainment of kingship and of rule over all earth and sea and sky, if only by leaving and overlooking them he can turn to That and see. (I.6.7.30–9)

This passage describes and promotes qualifiedly a world-renouncing conversion. The conditional clause in the last sentence leaves open the possibility that total renunciation of worldliness is not the only way to achieve the blessed sight. We can clarify the alternatives, however, and remove the conditionality if we describe them as opposite orientations. The opposites are: embodied states as strictly instrumental and subordinate to the disembodied state of eternal contemplation and embodied states as held to be intrinsically desirable. If the alternatives are stated thus, there is no doubt that Plotinus believes that one cannot have it both ways. The second alternative, no matter how described, is inferior to the first because they are just further states of an incarnated soul.

Let us remember that this call to holiness, if we may describe it as such, is located in the middle of a discussion of beauty. This remarkable association of the religious with the aesthetic is not of course uniquely Plotinian. But it is so to say naturally Plotinian. The most insignificant instance of physical beauty, a patch of color, for example, is directly connected to the source of beauty itself, as image to model. And if beauty is one dimension or facet of the universe, progress in appreciation of beauty results in achieving the goal of religion.

What is it that enables one man to appreciate non-bodily beauty and another not? It is the state of the soul. If the soul is not in a state akin to the non-bodily beauty with which it is confronted, then it cannot experience the delight caused by recognition of this kinship (I.6.9.29–30. See also V.8.2.42–5).[30] One cannot see god and beauty without first becoming godlike and beautiful. This explains why some are indifferent to non-bodily beauty, but it does not explain why someone who is indifferent owing to his non-beautiful soul should want to become a soul that delights in the beauty of other souls. Evidently, Plotinus thinks that it makes sense to exhort such a soul to self-improvement (I.6.9.7–15). He exhorts his imaginary interlocutor to "go back into himself" and if he does not see a beautiful soul, to undertake a project of self-construction until he is at home with himself in purity (σαυτῷ καθαρὸς συνεγένου) and a whole self (ὅλος αὐτὸς) emerges (I.6.9.15–18).[31] In other words, perfection here is viewed as an achievement in self-construction. What could the perfect achievement be other than to become identified with the true ideal self?

I take "at home with oneself in purity" to indicate a perfect coincidence between what the self thinks it wants and what it really or ideally wants. Only then is it in a position to recognize the beauty in another soul and in its activities. The "whole self" is one with a unity of purpose. It is a life that really makes sense because it has ordered the disjointed desires of the endowed self. The rational desire to be eternally an agent of rational activity is in charge.

The exhortation to become the sort of person who delights in things hitherto found undelightful only makes sense if there is the unusual sort of personal continuity we have discovered between the endowed and the true ideal self. It is not an exhortation to a conversion to a *different* self, which at any rate seems incoherent. Logically, it does not seem possible for a person to want to become something which would recognize no continuity with the previous self. If one were to want this, it would presumably make sense to ask why. And the answer, in order to be intelligible, would have to leave enough of the self after the fact for there to be continuity with the previous self. For example, if one said, "I want to become a physician," it would be perfectly sensible to reply to the question "why?" by saying, "So I will be respected or fulfilled" or whatever. I do not see how any similarly intelligible answer could be supplied when what is wanted is for a new individual to come into being, entailing the destruction of the old one and so discontinuity with it.

If this is so, then the exhortation to self-construction, which is at the same time an exhortation to the appreciation of beauty hitherto insufficiently appreciated, is based on the confidence of such continuity. The principal reason for confidence supplied is that everyone, even bad souls, sometimes experiences non-bodily beauty.

Surely, an important facet of Plotinus' religion is education and habituation which cultivates such experience. Plotinus advises different approaches for the lovers of beautiful sounds, called musicians (μουσικοί), and the anonymous lovers of the visual beauty of bodies (I.3.1–2).[32] In both cases the strategy is to lead them by reasoning to see the true cause of their delight, namely, the recognition of that which they unknowingly already possess (I.3.1.34). Once delight is revealed as delight in an image, one will be immediately drawn to the real thing.[33] This suggests that even if everyone from time to time experiences non-bodily beauty, the reason why mass self-conversions are not occurring every day is that people do not normally relate bodily and non-bodily beauty as image to model. Rather, they view these as various species within a genus. So, one who doffs his hat to the virtuous soul sees no regress or irony in then turning to beautiful bodies. He simply prides himself on his catholic tastes.

The important distinction between images of true beauty and true beauty itself suggests an analogous distinction between the beauty of Intellect and the source of beauty, the One (see I.6.7.1–30). Is there in fact such a distinction? Is it desirable or even possible that just as we are bidden to go beyond virtue to Intellect, we ought to go beyond Intellect to the Good itself?

217

The answer to these questions takes us on to very rocky terrain, that of Plotinus' so-called mysticism.

3 Mysticism and Philosophy

The reader of this book will perhaps have already experienced some puzzlement over my lack of attention to an important feature of his philosophy, namely, his mysticism. The simple explanation is that I have hitherto found no need to introduce the concept of mystical experience and related concepts in order to explain anything in Plotinus. This may surprise some who simply assume that mysticism is more or less what Neo-Platonism is all about.

In this book I do not wish to challenge that assumption for anyone but Plotinus. I am not concerned here with what Plotinus' successors made of his thought or the thought of Plato. On the other hand, I do not deny that there are important features of Plotinus' thought (and life) which are not easily captured by the conceptual categories employed by his predecessors and indeed by Western philosophy generally. Roughly, these pertain to the interstice between the One and Intellect viewed from the perspective of the individual self. Sharing in the life of Intellect or contemplation of Forms can, for example, be explained along Aristotelian lines. That is, Plotinus is talking about the life that Aristotle says god has always and we have occasionally. And no one supposes that Aristotle is being a mystic when he does this. It is true that Plotinus' account of the details of this life is importantly different. But it is still an account based on similar concepts. Further, much of what Plotinus has to say about the One is inspired by Plato and based on arguments which have a lot more to do with scientific realism than they do with mysticism. The elements in Plotinus' thought that can usefully be labeled "mystical" are rather easily isolated from his other epistemological doctrines.

Undoubtedly, what some philosophers have in mind when they allude to Plotinus' mysticism is the report by Porphyry in his *Life of Plotinus* that, while he was with him, his master achieved his goal of being united (ἐνωθῆναι) with god four times (*Life of Plotinus* 23.15–16).[34] There is also Porphyry's report that in his 39th year Plotinus planned to join the expedition of the Emperor Gordian to Persia in order to make a study of Persian and Indian thought (3.13–19). The expedition was aborted and Plotinus never did make the excursion. It would surely be a mistake to conflate his curiosity about Eastern thought with an actual incorporation of features of it into his own, without substantial supporting evidence.

Let us begin by distinguishing (1) Plotinus' personal experience as mentioned by Porphyry, (2) his account of the method preparatory to such an experience, in so far as it is something one can prepare for, and (3) the doctrines associated with the experience. If we approach the issue of Plotinus' mysticism in this way, it is easy to bring the discussion to a rapid conclusion.

For (2), the answer is basically education in beauty, the practice of virtue, and theoretical philosophy. For (3), the answer is truly and without exaggeration all of the doctrines discussed in this book. As for (1), there really is not much to say about experience that is in the nature of the case ineffable.[35]

Of course, there is somewhat more to the matter than just this. The fact that Plotinus had four distinct mystical experiences of the One already tells us a lot. Their transitory character distinguishes them sharply from the eternal primary activity of Intellect and, more importantly, from the experience of an individual self in communion with Intellect. In the case of Intellect and the self, we have already seen that they attain the Good in so far, and only in so far, as they contemplate Forms. If Plotinus' personal experiences were something other than this, as they seem to have been, then they are a sort of accidental feature of his philosophy. By this I mean that all of his attention to the ascent of the self to Intellect, from the outer to the inner and from the lower to the higher, is directed not to producing occasional visions or states, but rather to more enduring states of contemplation.[36] Indeed, "enduring" is hardly an adequate description of the eternal. It is true that the discarnate state that the philosopher can look forward to is bound to be qualitatively different from particular intuitions of eternal truth and that the latter provides only an inkling of the former. But it is also true that the discarnate state that is the goal of all incarnate activity is not a mystical experience if this is understood as a "leap" beyond Forms to their virtual source.

Another important feature of a putative mystical experience of the One is that, owing to what the One is and to the nature of all cognition, including the highest, this experience is trans-cognitional. Recall that the activity of Intellect is the paradigm of cognition. So, all cognition implies a residual duality of subject and object, as we have seen. And the only way to experience the One as an object distinct from that subject is via the intelligible objects. There is no doubt that the "unspeakable actuality" of Plotinus' mystical experience, as Porphyry calls it, is not cognitive identity with all Forms, for *that* is described by Plotinus at length. The problem in characterizing this experience is analogous to the problem encountered earlier in characterizing the activity of the One, which is super-cognitional.[37] What is needed is an appropriate language to indicate an experience which can only be represented cognitively in demonstration and in contemplation of Forms by Intellect.

Further, there is no indication either in Porphyry's account or in the treatises themselves that an experience such as Plotinus himself underwent would henceforth obviate the need for continual striving to identify with the true ideal self. A glimpse of the transcendent, as we might describe that experience, still leaves the incarnate individual with a residually disassociated self. The mere fact alone that after having undergone his mystical experience Plotinus could continue to engage in discursive reasoning testifies to this.[38] Certainly, what he longed for was permanent union, something besides which the four episodes must pale by comparison. The interesting question is whether the goal of permanent union is to be conceived as qualitatively different from those transitory visions. I have argued that it is, for the permanent union is to be conceived of as cognitive union, which is just the relation of Intellect to the One through the intelligibles.[39] Consequently, the value of Plotinus' mystical experience beyond the momentary delight in beauty itself and the lingering memory of that delight must remain problematic. Perhaps its chief value lay in its confirmation of the correctness of his approach and as a foretaste of eternal delight.

As for any benefit to others, Plotinus' personal mystical experiences seem to be nugatory. They are ineffable, and so incapable of being used as confirming evidence for anyone else. It is true that Plotinus apparently lived an exemplary life and even inspired the conversion of others by example as well as precept. One should not discount out of hand how impressive a way of life can be as evidence for the truth of a theory, particularly when the way of life is so closely tied to the theory. Nevertheless, Plotinus' exemplary life is quite distinct from his four isolated mystical experiences, as least in so far as that life could affect others.

It is important to stress that, in sharp contrast to the doctrines of many mystics, Plotinus' own experience or even a claim he might have made that such an experience is possible for anyone are logically disengaged from his entire philosophy.[40] That is, his experience of union with the One is not a substitute for a proof of its existence, nor is its possibility entailed by it. Nothing in that experience is taken to disclose what is not otherwise knowable, apart from the knowledge by acquaintance that the experience involves. If one simply ignores that experience, the arguments, including those pertaining to Intellect and the One and the true ideal self, remain intact and open to inspection. Certainly, the invitation to detachment from the endowed self and to ascent to an ideal self is not usefully or fairly identified as an extrusion of mystical experience as opposed to a consequence of metaphysical, epistemological, and psychological arguments.

It might perhaps be objected that my discounting of the importance of Plotinus' personal mystical experience misses the mark. There is another facet of his philosophy that might usefully be termed mystical, namely, the concept of θεωρία or contemplation. Indeed, far from holding that contemplation is unique or idiosyncratic, Plotinus is at least prepared to consider the possibility that "all things desire to contemplate" (III.8.1.2).[41] Surely, this dark saying, whether we call it "mystical" or not, lends an unusual cast to his overall account of this world. What are we to make of it?

Contemplation is the name of the primary activity of Intellect. Consequently, whatever else engages in contemplation besides Intellect is said to do so in a derivative sense determined by its nature (III.8.1.4–5). Even the contemplative activity of embodied selves is not the same thing as the activity of Intellect. Only the true ideal self, of which we are not conscious, is a perfect contemplator because it is identical with Intellect. When in the *Symposium* the story is told by Alcibiades about Socrates standing transfixed in one place and lost in thought, his contemplation was not primary contemplation (220cff.). There is, however, a distinction among forms of contemplation derived from the primary. The distinction is between what those do who possess intellect, namely, endowed selves, and everything else. Because endowed selves, and they alone, are ideally members of a community of discarnate intellects, they are able to engage in a form of contemplation unavailable to everything else.[42]

At this point, it must be recalled that it is not exactly true that lower members of the metaphysical hierarchy actually possess higher members or their properties. On the contrary, the One possesses Intellect, Intellect possesses Soul, and Soul possesses the body that is nature (see V.5.9.31–2). So, when Plotinus entertains the speculative notion that everything contemplates, he is considering the consequences that what is possessed (the lower) manifests the properties of the possessor (the higher). Elsewhere, he does exactly the same thing for the One. He says that everything is one derivatively by the presence of the One (see III.8.10; VI.9.9.7–11). Nothing is cut off from it, but nothing is identical with it either. Everything other than the One exists because the One is present to it. Similarly, whatever is beneath Soul, until we come to matter, manifests derivatively the property of Soul in some way. The ordered hierarchy modulates the manifestation of the higher in the lower. That is, Intellect is the highest form of manifestation of the One, Soul is the highest form of the manifestation of Intellect and a lower form of manifestation of the One, and so on.

The idea that everything contemplates is meant to be explored as one facet of the hierarchy. Contemplation is paradigmatically a property of Intellect. It is the activity by which it eternally attains what it desires, namely, the Good (III.8.11.23–4). Accordingly, the desire to contemplate in everything else should be another name for the manifestation of the activity of desiring the Good. Only in the paradigmatic case, however, is the desire for the Good coincident with the attainment of it. Actual contemplation in everything else should be the attainment of the Good to the extent that their natures allow.

Further, the identity of Intellect and οὐσία means that whatever participates in or possesses οὐσία possesses Intellect in some sense. This is what Aristotle *should* have said when he concluded that primary entity was self-thinking intellect and that the being of everything else is to be understood in terms of that which is primary. For Plotinus, participation in οὐσία without participation in Intellect is logically impossible. We have seen, though, that there are two "tracks" leading to and from Intellect, the one traversed by individual selves and the one traversed by the products of the universal soul, which have no independent access to Intellect. So, the manner in which each can contemplate or participate in Intellect is different. That which belongs exclusively to persons – higher cognitive functioning – cannot then be part of the essence of contemplation. The manner in which persons contemplate is but one species of activity in relation to the Good.

The sign indicating that all things desire the Good is their activity in behalf of a goal, the fulfillment of their natures.[43] Every organism strives to become what it specifically is. The justification for this claim is just the intelligibility and explanatory power of teleological analysis. The sign that there is some measure of attainment of the Good, that is, that a manifestation of contemplation is actually occurring, is production or action.[44] Doing or making must be construed as analogous to the stratification of contemplating itself.

First, we must distinguish the spontaneous or natural consequence of contemplation from a weakening of it, corresponding respectively to true and mimetic contemplation (III.8.4.41–3). The first sort of doing or making is just the secondary activity of the contemplator. The second sort is a corruption of contemplating, for in this case it aims at a state "outside" itself, a state which includes enjoyment of a bodily product. He who engages in bodily actions or in productive activity for its own sake shows an orientation in a direction opposite to that of the Good. We recall here Plotinus' reservations about the benefits of sexual intercourse. Second, we must distinguish among various forms of the weakening of contemplation corresponding to forms of the images of contemplation, including presumably artistic creations.

Where do we draw the line between consequence and weakening of contemplation? Plotinus says that it is drawn between Intellect and Soul or more precisely between the actions done as a result of the use of Intellect and all psychic actions (III.8.5.19–22).[45] Such action is a weakening of contemplation because the contemplation of soul is merely an image of the true contemplation of Intellect. So, there are two forms of weakening of contemplation, the actions of soul apart from Intellect, and the actions of persons who, having intellects, do not act according to it. In effect, there is little difference between these, for they are species of organic activity. In so far as persons act or produce things as organic individuals, they are comprehensible according to the principles by which nature generally is to be understood. In so far as the endowed self aims to be identified with the true ideal self and partially succeeds in a true form of contemplation, its actions are a consequence of this, not a diminution. The actions undertaken are then directed to further contemplation.[46] The difference between action that is a consequence of contemplation and action that is a weakening of contemplation is in the object desired, either the Good or anything else (III.8.5.36–7).[47]

The claim that everything contemplates, when submitted to scrutiny, amounts to neither animism nor pantheism.[48] But it does rest upon the principle of an integrated hierarchical order within the universe, beginning with the primary ἀρχή and ending at the limit of intelligibility. It attempts to relate all activity to the first principle of all. In answer to the question, "why do things do what they do?" popular replies are either that there is no answer to the question or that they do what they do out of mechanical necessity. The Plotinian answer to this question is not one which is inferior in subtlety or power to either of these. It is not usefully dismissed with the pejorative label "mystical."

It will be recalled that Plotinus distinguishes two "phases" in the production of Intellect, first, its desire for the Good and second, its achievement of that desire in contemplation of Forms. As I argued in chapter 2, these phases must be seen as a logical fiction. We are now finally in a position to see the point of that fiction. Mystical union with the One or Good for an incarnate individual is an image of the first phase.[49] Eternal, discarnate identification with Intellect which we aim for as a result of having that mystical experience is the second phase. We aim for this owing to our experience of the existence of the Good, the ἀρχή of all. There is indeed a logical fiction in speaking of phases of the life of Intellect. What is eternal and perfect is, for us, temporal and imperfect.

There is a widely misread text that actually supports this interpretation.

> Intellect also, then, has one power for thinking, by which it looks at the things in itself, and one by which it looks at what transcends it by a direct awareness and reception (ἐπιβολῇ τινι καὶ παραδοχῇ), by which also before it saw only, and by seeing acquired intellect and is one. And that first one is the contemplation of Intellect in its right mind, and the other is Intellect in love, when it goes out of its mind "drunk with the nectar"; then it falls in love, simplified into happiness by having its fill; and it is better for it to be drunk with a drunkenness like this than to be more respectably sober. (VI.7.35.19–27. See also III.8.9.29–32; V.3.11.4–12; V.4.2.4–7)

The misreading I have in mind is the identification of "Intellect in love" with a "higher" state of Intellect, one which transcends the activity of contemplating the One by means of Forms.[50] In Intellect, it is clear that the power of this direct awareness is the same power in virtue of which Intellect desires the Good "prior" to its achieving what it desires via contemplation. As we have seen, the distinction between desire and achievement is a logical fiction. Even if the state in which Intellect is "drunk" is supposed to be a state logically distinct from the state in which it desires the Good prior to contemplating it, there is no question that it cannot be really other than the eternal state of Intellect, whereby it contemplates Forms. If we ask once again for the point of the logical distinction, then the most natural interpretation is that it is intended to provide the explanation for an experience Plotinus himself had, the transitory intuition of the One.

The most circumspect way of representing this intuition propositionally is to say that the Good is the One.[51] Someone who had this experience is perhaps correctly described in the enthusiastic language used by Plotinus in our text. And though the "drunkenness" of such a person may be better than "a more respectable state," this is analogous to the claim that virtue is better than vice even though it is still inferior to the activity of Intellect. It is not implausible that Plotinus, like others before and after him, should have described himself as "drunk" and "in love" and "blissful" after having had his mystical experiences. But since these experiences are only intimations of the eternal life of Intellect, it is implausible to suppose that they represent the summit of the philosopher's quest.

Some Concluding Remarks

I am aware that this is a difficult book. I wish I could claim that it is all Plotinus' fault. Yet, he should bear some of the blame. His use of the Greek language is often hard to comprehend. His arguments and the exposition of his thought generally are fraught with ambiguity. His treatment of many secondary yet important matters is far from thorough. For example, the doctrine of reincarnation is not smoothly integrated into the main lines of his thought. Despite these difficulties, however, I am convinced that his philosophical achievement is remarkable.

As a critic of Aristotle, Plotinus deserves at least as much attention as does Aristotle as a critic of Plato. The responses to Aristotle's philosophy by his successors have been basically of three sorts: uncritical approbation, contemptuous dismissal, and uninformed criticism. Against this sorry background, Plotinus' achievement is all the more worthy of admiration. Even those who have little patience for his constructive philosophy can profit from reading the *Enneads* as a paradigm of anti-Aristotelianism. The principal feature of this anti-Aristotelianism is the rejection of a substance ontology. From this follow the rejection of the hylomorphic analysis of the human person and the rejection of the absolute primacy of substance in the universe.

Plotinus' demolition of Aristotle's philosophy prepares the way for his own reconstruction of Platonism. Out of the debris he retains a number of Aristotelian distinctions and principles to be put to Platonic purposes. Notable among these are Aristotle's concept of ἐνέργεια and his claim that in the highest form of thinking, there is a kind of identity of subject and object. Calling the result of Plotinus' efforts a "reconstruction" of Platonism is of course tendentious. Plotinus probably did not see himself as an innovator in any serious way. Rather, he saw himself as an expositor and defender of the font of wisdom, Plato's writings. One may usefully compare in this regard a theologian who attempts to systematize what he takes to be the true meaning of his scriptures. For example, the doctrine of the Trinity is not literally in the New Testament. But many theologians believe that that doctrine faithfully represents what is contained in the primary texts. I am glad to leave these hermeneutical questions to others to decide.

The core of Plotinus' reconstructed Platonism as I have interpreted him is the doctrine of instrumental creation and the dualism of endowed and ideal selves. From the first doctrine follows a subtle version of Platonic ontology wherein effect is related to cause as image to model. From the second doctrine follow an austere ethics and religion wherein the goal is to awaken incarnate individuals to a personal goal that is in principle beyond their ability to experience.

The two doctrines are mutually supportive. Although we cannot experience the ideal here below, we possess various images of it. The ideal is thus in a way already ours. Similarly, our discovery that we are at least cognitively an image of an eternal model is a starting-point for the argument for the existence of eternal truth, which in turn is shown to belong to Intellect and to be an image of the creator. The perfect simplicity and unicity of this creator entail that it operates instrumentally. Intellect becomes an instrument of the creation of images. Ordinary human life is lived amidst these images. But it is not cut off from their source or their cause.

I would like to end with the following observation. Most of the readers of this book will recall the time when they were first introduced to Plato, probably as university undergraduates. Many will also recall the thrill of the discovery of Plato's extraordinary doctrines. Sometime later in the term, they encountered Aristotle and his massive attack on Platonism. Typically, one would feel somewhat deflated at this point and persuaded that Aristotle had pretty well laid the Platonic spirit to rest. At this point the young philosopher, Peripatetically inclined though he might be, longed to hear what Plato would have said to Aristotle in his own defense. Could there even be a defense? Alas, Plato himself said nothing. If, however, one still longs to know what a Platonist could or should say to an Aristotelian, there is one outstanding remedy. Read Plotinus.

Notes

Chapter I An Argument for the Existence of a First Principle of All

1 The standard manner of referring to the writings of Plotinus is: *Ennead*, treatise, chapter, and line numbers (according to the critical edition of Henry and Schwyzer). Sometimes the chronological position of the treatise is given in brackets. I have provided a list of these separately.

2 On wisdom, see I.4.9.19; on matter, I.8.15.2; on love, III.5.3.1; on numbers, VI.6.5.17; on relations, VI.1.7.26–7; on time, III.7.13.49; on motion, VI.6.16.41. See Dörrie (1976a: 49, 51), Oosthout (1991: 17–19), and Paoli (1990: 4, 9–10). It is important to realize that treatises V.1, "On the Three Primary Hypostases," and V.3, "On the Knowing Hypostases and That Which is Beyond," are so titled either by Porphyry or by common consent among Plotinus' pupils. They are not Plotinus' own titles, nor do they reflect a technical use of ὑπόστασις by him.

3 At VI.2.13.27–8 the contrast ὑπόστασις – ἐπινοία, meaning extramental and mental existence, is clear. I assume that this contrast is implicit in other passages as well. In any case, I can find no instance where Plotinus uses the term ὑπόστασις for something that exists in thought alone. It has become fashionable among some scholars to characterize Plotinus as an idealist. For example, Lloyd (1990: 126) says that "the hypostases are experiences." For Plotinus, everything besides the One is a dependent existent and therefore the sensible world consists of dependent existents. Further, in a technical sense everything "below" Intellect depends on Intellect (not for its existence but) for that of which Intellect is an ἀρχή or principle. If "idealism" is understood as the doctrine of some sort of mind-dependent existence, then, as I shall try to show in chapter 2, Plotinus is not an idealist.

4 At V.1.8.27 he refers to them as "the three natures" (ταῖς φύσεσι ταῖς τρισίν). See also II.9.1.20.

5 See Rist (1962c) on the many passages in the *Enneads* where Plotinus uses θεός or ὁ θεός for the ἀρχή or first principle. The term θεός refers generally to anything more powerful than humans and everlasting. It is naturally applied to a first principle which, by definition, is contingent on nothing outside itself. Arnou (1967: 133) takes VI.9.8.8, "for a god is what is linked to that center [i.e., the One]," as implying a denial that the One is god. But the context of this passage indicates that Plotinus is referring merely to the relation of gods to the first principle. The investment in this ἀρχή with "personal" attributes must of course be viewed apart from the traditions of the revealed religions. For Plotinus and virtually all pagan Greek philosophers, the extent of the personalization of the

first principle is problematic and has to be worked out according to philosophical principles of reasoning. It was just obvious to philosophers of late antiquity that Plato's Form of the Good would reasonably be called θεός even though it has no apparent personal attributes.

6 See Gerson (1990) for a treatment of the major arguments in their historical and philosophical context.

7 That is, the first ἀρχή of the three ἀρχαί that there are: II.9.1.11–16. See also I.3.1.4–5. At III.8.9.19–32 and 10.31–5 there seem to be allusions to other possible arguments from degrees of perfection and from effect to cause, but these are nowhere worked out with any care. In two passages, III.8.9.1–3 and III.8.11.8–11, arguments for the existence of a first principle are adduced on the premise of the insufficiency of Intellect as a first principle. Either these arguments should be interpreted as presuming the existence of Intellect, in which case they are question-begging, or they should be interpreted as merely using Intellect as an example of the insufficiency of anything complex as first principle. In either case, Intellect is not uniquely or directly part of a proof of the existence of the One. See Armstrong (1940: 12) and Deck (1967: 7–9), who both regard the proof of the existence of the One (as opposed to the personal ascent to it) as depending on Intellect. Armstrong says, "the One as supreme source of being is really Aristotle's god carried to a yet higher degree of remoteness by identification with the αὐτὸ τὸ ἀγαθόν, and by the same identification brought into relation with the νοητά." And Deck says (9), "The One, or Good, was demonstrated by the need of the Nous [Intellect] for a principle and a good."

8 See Hager (1970: 244–50) for an analysis of this argument.

9 See VI.8.9.13: "this uniqueness comes from the principle itself." See also VI.8.7.38–9.

10 *Republic* 597c7–9: "If god made two [Forms of] Beds, necessarily there would appear one Form that both of those had and *that* would be the Form of Bed, not those two." See also the similar argument in *Timaeus* 31a6–7 for the uniqueness of the world based on the uniqueness of its model.

11 *Metaphysics* 12.8.1074a35–7: "The primary essence has no matter, for it is actuality. Thus, the first immovable mover is one both in formula and in number."

12 Throughout the beginning two chapters of VI.9 there is a sustained ambiguity in the meaning of τὸ ἕν between "the One" and "oneness." See Meijer (1992: 94–5). This ambiguity is established in the first line: Πάντα τὰ ὄντα τῷ ἑνί ἐστιν ὄντα ("all beings are beings by the One"). Two lines later the explanation is given: ἐπείπερ αφαιρεθέντα τοῦ ἕν ὃ λέγεται οὐκ ἐστιν ἐκεῖνα ("for if things are deprived of the oneness which is predicated of them they are not those things"). The first reference cannot mean "oneness" and the second cannot mean "the One." There are a number of places where it is impossible to tell for sure which is meant. Nevertheless, it is certain that the presence of oneness in something entails the causal agency of the One and that the effect of the causal agency of the One is always oneness in the effect. Thus, for an individual to lose "the One" is for it to lose its oneness.

13 See Hager (1970: 255–71) on the entire argument in VI.9.1–2.

14 See Hager (1970: 265).

15 On the received text it is puzzling what "man" adds to the complex of "rational living being." Perhaps it is meant to add either the matter or the individual characteristics. One editor emends the text slightly so that the translation reads "man is a rational living being, that is, [man] is made up of many parts." This meaning is certainly easier to interpret, but it cannot be said to have any support in the MSS. The point I am concerned with, however, is the same in either case.

16 Some will notice here a comparison with Meinong's "incomplete objects" which

have *Sosein* or essence that is incompletely determinate. Thus, the whale has no determinate weight. Further, an incomplete object is implicated in every complete object with that *Sosein*. According to Chisholm (1982: 49–52), the nature of this implication is obscure, but the relevant point for our purposes is that an additional explanatory factor is required to account for the difference between an incomplete object and a complete version of it.

17 Corrigan (1984: 228ff.) argues for a real distinction of existence and essence in Plotinus' metaphysics along somewhat different lines. He cites VI.7.2.3–4, where Plotinus distinguishes the "that" (ὅτι) and the "why" (διότι) of Intellect, probably using the distinction established in *Posterior Analytics* 1.13.78a22. But there no real distinction is clearly present, even though Plotinus implies that the διότι is separate (χωρίς). So I would not rely on this text. Corrigan also cites VI.7.21.12–14, where Plotinus says that Intellect, being what it is, receives something additional from elsewhere. Perhaps this something additional should be understood as existence. Still better evidence cited by Corrigan is VI.8.21.32–3, where Plotinus says of the One "[it] is only itself and really itself, while every other thing is itself and something else." This line has often been understood to mean simply that the One, in contrast to everything else, has no accidental attributes. This is true, but the point is more general. For the One cannot even be said to exist, although existence surely belongs to the One non-accidentally. The One has no compositeness, including the composition consisting of whatness and thatness. Finally, there are VI.8.13.56–7, where Plotinus says that the One is "the same as its existence" (ὑποστάσει), and VI.8.20.15–16, where the ὑπόστασις of the One is identified with its activity (ἐνέργεια). See also VI.8.12.25–7. So, by implication, nothing else is the same as its existence, that is, everything else is really distinct from it. This is confirmed by VI.6.13.50: [the One is needed] "for the existence of each essence" (οὐσίας). The last four passages seem sufficient to refute the claims by Fabro (1970: 91, 93–4) that "neither in Plato nor in Aristotle and not even in the schools derived from them is God ever indicated as the *esse subsistens*" and that "there is no composition of essence and existence in creatures in neo-platonism."

18 At III.8.10.1–2 there is a very strong assertion of this claim: "What is it, then? The productive power of all things; if it did not exist, neither would all things." See also V.3.17.10–14; V.3.15.11–12, 28; V.5.9.1–4; V.5.11.10–11. Also, VI.9.1.1–2 says: "It is by the One that all beings are beings, both those which are primarily beings and those which are in any sense said to be among beings," and I.6.7.11–12 says: "for it is cause of life and mind and being." But VI.8.15.28–9 seems to contradict this: "as first existence it is not in the soulless and not in irrational life." I suggest that the distinction between being contained in the One and the One being in something is operating here. Everything is in the One; the One is, in another sense, in everything capable of returning to the One by itself. It is because the One is in it that something can return to the One. Sweeney (1961b: 510–11), among others, argues that the basic principle of Plotinus' metaphysics is that "whatever is real is one." The startling conclusion Sweeney draws from this is that Plotinus is inclined to disregard the law of non-contradiction in order to retain the unity of all things. Yet surely this conclusion does not follow from the principle enunciated by Sweeney. A more accurate formulation of the principle would be that whatever is (finitely) real is so by participation in the One. So Rist (1973: 83).

19 This may be inferred from VI.8.12.34: "this [the One] was the same thing as essence" (οὐσία) when compared with ll. 14–16, where Plotinus says of Intellect that "it is not one thing and its essence another." The identity of νοῦς with its own οὐσία must nevertheless entail a complexity that is being denied of the One.

Line 32 says that in Intellect οὐσία and activity are somehow (πως) two, as is not the case with the One. See also V.5.3.23–4. Since the One is absolutely simple, it would seem to follow that the existence and the oneness given by the One to beings are two names for the same thing. So too VI.9.1.1: "It is by the One that all beings are beings." At VI.8.8.8–9 Plotinus says that the One is and is not the ἀρχή of all the "noble and majestic things" that come after it. Presumably, these "noble and majestic things" are the Forms. It is their ἀρχή because it is the cause of their εἶναι; it is not their ἀρχή in the sense that Intellect is itself an ἀρχή of essence and there is no other ἀρχή of this.

20 Plotinus distinguishes between (a) the One, (b) "essential" or "substantial" oneness, which is an attribute of οὐσία, and (c) the ἀρχή of number, one. See V.5.4.20–5; V.5.5.1–6; VI.2.9.5–9; VI.6.9.7–8, 33–4; VI.6.11.19–24, Roloff (1970: 110–13), and Krämer (1964: 292ff.). It is according to sense (b) that Forms are called "henads." It is according to sense (c) that things are numerable. By participation in Forms, things participate in essential oneness. The fact that we can count five horses and five dogs is attributable to the ἀρχή of number. So VI.9.5.38–46. The One is not the cause of oneness in anything in the sense of (b) or (c).

21 So Meijer (1992: 58–63), who thinks that "Supreme Entity" is the least misleading way to talk about that which is called "One" or "Good" in Plotinus so long as "Entity" is divested of connotations of limitedness.

22 See Gerson (1987: especially 133–41) and Kvanvig and McCann (1988: especially 18–19) for two arguments that a creator must be indistinguishable from a sustainer of existence. The basic argument is that "causing to be" is essentially a non-temporal relation, and so it is not possible to say that one thing caused something to be at one time and another thing caused it to be at a later time. A succession of causes of being is conceptually excluded. A similar argument is provided by Duns Scotus in Question 12 of his *Quodlibetal Questions*.

23 At VI.4.10.1–31 Plotinus argues that the first principle cannot be merely epistemologically first; it must be an ontologically first principle. This is so because the existence of composites is the datum to be explained, not their being objects of cognition. At VI.8.14.31–2 the One is called "the source therefore of being and the why of being, giving both at once." It is clear from lines 28–9 that the word "why" (διὰ τί) refers to essence or whatness. Cf. VI.8.18.7: "in that it [Intellect] has from him [the One] its being Intellect." This is not contradicted by III.1.1.8–9: "Well, then, among the eternal realities it is not possible to refer the first of them to other things which are responsible for their existence, just because they are first." What this means is that what is first, or an ἀρχή, in so far as it is first, has no cause. Thus, Intellect has no cause of its essence as such, of which it is the ἀρχή. But Intellect is not first overall and so requires a cause of that which is derived from the One, namely, its existence.

24 Cf. V.1.7.24–6: "Being must not fluctuate, so to speak, in the indefinite, but must be fixed by limit and stability; and stability in the intelligible world is limitation and shape, and it is by these that it receives existence." This passage, in addition to VI.8.18.7, cited in n23, seems sufficient to refute the contention of Covotti (1935: 165) that "Egli [Plotinus] nega, che l''uno' sia la semplice causa dell'esistenza delle cose: le quali, per contrario [mondo intelligibile] hanno, in se stesse, *la causa della loro esistenza*."

25 The reason given for this in the next line is that the One is "primarily itself" (πρώτως αὐτός). As an ἀρχή, it is identitatively what everything else is by participation. If the One were not unqualifiedly simple, what it is would be caused to be by its own existence, which would be other than it. Cf. VI.8.16.14–15, where the One "gives itself existence" (ὑποστήσας αὐτόν) and VI.8.13.55, where the

One "has brought itself into existence" (πεποιηκέναι αὑτὸν). So VI.8.7.53; VI.8.15.8–9; VI.8.20.21–2. Kremer (1966: 135–9; 384–8) takes the incomposite self-causation of the first principle to be the foundation of an ontological argument for the existence of god in Plotinus. I believe this is false, and the simplest way to show this is to point out that any predication of god or the One must be prefaced by οἷον or "sort of", for Plotinus. So we *could* say: "god is οἷον that than which none greater can be conceived" or "god is οἷον perfect" or even "god οἷον exists." But then of course the justification for these claims assumes that god exists. See Leroux (1990: 341–3) on the meaning of "self-caused." Leroux notes that one motive for saying that the One is self-caused when this is in fact the same as saying that it has no cause is to indicate that it is necessary and in no way contingent. Whittaker (1975) provides a rich selection of pre-Plotinian texts employing the idea of the self-generation of the universe and of a transcendent divinity. As Whittaker shows (217–18), Proclus thought that self-creation involved complexity and so denied it to the ἀρχή of all. He also thought that it was a mistake to assimilate self-causing to having no cause. If this refers to Plotinus, as I believe it does, it supports my interpretation of his understanding of self-causing as having no cause.

Chapter II The Attributes of the One

1 At VI.7.36.6–10 among the methods for learning about the One is abstraction (ἀφαίρεσις), removing from it anything inconsistent with its nature. This would include all predicates that entail complexity in the One.

2 For example, at VI.8.7.47 the sort of existence (οἷον ὑπόστασις) of the One is identified with its activity. See also VI.8.20.10–11 and Hager (1970: 246–7). It is just perverse to deduce from these and a number of other passages like them that the One does not exist. It would be more correct to say that the One does not exist in the manner in which anything else exists, or even better, the One does not have finite existence. The word οἷον does not mean "not."

3 The last-mentioned category of description is most clearly stated at VI.7.38.4–9, where Plotinus argues that we can call the first principle "Good" but we cannot say that it is good, where the latter would indicate compositeness. The former indicates the One just from the perspective of the end or goal of all things. See III.8.11.12–13 and Huber (1955: 80ff.).

4 Baladi (1970: 22) seems wrong to hold: "Formellement parlant, on ne peut remonter d'une qualité dans l'effet, à la même qualité ou même à une qualité analogue dans la cause. Au sens où l'emploi du terme 'cause' est relatif, il n'a nulle place en théologie." Kremer (1966: 195) argues that in identifying the One and the Good Plotinus is violating the absolute simplicity of the first principle. But to understand the first principle variously according to its multiple effects does not in fact lead to this result. The One is merely conceptually distinct from the Good. Cf. Meijer (1992: 184): "To speak about the One is not to speak categorically about the nature of the One but rather about its relations with what follows . . . leading to conclusions about the One."

5 Plotinus had before him two models for the jejune deduction of the attributes of a first principle so conceived, the poem of Parmenides and the first hypothesis of the second part of Plato's dialogue *Parmenides*. The Platonic source is of course more important; Parmenides himself is only a distant inspiration. However, though Plotinus seems to have thought that he was following Plato in the *Parmenides* when speaking of the One, I do not think that he interpreted the dialogue correctly, at least with regard to what Plato was doing in the desperately

difficult second part. But that is really not my concern. As Dodds (1973: 128) aptly states it: "[Plotinus] does not believe in the One because he has found it in the *Parmenides*; on the contrary, he finds it in the *Parmenides* because he already believes in it". See also Jackson (1967: 318–22) and Charrue (1978: 59–84), who, building on the seminal article of Dodds (1928), list the numerous parallels between the deduced attributes of the One and those of the subject of the first hypothesis of the *Parmenides*. A similar list is in Schwyzer (1944: 87–9). That Plotinus identifies his One as the Good and with the Form of the Good in the *Republic* is sufficient proof that he interprets the *Parmenides* incorrectly. That Plotinus further identifies the Good with "the One," co-principle with the Indefinite Dyad in Plato's "unwritten doctrines," is natural enough, particularly if he is relying on Aristotle's testimony in *Metaphysics* 1.6.988a7–17; 14.4. See D'Ancona (1990: 438 and n2) for references to the scholarship on Plotinus' use of Aristotle to interpret the Platonic doctrine of principles. That "the one" of the first hypothesis of the *Parmenides* is not to be equated with the Form of the Good in the *Republic* is evident from a comparison of 142a3–4 of the former with 505a2 and 519c9 of the latter. See Bonetti (1980: 18, 25), who recognizes that the cornerstone of a metaphysics justifiably called "neoplatonic" is just this identification. Schiller (1978: 38–41) gives a good example of a doomed attempt to give a positive interpretation to the first hypothesis of the *Parmenides* and thereby to justify Plotinus' identification of that with his own One. For Schiller, the one of the first hypothesis becomes a "necessary condition for the existence and knowledge of the universe." This is simply not warranted by the text. In interpreting Plotinus I shall try to make explicit the distinction between arguments based on his own principles and arguments from authority. Fortunately, the latter are quite rare and in any case do not directly involve the One. Meijer (1992: 6–26) provides the most recent history of the antecedents of the concept of "the One" and the relevant scholarship. Meijer argues that Plotinus' position constitutes a substantial innovation in the tradition, although Meijer regards the innovation as a development *within* Plotinus from an earlier pre-critical period. Gurtler (1992: 443–5) argues that Plotinus is not committed to an interpretation of the first hypothesis of the *Parmenides* as equivalent to the One. I think the end of V.1.8 is against this. But Gurtler is right to discount attempts to try to interpret Plotinus' One as if it is identical with the subject of the first hypothesis of the *Parmenides*.

6 At VI.4.11.15–16 it is clear that "simple" does not imply "one," although "one" implies "simple," for Intellect is simple but not unqualifiedly one.

7 The last line says that the One has everything but indistinctly (ὡς μὴ δια-κεκριμένα), which is intended to exclude the implication that it must be a multitude (πλῆθος) if it has all things in it. This is evidently what Plotinus means when he says that the One is all things and no one of them. See V.2.1.1; V.4.2.16; VI.7.32.12–14; VI.8.18.3; VI.8.21.24–5. See also Kremer (1966: 127–9).

8 Cf. *Metaphysics* 5.5.1015b9–12, where Aristotle claims that necessity in the primary sense belongs to the simple and that other things that are necessary are so because of a cause outside themselves. In relation to these claims, all that Plotinus has done is to deny that Intellect is unqualifiedly simple and so unqualifiedly necessary.

9 Plotinus typically uses the expression οἷον in a technical sense. For example, this is so at VI.8.7.31–2 and VI.8.11.9–10, where he says that using this expression of the One "is to enquire what attributes it has, which has no attributes." See Anton (1982: 24–33), nn11–12 (158–9); Heiser (1991: 62–72).

10 At V.5.10.21–2 and VI.9.6.10–12 the One is said to be ἄπειρον or unlimited in power. A limit to something may be external or internal. There is obviously no

external limitation to the One owing to its self-sufficiency. There is no internal limitation because of the One's incompositeness.

11 Cf. V.5.6.14–15, where the One is said to have a boundless nature (ἄπλετον φύσιν); VI.7.33.4, where the One is said to be formless form (ἄμορφον εἶδος), far from contradicting this, reinforces the denial of limitation, as the context shows. So Hadot (1988: 47–9). Plotinus is doubtless following the *Republic* 509b6–10, where it is said of the first principle of all: "the Good is not οὐσία, but beyond (ἐπέκεινα) οὐσία." But it is equally clear that he is going beyond Plato in his deduction of the attributes of this principle. Sweeney (1957: especially 527–31; 718; 731–2) has made the provocative argument that in calling the One "infinite" Plotinus does not intend to indicate that it is infinite in its nature, but only in its effects. I believe that Sweeney's claim has been refuted both by Clarke (1959: especially 86–92) and Rist (1967b: 28–9). Rist cites V.5.11.2–3, which I think cannot mean anything but that the One, absolutely simple in itself, is therefore absolutely infinite or unlimited. If the One had some intrinsic limit, it would not be simple. However, II.4.15.17–20 is an important passage for Sweeney. Of the generation of intelligible matter from the One it says "it would be produced from the unlimitedness or the power or the everlastingness of the One; unlimitedness is not in the One, but the One produces it." I read these alternatives (ἢ. . .ἢ) as inclusive, not exclusive. If they were exclusive, this would imply some complexity in the One. It is from the intrinsic infinity of the One that its infinite effects flow. Sweeney (1961b: 515 n24) seems to concede to Clarke that the One is intrinsically infinite.

12 V.5.11.1–4: "And this [the One] has infinity by not being more than one, and because there is nothing in which anything belonging to it will find its limit: for by being one it is not measured and does not come within range of number. It is therefore not limited in relation to itself or to anything else: since if it was it would be two." The oneness of the One should be understood here as indicating its incompositeness.

13 VI.8.20.17–19: "Now certainly an activity not enslaved to οὐσία is purely and simply free, and in this way he himself is himself from himself." See also V.5.6.5–7; V.5.10.19–20; V.5.11.1–4; and most clearly V.1.7.24–6. Clarke (1952: 184–8) shows how making form a limiting principle in Plotinus is an inversion of the position of virtually all his predecessors.

14 At VI.7.33.7–9 form is a principle of limitation to Intellect, for when Intellect is identified with one Form it is limited by it. The role of form generally as principle of limitation is invariant whether the form receives existence or is itself received by Intellect.

15 See O'Meara (1980b).

16 Aristotle, *Metaphysics* 13.4.1079a31–2 and 5.1079b35–1080a2, referring to the *Phaedo* in the later passage, says that "they" [the Platonists] separated (ἐχώρισαν) the Forms, which are nevertheless supposed to be the causes of the existence and coming to be of things. I mention Aristotle's interpretation here because Plotinus frequently follows Aristotle (especially the *Metaphysics*) in interpreting Plato's metaphysics.

17 V.1.8.6–10, where Plotinus quotes from *Republic* 509b8–10. See Hager (1970: 102–56) and (1976: 17) and Krämer (1969), who basically endorse the identification of the One with the Good in Plato both via the *Parmenides* and the indirect tradition regarding Plato's "unwritten doctrines." There are many complicated issues here. See Gurtler (1992) on the lack of evidence regarding Plotinus' interpretation of the first hypothesis of the second part of the *Parmenides*. Speaking summarily, I would reject the *Parmenides* as evidence for this identification and with qualifications accept the fundamental point of the indirect

tradition that Plato did at least consider seriously the postulation of a first principle of all which could be called both "Good" and "One." Hager (1976: 20–2) misinterprets *Parmenides* 142a6–8 to mean that Plato is there denying the negative deductions regarding the subject of the first hypothesis.

18 See I.8.2.2–4: "It [the nature of the Good] is that on which everything depends and 'to which all beings aspire'; they have it as their principle and need it." Also, VI.7.27.24–7. The Good as final cause of the activity of Intellect is expressed at III.8.11.8–11, 15–19.

19 See Schwyzer (1960: 355–6), Rist (1967b: 38–52), Gatti (1982: 13–28), Schroeder (1987), and Bussanich (1987) on the cognitive vocabulary applied to the One. Rist (1964a: 86–7) suggests both "suprapersonal" and "semi-personal" as appropriate for the manner in which cognitive attributes are applied to the One, wishing to stress that in denying "personal" attributes to it, Plotinus does not mean to make it "impersonal." I agree with Bussanich's conclusion (183) that the One is both "totally self-regarding" and "self-revelatory." Meijer (1992: 42, n150) thinks it an "awful misunderstanding" not to distinguish the terms κατανόησις and ὑπερνόησις as applied to the One. The former is said to have "a cognitive ring," whereas the latter "is part of a voluntative process and fundamental to the [One's] process of self-creating." It seems to me correct to distinguish the cognitive and the volitional in the One, but there are no grounds for finding this distinction in the two Greek terms.

20 I find it puzzling that Leroux (1990: 52) identifies "la volonté de l'Un et la volonté du Bien [of Plato]," citing the *Republic* and the *Symposium*. I can find no trace of a description of the Form of the Good as having a will in Plato.

21 See VI.7.37–42, where the discussion of the cognitive life of the One begins with the rejection of Aristotle's claim, *Metaphysics* 129.1074b23–35, that the ἀρχή of all thinks itself. See Siegmann (1990: 168–72). As Siena (1985: 319) notes, the rejection of "Aristotelian personalism" for the One seems to entail the rejection of pantheism. But this also follows from any of the "negative" attributes of the One.

22 See V.3.15.29–31 and V.5.9.35–7: "nor is there anything which possesses the First, but it possesses everything. Therefore it is in this way also the good of everything, because all things have their being directed towards it and depend upon it, each in a different way." At V.5.13.37–8 and VI.8.9.9–10 Plotinus says that the cause is greater or better than the effect, which perhaps amounts to the same thing. At V.2.1.1–2 he says that the One is all things, not as their "sum" but as their cause. See Kremer (1969: 61): "Das Insein erweist sich daher als die Signatur der radikalen Abhängigheit des Geschöpfes von seinem Schöpfer, alles Nichtgöttlichen von seinem Gott." Kremer is here speaking about an entire tradition's understanding of how a first principle contains what it is a principle of, not just Plotinus.

23 VI.7.15.10–11: "That [the One] then is the Good, but Intellect is good by having its life in that contemplation."

24 Aristotle does go on to say that "life belongs to god, for the actuality of intellect is life, and he is actuality (26–7)." But he does not say why activity is to be identified with intellect, which is precisely the problem.

25 In the lines immediately following the last text Plotinus makes the important claim "if then the activity is more perfect than the οὐσία, and the first is most perfect, the first will be activity." This, I think, indicates decisively that Plotinus does not identify οὐσία with being absolutely and that the denial of the former to the One is not the denial of the latter.

26 For example, Armstrong (1940: 12) holds such a view. Graeser (1972a: 103) says, "Being 'beyond οὐσία' the *One* is a set of logico-metaphysical devices, but is

itself no more involved in Being and in that which is derived from it than the meta-spatial God in Aristotle's *Metaphysics*, who is regarded as the ultimate final cause." This cannot be the case, if only because of the doctrine of an activity outside itself in the One. Aristotle's god, by contrast, has no actuality outside itself and hence no activity outside itself.

27 Aristotle, *Metaphysics* 9.8.1050a23–9, makes a distinction between an "internal" and "external" activity, as in the case of sight, in the first case, and the building of a house, in the second case. He does not, however, suggest that an "external" activity is necessarily entailed by an "internal" one. What would be the "external" activity of seeing? And he certainly does not countenance an "external" activity for that which is perfectly actual.

28 I doubt that V.3.12.20ff., which seems to hold that the first activity is Intellect, should be taken to indicate that the distinction between first and second activity does not apply to the One. First, this is contradicted by VI.8.20.9–15. The ἀρχή Intellect is the first activity of οὐσία. Against Büchner (1970: 99ff.), I.7.1.17–20 does not imply that there is no activity in the One. Rather, it implies that the activity in the One, though producing a secondary activity, does not thereby erect a real relation between the One and everything else. The two texts – V.5.3.23 and VI.8.7.46–54 – where Plotinus speaks of οἷον ἐνέργεια of the One do not contradict VI.8.20.9–15, where the One, beyond οὐσία, is identified with activity unqualifiedly. For those two texts qualify activity in the sense in which it is attributable to what has οὐσία and is something distinct from existence. See Hager (1970: 428, n414): "die Denkenenergie des göttlichen Geistes [ist] die erste Energie und das erste Denken überhaupt . . . Gemeint ist aber die erste erkennende Energie und das erste seiende Denken, was mit der übergeistigen Energie und dem überseienden Denken d.h. dem über-Denken des Einen nicht im Widerspruch steht."

29 Lloyd (1990: 100) holds that fire, light, perfume, snow, etc. "are not mere analogies or metaphors," that is, the principle is universal. From this it does not follow that the principle is nevertheless not differently applied to eternal and temporal beings. See IV.5.7.17ff. on the universality of the principle.

30 See *Physics* 3.3.202a13ff., where it is said that the actuality of an agent is in the movable, which implies that the agent is in potency to the movable, even if it is itself the movable. Lloyd (1987: 167–9) and (1990: 99–101) makes the connection between the discussion of activity here and the *Physics* doctrine. In the first article, he says that Plotinus' account here of efficient causality differs from Aristotle's only in the inferiority of the patient compared to the agent. I do not think this is the main point, for Aristotle would agree that everything is inferior to god with respect to actuality. I also do not agree with Lloyd that Plotinus does not admit that he is departing from Aristotle. It is true, as Bussanich (1988: 28–31) notes, that in *Metaphysics* 12.7.1072b13–14 Aristotle implies that the world depends upon an activity, the ἀρχή of all. But it is precisely the perfection of this ἀρχή that requires the dependence to be that of finality and not efficiency. De Vogel (1969b: 406) says that the One "creates as a by-product of its self-orientated, completely internal activity." There is no basis for speaking about the secondary activity of the One as a "by-product." Furthermore, it is in *contrast* to the "self-orientated" activity of Aristotle's unmoved mover that Plotinus describes the activity of the One.

31 Kremer (1987: 1002–11) argues that Plotinus holds that self-diffusion is just a property of goodness and that is why the One overflows. He finds this in Proclus, *Elements of Theology*, pr. 122. I believe that it is via the concept of activity and not the concept of goodness that Plotinus argues for the self-diffusion of the One.

32 At VI.9.2.5–8 Plotinus is expressing a view he rejects.

33 See also V.4.2.35; VI.8.7.46–8; VI.8.12.22–3; VI.8.13.6–8; VI.8.16.15, 25, 30, 31, 35 and Kremer (1966: 12–13).

34 In *Metaphysics* book 2, chapter 1, Aristotle does seem to consider the possibility of divine efficient causality. I have argued elsewhere (Gerson 1991) that this possibility is removed with the doctrine of the equivocity of being in book 4. Hence, in book 12 the divine can operate only as a final cause.

35 A similar point is made by Brunner (1973a: 33–63).

36 See, for example, *Summa Theologiae* I.q.45.a.1, contra: "Sicut igitur generatio hominis est ex non ente quod est non homo, ita creatio, quae est emanatio totius esse, est ex non ente quod est nihil." H. Dörrie (1960: 211–28) provides a useful survey of the literary uses of the language of emanation.

37 *Summa Theologiae* I.q.46.a.5, contra: "Illud autem quod est proprius effectus Dei creantis, est illud quod praesupponitur omnibus aliis, scilicet esse absolute." But how can we distinguish an eternal creature from a part of the eternal creator? I would hold that it is by an analysis showing the necessary compositeness of the former and the necessary simplicity of the latter. The existence of the creature is really distinct from its essence.

38 Cf. Büchner (1970: 36–41), who rightly stresses Plotinus' innovation with respect to the Aristotelian distinction of act and potency by its importation into a non-temporal context, where its use is strictly logical. Huber (1955: 78) claims that Plotinus cannot account for the production of a multiplicity from a transcendent One. He does not recognize that production just means eternal dependence. It is clearly tendentious and question-begging to suppose that an account of production means an account of how something came from nothing.

39 Armstrong (1937: 63) writes, "the confusion of thought involved in the doctrine of emanation becomes even more remarkable when we realize that it involves a concealed admission of Stoic materialism into the system." It is difficult to see what Armstrong thinks the confusion is, since he does not analyze the metaphor of emanation in the texts. I take the metaphors to represent a doctrine of creation, which is complex and obscure but not confused.

40 See Oosthout (1991: 73–4, 165–6).

41 The general principle of necessity is expressed at II.9.3.7–8: "But each of necessity must give of its own to something else as well."

42 See Kremer (1987: 1005–17), with extensive documentation showing the prevalence of the view that the necessity Plotinus attributes to the One's productive activity is identical to the necessity denied of the activity of God in creation metaphysics.

43 VI.8.8.12–15: "But we must say that he [the One] is altogether unrelated to anything, for he is what he is before them; for we take away the 'is,' and so also any kind of relations to the real beings." There is a remote Aristotelian parallel to this at *Metaphysics* 5.15.1021a26–9, where Aristotle envisages a relation with only one real relatum.

44 See Gorman (1940: 379–405), who uses the phrase "progressive unfolding of reality" (404) to characterize the One's relation to its products. Gilson (1962: 41–8) tries to distinguish what he calls Plotinus' "énologie" from an "ontologie." "Dans une doctrine de l'Etre, l'inférieur n'est qu'en vertue de l'être du supérieur. Dans une doctrine de l'Un, c'est au contraire un principe général que l'inférieur n'est qu'en vertu de ce que le supérieur n'est pas; en effet, le supérieur ne donne jamais que ce qu'il n'a pas, puisque, pour pouvoir donner cette chose, il faut qu'il soit au-dessus d'elle." This is a specious contrast. Gilson supposes that the One is the cause of being simply rather than finite being, as I have argued. If this precision is made, there is in fact no difference between Plotinus' basic metaphysics and what Gilson describes as a "doctrine de l'être." The unique

ἀρχή of finite being is virtually all that it creates, just as is the first cause in a "doctrine de l'être." Cf. O'Meara (1975: 103–4), who seems to follow Gilson in holding that Plotinus "emploie une 'hénologie' dans l'analyse de la réalité. Cette hénologie consiste à rapporter l'être des choses au principe d'unité que suppose leur être particulier." So too Bousquet (1976: 25–31). That Plotinus uses the concept of unity to analyze proximity to the ἀρχή of all should not be taken to exclude the fundamental point that this ἀρχή is the cause of the being of everything. Kremer (1966: 166) resists Gilson's distinction, insisting that Plotinus' metaphysics is a "hénologie ontologique." But he ignores a distinction between finite and infinite being, so it is not clear to me what the first principle is supposed to be in this interpretation. Schürmann (1982: 337–8) takes the interpretation of Gilson to an absurd extreme, denying any causality to the One, and holding that the One is just the condition for the possibility of any being. A slightly more nuanced version of this interpretation is provided by D'Ancona (1990: especially 446–54).

45 In IV.5.7.16–17 the example is given of the light within the sun (first activity) and the light flowing out from it (second activity). The second activity is said not to be separated (ἀφισταμένη) from the first. We get some idea of what this denial of separation means when Plotinus goes on to explicate the second activity as image or likeness of the first. Thus, absence of separation means basically dependence. On Intellect as image of the One see V.1.7.1ff.; V.2.1.19; V.6.3.1ff.; VI.7.17.39; VI.7.40.19; VI.8.18.15ff.

46 Müller (1913: especially 416–22) argues with considerable force against an emanationist interpretation, understanding "emanation" as the view that the first principle is diminished in producing anything else. By this criterion, Müller is certainly correct. As he puts it (418), "Das fest in sich geschlossene Eine und Gute fliesst nicht, es schafft."

47 There is another group of texts which may be taken to indicate that the One is not the unique cause of existence: III.1.1–8; III.2.4.17–20; III.3.4.23–35; III.6.6.8–23; V.2.1.13–15; VI.2.20; VI.7.2.19–37. See Fuller (1912: 306): "Just as the One overflows into Mind and Mind into Soul and Soul into the world, so the latent powers of Soul in their final exhaustion pass over into blank nothingness, or, in other words, beget or produce it." But cf. I.7.2 and IV.8.6.16–18, where participation in the One (Good) is ubiquitous.

48 *Summa Theologiae* I.q.45.a.5, respondeo: "Unde non potest aliquid operari dispositive et instrumentaliter ad hunc effectum, cum creatio non sit ex aliquo praesupposito quod possit disponi per actionem instrumentalis agentis."

49 There is some textual support provided for this in the conditional clause at III.8.10.1–2: "if it [the One] did not exist, neither would all things."

50 Hadot (1960: 107–41) richly documents his conclusion that "la triade être–vie–pensée révèle la structure de l'Intelligence."

51 At IV.8.6.1–3 Plotinus says: "If, then, there must not be just One alone – for then all things would have been hidden, shapeless within that One, and not a single real being would have existed if that One had stayed still in itself," which I understand as supposing the argument: since a multiplicity necessarily exists, the explanation of its existence, namely, the One, must necessarily exist.

52 Cf. O'Meara (1975: especially 120–4) for a study of the texts indicating the hierarchical structure of Plotinus' metaphysics. As O'Meara points out (120), there is no simple term for "hierarchy" in Plotinus. Nevertheless, there is ample evidence that Plotinus has a concept of an ontological and causal gradation of being, with the One at the apex.

53 At VI.7.2.16–17 Plotinus says that form (εἶδος) is the cause of existence (αἴτιον τοῦ εἶναι) for each thing. This use of this phrase for essential causality rather than

efficient causality has its precedent in Aristotle: see *Metaphysics* 5.8.1017b15; 7.17.1041b26–9; 8.3.1043b13–14; 8.6.1045a8–b20, etc. The function of form of course does not usurp the causal function of the One. By making the ἀρχή of all an αἴτιον τοῦ εἶναι as well (see I.6.7.11–12; V.1.4.29–30; V.1.5.5; VI.7.42.11; VI.8.14.29), Plotinus seems to court self-contradiction. For an ἀρχή is different from what it is an ἀρχή of, whereas an αἴτιον must be like its effects. Plotinus overcomes this dilemma in the only logically possible way, by making the cause the cause of the only facet of finite being which could not be like its cause, namely, its existence. That is, the likeness of cause and effect, as this was understood by all Plotinus' predecessors, was likeness in kind, for example, in the begetting of the child by the father. But the One is not a kind at all.

54 III.8.9.39: "the origin of Intellect and of all things." See Kremer (1966: 306, 421–2) on the necessary instrumentality of Intellect and how this makes Plotinus' creationism different from a metaphysics of *creatio ex nihilo*.

55 See VI.7.42.21–3: "But since Soul depends on Intellect and Intellect on the Good, so all things depend on him through intermediaries, some close to him, some neighbors of those close to him." That Soul should depend on Intellect and Intellect on the One is compatible with instrumental causality. For Soul depends on Intellect for οὐσία and life and thinking, whereas everything including Soul depends on the One for existence. At V.2.1.16 Plotinus does say that the ἐνέργεια ἐκ τῆς οὐσίας of Intellect is Soul. But Intellect gives οὐσία, life, and thinking to soul, not existence. See also V.1.3.6–12; V.1.6.45.

56 See Anton (1977: 258–71) on the meaning of "existence" (ὑπόστασις) when applied to the One and his criticism of Deck (1967), who argues that the One is not an ὑπόστασις at all. In saying that the One is cause of itself, Plotinus apparently violates the principle that a cause or principle is other than what it is a cause or principle of. It must be remembered, though, that the One is only analogously said to be anything, including a cause. So, it is not a cause of itself in the way it is a cause of everything else. See VI.9.3.39–40; VI.9.6.54–5 and VI.8.11.8–9: "there is no ἀρχή of the ἀρχή of all," and Marucchi (1935: 174–5). Gandillac (1966: 161) is surely right to stress the context of this description of the One, which is a discussion of its freedom. He interprets "cause of itself" negatively as meaning "without external cause or constraint." This does not of course preclude a positive implication, namely, that the ὑπόστασις of the One is identical with its activity. See VI.8.7.47. Bales (1982: 46–50) misunderstands the phrase in arguing that the concept of self-causation is self-contradictory. Bussanich (1987: 178–9) has pointed this out as well.

57 See *Summa Theologiae* I.q.14.a.11, respondeo: "Omnes enim perfectiones in creaturis inventae, in Deo praeexistunt secundum altiorem modum." Also, I.q.4.a.2, respondeo: "Cum ergo Deus sit prima causa effectiva rerum, oportet omnium rerum perfectiones praeexistere in Deo secundum eminentiorem modum."

58 Leroux (1990: 96, 108) seems to unpack the metaphorical representations of the One in terms of eminence, a position that is in conflict with his basic thesis that the simplicity of the One entails its impersonal nature. So too Beierwaltes (1985: 49–50 and n47), who seems to take the phrase εἶδος εἰδῶν at VI.7.17.35 to refer to the One, whereas in fact it alludes to Aristotle, *De Anima* 3.8.432a2, who so designates νοῦς. The One, says Plotinus, establishes (ἱδρύσῃ) the Forms. It is not their paradigm.

59 See VI.7.2.40–3: "If then the intelligibles have no cause of their being but are self-sufficient and independent of cause, they would be in possession of their cause in themselves and with themselves." Also, VI.7.17.6–9; VI.7.40.21–4; Rutten (1956: 104–5) and Bussanich (1988: 163–5).

60 V.6.5.8–9: "And this is what thinking is, a movement towards the Good in its

desire of that Good." See also VI.7.15.11, 16. At V.4.2.4, 12, 13 Plotinus seems to hold that the One is intelligible (νοητόν), roughly, that it is the intentional object of intellection (νοεῖν). On my interpretation, the One is called intelligible here because the good is achieved by Intellect by contemplating, that is, having an intelligible object. At III.8.9.10–11 Plotinus denies that the One is intelligible. The assertion and denial that the One is νοητόν are parallel to the statements that the One does and does not contain all the Forms and should be interpreted accordingly. I believe this interpretation helps explain why in the notorious text at V.1.7.5–6 Plotinus should not be taken to be saying that the One looks at itself by turning back upon itself and in this way produces Intellect. The generation of Intellect in this passage refers to the achievement of Intellect in identifying itself with what the One virtually is, all Forms. So O'Daly (1973: 71–2). On this difficult passage see Igal (1971a), Atkinson (1983: 156–60), and Bussanich (1988: 37–43). Should V.1.6.17–18 be read differently? See Lloyd (1987: 159–60).

61 If this were not so, then a real relation between the One and Intellect would be erected. It is pertinent to recall *Parmenides* 132de, where Parmenides derives a regress from Socrates' argument that Forms are models (παραδείγματα) whereas their instances are images or likenesses (ὁμοιώματα) of these. Parmenides' argument is that we can consider model and copy in so far as (καθ' ὅσον) the one is like the other. This symmetrical likeness presumes a real relation is possible. Szlezák (1979: 164 n539) is too quick to dismiss the containment of Forms in the One as inconsistent with Plotinus' general doctrines. See V.1.7.10–13: "The things, then, of which it [the One] is the productive power are those which Intellect observes, in a way cutting itself off from the power; otherwise it would not be Intellect. For Intellect also has of itself a kind of intimate perception of its power, that it has power to produce οὐσία" and the analysis of this passage by Igal (1971a: 142ff.). As Igal argues, the subject of "has power" (δύναται) is Intellect. So Lloyd (1987: 161). Since Intellect is eternally contemplating Forms, the sense in which the One has all Forms indistinctly in it ought to mean that goodness for Intellect is just contemplating Forms and that the One is the cause of the existence of this activity. At VI.7.17.3–6 Plotinus suggests that the One is "greater" than Intellect and the Forms, but since the One does not have that which it gives, its greatness can hardly be eminence in form. D'Ancona Costa (1992: especially 108–9) argues that the One is analogous to Forms, a kind of Form of Forms. Its superiority consists in its absolute universality. This interpretation, I think, results from supposing that the One must be somehow a Form if it is the cause of the being of Forms. But if the One is considered to be the cause of the existence of Forms, we need not hold to an interpretation which after all is contradicted by the text.

62 If I understand Lloyd (1987: 175–6) rightly, my interpretation is consonant with his own. Lloyd thinks that it is the One as object of thought which acts on Intellect and produces οὐσία, whereas I have said that it is the One as object of desire. Perhaps these amount to the same thing if the desire of Intellect is just βούλησις, an intellectual desire. See VI.7.15.14–16: "For that Good [the One] is the principle, and it is from that that they [the Forms] are in this Intellect, and it is this [Intellect] which has made them from that Good."

63 V.5.12.44–7: "He [the One] would not have cared if it had not come into being; and if anything else could have been derived from him he would not have grudged it existence; but as it is, it is not possible for anything else to come into being: all things have come into being and there is nothing left." Kremer (1987: 1017) thinks this passage and VI.7.8.13f. and IV.8.6.1–6 indicate that the necessity according to which the One operates is not logical necessity or the impossibility of the contradictory, namely, that there should be nothing in the world besides

the One. But the condition contrary to fact "he would not have cared if it had not come into being" does not have to mean that this is a real possibility.

64 In this claim is "classical theism's" response to the attack by Hartshorne (1967: 60–75) that God must be really related to the world either internally or externally. If the first, then God is altered by what happens in the world; if the second, then God is unaltered by what happens in the world, in which case God does not have knowledge of this changing world. The dilemma is a false one, for the ἀρχή and cause of all finite being is not really related to the world at all.

65 For example, the central thesis of Pistorius (1952) is that the three ἀρχαί are different "aspects" of "one Godhead." Accordingly, gradation or hierarchy among these is denied. It will become clear as we proceed why I regard this as fundamentally mistaken.

66 See II.9.3.11–12: "Of necessity, then, all things must exist for ever in ordered dependence upon each other: those other than the First have come into being in the sense that they are derived from other, higher, principles." This passage goes on to emphasize the eternal necessity of the ordered tableau of principles.

67 We shall see in the next chapter that the point of the obscure characterization of the "generation" of Intellect is its acting as an instrument in its own production.

68 Cf. II.5.1.24–8, where this sense of δύναμις is distinguished from that according to which something is viewed as incomplete relative to a future activity. Also, VI.8.1.10–11, where the One is said πάντα δύνασθαι, that is, to be omnipotent.

69 See Büchner (1970: 50–1).

70 It is said of the One at V.2.1.1–2: "it is the principle of all things, not all things, but all things have that other kind of transcendent existence; for in a way they do occur in the One; or rather they are not there yet, but they will be." When taken together with the claim that the One is the cause of all things and the underlying assumption that Parmenides' dictum that "something does not come from nothing" must be observed, I think it is necessary to interpret this claim in terms of virtuality. Cf. Büchner (1970: 105), who understands the One to be all things because it has in it all Forms "latently" or "amorphously." This seems to me to get things backwards if the latent or amorphous is understood as in any way inferior to the overt or formed. The perfection of all that Intellect is is in the One, where it cannot exist as it does in Intellect and where it is knowable only by the One. When at V.3.15.1ff., 35–6 Plotinus says that the reason the One can give everything is that it is or has nothing, this should be interpreted in terms of virtuality. Similarly, VI.8.18.39–41 says of the One: "He is then in a greater degree something like the most causative and truest of causes, possessing all together the intellectual causes which are going to be from him and generative of what is not as it chanced but as he himself willed," which must indicate virtuality. See also VI.7.32.12–16; V.2.1.1–3; V.2.2.24–6.

71 See V.3.17.12, where the One is said to be ποιητικὸν οὐσίας; VI.7.32.2, γεννήσας οὐσίαν. Also, II.8.19.12–20. As I have already argued, from these passages one should not infer that the One is eminently all that it produces; it is only virtually all that it produces.

72 It is true that a phrase such as ἐν ἄρα πάντα τὰ ὄντα (VI.5.1.26) encourages the monistic tendency of interpretation, but, in contrast to Spinoza, the unity of all things is not owing to the uniqueness of substance. Such a passage must be balanced by one like V.5.12.47–50, where Plotinus denies that the One is all things. For Spinoza, the uniqueness of substance is not attributable to substance being a unique nature possessed by other natures. The heart of the difference between Plotinus and Spinoza is that for Plotinus, being is equivocal and for Spinoza, being is univocal.

73 See V.5.10.3–4: "all things have a share, though nothing has it." The meta-

phorical language which is frequently employed by Plato to describe participation is also regularly employed by Plotinus for everything in relation to the One. See I.1.8; V.5.5.13; VI.4.15; VI.9.1.27.

74 For example, at III.8.9.23–4 we read: "For there is something of it in us too; or rather there is nowhere where it is not, in the things which can participate in it." See also VI.9.7.29–30; VI.9.8.33–5. Bréhier (1928: especially ch. 7) was perhaps the most influential exponent of the view of Plotinus as pantheist and agent of Orientalism in Hellenic culture. The opposite and for me decisive argument was put earlier by Müller (1914a), of whom Bréhier takes no notice. Among other things, Müller points out that Plotinus' devotion to Plato (76) and to the method of dialectic (81) are strong indications of Plotinus' thoroughly "Hellenic" orientation. Armstrong (1936) provided a direct response to Bréhier, defending the location of Plotinus' roots within Greek philosophy. Cf. the more recent work of Wolters in Harris (1982b: 293–308). I have no idea whether or not Plotinus was acquainted with "Oriental" philosophy. In these matters, I think the only sensible approach is to start with the arguments in the text and with his known sources. On that basis, I have found nothing in Plotinus which is so at odds with his own tradition that I felt a need to go outside it to understand what he was saying. That certainly may indicate a failing in me, however.

75 See Gorman (1940: 389–97) for a most insightful discussion of this point.

76 Leroux (1990: 50–3) stresses that the necessity here is intended as a denial of contingency, not as an assertion of external constraint. But cf. VI.8.10.25–6, where Plotinus says that the One is what it is not because it cannot be otherwise but because, being what it is, it is the best. The inability to deteriorate, the only theoretical option for the One, is not a defect or an indication of impotence. See Henry (1931: 320–30) and Armstrong (1982b). For a Christian creationist like Aquinas, the distinction of the will and nature of God is absolutely essential to preserving divine freedom and thereby to rejecting emanationism. See *Summa Theologiae* I.q.19.a.4, respondeo: "Dicendum quod necesse est dicere voluntatem Dei esse causam rerum, et Deum agere per voluntatem, non per necessitatem naturae, ut quidam existimaverunt." In the first objection in this article Aquinas quotes Pseudo-Dionysius (*De Div. Nom.* IV. 1 = *PG* 3, 693): "'Sicut noster sol, non ratiocinans aut praeeligens, sed per ipsum esse illuminat omnia participare lumen ipsius valentia; ita et bonum divinum per ipsam essentiam omnibus existentibus immittit bonitatis divinae radios.' Sed omne quod agit per voluntatem, agit ut ratiocinans et praeeligens. Ergo Deus non agit per voluntatem. Ergo voluntas Dei non est causa rerum." Aquinas' reply to this objection is curious: "Dicendum quod Dionysius per verba illa non intendit excludere electionem a Deo simpliciter, sed secundum quid; inquantum scilicet non quibusdam solum bonitatem suam communicat, sed omnibus; prout scilicet electio discretionem quandam importat." Does this not just beg the question?

77 See Gorman (1940: 397): "Liberty in the god of Plotinus does not depend upon whether or not he must produce; it depends upon whether or not he must be himself. God is free to be what he wills, he is free to have the essence he ought to have, but that essence is precisely to be the Good which must diffuse." A similar position, richly documented, is argued for by Kremer (1965: especially 249–54). Marucchi (1935: 169) rightly derives the One's freedom from its creative activity.

78 Cf. VI.8.17, where Plotinus succinctly defines providence as the disposition of Intellect, which itself "comes after" the One, which is "beyond" providence. As Schubert (1968: 27–33) notes, Plotinus' concept of providence is thus separated from its traditional association with care (ἐπιμέλεια). If the One is infinitely diffusive of its goodness, nevertheless, it operates *through* providence,

which is in a distinct ἀρχή. In other words, our knowledge of how precisely god cares for us is reducible to our knowledge of the eternal realm of intelligible being. The One could not exercise benevolence in any other way, say, by miraculous intervention, circumventing or ignoring Intellect.

79 Divine providence via the presence of god in the universe is affirmed at II.9.16.24–7, where Plotinus is reticent regarding the manner of presence but does claim that owing to the presence the universe participates (μεθέξει) in god. See also II.9.9.64. At III.3.2 Plotinus recalls Aristotle's *Metaphysics* 12.10.1075a13ff., where god is compared to a general leading an army. Whereas in the *Metaphysics* passage the type of causality exercised by god is unclear, in the *Ennead* passage it is rather more clear that god is being compared to an efficient cause who arranges things according to a plan.

80 To treat exemplification as a relation is dubious, particularly if we take the eternal relatum to be a universal. But for Plotinus the eternal relatum is Intellect, and the relation is that which obtains between a mind and a state of affairs, a relation which, whatever else it might be, is a real relation between entities.

81 The basic meaning of κύριος is "being authoritative." Having authority over providence can only mean within the context of Plotinus' metaphysics ultimate causality. Another way of stating this is to say that Intellect has a qualified authoritative role within a finite context, but that unqualified providence derives from the One. One may compare in this regard the ἀρχή of all as freedom-maker (ἐλευθεροποιόν, VI.8.12.19). At IV.4.9 providence is the preserve of Intellect, according to the principle enunciated in IV.4.8.7: "particulars are included in the knowledge of the whole." See Parma (1971: 43–74).

82 It is most illuminating to see the Stoic account of providence as a subset of the Plotinian. For the Stoics, providence is also identified with what happens κατὰ νοῦν, but for the Stoics there is nothing beyond νοῦς to which it is responsible or subordinate. The One is "beyond" providence analogously to the way it is beyond being.

83 For the basic contrast between νοῦς and ἀνάγκη in Plato see *Timaeus* 47eff. On Plato's assimilating fate to necessity see *Timaeus* 89b8 and *Laws* 873c4, where it refers specifically to the decay of the body that is the inevitable result of its nature.

84 See Wallis (1981) for an interesting comparison of Neoplatonic and Christian accounts of omniscience. Wallis, though, is speaking of omniscience in Intellect and Soul primarily.

85 For example, at III.2.15 we find a description of conflict in the sensible world which seems to be based on the idea of natural necessity. In causing the existence of everything that can exist, conflicts arise owing to the natures of these things. Thus, if the One is only the ἀρχή of existence, then such conflicts are ultimately attributable only to the ἀρχή of essence, that is, Intellect. See also III.2.11.1–8.

Chapter III Intellect and Soul

1 Perhaps Plotinus has in mind the implicit Stoic rejection of the separation of intellect affirmed by Plato, for example, in *Timaeus*, *Philebus*, and *Sophist*. Aristotle obviously views the separability of intellect as a problem in *De Anima* 2.2.413b26–7 and 3.5.430a22–4. The problematic nature of this is reflected in the commentary tradition, especially in Alexander of Aphrodisias. As I noted in the last chapter, in the *Metaphysics* Aristotle does not argue for the existence of separate intellect, but simply assumes that the unmoved mover that is pure activity must be an intellect.

2 See also VI.2.20.10ff., where Plotinus distinguishes general Intellect (νοῦν τὸν

ξύμπαντα) from particular intellects where the former contains the latter in potency (ἐν δυνάμει) and universally (καθόλου) and the latter contain the former as particular bodies of knowledge contain knowledge.

3 See also VI.4.3–4; VI.5.7.1–6, where the unity of Intellect does not imply a denial of a multiplicity of intellects.

4 A Stoic, hence relatively late, innovation is to identify the content roughly as a proposition or a part of a proposition.

5 At V.1.8 Plotinus interprets Plato so as to find the three ἀρχαί in his writings. But it is not often enough noticed that Plotinus says that Plato recognized that this was not Plato's own innovation, but rather that it belonged to an older tradition. If, therefore, Plotinus holds what he thinks Plato holds, he does so not because Plato said it but because what Plato said was true, as evidenced in part by the authority of tradition. See Eon (1970: 259–64).

6 See II.9.6; III.9.1; VI.2.22 for Plotinus' reading of the crucial passage *Timaeus* 39e7–9; Rich (1954) and Armstrong (1960) on Plotinus' interpretation of Plato on the demiurge and Forms. Charrue (1978: 126) is, I think, wrong in arguing that Plotinus "n'a pas véritablement besoin du démiurge" and that his only reason for affirming its existence is "son désir de se mettre en relation avec les idées de Platon." On the other hand, the work of Plato's demiurge, and even the name (see II.9.8.2), will devolve upon Soul rather than Intellect, and in this sense Charrue (138) is correct to signal a qualified allegiance to the letter of Plato's doctrine. Cf. Pépin (1956: 48).

7 In *Metaphysics* 12.7 Aristotle seems to infer that the unmoved mover is νοῦς because it is perfect actuality and that it is life because life is the actuality of νοῦς. The refutation of the claim that the ἀρχή of all can be intellect is the main subject of an entire treatise, V.6. At III.8.9–11 we find the argument that *because* Intellect exists, a superior principle, the One, must exist. See Szlezák (1979: especially ch. 3 and the critical notes on Krämer (1964), Hager (1970), and Armstrong (1967)). Szlezák's position on Plotinus' relation to Aristotle and Plato is similar to mine. Szlezák recognizes in Plotinus both a critical appreciation of Aristotle and a fundamental fidelity to Plato which is shaped by the results of his criticisms of Aristotle, particularly in the matter of the first principle. See also the still useful remarks of Covotti (1935: 189–93; 226–8). It is to be particularly noted that Aristotle's first principle is precisely not νοῦς but the activity of thinking of thinking (νόησις νοήσεως). As such, to the extent that Plotinus retains a subordinate role for what Aristotle made primary, what Plotinus is retaining is an activity without prejudice to what or who is supposed to be engaged in this. There is an illuminating comparison to be made between Plotinus' claim of the insufficiency of Intellect as an ἀρχή of all and Duméry's "henological reduction" (1964: especially ch. 2), in which he attempts to show that the complexity of consciousness is "reducible" to (i.e., presupposes) the existence of a transcendent one. At I.3.1.4–5 Plotinus says that the demonstrations of the first principle are themselves a kind of leading up (ἀναγωγή) to the One. This identification makes most sense if the demonstration is a kind of self-analysis as in a reduction of consciousness. See V.1.10.6, where Plotinus says that we ought to believe that the three ἀρχαί are in us (παρ' ἡμῖν). As Atkinson (1983: 212–15) shows in discussing this passage, that the ἀρχαί are "in us" means that they are virtually what we are and that we are capable of rising up, that is, identifying in some sense with those above us, namely, Intellect and the One.

8 Cf. *Metaphysics* 12.6.1071b19–20: "Therefore, there must be an ἀρχή of such a kind that its οὐσία is activity."

9 See Atkinson (1983: 196–8). Bertier et al. (1980: 180) list the actual divergences

from the second hypothesis of the *Parmenides* in Plotinus' account of Intellect as ἓν πολλά.

10 See Szlezák (1979: 55). I suppose that we might produce the following argument. If the absolutely simple is unique, then whatever it produces will be not simple. But this argument does not tell us that Intellect will be a product of the One or that it is the "first" product. We might add the following premise to the argument. If the absolutely simple produces, its primary product must be that with minimal complexity. This would be analogous to saying that if one walks from A to B, then the first step in the direction of B will be minimally removed from A in comparison to any other step. We would still then need to show that Intellect is implicated in minimal complexity.

11 All these passages analyze the generation of Intellect into a twofold process or presume such an analysis. The point of this logical analysis, which is couched in temporal terms only for heuristic purposes, is to indicate both the priority of being and desire to knowing and the essential complexity of the activity of cognition. At V.9.8.8–22 it is made abundantly clear that the derivation of νοῦς is logical. I will consider one motive for this logical fiction in the last chapter.

12 Thus V.I.7.5–6 with its awkward grammar almost certainly means that Intellect is oriented towards the One, not that the One is oriented towards itself. See Igal (1971a: 131–7), O'Daly (1973: 70–3), and Atkinson (1983: 157–60). Bussanich (1988: 37–43) gives an excellent summary of the debate on this passage between 1983 and 1988 and argues for the position originally defended by Hadot that the One is the subject of the return (τῇ ἐπιστροφῇ). But I am not convinced by his argument that this term makes sense if used of the One. Nor am I persuaded that the texts he cites are true parallels. More importantly, if the One is the subject, the generation of Intellect is not explained at all.

13 V.4.2.6–7: "[Intellection] is itself indefinite like seeing, but is defined by the intelligible." At V.2.1.12–13 after the text quoted above, the logical priority of τὸ ὄν to the gaze (θέα) upon the One is clear. It is tempting to gloss τὸ ὄν with τοῦ νοητοῦ above. The explicit identification of the objects of Intellect with Forms is made at V.9.8.1–4. See also I.6.9.41–2; VI.7.15.9–13.

14 See VI.6.6.8–10: "For it is not because the thinker thought out what righteousness is that righteousness existed, or because he thought out what movement is that movement existed." See also ll. 31–3 and V.9.7.11–12; VI.2.8.14–16; VI.2.19.18–21; VI.7.8.4–8. Plotinus is perhaps making use of *Parmenides* 132b7–10, where it is argued that τὸ νοούμενον is prior (logically, though the text is not explicit) to a νόημα of it. Cf. VI.7.40.6: "all thinking is from something and of something." Oosthout (1991: 68), puzzlingly, argues against the logical priority of being to knowing, even though earlier (64) he asserts it. See also Corrigan (1986b) and Bussanich (1988: 11–14).

15 See III.8.11.23–4: "so that in Intellect there is desire, and it is always desiring and always attaining." See also V.3.11.1ff.; V.6.5.9–10. At III.5.9.24–9 Plotinus tells us that "myths" "make generations of things ungenerated, and separate things which are together."

16 At V.9.8.16–17 Plotinus stresses that, whereas Intellect is an activity really distinct from the One, Intellect and Forms are the same activity or the same nature and so the distinction between them is not a distinction among different entities. See Lloyd (1987: 180–1). If we compare Aristotle's point that the actuality of the mover and the moved are the same numerically but different in definition (*Physics* 3.3.202a13ff.), we may be tempted to say that Intellect and Forms are only distinct in definition, though numerically one. But if this were so, then Intellect would not be many, owing either to the duality of subject–object in cognition or to the

manyness of Forms. So, we should say that Intellect and Forms are really distinct parts or aspects of one entity, not a whole made of distinct entities.

17 See VI.9.1 in general and ll. 26–8 in particular: "For of the things which are said to be one each is one in the way in which it also has what it is, so that the things which are less beings have the One less, and those which are more beings, more." The phrase "each is one in the way in which it also has what it is" reveals that oneness is not simply provided by the One. What something is is due to Intellect and the Forms. By participating in Intellect, a thing thereby receives the existence that sort of thing is capable of having.

18 At VI.9.1.30–2 in referring to Soul in relation to the One, Plotinus notes provocatively: "It [Soul] is certainly not the One itself; for the Soul is one and the One is somehow incidental to it, and these things, Soul and One, are two, just like body and One." The One is obviously not a predicamental accident of Soul. It is an accident in the sense that the existence of Soul is distinct from what Soul is.

19 At VI.2.11.9–18 grades of unity are considered. For example, a chorus has less unity than a house and so is further removed from the One, even though it is not less of a being. More or less unity does not imply that the One is a nature variously approximated. Things are more or less one because they have more or less undivided finite being, where the paradigm of finite being is Intellect. They exist simply because they are caused to exist by the One. Their existence does not admit of degrees.

20 At VI.7.13.11ff., where Plotinus speaks of the motion of Intellect, this should be understood as following Plato in *Laws* 897c5–6. Plotinus more or less consistently insists on activity without motion for Intellect, where motion is understood as implying imperfection of any sort, excluding of course the imperfection of multiplicity. See Armstrong (1971: 67–74), who perhaps makes too much of the apparent contradictions in those texts which speak of Intellect as immutable and those texts which speak of it as changing or in motion. Beierwaltes (1985: 97–100) rightly traces the paradoxical use of temporal language in reference to the eternal to Plotinus' effort to explain the complexity of Intellect, a one-many. Perler (1931: 9–17) thinks that Plotinus has three arguments for the existence of νοῦς: (1) from the presence of form in the sensible world; (2) from the presence of discrete quantities (numbers) in the sensible world; (3) from the presence of imperfect beauty in the sensible world. But these are the basis for arguments for the existence of Forms. Thus they are only indirectly arguments for the existence of Intellect, as Perler seems to recognize in his use of V.9.6.20ff. (46–8).

21 Let us note that this argument ignores the priority of Forms to Intellect, but it does not deny it. For it is also true that eternal Intellect would not exist if Forms did not exist. The priority of Forms to Intellect is just priority in our understanding. The primary activity of Intellect is cognitional identity with Forms, but cognitional being is posterior in our understanding to real being.

22 The Platonic warrant for employing a principle which maximally generates Forms comes from *Republic* 596a and *Epistle* VII 342de. This principle, however, is defeasible and allows for reductionism. That is, if it should turn out that f is not an intelligible predicate itself but is rather really reducible to g and h, then there is no ground for positing a Form of Fness over and above Forms of Gness and Hness. I do not find Plotinus actually being very interested in reductionist questions, although I suspect that he supposed some sort of reduction was in order.

23 See VI.3.9.24–9: "For Literary Skill is not posterior to the particular literary skill, but rather it is because Literary Skill exists that that in you exists; since that in you is particular by being in you, but in itself is the same as the universal. And Socrates did not in his own person give being human to the non-human, but

Humanity gave being human to Socrates: the particular human is so by participation in Humanity."

24 I discuss this further in the next chapter. Here I note only that we should distinguish three different claims: (1) there are no eternal possibilities; (2) there are no eternal possibilities with distinct truth conditions; (3) we have no cognitive access to eternal possibilities other than through their actualizations. It is only (1) that unqualifiedly contradicts the Platonic argument.

25 See especially V.5.1.30–8; 65–8: "So if there is not truth in Intellect, then an Intellect of this sort will not be truth, or truly Intellect, or Intellect at all. But then truth will not be anywhere else either." Also, V.5.2.17; V.5.3.2. See Siegmann (1990: 70–1).

26 It might be noted that book 6 of the *Metaphysics* is the only book of that work which is not explicitly referred to by Plotinus. Nevertheless, it can hardly be doubted that he knew and used the book.

27 As Plato argues in *Phaedo* 102–7. See V.8.4.1–11.

28 Cf. *Parmenides* 133e, where the Forms of Mastership and Slavery appear to be necessarily connected, and the example of the Forms of Threeness and Oddness and so on in *Phaedo* 104a.

29 G. W. Leibniz, *Discourse on Metaphysics*, VIII.

30 At II.5.3.38–40 and VI.4.4.40 Plotinus emphasizes that in the intelligible world everything is in activity and activity. On the eternal separateness of Forms see VI.6.7.8–10: "But though all things are together each one, on the other hand, is separate; but Intellect sees them, the things that are in Intellect and being, not by looking at them but by having them, and does not separate each individual thing: for they are already separated in it for ever." Also, V.8.4.11–18; VI.2.21.55; VI.4.4.43–4 and Büchner (1970: 90–7). "Separate" would seem to indicate here really distinct "parts" of one entity, not really distinct entities.

31 See 257cd, where the examples are the parts of the Form of Knowledge, that is, Forms of types of knowledge and the parts of the Form of Difference, for example, the not-Beautiful and the not-Tall. See Findlay (1974: 460–2) on the notion of partial identity among immaterial entities.

32 At VI.2.21.56 Plotinus calls it a sort of interweaving or construction (οἷον συμπλοκὴ καὶ σύνθεσις) emphasizing the complexity.

33 For this reason, we must reject the argument of Bréhier (1928: 100) that to identify Intellect and intelligibles "c'est nier toute différence dans le monde intelligible." This would only be so if Plotinus conceived of Intellect according to the Aristotelian model he rejects.

34 See I.8.2.15–19: "Intellect there is not like this, but has all things and is all things, and is with them when it is with itself and has all things without having them. For it is not one thing and they another; nor is each individual thing in it separate: for each is the whole and in all ways all, and yet they are not confused, but each is in a different sense separate; at any rate what participates in it does not participate in everything at once, but in what it is capable of." At VI.7.14.12–16 Plotinus compares the one-many to a λόγος πολὺς ἐν αὑτῷ, where the division is not of parts outside parts but "moves always to the interior, as the natures of living beings are included in and belong to the universal living being." See also V.9.10.9–10. The division continues until the indivisible "species" is reached. The text is probably an echo of *Timaeus* 30c7–d1, where the demiurge looks to the Form of Living Creature, which contains as parts all "living intelligibles." At VI.6.7 it is stressed that the relation of Intellect to Forms is not looking (ἐπιβλέπων) but having (ἔχων). Since this "having" is of course not adventitious, each Form in a way describes what Intellect is. Thus a reference to Form F and a reference to Form G is a reference to the same οὐσία. See also VI.7.2.24–5 and

especially VI.7.15.24, where Intellect is called a "variegated good." On these
two passages see Siegmann (1990: 36–7; 70–4). See also II.4.4.16, 18; V.3.1.1;
VI.3.2.3; VI.7.13.2. Cf. Lloyd (1990: 165), who construes one-many here as
intensionally one, extensionally many. This is, I think, an oversimplification and
does not account for a multiplicity of species within a genus. Plotinus rejects the
ontological priority of species to genus in Aristotle but does not invert it. The
parts of Intellect are not posterior to it.

35 Cf. Aquinas, *Summa Theologiae* I.q.15.a.2, respondeo: "Ipse [Deus] enim
essentiam suam perfecte cognoscit; unde cognoscit eam secundum omnem
modum quo cognoscibilis est. Potest autem cognosci non solum secundum quod
in se est, sed secundum quod est participabilis secundum aliquem modum
similitudinis a creaturis. Unaquaeque autem creatura habet propriam speciem,
secundum quod aliquo modo participat divinae essentiae similitudinem. Sic igitur
inquantum Deus cognoscit suam essentiam ut sic imitabilem a tali creatura,
cognoscit eam ut propriam rationem et ideam huius creaturae." Where Plotinus
would demur is at Aquinas' additional claim that this fact does not undermine
the divine simplicity. This is so because the ability of things to participate
variously in the divine essence has its foundation in the complexity of οὐσία. In
other words, if one way of participating in F is to be a and another way of
participating in F is to be b, then there is a complexity in F such as to justify
saying that a is not identical with b. By contrast, there may be two different
instances of one Form, say, the beauty in a law and the beauty in a body, and this
possibility is to be explained not by complexity in the Form, but complexity in
the underlying elements receiving Forms.

36 In the *De Anima* passage Aristotle is evidently speaking about the passive
intellect. But it is natural for Plotinus to infer from Aristotle's own account of the
agent intellect in 3.5 that what enables the passive intellect to attain to truth in
judgment is the identity of the agent intellect with that which is the locus of eternal
truth, the Forms.

37 In this passage, Plotinus uses the term τύποι for the putative impressions or
representations in Intellect. I take it that the argument is generalizable whatever
the exact nature of the representations, so long as they are distinct from Forms.
At line 55 he uses the more general term εἴδωλα.

38 The obvious Platonic text in support of this is *Philebus* 65d2–3, where intellect
is said either to be identical with truth or "most like" it and "most true." At
V.5.2.8 Plotinus characterizes the identification as a kind of fusing (συγκραθέντας)
with Forms. This indicates well the real identity of that which is nevertheless
distinct. Emilsson (1988: 1–20) offers a similar interpretation, emphasizing that
the rejection of representationalism is a function of Plotinus' repudiation of
scepticism. Oosthout (1991: 105–8) questions whether there can be a subject of
thinking if thinking is identified with the object of thought. The answer should be
"no" if the subject is supposed to be in potency to the activity of thinking. But
if, like Aristotle's god, the subject is wholly and essentially absorbed in thinking,
it is not clear to me why there cannot be a subject distinct from thinking.

39 See *De Anima* 3.4.430a3–5; 7.431b17; *Metaphysics* 12.9.1075a3–4. Alexander of
Aphrodisias, *De Anima* 86.14–18; 89.18–23; 109.4–7, amplifies the Aristotelian
doctrine. Plotinus echoes this at V.4.2.47–8.

40 The identification of the agent intellect with Aristotle's god goes back at least to
Alexander of Aphrodisias. See his treatise *De Anima* 89.16–23 and *Mantissa*
112.18–113.2. There are two texts in Plotinus, V.9.2.21–2 and V.1.3.20–3, which
are often held to show that he followed Alexander in this interpretation. I believe
these texts are inconclusive. Nevertheless, it is likely that Plotinus held that his
account of eternal Intellect is the correct amalgamation of what Aristotle says

about god and about the agent intellect. See Schroeder (1984: 244–6). It may be added that Plotinus is encouraged by Alexander's interpretation of the agent intellect which assimilates it to the mind of the unmoved mover. This is convenient for Plotinus because in tending to identify the mind of the unmoved mover with the demiurge, he can treat Intellect generally as if its nature is the same in agent intellect and demiurge.

41 See IV.7.9.14–15. Hadot's paper (1960) is the starting-point for present-day discussion of the unity of these facets of Intellect. See Kremer (1966: 86–108) for further discussion and extensive documentation.

42 The connection between intellecting and "the truest life" is made explicitly at III.8.8.26–30, glossing *Metaphysics* 12.7.1072b26–7: "life is the activity of intellect." In the light of these texts, I cannot agree with Rist (1973: 78–80), who claims "that Plotinus is fully aware of the problem of self-awareness, but argues that far from its being the major characteristic of mind, it ceases to exist on that level" and that "Plotinus is certainly arguing that self-consciousness is something to outgrow."

43 My use of the rebarbative "intellecting" is purely heuristic. I wish to emphasize that this is the activity of Intellect. In fact, this activity can be understood as knowing or even thinking so long as we add "in the highest or primary sense."

44 See also 9.1074b33–5. *De Anima* 3.6.430b25–6 also says that intellect knows itself.

45 V.6.1.22–3: "making itself two because it thinks, or, better, because it thinks it is two and because it thinks itself, one." See also V.3.5.1ff.; V.4.2.9–12; V.5.2.15; V.6.1.22–3; V.6.5.10–12; V.8.4.1–4; VI.7.39.11–14; VI.7.40.6; VI.9.2.36–7. On the ineliminable duality of intellect and intelligibles and on why this disqualifies Aristotle's unmoved mover as first principle of all see Hager (1970: 309–15).

46 See Pépin (1956: 54–5) and Wallis (1987: 922–5) on the sceptical background of this argument. Sextus Empiricus, *Against the Logicians* 1.310–12, states the dilemma faced by those who hold that cognition is an identification: "For if the mind apprehends itself, either it as a whole will apprehend itself, or it will do so not as a whole but employing for the purpose a part of itself. Now it will not be able as a whole to apprehend itself. For if as a whole it apprehends itself, it will be as a whole apprehension and apprehending, and the apprehending object will no longer be anything; but it is a thing most irrational that the apprehending subject should exist while the object of the apprehension does not exist. Nor, in fact, can the mind employ for this purpose a part of itself. For how does the part itself apprehend itself? If as a whole, the object sought will be nothing; while if with a part, how will that part in turn discern itself?"

47 This is most clear at II.9.1.36–9; 46–54. See also V.3.1.15–28. The passage at II.9.1.53–4 ends: "what room is there for the distinction in thought which separates thinking from thinking that it thinks?" This would seem to indicate an absence even of conceptual distinctness between knowing something and knowing that one is knowing something. But if this is so, then the only way we can preserve distinct knowers is to say that p as known by s has some different quality from the way p is known by r. Thus, s knows p in a unique manner or from a unique perspective. This fact does not, however, entail an obliteration of the distinction between subject and object. If it did, there would be no reason for denying Aristotle's claim that intellect is unqualifiedly actual. See Hintikka (1962: 103–25) for a useful survey of various versions of the claim that knowing p and knowing that one knows p are mutually implicative.

48 V.5.1.1–2: "Could anyone say that Intellect, the true and real Intellect, will ever be in error and believe the unreal? Certainly not." See also VI.2.8.2–5, where the infallibility of Intellect is explained by saying that the being of the object of

intellection is just its being thought. With this passage should be read V.6.6.24–7, where Plotinus distinguishes "man" and "thought of man," "horse" and "thought of horse," etc. We can reconcile these two passages if we say that "man" and "thought of man" are distinct according to a real minor distinction in the latter passage, though in substance they are identical. See also Pépin (1956: 49–50).

49 Proclus, *The Elements of Theology*, prop. 15 (Dodds: 1963), states this with utmost clarity. Since a material entity has parts outside parts, there could never be literal self-reflexivity (πρὸς ἑαυτὸ ἐπιστρέφειν) in it. See the commentary of Dodds (202–3) on this passage with references.

50 V.3.4.1–4 seems to contradict this when it says that we are in accord with νοῦς in two ways: "either by having something like its writing written in us like laws, or by being as if filled with it and able to see it and be aware of it as present." I discuss the interpretation of this passage below in chapter 8.

51 For Plotinus the most important association of life with Forms is of course to be found in Plato's *Sophist* 248e. See IV.7.9.24; V.3.8; V.4.2.43; V.5.1.33ff.; V.9.8.1–8; VI.2.20. See Hadot (1960: 108–9). That each Form is an intellect means that the world of Forms is in fact also a community of distinct intellects. See also IV.3.5.6–8: "Now no real being ever ceases to be; since the intellects there too are not dissolved into a unity because they are not corporeally divided, but each remains distinct in otherness, having the same essential being." Himmerich (1959: 50) cites III.2.16.17–20, where Plotinus says that all life is activity. In connection with this statement, Himmerich argues, Plotinus employs Aristotle's principle that actuality precedes potency to conclude that primary life has primary activity. This is not strictly true, because the One is primary activity. See VI.8.20.9–16. Also, III.8.8.8; V.1.8.17; V.3.5.26; V.6.6.21; V.9.5.29; VI.6.2.9; VI.7.40.15 on the identification of thinking and object thought. As Schwyzer (1951: 553–4) points out, Plato nowhere explicitly identifies intellect and οὐσία, but this is a natural inference from *Republic* 507b, 508b, and 509b.

52 V.9.8.3–4. Cilento's translation is not so misleading: "E, precisamente, nel suo complesso lo Spirito è il complesso delle forme; ma la forma nella sua singolarità è lo Spirito preso come singolo." Similarly, but more literally Bréhier, "L'intelligence complète est faite de toutes les idées, et chacune des idées, c'est chacune des intelligences" and Harder-Theiler, "Und zwar ist der Geist als Gesamtheit alle Ideen, die einzelne Idee aber ist der Geist als einzelnes."

53 V.9.7.14–17: "It is, then, incorrect to say that the Forms are thought if what is meant by this is that when Intellect thought this particular Form came into existence or is this particular Form; for what is thought must be prior to this thinking [of a particular Form]." Roloff (1970: 18), commenting on III.8.8, where Plotinus explains how thinking and being are identical and Intellect is true life, says: "Der Geist ist als Subject zugleich das intentionale Objekt, wie dieses umgekehrt zugleich das – das Object denkende – Subject ist." See also 51. Against this view, I hold that the Forms are intentional objects of Intellect and that self-reflexivity means the subject thinking the subject thinking the intentional object, thereby maintaining the distinction between subject and intentional object. For at VI.2.8.4–5 Plotinus says: "but if things which are without matter have been thought, this is their being."

54 Cf. *De Anima* 3.4.430a1–2. Huber (1955: 22) argues that in the "Spiritualisierung des Eidos" Plotinus develops an idea beyond anything explicit in Plato or Aristotle. I think this is true only in that Plato is not explicit on the cognitive identity of Intellect and Forms, and for Aristotle, cognitive identity of intellect and its objects is not identity with Plato's Forms.

55 Trouillard (1961a: 137–8) notices a kind of intersubjectivity amongst the eternal

minds which he compares to the unity of species within a genus and particular souls within a universal soul. Trouillard's comparisons are, I think, inapposite, and the intersubjectivity that Plotinus clearly suggests in this passage is nowhere clarified in the text. Armstrong (1967b: 245) refers to the "interpenetration of a community of living minds" but does not explain what this is supposed to mean.

56 At VI.2.18.11–15 intellect is said to be a σύνθετον ἐκ πάντων [γενῶν] and not any one of them. "Synthesis" is a difficult expression here, for it seems to indicate that which is posterior to what it is a synthesis of. But perhaps "synthesis" just means "whole," which need only be logically posterior to its parts. See also VI.2.3.20–30. If this were not so, in no sense could anything other than the One be derived from the One.

57 III.5.9.19–20; V.1.3.9; V.1.6.45–6: "Soul is an expression and a kind of (οἷον) activity of Intellect, just as Intellect is of the One." See also III.2.2.17; IV.4.16.19; V.2.1.14–15; VI.4.11.16. On the use of λόγος in this regard see Rist (1967b: 88ff.). On Soul as an image (εἰκών) or trace (ἴχνος) of Intellect see I.8.11.17; III.3.3.34; V.1.7.44; V.3.8.36.

58 Oosthout (1991: 118), commenting on V.3.7.25ff., thinks that Plotinus just circumvents the problem by *positing* Soul as a secondary activity of Intellect.

59 One of the clearest statements of this instrumentality is at VI.8.15.33–6, where existence is endowed according to λόγος or forming principle. A λόγος is in this context a Form. Another is at VI.4.11.1–9, where the principle that being is present according to the capacity of the recipient is expressed. I interpret this according to the instrumentality of Intellect. That is, the One endows existence to a kind of being, or better, each kind of being receives existence in a specific way, via its participation in Intellect. See also I.8.2.19–21.

60 See Kremer (1966: 97–8). On the coherence of the concept of an eternal mind and eternal activity see Stump and Kretzmann (1981: 446–7).

61 The contrast between βίος and ζωή, where the former is an image or manifestation of the latter, is not always made consistently. See III.4.3.12 and Beierwaltes (1985: 100 n77). Typically, as in III.7.12, for example, βίος is associated with Soul. I can only find one passage where βίος is associated with Intellect, V.1.4.9–10. But in this passage Intellect is metaphorically identified with Kronos.

62 One important source for the idea is probably *Nicomachean Ethics* 10.7.1177n26–1178a8. In the Aristotelian passage the paradoxical assertion is made both that the god's life of contemplation is a life greater than human life and that it is a life to which we should and can aspire because it is a life lived according to the best part of our soul. Indeed, there is an even more explicit identification of a man with a rational faculty at 9.4.1166a17 and perhaps also at 9.8.1168b35. This claim is more intelligible on the basis of Plotinian than on the basis of Aristotelian principles.

63 See V.3.4.23; V.3.9.8, where discursive reasoning itself is called an image of Intellect (εἰκὼν νοῦ). Plotinus uses both τὸ διανοητικόν and λογισμός for discursive reasoning.

64 It is clear from I.8.14.34 that the soul includes many powers (δυνάμεις δὲ ψυχῆς πολλαί). It is in fact a locus of a range of organic activities. See II.9.2.6–9.

65 See III.8.2.25–34; III.9.1.34–7; IV.3.12.14–19; IV.3.20.38–9; V.1.6.45; III.7.11.27–8: "in the same way Soul, making the world of sense in imitation of that other world, moving with a motion which is not that which exists there, but like it." See also IV.3.12.30–2: "But Intellect as a whole is always above, and could never be outside its own world, but is settled as a whole above and communicates with things here through soul" and VI.5.12.1. See Rist (1967b: 95), Schubert (1968: 51–4), Früchtel (1970: 41–67), and Turlot (1985: 523): "Nous considérons donc que le *Logos* plotinien est essentiellement le principe

'subordonné' qui, issue du *Nous*, fonctionne comme act de l'Ame, en tant qu'il opère la liaison de l'intelligible et du sensible, en y transférant les formes intelligibles, permettant la constitution du monde." See also Santa Cruz de Prunes (1979a: 77–88), who convincingly refutes the contention of Armstrong (1940: chs 6 and 7) that nature and λόγος are ὑποστάσεις distinct from soul. Armstrong (1967b: 254) corrects himself on this. This is not contradicted by VI.5.8.20, where it is said that "there is nothing between" (οὐδενὸς μεταξὺ ὄντος) Forms and instances. The absence of mediation here is an absence of essential mediation. That is, instances of Forms are not instances of instances of Forms.

66 Counter to the claim made by Lee (1982: 97–103). Perhaps an appropriate analogue to the instrumentality of Soul in relation to Intellect is to be found in Aristotle's analysis of cognition. For Aristotle, imagination can be characterized as an instrument of the agent intellect which operates upon the passive intellect. The important difference between the analogues is that Intellect alone is not an efficient cause, whereas the agent intellect is. This follows from the fact that Intellect is not perfectly actual, whereas the agent intellect is.

67 See IV.7.2.24–5, where it is stressed that the λόγος that is added to matter to make body could come from nowhere but soul.

68 Cf. *Metaphysics* 5.4.1014b36ff. Müller (1916b: 234–5) lists all the texts in which φύσις is used in this sense.

69 See II.2.1.37–8 and III.8.3, where Plotinus describes nature as contemplating in the sense that it is ποίησις but not in the sense that it contemplates ἐκ λόγου. See Rist (1967b: 98–9).

70 According to Aristotle, *Metaphysics* 5.4.1014b18–20, φύσις is the ἀρχή of motion generally. But the soul is the ἀρχή of motion for ensouled things: see *De Anima* 3.9.432a17; IV.7.9.6 follows Aristotle.

71 III.7.11.15–30 contains the best description of the restless and externally directed soul. It is said of soul that it "had an unquiet power, which wanted to keep on transferring what it saw there to something else" (ll.21–2). See also V.3.3.17, where Soul is said to busy itself (πολυπραγμονεῖν) with externals (τὰ ἔξω), whereas Intellect is concerned with what belongs to itself and what is in itself (τὰ αὑτοῦ καὶ τὰ ἐν αὑτῷ). See also IV.8.4.12–21 and Armstrong (1991).

72 At IV.8.1.22–7 Plotinus expresses the hope that he can derive "something clear" from what Plato says about the soul.

73 *Philebus* 28c7–8 calls intellect king of heaven and of earth (βασιλεὺς οὐρανοῦ τε καὶ γῆς). At 30c9–10 Plato says that intellect does not exist without soul, and d1–2 attributes to the divine a royal soul (βασιλικὴν ψυχήν) and a royal intellect (βασιλικὸν νοῦν). *Timaeus* 29e1ff. implies that the demiurge has intellect and makes the soul of the universe.

74 It is true that in the *Phaedrus* 245c4 Plato calls soul the ἀρχὴ κινήσεως. And soul is the ἀρχή of all motion at *Laws* 1.896a5–b1, including the motion of bodies. But at *Laws* 1.897c5–6, d3 Plato refers to a κίνησις νοῦ. This would seem to contradict what the *Phaedrus* says unless either κίνησις is being used equivocally or intellect and soul are actually more closely connected than Plato explicitly indicates.

75 At IV.2.1.1–7 Plotinus describes the intelligible world, the world of Intellect, as a world of souls without bodies (ψυχὰς ἄνευ σωμάτων). At I.6.6.17–18 it is said that soul is really itself only when in the realm of Intellect. At VI.7.15.27 the purified souls (ψυχὰς τὰς καθαρὰς) seem to be simply identified with intellects. It is possible that sometimes a "purified soul" refers to some sort of intermediate state midway between incarnation and identification with intellect, either in the "downward" or "upward" direction of its path. This would be the temporary state in which memories of an incarnate life might still be retained. Perhaps in

this Plotinus is especially eager to be in accord with Plato, particularly in the *Phaedrus*, where discarnate souls are represented as having a complexity and activity different from that of intellect. See also III.4.6; IV.3.13.29–30; IV.3.17. But this possibility does not change the main point of the argument.

76 Beierwaltes (1985: 80–3) stresses the temporality of Soul compared with the eternality of Intellect, analogous to the description of time itself as an image of eternity. See also III.7.11.43–5; III.7.12.21–2. Being in time is the life of the soul.

77 On the ambiguous uses of the various forms of πᾶς and ὅλος with ψυχή see Hellemann-Elgersma (1980: 132–47). The main distinctions are (1) between two kinds of soul, the soul of the universe and the individual soul; (2) each of these as wholes and their parts; (3) each individual soul and the unity of all these in some sort of whole. Thus, for example, the part of our soul that does not descend is also a part of a unity of all souls. As Hellemann-Elgersma notes, these distinctions are made in response to opponents whose accounts of soul are thought by Plotinus to be inadequate.

78 They are of the same form (ὁμοειδὴς) (IV.3.6.1). See Hellemann-Elgersma (1980: 57–63) on the image of "soul-sister" and the differences between the individual soul and the soul of the universe.

79 The doctrine of the organic continuity of the universe is Stoic. Plotinus' principal innovation is to insist on the separation of Intellect.

80 It is perhaps possible that "partial intellect" refers not to discursive reasoning but to the separated intellect of each individual. But then the contrast between what the universal soul has as a model and what individuals have is greatly lessened or even eliminated. So, I am inclined to interpret "partial intellect" as our own discursive reasoning faculty, our access to which is evident. It is quite ordinary for Plotinus to use ἐν μέρει for an instance of a Form.

81 Plotinus is perhaps trying to be faithful to the somewhat ambiguous claims made by Plato in *Philebus* 23c–30e and *Timaeus* 34c about the relations among the demiurge, intellect, and soul. To these passages must be added the complication caused by *Sophist* 249a4–7, where Plato says that in perfect being intellect must be present *in* a soul.

82 So it would seem from IV.8.8.13–16, where it is said that soul orders the universe not by λογισμός, but by intellect.

83 Schubert (1968: 48), Pazzi (1979: 303–4), and Oosthout (1991: 31–7) seem to follow a similar interpretation, though they perhaps do not take account of what for Plotinus are obvious Platonic suppositions.

84 At IV.9.4.19–20 Plotinus compares the soul as one-many to a seal-ring in relation to its impressions in many pieces of wax. See also VI.5.6.10–12, where this image is used of a Form in relation to its instances.

85 At IV.3.5.8–9 Plotinus says: "So too it is with souls, which depend in order on each several intellect, and are expressions of intellects." At lines 17–18 Plotinus seems to describe the soul apart from incarnation as a single abiding expression of Intellect (λόγος εἷς τοῦ νοῦ ἡ μένουσα), whereas the incarnate versions are partial immaterial expressions (λόγοι μερικοὶ καὶ ἄυλοι) The phrase λόγος εἷς τοῦ νοῦ is difficult, but can perhaps bear the interpretation of it as an instance of universal intellect, as explained in the last section; VI.4.14.1–3 supports this if in πάσας ψυχὰς ἔχει καὶ πάντας νοῦς the καὶ is epexegetic.

86 Plotinus learned that the immortal soul is just an intellect both from Aristotle and from Plato. In Aristotle, it is just the agent intellect. In Plato, *Timaeus* 41cd, 69c8–d1, d5–6, 90a, it seems clear that the immortal part of the soul is intellect. What Plotinus has done has made explicit and prominent what is perhaps just a possible implication in Plato, namely, a distinction between an undescended intellect and its image which is the highest part of the incarnate soul.

87 See also VI.5.10.11–23, where the unity of souls is a unity in thinking.
88 See VI.5.9, where the unity of souls sounds very much like the unity of the realm of Intellect. Merlan (1968: 54–5) understands Plotinus' claim that soul is one (see VI.4.4.34–45) as meaning that "[i]t is one and the same soul, one and the same intelligence which is present in all men. This unique soul, this unique intelligence operates incessantly, though we are not conscious of it. Plotinus is, in other words, simply another representative of the famous doctrine *de unitate intellectus* and of monopsychism." This interpretation makes nonsense of the *personal* ascent which is the core of Plotinus' ethical and psychological doctrines. The urgent question at VI.4.14.2: "how is one soul evil and the other good?" would make little sense on Merlan's interpretation.

Chapter IV Truth and the Forms

1 Cf. VI.7.2.16: "For what a thing is is the reason why it is."
2 At VI.9.1.1 Plotinus says: "It is by the One that all beings are beings." See also VI.8.14.30–1. Meijer (1992: 94–5) denies that VI.9.1.1 means that the One is the cause of beings. He holds that "beings are beings in virtue of unity." This is implausible. It is not the unity that something has that causes it to be. And the unity of something is owing to the Form of Unity, which is not the cause of the being of anything. If the One were the cause of unity, then since the One is the cause of existence according to many passages, either it would be the cause of two things, existence and unity, or else, as I hold, the unity that the One causes is just the existence of a unity. Further, if the One were the cause of unity it would be, contrary to Plotinus' own words at VI.2.9.5–10, a genus. Intellect owes essence to its own activity but the existence of essence to the One. See also VI.8.7.25–6: "for it is impossible for a thing to make itself and bring itself into existence" (ὑπόστασιν). At VI.7.2.23–7 Plotinus says that Intellect "has in itself the cause of its existence" (ὑποστάσεως). The context of this claim indicates that it does not contradict the above interpretation. Plotinus is here talking about essence, not existence. For example, in the Form of Man in Intellect is found the reason why men have eyes. Thus, at line 17 a Form is said to be "the cause of existence for each thing [that is, each instance of the Form]." So, Intellect explains why eyes exist in men.
3 Cf. Wagner (1985: 282), "Intellect alone must be that principle which guarantees both its own identity and the identity of its content, for Absolute Truth, the source of true knowledge and its objects, must depend on nothing external to itself."
4 See, for example, Ross (1986: 315–34), (1988: 279–300), (1989: 251–79), and (1990: 171–98).
5 See Ross (1990: 173ff.). It should be noted that here Ross is arguing for an interpretation of Thomas Aquinas and is not explicitly endorsing this view, although elsewhere he seems to do so. The present discussion does not depend on the correctness of Ross's interpretation or whether he completely endorses the view he attributes to Aquinas.
6 See Ross (1989: 271–8).
7 See Plantinga (1974: especially ch. 9) and (1980: especially 126–46).
8 Ross (1989: 271).
9 The subject of this sentence must be supplied. It is perhaps easiest to make it Intellect. But there is nothing against the subject being the One. The point of the passage is the same in either case.
10 See V.8.3.1–3 and V.9.2.7–9, where the Form of Beauty is said to be the cause

of beauty in its instances. By implication, a *different* Form would be the cause of the instantiation of different natures.

11 Thomas Aquinas, *Summa Theologiae* I.q.15.a.2, respondeo, sees this clearly, although Aquinas mistakenly thinks that he is refuting a Platonic (read: Neo-Platonic) position because he understands emanation as a *per accidens* series: "Ordo igitur universi est proprie a Deo intentus, et non per accidens proveniens secundum successionem agentium; prout quidam dixerunt quod Deus creavit primum creatum tantum, quod creatum creavit secundum creatum, et sic inde quousque producta est tanta rerum multitudo; secundum quam opinionem, Deus non haberet nisi ideam primi creati. Sed si ipse ordo universi est per se creatus ab eo, et intentus ab ipso, necesse est quod habeat ideam ordinis universi. Ratio autem alicuius totius haberi non potest, nisi habeantur propriae rationes eorum ex quibus totum constituitur; sicut aedificator speciem domus concipere non posset, nisi apud ipsum esset propria ratio cuiuslibet partium eius. Sic igitur oportet quod in mente divina sint prioriae rationes omnium rerum . . . Hoc autem quomodo divinae simplicitati non repugnet, facile est videre, si quis consideret ideam operati esse in mente operantis sicut quod intelligitur quae est forma faciens intellectum in actu . . . Non est autem contra simplicitatem divini intellectus, quod multa intelligat; sed contra simplicitatem eius esset, si per plures species eius intellectus formaretur." Ross thinks that there is no need for the *propriae rationes* in God's mind. Aquinas (on the traditional interpretation) thinks that there is a need for them but that they do not compromise the divine simplicity. Plotinus thinks that there is a need for them and that they do compromise the simplicity of the first principle, so that a second principle must be posited to contain them.

12 By contrast, Plantinga (1980: 142–3) assumes that creation is temporal and that God is not absolutely simple.

13 See Ross (1990: 195).

14 See Plantinga (1980: 140–6).

15 Ross (1980: 626) argues that God is not really related to creation, whereas creation is really related to God. This is not in conflict with Plotinus' own view. If it is said that the first principle must follow rules in creation, the constraints of eternal truth, it does not follow that the first principle is not the cause of the being of these constraints. It only follows that there be an eternally subordinate mind.

16 For a thorough treatment of this argument in *On Ideas* see Fine (1993: ch. 9).

17 In this regard, Plotinus' problem is more like one faced by any creation metaphysics than it is like anything faced by a Platonic or Aristotelian metaphysics. Maurer (1982: 173) points out that according to Aquinas, God knows Himself as imitable not just by kinds but also by individuals. Hence, the divine mind includes the ideas of individuals. So, the Plotinian reason for positing Forms of individuals is similar to the Thomistic reason, except that Plotinus will put these in Intellect for the same reason he puts all Forms in Intellect.

18 I read καθὸ ἡ ψυχὴ καθέκαστα καὶ ἐκείνως λέγεται ἐκεῖ with Igal (1973: 91) and translate accordingly rather than καθὸ ἡ ψυχὴ καθέκαστα καὶ ἐκεῖ ὡς λέγεται <ἐκεῖ> with H.-S. or καθὸ ἡ ψυχὴ καθέκαστα καὶ <ὡς λέγεται> ἐκεῖ [ὡς λέγεται ἐκεῖ]. Igal's reading certainly seems to give a better sense.

19 The clearest statement of this is at VI.5.7.1–8, where the identity of the distinct members of the "family" of intellects with intelligibles is asserted several times. See also IV.3.5.6–8: "Now no real being ever ceases to be; since the intellects there too are not dissolved into a unity because they are not corporeally divided, but each remains distinct in otherness, having the same essential being." Cherniss (1962: 508) says that Plotinus limits Forms of individuals to individual souls. My intepretation is even more limited than this, since it includes only individuals having a unique place in Intellect. Rist (1967b: 86–8) rightly dismisses Cherniss's

conflation of Plotinus' position with things Aristotle says about individual forms. But Rist's objections to Cherniss's interpretation do not, I think, apply to my own. Rist (1970: 299) says, although "it is probable that Plotinus accepts Ideas of all individuals, he seems to find Ideas of men the most acceptable, Ideas of animals less so, and presumably Ideas of inanimate things least of all." It is not clear to me what Rist thinks is the principle of "acceptability" Plotinus employs. Cf. Rist (1982: 101): "I believe it may now be assumed . . . that Plotinus was one of those Platonists who subscribed to a heretical version of Platonism according to which there are not only forms of species but also forms of individuals, *at least in the case of individual men*" (my italics).

20 Rich (1957: 232–8) demonstrates amply the unambiguous character of Plotinus' fidelity to this doctrine. She points out in particular why the exigency of retribution combined with the doctrine of the soul's impassivity makes reincarnation attractive to him. This still leaves the problem, recognized by Plotinus, of how a person can be reincarnated into an animal. See also III.2.8; III.3.4; III.4.2; IV.7.14; VI.7.6. Mamo (1969: 94–5) is, it appears, alone among contemporary scholars in voicing strong doubts regarding Plotinus' fidelity to a belief in reincarnation or transmigration of souls. So, Mamo can hold that there is a Form for each and every individual human being or animal.

21 Cf. VI.5.12.15–22, where the accretion (προσθήκη) is identified with non-being. It is by eliminating this that one returns to the intelligible realm.

22 This is how I understand lines 19–22, which seem merely to be missing the words "at the same time" and which I supply from line 15, ἐν μιᾷ περιόδῳ.

23 At V.7.3.1–13 Plotinus considers but then seems to reject the possibility that indistinguishable individuals within a litter or twins might need have only one λόγος. That they are simultaneous individuals seems enough to guarantee more than one λόγος. This tends to confirm my interpretation of the restriction on transmigration. Otherwise, the individuality of Socrates would be utterly specious.

24 Cf. Igal (1973: 97 n1) on the text at this point.

25 We may note that V.9 is treatise 5 in Porphyry's chronological order and V.7 is treatise 18 and that both were written before Porphyry joined Plotinus in 263. In general, doctrinal divergences among these treatises are very difficult to discern. Blumenthal (1966: 61–80, reprinted in revised form in 1971b: 112–33), finds rejection of Forms of individuals elsewhere and arrives at the distressing fluctuation: "no" in V.9[5], "yes" in V.7[18], "no" in VI.4–5[22–3], perhaps "yes" in IV.3[27], "no" in VI.7[38] (p. 76). I discuss the other passages adduced by Blumenthal below. Cf. Mamo (1969: 79–83), who argues on grounds similar to mine that V.9.12 is not to be taken as contradicting V.7.

26 Igal (1973: 92–8). So Armstrong (1977a: 52–4).

27 Rist (1970: 299–301) rightly rejects the claim of Blumenthal (1966: 70–3) that this passage indicates a denial of Forms of all individuals. Blumenthal (1971b: 122–3 and n24) says that in the earlier article "I probably adduced VI.5.8 as negative evidence [for the existence of Forms of individuals] too confidently." Nevertheless, he does count it as such evidence along with V.9.12.

28 A similar conclusion is reached by Armstrong (1977a: 52–6). Nevertheless, it is wrong to assume that Plotinus *starts* from identity in difference as a datum to be explained. For Plato, it is possible to go from identity in difference directly to Forms; for Plotinus it is not, because of the mediating role of soul. See Pistorius (1952: 28), "For Plato the ideas were knowable by the discursive reason. Even the highest idea, the archetype or idea of ideas, could be reached by the power of human thought. Not so Plotinus. He does not go from the visible to the invisible, from the particular to the universal, but from the universal to the particular."

29 See Rist (1970: 301).

Chapter V Categories and the Tradition

1 See *Post. An.* 1.32.88b1. At *Metaphysics* 5.28.1024b9–16, he says that one of the meanings of "different in kind" (ἕτερα τῷ γένει) is different "categories of being" (κατηγορίας τοῦ ὄντος). See also *De Anima* 1.1.402a23–5. Rutten (1961: 43–8) thinks that Plotinus confuses categories and genera. But Plotinus is evidently relying on a well-established usage.

2 Perhaps Plotinus has in mind *Phaedo* 79a5–6, where Plato says: "let us posit two kinds of being, the visible and the invisible."

3 It is possible that Plotinus thinks of the Stoics as inheritors of the materialist metaphysics reduced to absurdity by Plato in *Sophist* 246a–248a. In this regard Plotinus is followed by later commentators. See Brunschwig (1988: 65–76).

4 The first is at VI.1.25.8–9 and the second at ll. 9–10. See Wurm (1973: 158–63).

5 Gandillac (1979: 249) cites 999a6–14 as the source, but this passage contains a continuation of the same point, namely, the predicative connection of the prior and posterior.

6 Graeser (1972a: 90) writes: "to infer, as Plotinus does, that τι, if it is to be, must be ἕν τι τῶν εἰδῶν (25.9) and, if not, Being would equal τὸ μὴ ὄν, is, firstly, to confuse reference and predication, and secondly, to conflate the predicative and existential function involved in the usage of the *copula*." This criticism seems to me to ignore the desperation of the version of the Stoic position that Plotinus is attacking and his accurate diagnosis of it: positing a highest genus which is also a genus of different *kinds* of things.

7 See Alexander of Aphrodisias, *De Mixtione*, 224.32–225.7 (*SVF* II.310).

8 I interpret thus the obscure argument at lines 6–7: "if they say that [act and potency] are simultaneous, they will put the principles in the realm of chance."

9 Because matter is not a τόδε τι, it cannot be primary οὐσία. See also 7.3.1029a26–8 and 7.6.1031a15–17, where Aristotle also says that *if* Forms exist, then the ὑποκείμενον cannot be identical with οὐσία. Perhaps it is this passage in particular which Plotinus has in mind.

10 See Graeser (1972a: 100).

11 See Graham (1987) for an extensive treatment of the claim that the theory of the *Categories* is fundamentally at odds with that of the *Metaphysics*.

12 See Hadot (1974: 31–47) on the attempts by Plotinus' successors, principally Porphyry, to reconcile the Aristotelian account of οὐσία with that of Plotinus. I believe that in this regard confusion arose because, although Plotinus accepted the equivocity of being, and perhaps accepted the equivocity of οὐσία (see VI.1.3; VI.2.1.29ff.; VI.6.13.27–8), he does not accept the Aristotelian hypothesis that being is substance, at least not in the sense in which Aristotle intended it. Hence, one cannot infer that the relation ἀφ' ἑνὸς καὶ πρὸς ἕν will be the same in both cases. See Gandillac (1979: 252–3). Thus Corrigan (1981: 101ff.) is misled into arguing that an Aristotelian doctrine of substance is retrievable basically intact from Plotinus' positive accounts. See also section 3 below. Strange (1987: 964–72) understands Plotinus' criticism of Aristotle's categories as rather more eirenic in tone and close to Porphyry's attempt to reconcile Aristotle with Plato. I think it is more likely that Plotinus wishes to show the severe limitations of the Aristotelian account.

13 At 5.8.1017b23–6 Aristotle says that οὐσία has two senses: (1) a subject and (2) what is separable and a "this something." He explains the latter by form or shape.

14 There are of course different senses of "separate" and "separable" in Aristotle. The phrase "unqualifiedly separate" (χωριστὸν ἁπλῶς) is the primary sense. It is used of the sensible composite at *Metaphysics* 8.1.1042a30–1. But it is also by implication used of the οὐσία that is ἀΐδιος καὶ ἀκίνητος at 12.7.1073a4

(κεχωρισμένη). The conflict is patent, both between the passages in books 7 and 8 and between books 8 and 12. Either the sensible composite and the non-sensible οὐσία are independent of each other or not. If so, then how is the science of οὐσία ἀκίνητος supposed to be the science of being qua being, as Aristotle says it is at 6.1.1026a29–32? If not, then presumably the sensible composite is dependent on non-sensible οὐσία, in which case it is called "separate" equivocally.

15 See Anton (1976: 87): "For it would appear that the Aristotelian categories are not simply inapplicable to the realm of the intelligible; they are inadequate even for the task of understanding the nature and properties of the sensible object. Recognition of this radical aspect of Plotinus' criticism makes him the theoretical forerunner of all modern thinkers who rejected Aristotle's conception of physical substance and the categories as the ultimate types of attribution and property analysis." This seems to go a bit too far, for Plotinus is prepared to allow a pragmatic function to the concept of οὐσία which is not disharmonious with at least one line of Aristotle's own thinking. Cf. Foss (1982: especially 77–83); Lloyd (1990: 86, 95–7). Lloyd speculates on whether the pragmatic function of the concept of οὐσία for Plotinus corresponds to the function of the discursive intellect as distinct from Intellect.

16 And, we may add, on Aristotle's claim that being is οὐσία, οὐσία cannot be a genus anyway. See Wurm (1973: 151–2). Rutten (1961: 59) thinks that this argument is a sheer confusion, but it is not clear why he thinks this.

17 But see 8.3.1043a30, where Aristotle seems to *contrast* the composite and the actuality or form. A few lines later, however, he adds, "But, although these distinctions [between composite and form in the cases mentioned] contribute something to another inquiry, they contribute nothing to the inquiry into sensible substances; for the essence belongs to the form or actuality. For a soul and the essence of a soul are the same, but the essence of a man is not the same as the man, unless also the soul is called 'a man.'" In this context, the words "for the essence belongs to the form or actuality" seem to apply to non-sensibles, and this implies that in the case of sensibles, the actuality and the composite are not distinct.

18 See Code (1985: 102): "a particular like Socrates is not, according to the hylomorphic analysis of *Metaphysics* Z, a primary substance, and he is not identical with his essence."

19 I take it that this is a direct denial of Aristotle's conclusion at *Metaphysics* 8.3.1043b3: "the essence of a man is not the same as the man, unless also the soul is called 'a man'". Note that Plotinus embraces the counterfactual condition. In VI.3.5.12–14 Plotinus adds: "so the form is not in the matter as in a substrate, nor is humanity in Socrates [in this way] since it is a part of Socrates," where the last clause must be intended to distinguish the sensible composite which is Socrates from his form.

20 Aristotle, at *Metaphysics* 9.8.1050b2–4, affirms both the identity of form and actuality and the priority of actuality to potency in οὐσία.

21 See, for example, VI.3.4.35–7, which looks like Plotinus' endorsement of the causal priority of sensible substance to its attributes.

22 Cf. *Metaphysics* 7.17.1041a17–22, which is perhaps the passage Plotinus has in mind. There Aristotle tries to show that to inquire into why something is itself is to inquire into nothing. As we have already seen, Plotinus would accept such a claim for primary οὐσία, that is, Intellect.

23 The instrumental causality of Forms, as in "Helen is beautiful because of Beauty," is only explained by such identity, as is the parallel self-identity of Form and instance in "neither is Tallness short nor is the tallness in us short." Cf. VI.5.8.22–6: "For if the Idea of Fire, for instance, is not in matter – let our

discourse take the matter underlying the elements as an example – the fire itself which does not come to be in matter will give the character (μορφὴν) of fire to all the matter made fiery."

24 One may perhaps compare Magritte's famous hyper-real painting of a pipe with the legend "ceci n'est pas une pipe." Or we might think of a drawn circle which is and is not a circle. If we think it is wrong to call the drawn circle a circle, is it equally wrong to call it a square? If not, why not? At V.7.1.21–3 Plotinus says that men are not related to their Form as portraits of Socrates are to their original. Here he is referring to the Form of the individual. Socrates is thus related differently to the Form of Socrates and to the Form of Man. The main difference is that the Form of Socrates and Socrates are in a one–one relation, whereas the Form of Man and Socrates are in a one–many relation. The same Form of Man is in Aristotle. But the "real" Socrates is the Form of Socrates, not the sensible Socrates.

25 Following Plato, Plotinus describes time as an image of eternity (III.7.13.24) and Forms as the παραδείγματα of which sensibles are images (I.2.7.28–30; V.3.13.30–1; V.8.12.15). Unlike Plato, however, Plotinus describes Soul as image of Intellect (V.1.3.8; III.8.11.29–30; V.3.4.21).

26 I take it that this is what Wagner (1985: 275) wishes to deny, but the texts do not support his argument. Fielder (1978a) and (1980) has an interpretation similar to mine. At IV.5.7.18 the secondary activity of Intellect is said to be an ὁμοίωμα of it. I take this to indicate univocity. Indeed, I am not sure what non-univocal likeness would be. Presumably, it would be something like resemblance. But resemblance is not clearly a two-term relation. If resemblance does not reduce to univocity, then to say that A resembles B is to say that A resembles B in some respect. Then, a four-term proportionality is erected: A:C::B:C. If this is an exact proportionality, then we have univocity once again. If it is not, then the proportionality needs also to be expanded, indefinitely, I should think. At V.8.8.17–21 it is said that things in the sensible world are beautiful because they are images of that which is beautiful itself. This passage says that imagery is the *reason* for predication, not that calling a sensible "beautiful" just means that it is an image. The latter is what I take a denial of univocity to entail.

27 A substance is in potency to its accidents and is their efficient cause. So, the substance is an explanation for the existence of the accidents. But it is not in so far as it is a potency that the substance explains; rather, it is in so far as it is form or actuality.

28 See Lloyd (1990: 89).

29 At lines 29–31 Plotinus says: "And the rational form (λόγος) of a man is the being a 'something' (τι), but its product in the nature of body, being an image of the form, is rather a sort of 'some such' (ποιόν τι)." It is clear from the text a few lines later (16.3) that τι stands for τόδε τι. It is also clear that λόγος is being used synonymously with εἶδος.

30 At VI.3.15.33–5 I follow H-S₂ in reading: οὕτως οὖν καὶ λόγου ὄντος, καθ᾽ ὃν Σωκράτης, τὸν αἰσθητὸν Σωκράτη <ὀρθῶς λεκτέον οὐ Σωκράτη>. The apparatus explains: "sensibilem Socratem aeque falso Socratem appellamus atque in exemplo Socratis effigies Socrates appellebatur." H-S₂ are followed by Igal and Armstrong.

31 Lloyd (1955: 68–71) agrees that the focus of Plotinus' argument against Aristotle's categories is the unity of the individual and that the result of the argument is the denial of the distinction between essential and accidental predication. This is particularly clear in VI.2.4–5.

32 See Wurm (1973: 254).

33 It is true that in this passage Plotinus proposes this description dialectically. But

at VI.3.10.15–16 and again at VI.3.15.24–7 he seems to embrace it as his own. See Wurm (1973: 255). The ultimate source for Plotinus' thus describing sensible individuals appears to be *Theaetetus* 157bc, where the term used is ἄθροισμα. Perhaps Plotinus shifts his terminology because Plato's term was taken up by Stoics (see Sextus Empiricus, *Against The Logicians* 1.277) and he did not wish to confuse his view with theirs. See Wurm (1973: 250–62).

34 Plotinus sometimes uses the language of substance and accident himself. See I.8.3.16–17; I.8.6.51–2. But in neither of these passages is he speaking of sensible substances. In the first passage he is speaking about the essence of evil and in the second, the essence of elements. Rutten (1961: 70) rightly says that "Plotin réduit l'οὐσία à sa *fonction de sujet logique*" because of its essential indeterminacy. By contrast, for Aristotle a sensible substance is a real subject because it is essentially determined by the secondary substances which are said of it.

35 Corrigan (1981: 120–2) writes: "The essence in the matter *makes* the sensible object. This is Aristotle's view of sensible substance. It is also that of Plotinus" (120 n82). But he seems to contradict himself a bit later when, referring to Plotinus' account of substance, he says, "although man *is* most fundamentally his essence ... nonetheless 'this' man and his essence are not *identical*" (122). Precisely because Plotinus does separate the essence of a sensible substance from that substance, in defense of Plato and directly counter to Aristotle, an Aristotelian account of sensible substance is forfeited. Thus Corrigan's attempt to make Plotinus a continuator of Aristotle in this regard rather than an opponent is misconceived.

36 See 254c2ff. Some scholars have argued that the μέγιστα γένη are not Forms, but Plato says explicitly that the five are selected from among all the Forms (πάντων τῶν εἰδῶν). At any rate, Plotinus unquestionably treats them as such. In what sense they are μέγιστα remains to be seen.

37 See Cornford (1935: 274–8).

38 As suggested by the ordinary usage of the Greek word οὐσία.

39 Plato's later dialectical method of collection and division presupposes this sort of account.

40 The role of the One in causing the existence of every composite is an expansion of the role of the Form of the Good, which gives existence only to other Forms. Plato does not explicitly account for the existence of anything other than Forms by means of Forms, even the Form of the Good.

41 Plotinus sometimes qualifies this slightly, calling Intellect ὄντως οὐσία (VI.6.8.2) or ἑστία οὐσίας (VI.2.8.7). In these cases, the contrast is presumably with οὐσία in the sensible world, which is only an image of true οὐσία.

42 See VI.2.18.12–15: "But Intellect, since it is being as intelligent and a composite of all [the genera], is not one of the genera; and the true Intellect is being with all its contents and already all beings, but being in isolation, taken as a genus, is an element (στοιχεῖον) of it." See also II.6.1.4, where Intellect is described as τὸ ὅλον. See Volkmann-Schluck (1966: 112–18). The use of στοιχεῖον for a genus is gotten from Aristotle, *Metaphysics* 5.3.1014b10–12.

43 The term οὐσία is used by Plotinus synonymously with the nominalizations of the verb "to be" (εἶναι) and the participle ὄν.

44 See VI.2.8.14–15: "For its self-directed activity is not οὐσία, but being (τὸ ὄν) is that to which the activity is directed and from which it comes: for that which is looked at is being, not the look."

45 At VI.2.7.26 movement is said to make being perfect (τέλειον), perhaps an echo of Aristotle's use of ἐντελέχεια for motion.

46 See VI.2.17.28–30: "the good for Intellect is its activity towards the Good; but this is its life; but this is movement, which is already one of the genera."

47 Aristotle says that rest is the contrary of movement at *Metaphysics* 5.2.1004b27–9, meaning that it is incorrect to say of something that it is at rest unless it could have been in motion. On the other hand, at 12.7.1073a4 he says that god is immovable. I assume that the kind rest is equivalent in meaning to immovable. Cf. VI.2.8.22: a rest that never started (οὐχ ὁρμήσασα στάσις), which seems to indicate an exclusion of movement unconditionally.

48 See Brisson (1991: 468): "Considérée comme l'acte de intellect en acte, la pensée peut être tenue pour un mouvement. Mais si on considère la pensée dans la perspective de son terme, la forme (ἰδέα), on peut la définir comme un repos. Bref, le repos se trouve du coté de la forme appréhendée comme la limite de l'intellect, alors que l'intellect, lui, se voit défini comme le mouvement de la forme."

49 At II.4.5.30–1 Plotinus says that movement was called (by Plato?) otherness both because they are the co-principles of intelligible matter and because they themselves "sprang forth together."

50 See VI.2.15.14–15: "but if it [Intellect] is many, it is also otherness, and if it is one-many, it is also sameness." I take "many" to indicate a real distinction within one entity.

51 On the complex historical background of Plotinus' concept of intelligible matter, born of an apparent conflation of Aristotle's account of the principle of the Indefinite Dyad in Plato and Aristotle's own concept of intelligible matter as both principle of individuation among mathematicals and as genus, see Rist (1962a) and Szlezák (1978: 72–85).

52 V.4.2.7–9: "from the Indefinite Dyad and the One derive the Forms and Numbers: that is, Intellect." See also V.1.5.13–19; V.2.1.7ff. and Szlezák (1979: 65). That the coming to be of intelligible matter or the Indefinite Dyad is to be understood only logically is clear from VI.6.6.4–5. *Metaphysics* 13.7 is the main source for Plotinus' information on Plato's unwritten doctrine of principles. Merlan (1964) argues that *Metaphysics* 1.6.987b20–5 is quite likely to be a source as well. What is at issue in Merlan's case for the importance of a brief reference as compared to a much longer discussion is whether Aristotle claimed that Plato held that Forms were in fact numbers or whether he claimed that Plato held that Forms and numbers both originated in the operation of the One on the Indefinite Dyad. The text Merlan refers to might well have been taken by Plotinus in the latter sense. In fact, I believe that Plotinus interprets Plato in a way which is different from Aristotle's interpretation in either case.

53 So Fuller (1912: 283): "In him [Plotinus] Matter is certainly not the principle of individuation in the intelligible world. It is rather the principle of its community and oneness, of that being and unity in which the Ideas all share in spite of their variety." At III.8.11.2–6 intelligible matter is described as the potency or first phase of the generation of Intellect. Actual contemplation of Forms is the second phase. As we have seen, this is a logical distinction only. See Schroeder (1986a: 189). This does not appear to represent a meaning different from that contained in the other passages cited above. See Bussanich (1988: 118–20) on III.8.11.2–6.

54 See Rist (1962a: 105).

55 See Hadot (1960: 111): "Les genres de l'être du *Sophiste* (254–5): être, mouvement, repos, identité et altérité, apparaissent comme les différents aspects sous lesquels notre intelligence morcelante saisit la vie unique de l'intelligence. Mais c'est bien parce que la réalité intelligible est douée de vie et de pensée que cette mutiplicité de points de vue est possible." See also III.7.3.11–17; Nebel (1929: 44–6) and Büchner (1970: 59–63).

56 At VI.2.14.5ff. Plotinus distinguishes a particular οὐσία from οὐσία itself. The former has qualities whereas the latter does not. Plotinus is here not making the

point that a universal is not an instance of itself. Rather, he is alluding to an inference from Aristotle's own claim that primary οὐσία is separated form. But form is neither universal nor particular. Primary οὐσία has no qualities not because it is a universal, but because it is unqualifiedly actual.

57 Plotinus rejects explicitly Forms for the following: things which are "contrary to nature" (V.9.10.2–3); artifacts and the arts which produce these (αἵ τέχναι ποιητικαί), except in so far as they make use of proportions and practical virtue and so are included in the λόγος of man (V.9.11.13–17); dirt, mud, and savage beasts (V.9.14.7–11); casual composites (τὰ σύνθετα εἰκῇ) (V.9.14.14–17); imitative arts (αἵ τέχναι μιμητικαί) except in so far as they are included in the λόγος of man (V.9.11.1–6).

58 Plotinus is clearly puzzled about Plato's understanding of the relation of νοῦς to the Forms. At VI.2.22.1–3, referring to *Timaeus* 31b9 and 39e7–9 Plotinus says: "And Plato speaks riddlingly of the way in which Intellect sees the Ideas in the complete living creature [observing] of what kind they are and how many they are." Plotinus interprets the relation between νοῦς and τὸ παντελῶς ζῷον as a relation between two parts of a whole, although he himself explicitly denies the adequacy of thus representing the relation of Intellect to eternal truth. The subject Intellect sees the Forms in its intentional object, οὐσία. The five greatest kinds are aspects of this "whole." See VI.2.21.58 and VI.6.17.34–40.

Chapter VI A Platonic World

1 There are three Platonic texts from which this distinction is derivable. First, at *Parmenides* 132d5–7 Parmenides responds to Socrates' suggestion that the theory of Forms can be saved if Forms are said to be παραδείγματα and instances are said to be ὁμοιώματα, that is, images of Forms. Parmenides says: "if a thing is made in the image of the Form, can that Form fail to be like the image of it, in so far as (καθ᾽ ὅσον) the image was made in its likeness (ἀφωμοιώθη)?" Thus, homonymy between Form and instance does not preclude synonymy. In fact, it entails it owing to the nature of instantiation. The second text is *Sophist* 236a8–b7, where the Eleatic Stranger in the course of the division leading to the definition of the sophist distinguishes between two kinds of μίμησις, εἰκαστική and φανταστική. The former is when the imitation is like what it imitates, though somehow different from it; the latter is when the imitation is not like what it imitates. The two ways of imitating a model are analogous to synonymous and homonymous images of Forms, respectively. The latter, however, cannot be instances of Forms. Cf. VI.5.8.25, where the Form of Fire gives the μορφὴν πυρὸς to sensible fire. This "form" is then identified with the "image" of Fire. So, there are a form of fire and an image of Fire in sensible fire. To insist on homonymy without synonymy is to conflate the two distinct features being explained in this passage. The third passage is *Timaeus* 53b, where Plato describes the state of the world before the imposition of "forms and numbers" on it by the demiurge. The result of the demiurge's activity is a realm of sensible images which nevertheless bear the mark of intelligibility. See Leroux (1992: 250–8) on the last passage.

2 It is also true for qualities themselves considered as individual subjects or particulars. Thus we must distinguish this white from the nature of white in it.

3 See Aubin (1953: 348–79), Schroeder (1978: 51–73), (1980: 37–60), Fielder (1976: 102–6), (1977: 1–11), Beierwaltes (1985: 73–113), Wagner (1986: 57–83), and Leroux (1992) on the metaphysics of imagery in Plotinus. Schroeder (1978) and (1992) names what I have called homonymous and synonymous images

"representation" and "reflection." A large part of the latter work is devoted to showing how this distinction is applied to various problems by Plotinus.

4 Plato himself in his later dialogues feels justified in using οὐσία in some sense for the sensible world, as in *Philebus* 26d8, 27b8–9, where he speaks of γένεσις εἰς οὐσίαν and γεγενημένην οὐσίαν. This fact undoubtedly supports Plotinus' confidence that there is some commensurability between what Plato and Aristotle believe about the sensible world.

5 V.9.13.9–11: "and there must be true knowledge in the souls which are in us, and these are not images or likenesses of their Forms as things are in the sense-world, but those very Forms themselves existing here in a different mode" (ἄλλον τρόπον). I understand "different mode" to indicate a synonymous image. By contrast, the mode of cognition in Intellect precludes imaging altogether, except of the One. Intellect is identical with Forms. This distinction allows Plotinus to attribute knowledge and the consciousness of knowledge to the individual without implying that the individual is thereby conscious of identification with Intellect.

6 See V.8.7.12–16: "The only possibility that remains, then, is that all things exist in something else, and since there is nothing between, because of their closeness to something else in the realm of real being something like an imprint and image of that other suddenly appears, either by its direct action or through the assistance of Soul – this makes no difference for the present discussion – or of a particular soul." Armstrong, in his note to this text, says, "[t]he insistence on the immediate and intimate relationship of the intelligible and sensible universes and the comparative unimportance of the mediation of soul should be noted." The possibility that is countenanced by the phrase "either by its direct action" I think refers to the images in soul rather than the images mediated through soul. The mediating role of soul is stressed elsewhere.

7 See V.9.2.16–18: "What then is it which makes a body beautiful? In one way it is the presence of beauty, in another the soul, which moulded it and put this particular form in it." See Lee (1979: 81–2).

8 See V.2.1.19–21; II.3.17.2–7; IV.4.13.2–13 on nature in plants and the absence of cognition in them. As Deck (1967: 70–2) argues, III.8.8.14–16, where Plotinus speaks of φυτικὴ νόησις, is not a contradiction of this, for this type of intellection is only a remote image of Intellect under the aspect of life.

9 See VI.3.15.24–38; II.7.3.4–5, where "body" (σῶμα) is defined as "qualities with matter." At VI.3.10.12–17 we read: "For since our discussion is about sensible substance (αἰσθητῆς οὐσίας) the division would not be out of place if it was taken to be made by the differences which present themselves to sense-perception; for this sensible substance is not simply being, but is perceived by sense, being this whole world of ours; since we maintained that its apparent existence was a congress of perceptibles, and the guarantee of their being comes from sense-perception." I believe that the last phrase of this passage indicates that Plotinus is using the term "sensible substance" equivocally. That is, what Aristotle would call a sensible substance is to be understood otherwise. Counter to the claim of Wagner (1982b: 67), this passage does not entail that "[t]he substances of the phenomenal world depend for their existence upon our perceptions rather than helping explain the phenomenal world. Phenomenal bodies are items that individual souls make by means of sensation, and their substance is a result of that making." Here Plotinus is only referring to a convenient manner of classifying the putative sensible substances. That πίστις arises from αἴσθησις is perfectly in line with Platonic doctrine.

10 See Code (1984: 105): "The separability of Forms goes hand in hand with the idea that Forms are participated in *accidentally*. If the Form of Man is separable, then particular men are accidentally, not essentially, men. Aristotle finds this

unacceptable." According to Plotinus, however, once Aristotle concedes that a sensible substance is not unqualifiedly identical with its essence, he no longer has the tools to defend the alternative.

11 VI.3.8.30–1: "And there is no need to object if we make sensible substance out of non-substances." See also II.6.1.48–52, *Physics* 1.6.189a33: "how could substance come to be from non-substances?", and *Metaphysics* 14.1.1087a29–b4. The absurdity is said to arise from the fact that substances do not have contraries, but if a substance is in a subject, that out of which it is made, it will have a contrary. Further, if non-substances are prior, what is the subject they are in?

12 I take it that at VI.3.1.13–16, when Plotinus proposes to order sensibles in terms of species and genera, he is doing this solely on pragmatic grounds.

13 At III.6.14.18–36 the description of the relation of matter to form in the sensible world is suffused with artificial imagery. See also II.4.5.18; II.5.5.22.

14 Benz (1990: 85–177) provides a comprehensive survey of the various accounts of matter in the *Enneads*.

15 In calling the receptacle "matter" Aristotle means "prime matter," as he says in *Generation and Corruption* 2.1.329a24.

16 At III.6.13.19 Plotinus quotes *Timaeus* 52a8–b1, where Plato identifies the receptacle as χώρα. So, when Plotinus further identifies the receptacle as matter, he seems to be endorsing Aristotle's interpretation of matter as space. See Matter (1964: 200–17) and Schwyzer (1973: 268–73).

17 Cf. *Metaphysics* 8.4.1044a18 and II.4.11.23–5, where the distinction is between unqualified (ἁπλῶς) and qualified (τούτου or ποιὰ) matter. See also II.5.5.8; III.6.10.3–5.

18 Aristotle, *Generation and Corruption* 1.5.320a2–3: "Matter, in the most proper sense of the term, is to be identified with the substratum which is receptive of generation and destruction." See also *Physics* 1.9.192a31–2.

19 Cf. II.9.3.12–18, where Plotinus argues that matter is indestructible because its existence is caused by eternal principles, which operate necessarily. So, if matter exists now it must always exist, otherwise its coming into being would be the result of a principle that is not operating necessarily. The argument appears circular, as Roloff (1970: 163–4) notes. Nevertheless, from the existence of matter now we can deduce its hypothetical necessity for the existence of any images of Intellect. And from the hypothetical necessity of matter for the existence of any images we can perhaps then deduce its unqualified necessity if the One operates necessarily below Intellect.

20 If matter had no φύσις, there could be no distinction between what matter is and its existence. The absence of a distinction between "what" and "that," however, belongs uniquely to the One. Φύσις appears to be a broader category than εἶδος, including εἶδος and matter as well. Since εἶδος and its synonyms generally connote transparency to an intellect for Plotinus, matter should be understood as intrinsically an unintelligible existent or principle of existents. Plotinus' willingness to attribute a φύσις to matter is thus traceable ultimately to his creation metaphysics. From the fact that matter has a φύσις, it does not follow that matter is substance, because φύσις does not determine individuality in a bit of matter.

21 See Wurm (1973: 237–8 and n27, 253), Santa Cruz de Prunes (1979a: 129).

22 See also IV.7.2.24, where it is said that matter plus λόγος equals body (σῶμα), and IV.3.20.37–8: "the form in matter is inseparable" (ἀχώριστον γὰρ τὸ ἐν ὕλῃ εἶδος). This is inseparability in reality. The form can be separated in thought. Then it is the same as the universal.

23 See Schwyzer (1973: 266–80), who holds that since matter is not generated in time it is simply ungenerated. Cf. O'Brien (1981: 112), (1991: chs 1–3), and (1993: 21–7 and 61–8), who rightly rejects Schwyzer's argument. At IV.8.6.18–23

Plotinus contrasts two possibilities for matter: either it is eternal or it was generated. In the latter case, its being was a sort of gift from its cause. Plotinus does not unambiguously opt for either alternative, perhaps thinking of the *Timaeus*. However, several points need to be stressed. Even in the case of the first alternative, *dependence* is not necessarily denied, as is evident at II.4.5.24–8, where Plotinus says that, although intelligible matter is not in time and so is eternal (ἀεί), it has an ἀρχή. And just because it has an ἀρχή, it has in some sense γένεσις. The eternal γένεσις of matter is its dependence on the One via Soul. So, Plotinus uses γένεσις and its various forms in two senses: (1) having an ἀρχή eternally and (2) having an ἀρχή in time. (3) There is yet another sense of γένεσις, that of undergoing change. This is related to (2) but not identical with it: (3) refers to the lack of completeness and successive states either of that which also has an ἀρχή in time, such as individuals in nature, or to what has no beginning in time but is always in process (γινόμενα ἀεί), like the universe itself (see II.4.5.27). In no sense does it refer to things under (1). Matter is not exactly like things in (3) because it has no shape sufficient for a change (see II.5.5.12). What would it change into? What would it become?

24 He adds that the identification depends on defining στέρησις as "opposition to the things that exist in rational form" (ἀντίθεσις πρὸς τὰ ἐν λόγῳ ὄντα). See also I.8.11.1–7. Plotinus appears to equate στέρησις with ἐλλείψις or lack, which he identifies with matter at I.8.5.6–13.

25 It is not clear, however, that in this passage Aristotle is referring to unqualified matter rather than to designated matter. If he is referring to the latter, then Plotinus is extending the meaning of στέρησις rather than denying Aristotle's claim in regard to a proposition containing the same meaning.

26 It is clear from *Metaphysics* 5.22 in Aristotle's discussion of the meanings of στέρησις that unqualified privation has no place. All of the senses of privation discussed refer to the absence of a particular characteristic that is either suitable or at least possible for an individual to have. I take it that the concept of unqualified privation represents Plotinus' innovation. He does, however, employ the Aristotelian distinction at I.8.11.10ff.

27 Recall that at VI.1.2.10–12 Plotinus notes and approves of Aristotle's claim at *Metaphysics* 7.3.1029a29–30 that the form and the composite would both seem to be more οὐσία than the matter. See also VI.3.7.12–16.

28 VI.3.7.28–9: "So here also [in the sensible composite] being is different in matter and form." See also VI.3.3.1–3, where he adds that the being of the composite differs from the being of the other two as well, and II.5.2.10–12; VI.3.2.7–8.

29 Simons (1985: 62) aptly states: "Plotinian matter is not designed to account for the presence of authentic Being in sensibles. To the contrary, it is designed to justify the antithesis, namely, that the sensible realm is not the locus of εἶδος."

30 Spurious reasoning (νόθος λογισμός) is the way to describe cognition of the receptacle in the *Timaeus* presumably because of the "puzzling way" that the receptacle partakes of the intelligible (51b). The way is puzzling because the receptacle is without form (ἄμορφον). It is a peculiar form of reasoning that can grasp what is without form.

31 This description is reminiscent of *Sophist* 240b, but there it is applied to the semblances produced by the sophist, i.e., false propositions and beliefs. Plato nowhere describes the receptacle in this way, although he does say at *Timaeus* 52c2–4 that what is present in the receptacle is an image (φάντασμα), "an ever moving semblance of something else, clinging in some sort to existence on pain of being nothing at all." At I.8.3.8–9 evil, which is elsewhere identified with matter, is said to be an "image of being or even something more non-existent"

264

NOTES

(εἰκὼν τοῦ ὄντος ἢ καὶ μᾶλλον μὴ ὄν). Plotinus appears to identify matter with Plato's images of reality, or at least with the unintelligible "aspect" of images.

32 See I.8.3, where Plotinus carefully distinguishes the non-being of matter from unqualified non-being. O'Brien (1981: 110), citing III.6.11.31–42 and III.6.14.18ff., points out that the participation by matter in goodness is strongly qualified. Indeed it is so, because matter does not participate through form in goodness, as does everything else. It retains a dependence relation to the One, though the power of form has dissipated completely.

33 The assocation of matter with a necessary condition for contraries is an argument based on *Timaeus* 47e5–8b1, where Plato identifies necessity with the "errant cause" that the demiurge was forced to overcome in bringing order to the world. This is a particularly inappropriate comparison for Plotinus, since the independence of necessity in Plato's account is clear. Such independence is of course inconsistent with the argument that *everything* proceeds from the first principle.

34 See III.7.5.12–18, where αἰδιότης is defined as the condition of the substrate (κατάστασις τοῦ ὑποκειμένου) (i.e., Intellect) and αἰών the ὑποκείμενον itself. But cf. III.7.3.23–4, where Plotinus says that αἰών is not the ὑποκείμενον itself but something that is attributed to it indicating that there is nothing it is going to be.

35 Stump and Kretzmann (1981: 432) want to distinguish the eternal from the atemporal, where the latter covers numbers and truths and where the former alone applies to life. Such a distinction is not appropriate for Plotinus. Atemporal entities without life are impossible for the reason given in chapter 3.

36 I agree with Sorabji's conclusion (1983: 125–7) that strict timelessness is a concept not to be found in Aristotle's texts. Nevertheless, as Sorabji points out, on Aristotle's definition of time, whatever is everlasting is not in time, although obviously in some sense temporal predicates are applicable to it.

37 See V.1.4.17–19, where Plotinus distinguishes ὁ ὄντως αἰών of the blessed life of Intellect from time's imitation of it.

38 See Sorabji (1983: 138).

39 See IV.4.1.12–16: "But if, as we believe, every act of intelligence is timeless, since the realities there are in eternity and not in time, it is impossible that there should be a memory there, not only of the things here below, but of anything at all. But each and every thing is present there; so there is no discursive thought or transition from one to the other."

40 Aristotle argues that time is a measure of motion with regard to prior and posterior. He demonstrates that motion is everlasting and therefore that time is as well. But time as such is not an attribute of motion and so not dependent on it in being. This is so because time can measure the non-existent past.

41 See Plass (1977: 18–19). Plato in the *Timaeus* 35a describes the construction of the world-soul by the demiurge as a mixture of the "stuff" of eternity and becoming. But it is clear that this mixture is properly so-called only because it is everlasting, that is, everlastingly in time.

42 Difference and sameness are, as we have seen, two of the greatest kinds. What Plotinus means here is that the life that is in time instantiates difference rather than sameness because its parts are spread out rather than all at once.

43 It might be objected that this claim is simply false, for a substance is ontologically prior to its accidents, but the accidents are predicated of the substance. This is true for sensible substances, but the ἀρχαί do not have accidental attributes. Whatever is predicated of them is done so essentially.

44 See III.7.6.21–36, where Plotinus emphatically distinguishes the durationless life of Intellect from that which has no beginning and no end but endures forever.

45 III.7.7.4–5: "We too, then, must have a share in eternity. But how can we, when

we are in time?" See also III.7.6.47–50. At III.7.13.1–4 he says that time (i.e., the life of Soul) cannot be "in time." Being "in time" then is a dependent relation for everything "in", that is, dependent on, Soul. And this includes things at rest. Thereby Plotinus provides one reason for rejecting Aristotle's account of time as a measure of motion alone.

46 So Lassègue (1982: 418).

47 Plotinus is here following Aristotle, *Physics* 4.11.219a1–10.

48 So Aristotle, *Physics* 4.12.221b7–9.

49 Trotta (1992: 351–65) argues that Plotinus confuses the ontological with the mathematical in his criticism of Aristotle's account of time in the *Physics*. For when Aristotle says that time is a number of movement, he does not mean an abstract counting of it, but a property of movement itself. As Aristotle says, 219b6–9, time is a number in the sense of that which is numbered, not in the sense of that by which we number. It seems, though, that Plotinus at III.7.9.68–73 does consider the possibility that "number" means either that which numbers (measures) or that which is numbered (measured). In the latter case, Plotinus argues that, assuming time is different from movement, Aristotle has not explained why if there were movement and a "before" and "after" there would be no time without that which is measured or numbered. In other words, if time is numbered and not that which numbers and yet is different from movement, why is it that for Aristotle there is no movement without time or time without movement?

50 Epicurus apparently used the term σύμπτωμα. Sextus Empiricus, *Adversus Mathematicos* 10.219, interprets Epicurus as meaning that time is a σύμπτωμα συμπτωμάτων, for movement itself is a σύμπτωμα of entities. So little is known about Epicurus' account of time (if indeed he had elaborated one) that these distinctions need not concern us.

51 See Clark (1944: 349–58). Trotta (1992: 362–5) points out that regarding soul and its relation to time, Plotinus grafts the Aristotelian account on to the Platonic. For Aristotle says, *Physics* 4.14.223a16–29, that time exists actually as opposed to potentially only if there is a soul to measure it. For the specification of a unit of numbering depends on us. Plato holds that soul produces the orderly and hence temporalized movement of the universe. But since time seems to be independent of the numbering by any particular soul, Plotinus wants to identify it with the everlasting life of the soul of the universe. This is presumably what Aristotle should have concluded, according to Plotinus.

52 III.7.12.24–5: "For it is in activity of this kind that this universe has come into being; and the activity is time and the universe is in time."

53 See Beierwaltes (1967: 267). At the end of the treatise, 13.66–9, on the question of whether time is "in us" as it is in the "soul of the all" he replies: "Is time, then also in us? It is in every soul of this kind, and in the same form in every one of them, and all are one. So time will not be split up, any more than eternity, which, in a different way, is in all the [eternal] beings of the same form." This is disputed by Jevons (1964: 70), who argues: "The soul-movements of which time consists are on (or rather towards) the level of individuals, rather than of the whole world."

54 See Beierwaltes (1967: 286–7).

55 See ibid., 260–2.

56 At III.7.11.31–5 Plotinus represents the distinction as between soul which temporalized itself (ἑαυτὴν ἐχρόνωσεν) and everything else which is "in time." See also III.7.13.30–40 and Manchester (1978: 126–7). Guitton (1971: 64) aptly states: "Plotin intériorisait le temps, mais il spiritualisait le mouvement." Cf. I. Kant, *Critique of Pure Reason*, 77, "Time is nothing but the form of inner sense, that is, of the intuition of ourselves and of our inner state." "Time is the formal

a priori condition of all appearances whatsoever." The priority of "psychical time" is of course the Kantian analogue.

57 See III.7.11.45–8, where Plotinus says that time stands to eternity as "this all" stands in relation to "the intelligible all" that is, in the relation of becoming to being. The remainder of this chapter (ll. 48–62) goes on to contrast time and eternity in the terms in which becoming and being are traditionally contrasted in Platonic metaphysics.

58 See Stump and Kretzmann (1981: 444–5) for a similar argument that the concept of temporal or "apparent" duration is parasitic upon the concept of atemporal duration. I think Plotinus would simply contrast the temporal with the eternal, since there is no eternal duration. It should be noted in this regard that although Plotinus follows Plato's general approach to the priority of being to becoming, he does appear to invert Plato's ordering of space and time. For Plato in the *Timaeus* 38b6, 52a8, clearly makes space prior to time by making space eternal but time generated. See Helm (1981: 237–8). It may be objected that since Plotinus believes that *everything* besides the One is generated and that since he also believes the *Timaeus* is not to be taken literally in any case, the priority of time to space is mitigated. This objection is weak, for even on a non-literal interpretation of the *Timaeus*, the priority of space to time remains. That is, space is independent and time is dependent. Plotinus cannot have been unaware of his admittedly tacit divergence from Plato on this point.

59 On the entire passage see Beierwaltes (1967: 249–62).

Chapter VII Human Psychology

1 See IV.7.10.1–3, which seems to rely both on the so-called affinity argument in the *Phaedo* (78b4–84b8) and the argument at *Republic* 611a–612a. Contrast the Stoic position, which is that the soul survives the dissolution of the body, but not indefinitely: Eusebius, *Evangelical Preparation* 15.20.6 (*SVF* 2.809).

2 The Greek here is very difficult to translate. The words ἐλέγχοιτ' ἂν καὶ τῇ παραθέσει μὴ δι' ὅλου δέ . . . are almost unintelligible if we do not take them as a clumsy gloss on the passage from the *Letter to Herodotus* quoted below. I cannot improve on Armstrong's translation.

3 See Schwyzer (1960: 341–78); Emilsson (1988: 164–5).

4 Schwyzer (1960: 373) notes that in Plotinus συμπάθεια is a synonym for συναίσθεσις, which is the term he most frequently uses for self-reflexivity. But Schwyzer takes the terms as synonymous only when Plotinus is referring to "Miteinanderfühlen." In our text it is clear that συμπάθεια does not have this meaning in referring to soul. I think it is synonymous with συναίσθεσις nonetheless. See Gurtler (1988a: 91–137) for a careful survey of the various uses of συμπάθεια in Plotinus.

5 Searle (1992) presents a valuable contrasting argument. He agrees that mental activities or properties like intentionality and consciousness are ineliminable, but he denies that these cannot be accounted for by the sciences that explain bodies. "One can be a 'thoroughgoing materialist' and not in any way deny the existence of subjective, internal, intrinsic, often conscious, mental phenomena" (54). Epicurus and the Stoics, unlike some contemporary materialist philosophers, would not wish to deny "mental phenomena" either. Searle and Plotinus would differ on the description of the phenomena which they seek variously to explain: Plotinus would say that no body could account for mental phenomena and Searle would say that mental phenomena are merely sorts of "emergent properties" of bodies, albeit very unusual bodies (111–12).

6 Rist (1982: 102) argues that, given that there are Forms of individual souls, an ideal self will retain something of its "personality" in union with the One. I cannot see how this personality could involve more than numerical distinctness in the activity of the individual contemplator. That is, everyone would be contemplating the Forms, and hence attaining the Good, and there would not be different "versions" of this. There would be just multiple cases. Some find the prospect of the absence of the idiosyncratic repugnant. For example, Nagel (1986: 219) writes: "I would rather lead an absurd life engaged in the particular than a seamless transcendental life immersed in the universal." Plotinus would, I think, reply to this by saying that personal preference is not here the fundamental issue. First, it must be determined whether the ideal self is an incarnate or a discarnate agent. The answer to this question ought to guide preference.

7 See Diogenes Laertius 7.156; Hierocles, 1.20; Nemesius, *On the Nature of Man* 2 (*SVF* 2.773).

8 Proclus, *Elements of Theology Propositions* 15–17, seems also to have the Stoics in mind in arguing that the agent of intellection cannot at once be material and self-reflexive. See Inge (1929: I.124–8) and Emilsson (1988: 154–8). Aquinas, *Summa Contra Gentiles* II. 49; *In II Sentences* d.19 q.1.a.1, solutio, develops at some length this argument, which perhaps originates in Aristotle's *De Anima* 3.4.429b9–430a9; 3.2430b24.

9 Plotinus' account of the Stoic position is exactly confirmed by Aëtius, *Placita* 4.23.1 (*SVF* II.854): Οἱ Στωϊκοὶ τὰ μὲν πάθη ἐν τοῖς πεπονθόσι τόποις, τὰς δὲ αἰσθήσεις ἐν τῷ ἡγεμονικῷ.

10 At IV.4.19.26–9 Plotinus explicitly distinguishes between a pain, which is a πάθος, and sense-perception of a pain, which is a kind of cognition. But my perception of my pain would not in principle be different from my perception of your pain on a materialist conception of the soul. Plotinus perhaps has in mind *Republic* 462d, where Plato makes the point that a man can be said to have a pain in his finger owing to his organic unity. The pain is both in the finger and in the man himself.

11 O'Meara (1985: 252) summarizes the underlying central argument thus: (1) soul is responsible for the life or living functions of body; (2) the nature of body is such that it could not be responsible for such functions; (3) therefore soul is not body.

12 See the affinity argument in the *Phaedo*, where the soul is shown to be connatural (συγγενές) with Forms, and *De Anima* 1.3.407a18; 3.4. See also Emilsson (1991: 162–3).

13 When at IV.7.8⁵.1–5 Plotinus paraphrases this definition, he leaves out the crucial qualification that the soul is the *first* actuality.

14 So Verbeke (1971: 200–4).

15 Verbeke (1971: 207–10) seems to miss the point of this criticism. He takes the conflict to which Plotinus is referring as one between bodily and spiritual desires and Plotinus' claim against Aristotle that the ἐντελέχεια doctrine of soul cannot account for this.

16 See I.8.4.6–25 for the fullest description of the phenomenon. Also I.1.9.6–8; II.9.15.34–8.

17 Perhaps Plotinus also has in mind the famous text from *Generation of Animals* 2.3.736b27: "It remains, then, for the reason alone so to enter and alone to be divine, for no bodily activity has any connection with the activity of reason." This text seems to suggest a difficulty Aristotle faces in unifying the cognitive life of the organic individual. See Blumenthal (1972: 345), who calls this "a thoroughly cavalier treatment of the basis of Aristotle's psychology." I think that it is more aptly characterized as an attack on hylomorphism for its inconsistencies

in the treatment of the person or self. Verbeke (1971: 218), who thinks that Plotinus misunderstands Aristotle on many points in this text, still concedes (218): "Il fault avouer cependant que dans le cadre de son entéléchisme, il n'est pas arrivé à déterminer la place de l'intellect humain." I take it that that is precisely the main claim Plotinus is making.

18 At IV.3.20.36–9 in arguing against various ways of understanding the relation of soul to body, Plotinus rejects the view that it is present as form to matter: "But it [soul] is not, either, present like the form in matter: for the form in matter is inseparable, and it comes afterwards to the matter which is already there. But soul makes the form in matter and is other than the form [which it makes]." Presumably, the matter here is designated matter. See also VI.4.3.17–22; VI.7.4–5. See Blumenthal (1968: 254–61), Hager (1964: 174–87), and Rist (1966: 82–90).

19 See I.1.6.8–9, where the *living* composite is distinguished from the soul (i.e., the self). See Trouillard (1956: 68), "Le dualisme du pur et de l'impur n'est pas celui de deux substances, mais de deux structures mentales: il n'est pas celui de l'esprit et de la matière, mais celui de la pensée affranchie de la raison confisquée, de l'esprit éveillé et de l'âme en sommeil." Also, O'Meara (1985b: 254ff.) and Oosthout (1991: 42–58). On some differences between Plotinian and Cartesian dualism see Emilsson (1991: 162–4).

20 See I.7.2.9–11: "Life, then, is the good to that which lives, and intellect to that which has a share in Intellect; so that if something has life and intellect, it has a twofold approach to the Good." Also II.1.5.18–24, where Plotinus expresses the dualism in terms of two souls, one governing our association with the body and the other, by which we are ourselves (καθ' ἣν ἡμεῖς), being the cause of our well-being, not the cause of our being. That is, it is not the cause of our composite being. See also I.1.3.21–3 and Himmerich (1959: 73–83).

21 See also IV.7.11.11–14; V.1.2.1–9. At IV.7.11–12 three of the four arguments for the immortality of the soul in the *Phaedo* are summarized: the recollection argument (72e3–78b3), the affinity argument (78b4–84b4), and the exclusion of opposites argument (102a10–107b10). See Charrue (1978: 195–204). Space forbids a detailed discussion of these arguments and the complex Platonic background.

22 See also 245c7–9, which Plotinus repeats at lines 7–8.

23 See Dodds (1960a: 385–6). The most extensive study of the concept of the self in Plotinus is O'Daly (1973): see chs. 4–6 and notes for references to previous works on this subject.

24 See IV.7.1.24–5: "the soul is the self" (ἡ ψυχὴ αὐτός). This evidently goes beyond what is presumably Plotinus' authoritative text, *Alcibiades* 130c, where the self is identified with the soul. It shows how Plotinus maintains a Platonic position while absorbing an Aristotelian lesson. See also II.2.2.3–5 and IV.3.7.25–8, where "two souls" are posited, one of which belongs to that which is a part of the All, namely, the non-hylomorphic composite, and one of which is a personal whole (οἰκεῖον ὅλον). At IV.3.4.21–37 there is a vivid metaphorical comparison of the two souls to a healthy man, on the one hand, at the service of a sick neighbor, and the sick neighbor, on the other hand, absorbed with concern for his body. See de Vogel (1976: especially 152–3).

25 Aristotle, *De Anima* 3.4.429a22–5, says: "so the part of the soul which is called 'intellect' (by 'intellect' I mean that by which the soul can think and believe) is actually none of the things prior to thinking. In view of this, it is not even reasonable that it should be blended with the body." If intellect is not blended with the body, it would seem to be a separate actuality in addition to the agent intellect. That would leave the other "parts" of the soul as the actuality

contributing to the hylomorphic composite. But then the unity of the form of this composite with the intellect is obscure. How are they one soul?

26 This suggests that to some extent the endowed self is formed by empirical experience. See O'Daly (1973: 49) with references to earlier debates over this implication.

27 Rist (1967a: 418ff.) distinguishes between an "empirical self" and a "second self" or "eternal self," meaning Intellect. This is the essential distinction. But it is also necessary to distinguish "self" from the continuum of psychic powers. Rist (1982: 99–101) more or less does this.

28 At VI.9.7.33–4 Plotinus says: "he who learns who he is will also know where he came from" (ὁ δὲ μαθὼν ἑαυτὸν ειδήσει καὶ ὁπόθεν). The learning indicates the recognition of the true ideal. Appropriating it affectively, as it were, so that one actually desires to achieve that ideal, is another matter.

29 This is akin to Plato's characterization of types of persons according to their predominant interests at *Republic* 475aff.

30 VI.7.6.17–18: καὶ ἔστιν ἕκαστος καθ' ὃν ἐνεργεῖ. The predicate going with ἔστιν is ἄνθρωπον from line 12. But in this context "man" is shorthand for "kind of man," which should be glossed by "a life in which a kind of activity is dominant."

31 See III.4.2; IV.8.3.10–13; IV.9.5.7–26 and Deuse (1984: 122ff.) on how the concept of activity is used to explain the claim that the soul is one and many.

32 The best text for this claim is I.4.9.18–30, where Plotinus compares the activity of Intellect with vegetative activity. We do not have an apprehension (ἀντίληψις) of the latter activity, yet it is *our* activity nevertheless, that is, the activity of the composite that belongs to us. At IV.3.30.13–16 Plotinus says: "The intellectual act is one thing and the apprehension of it another, and we are always intellectually active but do not always apprehend our activity; and this is because that which receives it does not only receive acts of the intelligence, but also, on its other side, perceptions." Does this mean that we are sometimes aware of it? What does this awareness consist in? At I.4.10 Plotinus strongly suggests two things: (1) awareness consists in an experience of a "reflection" of the activity of Intellect in our discursive intellect and (2) awareness is of the fact that Intellect is active as opposed to an actual experiencing of the activity of Intellect. Extending the analogy of vegetative activity, this would mean that (1) we can see the results of growth in ourselves from time to time and (2) we can therefore infer that growth is occurring even though we do not experience growth.

33 This is precisely the question D. Parfit (1971) means to address with his notion of q-intentions. Roughly, q-intentions are like ordinary intentions except that they may be intentions that another person perform some action, namely, the person who is the psychological successor to the original intender. Jonas (1964: 163ff.) criticizes Plotinus for holding that the goal of temporal existence and of virtue can ever be an eternal state. It is just because the temporal cannot mutate into the eternal that Plotinus posits the undescended self. The psychological problem is perhaps more acute. What reason have I to believe that the temporal "I" would recognize the eternal contemplator as the real me? But consider Gauguin before he realized his vocation as a painter. Might he not have said, "I cannot imagine myself as an artist. That would not be me"? Why not suppose that the imaginability is only ex post facto? That is, only when engaging in the ideal activity does one recognize that it is really one's ideal self that is doing it.

34 At I.6.5.6–8 in a remarkable adaptation of Plato's account of the erotic in the *Phaedrus* Plotinus characterizes those who see their own inner beauty as those who "long to be with themselves, gathering their selves together away from their bodies."

35 At V.8.11 there are a number of remarkable phrases, such as "comes to unity with himself" (εἰς ἓν αὐτῷ ἐλθὼν) (4) and "we understand ourselves best when we have made our self-knowledge one with ourselves" (μάλιστα πάντων ἐσμὲν αὐτοῖς συνετοὶ τὴν ἐπιστήμην ἡμῶν καὶ ἡμᾶς ἓν πεποιηκότες) (32–3), which indicate the paradoxical nature of becoming what one already is. I understand phrases such as "becoming one" as the achievement of an ideal self. It is not so clear what Hadot (1963: 23–39) means by "niveaux du moi," but his basic distinction between "moi" and "vrai moi" is roughly my distinction between the endowed and the true ideal self. Bousquet (1976: 47) neatly describes the soul as "auto-constituante et dérivée," which indicates the same thing as the more paradoxical-sounding "becoming what you are already."

36 See also IV.8.1.1–2: "Often I have woken up out of the body to my self and have entered into myself, going out from all other things." This seems to be the recognition of the true ideal self. Plotinus goes on to say in this passage that he "felt assurance that then most of all I belonged to the better part" and "I have come to identity with the divine." But from this it does not follow that he has actually had the experience that a discarnate intellect has as opposed to recognizing that there is such an intellect and that he is ideally identical with it.

37 In distinguishing the principle of the rational animal from the composite and, by implication, the form of that composite, we see the origin of the problem of the unity of man caused by postulating a plurality of forms. This is a problem that was to surface persistently in medieval philosophy in the light of theological principles of immortality and resurrection. How can that which exists separately from the body be identical with that which is embodied once and again? It is important to grasp why for Plotinus this is not a problem, or at least the same sort of problem. For Plotinus, the incarnate composite is an image of the true being, a diminished and imperfect version. Reincarnation is not the perfecting state that resurrection is supposed to be. Aquinas agrees with Plotinus in accepting the equivocity of the incarnate and discarnate states, but reverses Plotinus' position, attributing perfection to the former. The problem of the unity of man with a plurality of forms remains only for philosophers and theologians who would insist on univocity for the two.

38 See also VI.7.5.1–5, where the soul of the composite is said to be a type of activity distinguished from the agent of the activity.

39 See Smith (1978: 292–3): "It is important here to distinguish the higher self (our ever active νοῦς) and the empirical self from a vague 'we,' a sort of floating ego, which determines the particular level of being which one may choose to dominate our lives."

40 I.4.14.1–4: "Man, and especially the good man, is not the composite of soul and body; separation from the body and despising of its so-called goods make this plain." By "composite" Plotinus means "hylomorphic composite."

41 See Rich (1963: 8–9).

42 I.1.9.15–18: "So we have distinguished what belongs to the joint entity and what is proper to the soul in this way: what belongs to the joint entity is bodily or not without body, but what does not require body for its activity is proper (ἴδια) to the soul." Given what has been said in the last section, I take it that "soul" in this passage refers to the self. That the self exists discarnately implies that its properties are non-bodily. See also I.1.6.8–9: "Certainly the life of the composite will not be that of the soul."

43 At VI.9.1.39–42 Plotinus contrasts the views of psychological activities and states as parts and as faculties or powers, apparently opting for the latter. It seems clear that the parts of the soul in Plato's *Republic* – desiderative (τὸ ἐπιθυμητικόν), spirited (τὸ θυμοειδές), and rational (τὸ λογιστικόν) – cannot be δυνάμεις, for

faculties can neither be at war with each other nor fail to perform their functions, as is the case with the parts of the soul. See also *Republic* 440e5, 442ab, 443d3–6, 586e5. At IV.7.14.8–14 Plotinus refers to the language of tripartition dialectically, that is, he does not definitely endorse it. He does, however, endorse the view that if the soul were tripartite, only its highest part would survive the death of the body. See also III.2.18.3–5, where tripartition is explicitly used. Blumenthal (1972: 348–50) suggests that Plotinus reserved the language of tripartition for use only in ethical discussions, as in I.2.1.15–21. I think Plotinus is wholly committed to the psychological account which tripartition is intended to support and tries to supplement the account in terms of parts of the soul with the language of faculties of the soul. Perhaps this is ill-advised.

44 See I.1.7.21–3: "Since man coincides with the rational soul, when we reason it is really we who reason because rational processes are activities of the soul," and I.1.10.5–7: "So 'we' is used in two senses, either including the beast or referring to that which even in our present life transcends it. The beast is the body which has been given life. But the true man is different, clear of these affections."

45 See I.4.15.15–21, where Plotinus compares the rational faculty in relation to the lower parts of the soul to a man in relation to a child. Also, I.2.5.25–7 and I.2.6.1–11.

46 See Baladi (1970: 90–8).

47 Following Plato in *Republic* 580d, 581a, where he attributes πάθη to the two lower parts of the soul.

48 The list of basic πάθη among the Greek philosophers is fairly consistent. Plato, *Timaeus* 42a, gives "sexual desire mixed with pleasure and pain, and in addition fear and anger and whatever follows these and their contraries." Aristotle, *Nicomachean Ethics* 2.4.1105b22–4, says: "by πάθη I mean, for example, appetite, anger, fear, envy, courage, gladness, friendly feeling, hatred, longing, emulation, pity, and, in general, whatever is accompanied by pleasure and pain." The Stoics, says Diogenes Laertius, 7.110, give four genera of πάθη, grief, fear, appetite, pleasure. The Stoic definition of πάθος, "an irrational movement or excessive impulse in the soul contrary to nature," of course guarantees the possibility that the soul should have πάθη. For Plotinus, this view is eliminated with the refutation of the Stoic materialistic conception of the soul.

49 See II.5.2.34–5, where Plotinus follows Aristotle in identifying a virtue as a habit and distinguishing it from the activity that follows from it.

50 See also IV.4.19.26–8: "But, then, the perception itself is not to be called pain, but knowledge of pain; but since it is knowledge it is unaffected, so that it can know and give a sound report."

51 In the next chapter Plotinus seems to imply that the specific activity of the part of the soul involved with emotions is that of having an image or φάντασμα. Plotinus' account follows that of Aristotle in *De Anima* 1.4.408b1–18, especially with regard to the distinction between soul and subject of emotional experiences.

52 In the previous chapter (lines 29–31) Plotinus says, "when man has an appetite for sexual pleasures, it will be the man that desires, but in another way it will be the desiring part of the soul that desires."

53 III.6.5.22–5: "But the purification of the part subject to affections is the waking up from inappropriate images and not seeing them, and its separation is effected by not inclining much downwards and not having a mental picture of the things below." The entire chapter should be consulted.

54 At IV.4.19.12ff. Plotinus argues that the soul perceives a πάθος of pain in the body but is itself unaffected. The reason is that if it were affected itself, being wholly present in the body, it would not have indicated the affection in a particular part of the body, e.g., the finger. This argument is sophistical unless Plotinus is

(1) taking pain to be an intentional object logically distinct from that which perceives the pain and (2) distinguishing soul from self, for otherwise the perception of a pain in my finger would not be painful to me and (3) making the self the subject with this intentional object.

55 At IV.4.44.1–4 Plotinus makes the same point in a powerful extended metaphor of enchantment (γοητεία): "Contemplation alone remains incapable of enchantment because no one who is self-directed is subject to enchantment: for he is one, and that which he contemplates is himself, and his reason is not deluded, but he makes what he ought and makes his own life and work."

56 Arnou (1967: 63).

57 See especially *Republic* 485d6–7 and 580d7–8 and the discussion of the lower mysteries in the *Symposium* 201d–209e.

58 I suppose these are the sorts of texts which encouraged Plotinus to believe that there is not much difference between parts and faculties of the soul.

59 At *Rhetoric* 1.10.1369a3 Aristotle says that βούλησις is ὄρεξις for the good, implying that this distinguishes βούλησις from other forms of ὄρεξις. If to this we add the first lines of the *Nicomachean Ethics* where he says that every πρᾶξις aims at some good, we should perhaps conclude that animal motions springing from either ἐπιθυμία or θυμός are not unequivocally actions. Plato, on the other hand, does not seem to regard the motions of human beings springing from ἐπιθυμία or θυμός as anything other than actions and as aiming for some good. Of course, Aristotle would no doubt agree that for an animal in whom there is no question of rationality nevertheless this animal moves towards what it in some sense takes as its own good. Accordingly, I do not think that the differences between Plato and Aristotle in this regard are anything more than apparent.

60 Thus, Plotinus' use of the term οὐσία here is not a concession to Aristotle, for Aristotle specifically rejects the claim that the soul is a substance.

61 At I.4.6.19–24 Plotinus stresses that βούλησις in the proper sense cannot be said to pertain to "necessities" or things unpleasant, although of course in some sense we may desire these. We go after these not because they are good but because they contribute to our incarnate existence. At I.8.15.7 he speaks of ὄρεξις for the good. Aristotle regularly uses βούλησις for a desire for the good. See *Rhetoric* 1.10.1369b2–3; *Nicomachean Ethics* 3.4.1111b26, 3.5.1113a5, 3.7.1113b3.

62 The entire treatise IV.8 is devoted to the descent of the soul into the body. At IV.8.8.9–11 Plotinus distinguishes bodily desires from our apprehension of them. Whether we ignore what we apprehend or embrace it as our own depends on our self-definition. The very possibility that a human soul should seek to satisfy these desires indicates that it is not absolutely oriented towards the good.

63 Generally, as for example in I.8.15.16–18, Plotinus uses ἐπιθυμία for desires of the incarnated composite. However, there is at least one passage where he speaks of ἐπιθυμία for the good (III.5.9.50–1), but here he is commenting on Plato's *Symposium* 203bff. and seems to be just following the usage there.

64 Plotinus appears to use the term πείσεις as synonymous with πάθη. See especially III.6.19.8–11.

65 Aristotle, *De Anima* 2.3.414b2, makes ἐπιθυμία a form of ὄρεξις. At *Nicomachean Ethics* 2.4.1105b21–2 he gives it as an example of a πάθος. At *Rhetoric* 2.2.1378a32 the πάθος anger is defined as a type of ὄρεξις. At *On the Motion of Animals* 8.702a15–19 in describing the steps leading to the actual motion of an animal, Aristotle says: "And for this reason, thinking that one ought to go and going are virtually simultaneous, unless there be something else to hinder action. The organic parts are suitably prepared by the affections, these by the desire, and desire by imagination. Imagination in its turn comes about either through thinking

or sense-perception." Here ὄρεξις and πάθος are distinguished as phases of one process.

66 Feelings accompanied by pleasure, unlike feelings accompanied by pain, do not seem to be necessarily connected to any particular desire, not even a desire that the feeling should continue or return. Plotinus takes pleasure as a πάθος at I.4.2.26; III.6.4.8; IV.4.28.3. It is not, however, clear in any of these passages with what ὄρεξις pleasure is to be associated.

67 Plato, *Symposium* 200b, is Plotinus' guide in this matter, for there he says that when the goal of all human striving in actually attained, desire (ἐπιθυμία) stops. Of course, one can desire to continue to possess what one already has, but only if one is in time.

68 Cf. *Phaedrus* 246a–257b, the myth of the charioteer and the two horses, which seems to presume tripartition in the discarnate soul.

69 Aristotle adds that if the agent would have acted anyway had he known, the action is not involuntary but non-voluntary (οὐχ ἑκών). Further, acting because of ignorance is distinguished from acting in ignorance, when the agent has, through, say, drink or passion, put himself into a situation where he forgets what he knew.

70 Aristotle says that we deliberate about means, 3.5.1112b11–12. The difference between choice and deliberation with regard to ends is that without desire, deliberation alone does not result in action and choice is the ἀρχή of an action.

71 See Henry (1931: especially 55–9), whose seminal paper has had the evidently permanent and salutary effect of steering scholarship away from an imputation of determinism to Plotinus. Following Henry is Rist (1967b: 130–8).

72 When Plotinus says here that (non-Epicurean) atomists would have to hold the absurd position that someone is compelled (ἀναγκασθήσεται) to follow a particular occupation, he perhaps has in mind that pursuing an occupation requires the actual presence of a goal in the mind of the agent and that this goal is crucial in explaining the agent's action in a way that the atomist cannot allow.

73 Cf. the questioning by Botros (1985) of the traditional attribution of soft determinism or compatibilism to the early Stoics and the response by Sharples (1986). Sharples, in defending the interpretation of early Stoicism which has them holding both to universal causal necessitation and human responsibility, is in accord with Plotinus' interpretation, allowing for the fact that Plotinus makes no chronological refinements among various Stoic positions. The Stoics held that the sage alone is free, which does not mean that his actions are undetermined. For this reason it would be a mistake to compare the Stoic sage to Plotinus' virtuous man.

74 On the meaning of the phrase τὸ ἐφ' ἡμῖν see Leroux (1990: 237–8).

75 Leroux (1990: 239–42) has some helpful remarks on the relevant background to this discussion including the dimension of fatalism, which is not in Aristotle's discussion but is in Alexander's *De Fato*. Thus, the present account is not exclusively ethical, but is metaphysical as well.

76 Graeser (1972a: 117) compares Plotinus' dialectical definition of ἐφ' ἡμῖν with one which is reported as Stoic by Alexander (*SVF* II.984): "these things are in our power, the contraries of which we are able to perform." Even if Alexander is being more polemical here than accurate, it is reasonable to suppose that Plotinus' understanding of the Stoic position is influenced by his reading of Alexander. Graeser, however, does not see that if Plotinus does indeed have the Stoics in mind here, he is bringing into question their view. For the Stoics held that βούλησις is itself determined by antecedent causes. Hence, even if we do what we do according to βούλησις, we are not thereby unqualifiedly free. Cf. Cicero, *De Fato* 9 (*SVF* II.951), arguing against the Stoic view: "Non enim si alii ad alia propensiores sunt propter causas naturales et antecedentes, idcirco etiam

nostrarum voluntatum atque appetitionum sunt causae naturales et antecedentes; nam nihil esset in nostra potestate si res ita se haberet."

77 At IV.8.5 Plotinus says that necessity (ἡ ἀνάγκη) *includes* the voluntary, which seems to imply that an absence of necessity pertains only to that which is not voluntary in the narrow Aristotelian sense. Alexander of Aphrodisias (*De Fato*, 183.29–30) makes the distinction between ἐφ' ἡμῖν and ἑκούσιον that Plotinus is using. See IV.3.13.17 and O'Brien (1977: 401–22).

78 See also *Nicomachean Ethics* 3.3.1111a24 and Leroux (1990: 248–9). That Plotinus is closely following Aristotle here is evident from comparing the similar discussion of Alexander of Aphrodisias in *De Fato*, 183.30–184.9, where he is defending Aristotle against Stoic determinism.

79 Thus I interpret the argument from VI.8.2, which concludes (33–7): "And if reason itself makes (ποιεῖ) another desire, we must understand how; but if it puts a stop to the desire and stands still and this is where what is in our power is, this will not be in action (πράξει), but will stand still in Intellect; since everything in the sphere of action, even if reason is dominant (κρατῇ), is mixed and cannot have being in our power in a pure state." In order to understand this passage it helps to refer to the study of Arnou (1921, 1972), which demonstrates the distinction between πρᾶξις and ποίησις for Plotinus. The latter term is generally identified with θεωρία, whereas the former indicates that "qui incline vers le sensible et subit des influences matérielles (50)." Accordingly, no action can be unqualifiedly free (see also 23–5).

80 See also IV.8.5.8–10: "For everything which goes to the worse does so unwillingly, but, since it goes by its own motion, when it experiences the worse it is said to be punished for what it did."

81 Here it becomes clear that the activity of Intellect is not merely the paradigm of cognition but the paradigm of action as well because action (as opposed to motion) requires cognition. So, perfect free action is identified with the activity of Intellect. See also VI.8.6.19–22: "so that also in practical actions self-determination and being in our power is not referred to practice and outward activity but to the inner activity of virtue itself, that is, its thought and contemplation."

82 VI.8.3.21–6: "We trace back what is in our power to the noblest principle, the activity of Intellect, and shall grant that the premises of action derived from this are truly free, and that the desires (τὰς ὀρέξεις) roused by thinking (τοῦ νοεῖν) are not involuntary, and we shall say that the gods who live in this way have self-determination." I take it that the "free premises" are the universal premises in practical syllogisms. Thus, Plotinus will say that the good man acts κατὰ προνοίαν and not ὑπὸ προνοίας. See also III.2.9.21; III.3.5.34, 47–9. This distinction is an interesting application of the logical distinction between desire and achievement of desire in Intellect. If we act according to providence, we act on the basis of cognition of the good. To act by providence would mean acting according to the laws of nature. Anyone or anything can act "by providence" just by doing what comes naturally.

83 VI.8.4.15–17: "For the involuntary is a leading away from the good and towards the compulsory, if something is carried to that which is not good for it." This seems to be Plotinus' gloss on the distinction frequently made by Plato between doing what seems best (ποιεῖν ἃ δοκεῖ βέλτιστα εἶναι) and doing what one wants (ποιεῖν ἃ βούλονται). Cf. IV.8.5.8 and *Gorgias* 467b3–9. Müller (1914b: 488): "Wir sind frei, soweit wir den Guten anhangen und nachleben, unfrei, sofern wir uns vom Bösen überwältigen lassen."

84 On the doctrine that no one does wrong willingly in Plato see *Meno* 77b–78b; *Gorgias* 466e, 467b, 509e; *Apology* 25d–26a; *Protagoras* 358d; *Laws* 731c1–5,

734b, 860d5; *Timaeus* 86d. Cf. III.2.10. This claim directly contradicts what Aristotle says at *Nicomachean Ethics* 3.7.1113b6–7, namely, that wrongdoing is as much within our power as is virtue.

85 Cf. Combès (1989: 31): "Le plotinisme est une philosophie de la liberté créatrice de la nécessité dans son rapport à l'un, qui est le fondement transcendant de la liberté et du tout. Le stoïcisme est une philosophie de la liberté de consentement à la nécessité autosuffisante du tout . . . La nécessité est le détour que la liberté s'impose pour se poser soi-même radicalement."

Chapter VIII Some Epistemological Questions

1 See Lloyd (1987: 184): "The genesis analysed thought universally inasmuch as it analysed thought at its best in accordance with the widely accepted theory that to define 'x' is to define 'x at its best'".

2 Emilsson (1988) provides the best study of Plotinus' philosophy of sense-perception. Benz (1990: 178–283) provides an extensive treatment of the topic which unfortunately takes no notice of Emilsson's work.

3 On sense-perception involving affections see I.1.3.3–5; III.6.1.1–3; III.6.2.53–4; IV.3.3.21–5; IV.3.26.5–6; IV.4.23.19–32; IV.5.4.29; IV.6.2.16–18; VI.4.6.10–11. See also Emilsson (1988: 67–73). I say "involve" because Plotinus also says that individual acts of sense-perception are not themselves affections. See also III.6.1.1 and most clearly VI.4.6.14–15 and IV.6.2.16–18. On the composite, ensouled individual as perceiver see I.1.7.1–6; IV.3.20.44–5. Sometimes, e.g. example in IV.4.23.48–9, Plotinus will specify the subject as the soul in the body or working through the body: "But it is clear that sense-perception belongs to the soul in the body and working through the body." The "body" referred to here is elsewhere, IV.4.23.33, specified as an "organ." The equivocity is of course a function of the equivocity in the reference of "I."

4 Perhaps it is tendentious to say that Plotinus wants to distinguish a phase of αἴσθησις as sensation, when what is really meant is that what we would call "sense-perception" includes sensation. I should like to designate typical experiences involving our five senses and external bodies and some sort of psychological event expressible in words such as "I see the table in front of me" as taken together the process which both Plotinus and modern philosophers are trying to understand. Plotinus certainly emphasizes the latter phase of this process, although, as we shall see, he does not exclude the initial phase from it. See Blumenthal (1976b: 45–6).

5 See IV.4.8.9–13, where Plotinus strongly implies that sense-perception can occur without judgment. I take it that this refers to the first phase of the process. At IV.5.1.10–13 Plotinus says that a sort of ὁμοπάθεια involving the sense-organs must arise in order for sense-perception to occur. Since sense-perception is not an affection at all, although it can have an affection as object and it requires an affection to occur in the composite perceiver, this ὁμοπάθεια is perhaps close to what we would call "sensation." It seems that Plotinus might have gotten the distinction between sensation and sense-perception from Plato, who in the *Theaetetus* uses αἴσθησις both for a physical process (152c) and for that which includes judgments (158b, 161d, 178b, 179c).

6 So Blumenthal (1971b: 71–2), (1976b: 47); Contra Clark (1942: 360–2); Emilsson (1988: 113–21).

7 This claim is supported by III.6.1.1–7 and by IV.4.8.9–16, where Plotinus describes a case in which the subject is unaware of a perceptual act, as a result

of which memory is not possible. Armstrong adduces IV.9.2 and V.1.12 as parallels to IV.4.

8 See IV.6.2.1–3: "[The soul] speaks about things which it does not possess: this is a matter of power, not of being affected in some way but of being capable of and doing the work to which it has been assigned." Also, IV.3.23.1–21 distinguishes the potency of the animate body from the potency of the soul for actualizing the former. Aristotle, *De Anima* 3.3.428a6–7, says that αἴσθησις is a potency or an activity depending on whether we are speaking, say, of a faculty like sight (ὄψις) or of an activity like seeing (ὅρασις).

9 On sense-perception as activity see III.6.1.1–2; IV.6.2.1–6; VI.1.20.26–32.

10 When at IV.4.23.48–9 Plotinus says that sense-perception operates "through the body," he means of course an animate body, and this is in line with his peculiar form of dualism. The entire chapter is an argument for the need for a bodily instrument of sense-perception.

11 See I.6.3.9–15; III.6.18.24–8; IV.3.3.18–22; IV. 4.23.21. Cf. Aristotle, *De Anima* 2.12.424a17–19.

12 In general, a representationalist theory of sense-perception would hold that what is directly perceived stands to bodies as the images on a television screen stand to the actual events being televised.

13 Of course, for Plotinus the forms of sensible composites are not univocally actual in the way that the separated Forms are, but this is beside the present point. Moreover, Plotinus obviously cannot accept Aristotle's position that the accidental attributes which are the objects of sense-perception are actualizations of the substance. For Plotinus, they are nothing but items in the conglomerate of qualities.

14 On this passage see Emilsson (1988: 68–74).

15 For example, I.1.2.26–7. Even indirect or accidental sense-perception of that which causes a proper sensible (e.g., perceiving the man who is white) is not belief (δόξα). For we indirectly perceive the man even if we believe we are perceiving something else. Even indirect sense-perception is non-inferential.

16 So Emilsson (1988: 124).

17 Plato might be taken to imply at *Theaetetus* 158e–160c that αἴσθησις is ἀψευδές. Aristotle says this at *Metaphysics* 4.5.1010b2 and *De Anima* 2.6.418a12–16, although the latter text should be compared with his more nuanced statement at 3.3.428b19.

18 See IV.4.23.5–9, where Plotinus tries to understand sense-perception according to the model of intellection.

19 See also VI.7.6.1–11 and Clark (1942: 363–9).

20 In the same passage, lines 3–5, Plotinus also uses a metaphor of measurement when he says we perceive a beautiful object by using the form of beauty in us as we use a ruler for judging straightness. I take this as a variation on classification with no important difference.

21 See IV.9.3.26–7: "but sense-perception which judges with the intellect of each individual."

22 Perhaps I.8.14.5 and II.4.10.8–9 should be understood as implying a constructive power of imagination which is not memorial because there is no corresponding impression left by sensation.

23 The words ἀεὶ κινουμένης πρὸς νόησιν indicate the active potency of the soul, since the soul is a self-mover.

24 See I.2.3.27–31, where the λόγος in the soul is said to be an imitation (μίμημα) of Forms just as the verbal λόγος is an imitation of that in the soul. Also, V.1.3.7–9. It is no doubt odd to speak about a symbolic representation as a μίμημα. But Plato, *Cratylus* 423b9–11, even suggests that a name (ὄνομα) can

be called a μίμημα of that which it names, assuming, that is, that it is the "right" name.

25 I believe that when Aristotle says of the agent intellect χωρισθεὶς δ' ἐστὶ μόνον τοῦθ' ὅπερ ἐστί (3.5430a22–3) he does not mean to imply that it exists as it were in two states or forms. Rather, "having been separated" means separated in analysis. When we consider it separated in thought it is, being immaterial, just what it is. This is the same point Aristotle makes at *Metaphysics* 7.6.1032a5–12 and 7.11.1037bf. In any case, I believe that this is how Plotinus understands Aristotle and what Plotinus means in his own account of intellect.

26 Cf. Schwyzer (1960: 371) and O'Daly (1973: 44). Blumenthal (1971b: 107–8) refers to a number of passages – VI.5.7.1–6, V.8.3.9f., IV.3.30.7–15, V.3.3.26–9, I.2.4.25–7, V.1.10.5f. – which all speak of our participation in the primary activity of Intellect. None of these texts, however, suggest that we are aware that we are actually doing what it is that our intellect does while we are in the incarnate state. See Volkmann-Schluck (1966: 46–59) on the differences between the cognition of intelligibles by Intellect and by Soul, which has access to them only indirectly. The primary activity of Soul is discursive thinking and the *externality* of intentional objects in this mode of cognition is not able to be transformed within Soul itself. So Alfino (1988: 282), who says, "If the soul possessed direct access to Intellect, language would be superfluous."

27 In the first passage he says οἷον τοὺς τύπους. I presume that this indicates that τύπος is used equivocally for the sense and intellectual impressions.

28 Cf. V.8.1.1–4, for example, where Plotinus says that as a result of contemplation we come to a concept of the father of Intellect. A concept of the One is most definitely only an image of it.

29 See V.3.2.24–5: "it [the faculty of discursive thinking] has understanding of the impressions which it receives from both sides." The words "both sides" (ἑκάτερα) refer to ἐκ τῆς αἰσθήσεως (line 7) and ἐκ τοῦ νοῦ (line 9).

30 The intelligible image is an image because there can be numerically many, whereas there is only one Form. It is a synonymous image because it is just the nature that the Form's name names. Phillips (1987: 47) in a very helpful paper wishes to distinguish the adapting of a τύπος of sense-perception to a τύπος of Intellect from the adapting of the latter to Forms. He calls this a two-stage process of recollection. However, these must be radically different activities. In the putative second stage of the process, how are we to suppose that the soul has at once a τύπος of a Form and the Form itself available for comparison?

31 One might adduce V.8.3.10–16 as a possible parallel. In this passage, the having of images of Intellect is disparaged. Instead, we should aim to have Intellect as if we had a sample of gold. I confess that I am unable to make sense of this metaphor if it is intended as having a cognitive point. I would suggest, though, that the "sample of gold" corresponds not to a concept of the Form of Beauty (which is the subject of the chapter), but to a beautiful soul.

32 I follow Igal (1975: 175 and n1), H-S$_2$, and Armstrong in reading καὶ γὰρ αἰσθανόμεθα δι' αἰσθήσεως κἂν <μὴ> ἡμεῖς οἱ αἰσθανόμενοι· ἆρ' οὖν καὶ διανοούμεθα οὕτως καὶ διὰ <νοῦ> νοοῦμεν οὕτως; Oosthout (1991: 193–4) supports the manuscript reading, printed by H-S$_1$, which has καὶ instead of κἂν and omits the words μὴ and νοῦ. It seems appropriate, though, in the context of this treatise that Plotinus wishes to emphasize the distinction between the rational agent (the primary image of the discarnate true self) and the agent of sense-perception.

33 At V.3.3.8 Plotinus says that we have a rule (κανόνα) for goodness in us which enables us to make the predicative judgment "Socrates is good." How is

this rule present? By our being like the good (ἀγαθοειδής) and by Intellect illuminating us. It is not the Form that serves as a rule, but our inherent ability to imitate Intellect.

34 Plotinus found at *Phaedo* 66e–67b strong support for the claim that pure knowledge, hence identification with the activity of Intellect, is unavailable to the incarnate individual. See Smith (1981: 99): "intelligible reality when viewed through the medium of discursive reason appears to be plural and discrete". So Wurm (1973: 240–50).

35 V.3.2.7–9: "the reasoning power in soul makes its judgment, derived from the images present to it which come from sense-perception, but combining and dividing them." See Benz (1990: 273–82).

36 V.1.10.12–13: "intellect is of two kinds, the one which reasons and the one which makes it possible to reason." See also VI.9.5.8–9: "they must grasp that there is an Intellect other than that which is called reasoning and reckoning" and Blumenthal (1971b: 104–5). The intellect which reasons seems to be identical with what Plotinus calls "the middle region" at I.1.11.1–8, I.8.14.34, and II.9.2.8. See Schibli (1989: 207–15), who thinks that this middle region or discursive faculty has direct access to eternal Intellect. But this would mean direct access to Forms, and Plotinus says that this is possible only for that which is identical with Forms.

37 V.9.8.21–2: "For the dividing intellect is a different one, but the undivided Intellect which does not divide is being and all things." See also VI.2.7.16–20, O'Daly (1973: 50–1), and Szlezák (1979: 180–205).

38 At VI.9.5.16–20 Plotinus says of Intellect that it is a "multiplicity which is undivided and yet again divided" (πλῆθος ἀδιάκριτον καὶ αὖ διακεκριμένον) and that "it [Intellect] is as bodies of knowledge, where all the items are in a partless whole and yet each of them is separate" (ἐπιστήμαις πάντων ἐν ἀμερεῖ ὄντων ὅμως ἐστὶν ἕκαστον χωρὶς αὐτῶν). The divisions and separateness of the parts of Intellect cannot be the same as what is divided in discursive judgment. I think that what this does mean is that Intellect is virtually divisible in discursive judgments. Cf. VI.4.2.22–3 (with lines 17–9), where Plotinus says that that which participates in true being "encounters being, therefore, as a whole." O'Meara (1980b: 70) writes aptly of the "integral totality of Being" omnipresent to sensibles. But it can only be virtually present in an image. Lloyd (1986: 263), replying to Sorabji (1982) and (1983: 152–6), states the position I am defending with admirable lucidity and precision: "The *totum simul* which is associated with pure intellect neither is nor is known by a collection of propositions, but is what occupies the place of the genus of being. For that can be grasped as a merely undifferentiated whole, while in fact it contains a multiplicity of parts. It is the former aspect, Being as an intentional or phenomenological object, which is the content of the thinking qua thinking and whose non-complexity prevents it from being propositional." See also Rist (1989: 190–7) and Alfino (1988: 273–6), also replying to Sorabji. Oosthout (1991: 139) also rejects Sorabji's argument but makes the interesting criticism of Lloyd's interpretation that true self-knowledge is not exactly non-propositional, for the thought "I am x" where "x" is a Form is in a sense a proposition. Even self-reflexivity judgments are judgments and so involve complexity.

39 At I.2.3.25–6 Plotinus asks the question, "is thinking (τὸ νοεῖν) said homonymously?" No, he replies. It refers primarily to the Intellect and derivatively to our thinking, which is said to be a μίμημα of the former. Two points need to be stressed here. First, a μίμημα can be a non-homonymous, that is, synonymous, image. Second, since τὸ νοεῖν is the activity in which the thinker is identified

with form, the identification of form in derived thinking would seem to be a synonymous image of primary thinking. Thus, our thinking is not purely symbolic. When we think "2 + 2 = 4," the content of our thinking is a synonymous image of the content of an eternal intellect. Perhaps it will be objected that thinking could be synonymous without the contents of thinking being so. But thinking only occurs when an intellect is identical with truth, and this seems to preclude the possibility that its contents are mere homonymous symbols. Analogously, the claim that "x + y = z" is not true or false. The form of cognition of such a propositional function would be imagination, not thinking, for Plotinus.

40 Cf. Blumenthal (1971b: 96–7 and nn25, 26). McCumber (1978: 160–7) finds greater use of a doctrine of recollection by Plotinus than does Blumenthal, but he seems to understand this doctrine more as the result of a process of recollection than as the process itself. As the former, the issue is not contentious, for Plotinus certainly believes in a state of cognitive union with Forms in a manner similar to Plato. As the latter, the question is more problematic than McCumber suggests, for Plotinus does not hold that we can make direct use of the Forms in cognition.

41 See Oosthout (1991: 83–7) on this passage. At V.3.3.12 Plotinus uses the term ἴχνη instead of τύποι to make the same point. See also IV.6.3.10–12, where Plotinus says that the soul thinks (νοεῖν) of intelligibles when it arrives at the memory of them. Similarly, at V.3.3.35–6 we are said to think (νοοῦμεν) thoughts (νοήματα) in discursive reasoning (διάνοια). Yet at IV.6.1.1–5 Plotinus says that since sense-perceptions are not τυπώσεις, neither should memories be said to be these.

42 I think this interpretation accounts best for the curious claim at IV.3.31 that sensible and intelligible images "coalesce" in memory.

43 IV.4.3.1–3: "But if it comes out of the intelligible world, and cannot endure unity, but embraces its own individuality and wants to be different and so to speak puts its head outside, it thereupon acquires memory."

44 Cf. V.3.4.10–13, where Plotinus contrasts thinking as man and thinking in Intellect. This claim is probably connected with Plotinus' distinction (I.4.10.19ff.) of intellection and imagination, where Plotinus holds that the former can take place without the latter.

45 Warren (1964) briefly reviews the meanings of three terms used by Plotinus for consciousness: ἀντίληψις, παρακολούθησις, and συναίσθησις. Schroeder (1987) also discusses the terms συναίσθησις and σύνεσις as used for self-consciousness in Intellect. Warren (93) notes the essential connection between embodied consciousness and the faculty of imagination. Arnou (1967: 305) shows that the use of παρακολούθησις for embodied consciousness does not indicate that the discarnate self identical with Intellect is unconscious. Lloyd (1969–70: 263ff.) believes that for Plotinus self-consciousness is essentially propositional (i.e., "I am aware that I am aware of x") and for this reason denies self-consciousness to the non-discursive thinking of Intellect. As is evident throughout V.3, the consciousness of Intellect is always self-consciousness and is expressed generally in cognitive terms, including συναίσθησις. The distinction Plotinus is presupposing is basically ontological and only secondarily psychological. When embodied, the cognizing individual is identical with images; in Intellect its cognitive activity is identification with real being. What is of particular importance here, beyond a stipulative terminology, is that the former activity would not be possible were the latter activity not ongoing. See Schroeder (1987: 697): "It could be said that human awareness is triadic in that the awareness of any sensible object involves an illumination from beyond both of the object perceived and of the percipient subject." Warren (1966: 284)

observes that for Plotinus ordinary unconsciousness is a necessary prerequisite for true self-consciousness.

46 Cf. I.4.9.24–30, where Plotinus compares our unawareness of the activity of Intellect with the fact that we have no awareness of vegetative activity. Could we *ever* be aware or conscious of the latter? I think that with this analogy Plotinus means to indicate that we could be aware that it is occurring but we cannot as it were consciously vegetate. Oosthout (1991: 28) aptly states: "Self-knowledge, therefore, becomes a limiting concept. It functions as a fundamental category in the description of the world of experience, but its full realization falls outside the range of human experience."

47 At IV.4.5.13–24 Plotinus describes the passage of the soul through heaven, either ascending to Intellect or descending to an earthly body. In this middle state, memory is active, and even differences in characters (τῶν ἠθῶν) are discernible. By implication, these differences disappear in the ideal state. The middle state is a fiction evidently intended to mitigate the harsh discontinuity between idiosyncratic and non-idiosyncratic personal identity. If this state did not exist, then personal immortality would be radically equivocal in meaning. For if I am told that I shall survive the death of my body, what I take to be my self is more than an impersonal locus of contemplation. Heaven (ὁ οὐρανός) seems to be a place for preparing for an ascent into Intellect as well as a place for recovering the memories to be possessed by the reincarnated individual.

48 At IV.4.3.5–6 Plotinus in effect makes personal identity depend on memory: "in general, it [the soul] is and becomes what it remembers." This personal identity, depending on idiosyncratic experiences, must be distinguished from that of the personal identity of a locus of contemplation indistinguishable in its contents from any other. But if the content of every eternal contemplator's mind is identical, how does the awareness that each has of the fact that it is contemplating differ from any other?

49 Szlezák (1992) sees a greater continuity than I do between Plotinus' and Plato's accounts of νοῦς. I think he is right to emphasize that Plotinus wished to follow the *Republic* and the *Timaeus* in making the highest part of the tripartite soul identical with discarnate intellect. Szlezák (334) thinks that Plotinus holds that the highest part of the tripartite soul loses its habitual mode of discursive thinking upon achieving a discarnate state, when it becomes "pure νοῦς." For the reasons already discussed in this chapter, I very much doubt that the agent of incarnate thinking could, according to Plotinus, do what discarnate intellect does.

50 See I.5.1.2–4, where memory is said to have no role in happiness.

51 IV.4.2.30–2: "When therefore it [the soul] is in this state it could not change but would be unalterably disposed to intelligence while at the same time having a concurrent awareness of itself, as having become one and the same thing with its intelligible object." Cf. II.9.1.34–7. Warren (1965: 254–5) writes: "Plotinus wants to abandon the *notion* of memory, but he certainly does not want to abandon the content of those experiences. Whatever occurs spatio-temporally is a reflection of the forms in νοῦς and all that occurs here must exist there." This cannot be quite right as it stands. Plotinus evidently regards a state in which memory is obliterated as desirable.

52 I do not see how "intelligible realm" (ἐκεῖ) can refer here to Intellect, which is eternal and from which it is not possible to conceive of a motive for descent. Plotinus' claim makes somewhat more sense if it refers to the vaguely temporalized realm of discarnate existence for souls, a sort of staging area prior to final ascent to Intellect or to reincarnation. I am not, however, confident that this is what Plotinus means. And if it is not, I think his argument has gotten rather out of hand at this point.

Chapter IX Conquering Virtue

1 See *Nicomachean Ethics* 1.1.1094a26–b2 and the entire last chapter of that work, where Aristotle explicitly situates his ethical conclusions in a political context. By contrast, political virtue is for Plotinus an inferior form of virtue. The highest form of virtue is above politics.

2 See Himmerich (1959: especially 38–47).

3 The identification of the One as the Good has its origin, as we have seen, in an interpretation of Plato, according to which the subject of the first hypothesis of the *Parmenides* is identified with the Form of the Good in the *Republic*. The exegetical question this raises is, however, separate from the reasons independently supplied for making the ἀρχή of all a moral principle.

4 This is most clearly stated at VI.7.15.9–10: "but there [Intellect], Plato says, is the archetype, which 'has the Form of the Good' because it possesses the Good in the Forms." That is, in contemplation of Forms, the good is achieved.

5 Himmerich (1959: 19–28) takes this as a reductio ad absurdum of Aristotle's identification of happiness with an end or with "living well." But neither Aristotle nor Plotinus wishes to deny the general application of the concept of τέλος or goal beyond humanity. Aristotle does not define happiness as living well. Rather, at *Nicomachean Ethics* I.8.1098b20–1, he says that saying that the happy man is one who lives well harmonizes (συνᾴδει) with the λόγος of happiness or "the human good," given at 1098a16–18. Perhaps we need not accuse Plotinus of misreading Aristotle, but should say rather that he refutes an incautious interpretation of him.

6 At I.4.10 Plotinus is careful to distinguish the reflexive awareness in the ideal self contemplating intelligibles from the potential awareness that *we* might have that contemplating is occurring. The latter occurs with imagination (line 20); the former does not.

7 I.4.14.26–30: "When he finds himself in pain he will oppose it to the power which he has been given for the purpose; he will find no help to his well-being in pleasure and health and freedom from pain and trouble, nor will their opposites take it away or diminish it. For if one thing adds nothing to a state, how can its opposite take anything away?"

8 In one brief chapter Plotinus dismisses Epicurean hedonism, rejecting both the so-called "kinetic" pleasures and Epicurean static pleasures which require a body: I.4.12.

9 I.4.4.26–36; I.4.7; I.4.13. In the last passage Plotinus points out that it is silly to hold that being roasted alive in the bull of Phalaris is pleasant, even though the good man would still be happy if he suffered in this way. The torture is painful, but the pain does not matter to happiness.

10 At I.4.7–8 Plotinus does seem to approve suicide under certain extreme conditions. But these are such that none of the indications of wrongdoing are likely to be present.

11 See I.4.4.18–20: "What then is the good for him? He is what he has, his own good. The transcendental (ἐπέκεινα) Good is the cause of good in him; the fact that it is good is different from the fact that it is present to him." The Good is present with the instrumentality of Intellect and Soul.

12 See Rist (1976: 229).

13 See *Symposium* 206ff. on the task of knowledge of the beautiful and Aristotle's description of a friend as "another self" (ἕτερον αὑτον) in the *Nicomachean Ethics* 9.9.1169b6–7. But Aristotle adds that a friend is an "external good" which it would be absurd to deprive the happy man of.

14 When at II.9.15.38–9 Plotinus says: "In reality it is virtue which goes before us

to the goal and, when it comes to exist in the soul along with wisdom, shows god," I understand him to mean not that virtue is a condition for desiring the Good, but that it is a condition for attaining it.

15 See Himmerich (1959: 29–37).

16 Inwood (1985: 210–15), approaching the problem from within Stoicism, thinks that a good Stoic response would be to say that in effect the pursuit of things preferred (i.e., "externals") is defeasible, that is, potentially dispensable on those occasions when their pursuit conflicts with the pursuit of the good. But this does not seem to address Plotinus' criticism. See Bussanich (1990: 154–7) on Plotinus' critique of Stoic ethics.

17 So Costello (1967: 493ff.), who stresses the appropriateness of the placement by Porphyry of I.8 among the treatises dealing with morality rather than metaphysics. Costello is wrong, however, to suggest that a notion of metaphysical evil in Plotinus would imply the presence of evil in everything other than the One, including Intellect. Metaphysical evil stops at the immaterial world. The mistake here is to think that the existence of metaphysical evil would imply that Intellect is evil because it exists in separation from the One.

18 I think there is little to be said for Inge's intended exculpating assertion (1929: I.135): "When he attributes a positive evil nature to Matter, Plotinus is thinking of the materialist's Matter, not of his own doctrine." Inge cites II.9.12 as evidence that Plotinus believed that evil could be attributed to the soul rather than matter. However, Plotinus says this in a passage in which he is formulating a Gnostic position, not his own.

19 Plotinus makes the distinction in several ways. At I.8.3.24–5 he distinguishes evil itself (τὸ κακὸν αὐτό) and evil which derives from it [evil itself] and exists accidentally in something else (τὸ κατ' ἐκεῖνο συμβεβηκὸς ἑτέρῳ). At I.8.5 he distinguishes between evil simply or παντελὴς τὸ κακόν and particular evils. At I.8.8.37–44 he distinguishes between "primary" and "secondary" evil.

20 At III.2.5.25–6 it is stated most clearly: "In general, we must define evil as a falling short of good, and there must be a falling short of good here below, because the good is in something else." See also III.6.11.43–5.

21 Cf. I.8.14.37, where it is said that nothing exists (here below) without soul. This of course includes the soul of the universe. Its body, the material world, is as such not bereft of soul and so not what evil is primarily. See Himmerich (1959: 121): "Nur der Verstand findet in der Reflexion über die Struktur der Welt ein Erstes Böses an sich, so wie auch die Materie als das nichtgeistige Prinzip nicht in der Empirie begegnet, sondern nur von Verstande auszumachen ist." This seems to be the point behind the distinction between evil in itself and the evil that something has at I.8.3.23–4.

22 See also I.8.8.37–40: "So, then, let unmeasure be the primary evil, and that which is in a state of unmeasuredness by likeness or participation evil in a secondary sense, because its unmeasuredness is accidental."

23 At I.8.9.7 Plotinus says we know matter by ἀφαίρεσις or abstraction. The term ἀφαίρεσις is not used here in the precise Aristotelian sense in which it is used for quantitative abstraction. It seems rather to mean a separation of one or more parts from a whole of any sort. See, for example, I.2.4.6; I.4.14.29; I.8.14.23; III.2.15.42–3; III.9.9.23; IV.3.26.51–2; IV.7.5.27.

24 At II.5.5.22 Plotinus says that matter is unaffected by form, though this does not of course entail the opposite. However, at III.6.12.1–7, commenting on Plato's *Timaeus*, he seems to endorse an interpretation which does entail the impassibility of form to matter. I take it that he must be referring to the impassibility of form as such, which is really distinct from the enmattered image of it.

25 At II.3.18.1–3 Plotinus comes as close as he ever does to making evil explicitly

a hypothetical necessity: "then are the evils in the all necessary, because they follow on prior realities? Rather because if they did not exist the all would be imperfect." The "all" is the material universe. It is not of course unqualifiedly perfect. It is only a perfect image of its source.

26 I.8.11.10–11: "But if the privation is privation of a form which ought to be present, if the privation in the soul is a privation of good and produces vice in the soul corresponding to its own definition, soul then has no good in it, so then it has no life in it, though it is still soul." At I.8.3.14, it is formless (ἀνείδεον), and at II.4.16.23 ill-formed (δυσειδές).

27 The identification of matter with privation alters the Aristotelian account according to which matter is potency in contrast to privation. See *Metaphysics* 5.12 and 22. If, as I have argued, matter is understood by Plotinus as analogous to prime matter, then the potency that matter is in the first instance is a potency for generation and destruction. That this should be interpreted as a privation follows from the deficiency in being of everything contingent or sensible. The first meaning of "privation" Aristotle gives in his philosophical dictionary is "not having something which can be had by nature, even if that which does not have it would not by nature have it." Aristotle does not believe that anything can have eternal life "by nature." God's everlasting life is beyond nature. Plotinus would say that everything subject to generation and destruction has the privation of true life and oneness because these *can* be had "by nature," where "nature" is understood as referring to its paradigm. Fuller (1912: 255) makes a different and useful point: "To assert, as Aristotle does, that [good and evil] represent contrary formations of a neutral Matter is covertly to ascribe the cause of Evil to Form, not Matter."

28 Does this refer to men who are liberated from vice or whose incarnation inures them against it? The former seems most likely. I suppose that the virtue here is higher virtue, not the lower virtue. Cf. section 3 below. The Stoic sage is the appropriate model here, I suspect. On this textually difficult passage see O'Brien (1971: 129–30).

29 See Rist (1983: 136–40).

30 Vice is clearly defined at I.8.8.41–2: "Vice, which is ignorance and un-measuredness in the soul, is evil secondarily, not absolute evil." The primary evil is matter. See also IV.8.4.1–23. On the evil that is matter, and vice see O'Brien (1971: 113–46). Rist (1974: 496–7), replying to O'Brien, insists on the distinction between evil and vice, which are not clearly distinguished by O'Brien. Cf. Hager (1977: Nachtrag 1973 [469–74] to the article originally appearing in 1962) and (1987: 52–60), who basically supports Rist and Schwyzer (see n33 below), holding that in the lowest part of the soul there is "eine gewisse Bereitschaft . . . Böses in sich aufzunehmen (53)." This does not indicate a source of evil in the soul. Its susceptibility to evil exists despite the fact that no one does wrong willingly.

31 I.8.14.19–22, referring to *Phaedrus* 246b7–c1. It is to be noted in the text of Plato that there is at least a prima facie incoherence in speaking of a perfect soul "losing its wings." Fuller (1912: 101) holds that it is a contradiction to attribute proper perfections to Intellect and Soul because only the One is essentially good. Thus, because Intellect and Soul are not completely self-sufficient they cannot be perfect. Fuller's error arises from thinking that the goal of all creation is "to transcend and annihilate itself by absorption into deity."

32 I.8.14.49–50: "So matter is the cause of the soul's weakness and vice: it is then itself evil before soul and is primary evil." See also I.8.15.13–14. So Fuller (1912: 269–74). Cf. Hager (1962: 89), who views the weakness as a *conditio sine qua non* of the decline into evil, but distinct from evil itself.

33 See O'Brien (1971: 135–9). Schwyzer (1973: 275–7) contradicts O'Brien and questions whether I.8.14.49–54 can be understood to indicate that soul is in any way responsible for matter. Schwyzer grants that the language of the text is not decisive one way or another. It does not seem to me that Schwyzer's correct emphasis on the everlastingness of matter supports his case, because for Plotinus time is irrelevant to dependence in being. On the other hand, his reference to III.6.11.44, where matter is said to be impassive with respect to the Good (τοῦ ἀγαθοῦ ἀπαθής), is apposite. Matter, though it exists, is bereft of goodness because it escapes the instrumental agency of Intellect. Rist (1974: 502–4) argues that in I.8.14.49–54 Plotinus is distinguishing between moral and cosmological evil (matter), the latter being an actualization of the former. And with the actualization of matter comes the possibility of further moral evil or vice. This, I think, accounts well for evil in the soul which is not identical with matter. See Inge (1929: I.131).

34 See I.8.5.1–5: "But if lack of good is the cause of seeing and keeping company with darkness, then evil for the soul will lie in the lack and this will be primary evil – the darkness can be put second – and the nature of evil will no longer be in matter but before matter."

35 This is also a comment on a passage in the *Phaedrus* (256b2–3). In that passage Plato is talking about vice in the soul, but it is the incarnated soul that is the specific subject.

36 See Schubert (1968: 80), who, I think incorrectly, contrasts this with Plato's account of punishment. For Plato, judgment may be of the soul in the discarnate state, but punishment consists in some form of reincarnation.

37 See Schubert (1968: 122–5). Rist (1983: 139) stresses that matter is not the cause of vice.

38 See III.4.2.11ff., where the principle of decline seems to be: "when it [the soul] goes out of the body it becomes what there was most of in it, that is, what it had most of when in the body." The remainder of the chapter recounts the punishments following previous unhappy incarnations. See IV.3.24.20–8, which seems to suggest that punishment for previous incarnate evils must await reincarnation. Also IV.3.8.5–9. At IV.8.5.16–18 the error of the soul is said to be twofold: (1) "either owing to the cause of the descent" or (2) "doing evil when the soul has arrived here below." In the first case, the punishment (assuming Theiler's addition of δίκη to the text) is just the experience of the descent. In the second case, the punishment is reincarnation. So, in the first case something like an original incarnation must be supposed, else there would be no way of distinguishing the two kinds of error. Yet this original incarnation is not temporally first. It is conceptually first. That is, the nature of soul must explain the nature of that with soul, namely, the non-hylomorphic composite. See Blumenthal (1971b: 60–1).

39 At I.8.15.1–5 Plotinus stresses the necessity of the existence of matter (τὴν ἀνάγκην τῆς ὑποστάσεως αὐτῆς). This does not contradict I.8.5.5–12, where evil is said not to have existence. Plotinus is here simply following Plato in the *Sophist* (238c9–10 and 258b2–3) when he distinguishes between τὸ μὴ ὄν, the relatively non-existent, and τὸ μὴ ὄν αὐτὸ καθ' αὑτό, the totally non-existent. The former is not nothing. See also VI.9.11.34–8.

40 Fuller (1912: 323–8) thinks that the One is straightforwardly the cause of evil, but he does not take account of the instrumental causality of Intellect and Soul.

41 I take it that lines 21–2 repeat 17–18 and are not a new argument.

42 See Rist (1983: 146–9).

43 This is contradicted by Rist (1967b: 128), who says, "Matter is no metaphysical evil, for it only exists as 'non-being,' but its sheer lack of reality means that its

effects will be bad. This is the sense in which it is the prime evil." See the criticism of Rist by O'Brien (1971: 123–7), with which I basically agree.

44 The Platonic source for this idea is *Phaedo* 67c4–d8. At I.2.2.4, I.2.3.20, and I.2.7.28 he describes virtue as assimilation (ὁμοίωσις). I take it that this is the same thing as κάθαρσις viewed positively.

45 One might compare in this regard Martin Luther's polemical and tendentious claim that Christianity has nothing to do with virtue. Bodéüs (1983: 259–61) draws a clear contrast between Christian and Plotinian ethics, based upon the difference between incarnate and discarnate ideal states.

46 Cf. *Timaeus* 90bd. Müller (1917c: 57) writes, "Aus diesem Satze [*Theaetetus* 176ab] lässt sich wie aus dem Kern so ziemlich die gesamte Philosophie Plotins entwickeln." I think there is some truth in this extreme claim if we view Plotinus' philosophy from a practical perspective. Dillon (1983: 92) compares the distinction in the *Phaedo* 82a11–b1 between "popular" and "political" virtue, on the one hand, and philosophical virtue, on the other, with what he takes to be a unified account of virtue in the *Republic*, an account supporting the latter form of virtue. Dillon's point is that Plotinus is led to an account of different grades of virtue as an attempt to reconcile what is in Plato incompatible. But within the *Republic* at least a pejorative connotation does not attach to the account of virtue in Book 4.

47 As Jonas (1964: 144–5) points out, Plotinus' interpretation of the Platonic injunction to assimilate oneself to god is filtered through Aristotle, *Nicomachean Ethics* 10.8.1178b7–23, where divine happiness, understood as contemplative activity, is *beyond* virtue understood as action. Plato, however, seems to identify assimilation to god with virtue.

48 This instrumentality is clearly contrasted with happiness itself, which is not found in actions at all, even virtuous ones. See also I.5.10.20–3 and Arnou (1972: 17). As Arnou points out, action (πρᾶξις) is always directed to the "external," whereas contemplation (θεωρία) or production (ποίησις) is always directed to the "internal" or to the self. If happiness is virtuous activity, then virtuous activity can never consist in what would amount to a deconstruction of the self.

49 At I.2.2.21–6 Plotinus says that the lower virtues are likenesses to the paradigm of measure, Intellect, although he explains the recognition of this in a curiously pejorative tone. Soul deceives us into imagining that this likeness is true divinity. I take it that the point is that we must not mistake the lower virtues for the true likenesses of Intellect, the higher virtues, though we be apt to do so. Also, at I.2.1.23–6 Plotinus does admit that posession of the lower virtues does in a way contribute to making us godlike.

50 On this interpretation I do not think we have to admit the conflict between Plotinus' theory and personal practice that Rist (1967b: 166–8) suggests. The incarnate individual or the endowed self, even when perfected, is still operating under the exigencies of nature.

51 At III.6.2.22–32 Plotinus says that the vice of the reasoning part of the soul (τὸ λογιστικόν) is unintelligence (ἄνοια) and that false beliefs produce vice. By contrast, true opinion would govern the disposition to lower virtue. True opinion, however, is not knowledge, either for Plato or Plotinus. Cf. *Timaeus* 86bff., where Plato says that the ἄνοια of the soul is of two kinds, madness (μανία) and ignorance (ἀμαθία).

52 See Plass (1982: 250–6) on the man of higher virtue "going through the motions" of ordinary life. Ferwerda (1984) assembles the texts which together indicate Plotinus' in principle resistance to the idea that pity is a virtue. Yet as Ferwerda points out (68–70), this is in marked contrast to the way Plotinus is represented by Porphyry in his personal life. I suppose Plotinus' behavior in this regard would be more inconsistent with his theory if he thought that pity was a vice.

53 By distinguishing the virtue that is identical with true opinion from the virtue that is identical with knowledge, Plotinus is able to deny mutual implication for the lower virtues while retaining it for the higher. For example, one may have a true opinion that temperance is good for oneself but a false opinion that courage is not.

54 One might object that if virtue is a καθάρσις, then it would seem to admit of degrees, which is in contradiction to the Stoic doctrine. However, "virtue" in the principal sense refers to the higher virtues which indicate a state, not action in the ordinary sense. It is difficult to see what degrees of this state could be. I think that this can be said of the lower virtues as well, though for a different reason. Because they are a unity, they must be understood as a state or disposition of the agent, and only secondarily as referring to the agent's acts.

55 Cf. Rist (1976b: 229–32) on what the practice of the lower virtues by someone possessed of the higher amounts to. Rist quotes III.2.9.10–12: "But it is not lawful for those who have become wicked to demand others to be their saviours and to sacrifice themselves in answer to their prayers." Dillon (1983: 94) aptly compares the Plotinian just man and the Platonic just man, both of whom are disinclined to do the things ordinarily accounted unjust because of the kind of person each has become. I think the "attitude" inplicit in the quotation by Rist is not incompatible with what Dillon says. The Plotinian or Platonic just men will do their duty to others unfailingly, but will not mistake this for happiness or the pleasure associated with happiness. Beierwaltes (1985: 29–30) argues similarly.

56 Armstrong (1961: 115) writes: "A man, in [Plotinus'] opinion, will act more virtuously if, instead of thinking 'I propose to perform the following virtuous actions,' he simply concentrates his mind on virtue so intensely that the virtuous actions follow naturally and spontaneously as occasion requires. And this, apparently, was not only how he thought but how he lived." A similar interpretation is given by Bussanich (1990: 180–4).

57 See I.4.8.20–2: "it is the business of virtue to raise ordinary nature to a higher level, something better than most people are capable of; and it is better not to give in to what ordinary nature normally finds terrible." On this discontinuity see I.2.6.17–19 and Plass (1982: 242–3), where the relation of higher and lower virtue is aptly compared to the relation of Forms to their images. So too Lieshout (1926: 67–8) and Dillon (1983: 94–5).

58 See I.4.16 for a powerful description of the contrast between the σπουδαῖος and the ἐπιείκης ἄνθρωπος. The latter, though he be virtuous, contains a mixture of good and bad owing to his attachment to the bodily. I suspect that this contrast contains a veiled criticism of Aristotle, who in idealizing the contemplative cannot yet bring himself to disparage the practical. See Bodéüs (1983: 259), "il résulte alors que l'éthique plotinienne est essentiellement négative. Car, en soutenant que le sage parfait devient ce qu'il était 'en puissance' Plotin entend signifier seulement qu'il devient ce qu'il était déjà 'en partie'; et l'attrait positif du bien se réduit dès lors, à l'attrait du bien dans sa pureté. Or la 'purification,' par quoi se traduit l'effort moral, n'est en somme que l'opération qui consiste à retrancher l'âme (d'essence noétique) de la société du corps."

Chapter X Philosophy of Religion

1 See Armstrong (1974: 184–7) for some interesting remarks on Plotinus' likely attitude to the theurgic practices that constituted a part of the civic religion.

2 If Plotinus had established a "church" it would probably have had at least three essential dogmas: (1) that god exists; (2) that god is provident; (3) that there are

rewards and punishments meted out by god for our lives here below. Upon these claims Plato in the *Laws*, book 10, proposed to construct a civic religion, with notable lack of success. Plotinus, however, does not connect these claims with any proposed group practices. Perhaps he would have if he had had the opportunity to establish his Platonic utopia. The asocial nature of Plotinus' religion seems to me in this regard closer to seventeenth-century English deism than to Platonism. This is in line with Plotinus' propensity, unlike Plato, for detaching ethics from politics.

3 See Aubin (1953: 373–7) on ἐπιστρέφειν and ἐπιστροφή.

4 Trouillard (1954: 45) states this beautifully: "Il faut comprendre l'implication de l'idée dans l'action et de l'Un dans l'idée. On ne gagnera rien à chercher Dieu dans les prodiges dans la nature ou dans les états internes de la psychologie. Le dieu de ces phénomènes c'est l'âme; le dieu de l'âme c'est l'intelligible. Dieu se révèle à travers «l'intrinsécisme» de la vérité. Tant que nous comprenons la moindre proposition mathématique, l'absence de Dieu n'a pas de sens pour nous, car cette absence comprise serait encore une vérité qui nous donnerait accès à la divinité. C'est à dire qu'il y a identité entre la présence de Dieu et l'éveil de l'esprit."

5 See Roloff (1970: 165–226); Elsas (1975); Runia (1984).

6 See Hartshorne (1967: especially chs 1, 5).

7 See Atkinson (1983:1–21) for helpful philological notes and bibliographical references pertaining to this text.

8 Baladi (1970) has devoted an entire monograph to the concept of τόλμα in Plotinus. See ch.3 on this passage.

9 See I.1.12.24, where the inclination (νεῦσις) downward is said not to be an error, and IV.3.13, where it seems to be described in terms of a natural event, like the growing of horns on an animal. Baladi (1970: 78–80) agrees with Dodds that the descent of the soul is to be divested of any pejorative connotations. Baladi (116) goes so far as to identify τόλμα with contingency.

10 See Dodds (1965: 25–6). Puech (1960: 182–5) argues subtly that Plotinus was never drawn to Gnosticism himself but that he came to believe that an excessively gloomy view of the physical world in his earlier writings needed to be toned down in order to avoid confusion of his doctrines with those of the Gnostics. Puech takes II.9 as marking "la crise" when Plotinus resolved to draw back from a negativism which in fact he no longer wished to espouse. On problems in the interpretations of Dodds and Puech on τόλμα in V.1 see Atkinson (1983: 4–6). O'Brien (1993: 8–16) has noticed two defects in Dodds's interpretation. First, Dodds (25 n5) mistakenly took II.9 as treatise 23 rather than what it is, treatise 33. Consequently, the treatise that is supposed by Dodds to indicate a new optimism in Plotinus' view of the soul's descent, namely, IV.3, treatise 27, was actually written *before* the treatise that is supposed to indicate a pessimism on Plotinus' part. Second, Dodds and others assume that when Plotinus says in V.1.1 and IV.7.13 that the soul wishes (βούλεσθαι) to descend and descends voluntarily (ἑκούσιον), he must mean that the soul *chooses* to descend. Then, when in IV.7.13 Plotinus says that the soul is constrained to descend, this must indicate a change in his view. But O'Brien notes that neither in Plotinus nor in Aristotle does the voluntary entail choice. Thus, when Plotinus says that the soul is constrained, he is not exactly contradicting his earlier assertion. That is, the soul goes willingly but not with deliberation. O'Brien also accepts the emendation of Theiler at IV.7.13.17 from ἑκοῦσαι to ἄκουσαι so the text reads: "the souls neither go involuntarily nor are they sent" rather than "the souls neither go voluntarily nor are they sent," which is the correct translation of the text printed by Henry and Schwyzer. Thus, IV.7.13 is actually in accord with V.1.1.

11 Rist (1965: 337ff.) reaches a similar conclusion, in effect making τόλμα not a cause of descent but one (bad) response to descent. Rist (1975: 109, 111) points out that Plotinus never refers to the descent as a kind of προαίρεσις, which would suggest rationality or deliberation. Rather, the fall of the soul is non-rational. Rist says that the soul is seduced by pleasure or pride. But why do souls find these seductive? Evidently, it is because psychic desires are the incarnate image of intellectual desire. We cannot stop having these desires, but we can stop desiring to have them. O'Brien (1993: 17) holds similarly that the soul descends necessarily because of its nature and not because it has chosen to do so.

12 Cf. VI.9.7.33–4: "he who has learnt to know himself will know from whence he comes." In this passage, the ultimate source whence we came is the One. See also I.6.6.17–18; VI.9.11.43–5. Kremer (1981: 43–56) richly documents the historical and systematic background of Plotinus' idea of religious ascent as growth in self-knowledge.

13 Thus I think it is wrong for Inge (1929: I.246) to say: "the question whether it is *my* self that has its distinct place 'yonder' is simply meaningless." Equally mistaken is Pistorius (1952: 48–52; 58–66), who infers from V.3.6–7 that if self-knowledge is the manner in which Intellect knows the One, then Intellect and the One must be identical. For the One is *virtually* what Intellect is. See Salmona (1967: 30–70).

14 See VI.9.11.35–40: "For the nature of the soul will certainly not arrive at absolute non-existence, but when it goes down it will arrive at evil and in this way at non-existence, not at absolute non-existence. But if it runs the opposite way, it will arrive, not at something else but at itself, and in this way since it is not in something else it will not be in nothing, but in itself."

15 How could one ensure that resurrected persons possessing glorified bodies and free will would be unable to sin as Adam did? If one could not ensure it, then such a state would not be ideal, as Plotinus understands that concept. Should one reply that the resurrected state is actually an improvement over the prelapsarian state, Plotinus would no doubt say that if that state is necessarily a bodily one, then it is heir to all the evils that that state implies, whereas if it is not, then the ideal is not a resurrected state.

16 I think that Arnou (1967: 224–9) grasped this perfectly when he argued that Plotinus excludes absolutely the need for divine assistance or grace in effecting the ascent to the One. As Arnou puts it (228–9): "Tout le succès de l'enterprise est entre les mains de l'homme, qui, par ses efforts, est l'artisan de son salut comme de sa perfection: rien n'est plus opposé à la pensée de Plotin que la notion de grâce prévenante." See also Kremer (1981: 55–6).

17 See Deuse (1983: 123–8) for this solution.

18 This seems to be the implication of VI.4.15. Cf. VI.4.11, where the general principle that "what is present is present according to the capacity of that which receives it" is enunciated. Thus the animal body would be capable only of receiving a soul activated according to a particular pattern of dispositions which excluded rational activity. On the natural continuity of human and animal souls, particularly as this explains the possibility of transmigration, see Cole (1992: 83–90).

19 That there is punishment for wrongdoing Plotinus never doubts. See III.2.4.23ff.; 44; 5.17; 8.26ff.; 9.8–10. At III.4.2.16–24, Plotinus follows Plato in making the punishment a form of transmigration of the soul into some animal form.

20 Yet, at VI.7.36.6–10 Plotinus distinguishes the methods whereby we are taught about the One (ἀναλογίαι, ἀφαιρέσεις, γνώσεις, and ἀναβασμοί) from the means by which we are imported towards it (καθάρσεις, ἀρεταί, κοσμήσεις, and participations in the life of Intellect). The passages are reconciled if the distinction

indicates an ordered procedure: first demonstrations, then the moral ascent. See Hadot (1988: 347–50).

21 Cf. *Republic* 521c10–523a3, where the study of mathematics is constitutive of the ascent to the Good.

22 See also V.5.12, where the priority of the Good to beauty as it exists in Intellect is clearly expressed. Plotinus does not distinguish a Form of Beauty from other Forms. In fact, beauty is identified with Intellect, which is itself identical with all the Forms. See also I.6.6.26–7; V.8.3.9–10. Plotinus is perhaps encouraged in this approach by the *Symposium*, where a Form of Beauty is not obviously distinguished from the Form of the Good or indeed from the other Forms.

23 See I.6.5.17–20: "We love and delight in these qualities, but why do we call them beautiful? They exist and appear to us and he who sees them cannot possibly say anything except that they are what really exists. What does 'really exists' mean? That they exist as beauties." The last words are puzzling. The word καλά seems to explain the word ὄντως. Then it would indicate that beauty is a property of the really real as opposed to anything else. It is a property of the life of Intellect. See also V.8.9.43–7. At I.6.6.21 Plotinus employs an odd neologism to make a similar point about reality and beauty: "Or rather, beautifulness is reality" (Μᾶλλον δὲ τὰ ὄντα ἡ καλλονή ἐστιν). He proceeds to emphasize the identity of καλλονή with goodness and to add that together they produce τὸ καλόν, which is nothing but Intellect.

24 The objection from simplicity works better for simple objects than for the simple parts of complex objects. The proponent of symmetry need not concede that the parts of the complex have to be beautiful for the complex to be beautiful. Anton (1964: 233–7) examines some of the logical difficulties in the refutation of beauty as symmetry.

25 See also I.6.6.18–24, where the identification of beauty and good is strongly made.

26 See I.6.3.9–15, especially the uses of the metaphors σύμφωνον and συναρμόττον. Similarly, there is a lack of resonance when one encounters ugliness. See also I.6.2.4–6.

27 See V.5.12.23–4, where, following Plato, Plotinus says that people are often content with apparent rather than real beauty. By contrast, they are only satisfied with real goodness.

28 See also III.5.1.30–6, where this is said to be the error of those who are unable to grasp that bodily beauty is an image of true beauty.

29 This is not to associate Plotinus with the Gnostic belief that fidelity to "higher" beauty requires disdain for the lower. What one should disdain is the false belief that the lower is the higher. See II.9.17.32–8. For a highly positive view of Plotinus' propensity to asceticism see Dombrowski (1987). Beierwaltes (1985: 26–31 with n46) objects to Jonas's (1964) characterization of Plotinus' ethics as involving a "Weltflucht" or extreme "Weltlosigkeit" and "absoluter Solipsismus." Beierwaltes aptly cites I.8.6.10–13, where Plotinus, commenting on *Theaetetus* 176a, says that when Plato recommends a "flight from here" he means not a flight from earth but a flight from wickedness.

30 At IV.7.10 there is a remarkable description of the process of stripping off bodily accretions which leads to self-recognition. See Szlezák (1979: 170–6) who shows that here Plotinus is closely following *Republic* 611a–612a, as well as *Phaedrus* 247c6–7 and *Phaedo* 79d1–6, as others have pointed out.

31 Cf. VI.7.30.36–8: "what is really worth aspiring to for us is our selves, bringing themselves back for themselves to the best of themselves." See Trouillard (1955c: 202): "A la notion chrétienne de *rédemption* s'oppose l'idée néoplatonicienne de *purification*."

32 The term μουσικός in Plotinus refers usually to a practitioner of a "musical" art,

290

as opposed to one who appreciates these. See I.4.16.23; III.6.2.15–17; III.6.4.50–3; IV.4.31.20–2; IV.4.40.26–7; V.9.11.10. It is perhaps this sense which is to be understood here. In that case, the musician is a creative artist. See Anton (1967: 94–7) on the theory of artistic creation in Plotinus. Rich (1960: 236–7) points out how Plotinus recognizes the distinct character of artistic μιμήματα or εἴδωλα in comparison with natural images of Forms. This is perhaps a tacit clarification of Plato's *Sophist* 235a–236c. See IV.3.10.

33 One might compare the 1944 film *Laura*, in which an investigating policeman falls in love with the painting of a woman he thinks is dead. When he learns that Laura is really alive, he immediately transfers his love to her. The crucial psychological point in Plotinus' account is lost if there is no possibility of a dénouement in which the true nature of the image is revealed as such: III.8.4.43–4: "For who, if he is able to contemplate what is truly real, will go after its image?"

34 Against the contention of Eborowicz (1958: 26–31), I do not regard the opening passage of IV.8.1 as a personal testimony by Plotinus of many mystical experiences of the One, but rather of a consciousness of the identity of his true self with Intellect. See O'Meara (1974: 238–44), who argues for distinguishing the type of experience in Porphyry's account and in Plotinus' own testimony.

35 See Katz (1950: 24), who rightly distinguishes between Plotinus' experience and its interpretation, disparaging the alleged uniqueness of the former.

36 On the initial "interiorizing" aspect of the ascent to the One see V.5.7.32; V.8.11.10ff.; VI.8.18.1–5; VI.9.7.16–17.

37 See III.8.9.19–22, where Plotinus says that it is our likeness to the One that enables us to have a simple intuition (ἐπιβολῇ ἀθρόᾳ) of it. See Thesleff (1980) for a close study of the erotic metaphors employed by Plotinus in describing what Thesleff calls the *unio mystica*. The use of erotic imagery is appropriate, for the ecstatic experience of union is not reducible to the cognitive.

38 See Hadot (1988: 58–66) for a thorough analysis of the characteristics of mystical experience in Plotinus. According to Hadot, there are six: (1) momentary or transitory ecstasy; (2) feeling of presence of the One; (3) the presence is felt in terms of vision; (4) the vision is felt as loving union; (5) during the time of union, the mystic is aware of nothing else; (6) union is accompanied by a feeling of joy.

39 IV.4.4.1: "Now in the intelligible world the soul also sees the Good through Intellect." I.8.2.23–5: "And soul dances around Intellect outside, and looks to it, and in contemplating its interior sees god through it." See also VI.9.9.17, where life with the One is just the activity of Intellect. Also V.6.5.8, where intellection is described as motion towards the Good (κίνησις πρὸς ἀγαθόν).

40 See Inge (1929: II.132–63), whose works are still among the most acute and sensible expositions of Western mystical doctrine. Inge says (159): "The common impression about Plotinus, that ecstasy is an important part of his system, is erroneous ... the philosophy of Plotinus [does not] culminate in a 'convulsed state' which is the negation of reason and sanity."

41 See also III.8.7.17–18, where the qualification is added: "if the beginning for everything is the goal" (εἴπερ τέλος ἅπασιν ἡ ἀρχή). On the various applications of this doctrine see Arnou (1921, 1972), Eborowicz (1958), Deck (1967), Santa Cruz de Prunes (1979), and Gatti (1982).

42 See III.8.1.6–7, where Plotinus distinguishes "true" contemplation and an imitation of it. The distinction is *among* things other than Intellect. See the interesting account by Wallis (1976) of the experiential analysis of Intellect and the impressive analogues in other traditions. Wallis is not too clear, however, about whether the experience of Intellect is thought by him to be one of which we are aware when we have it. But unless we are in some sense aware when we

have it, how are we supposed to be aware later on that it was *we* who had it in the first place?

43 See V.6.5.9–10 and Arnou (1972: 81–3). Müller (1916b: 242–5) makes the interesting suggestion that the idea that all things desire the Good is an intended extension of the claim made by Aristotle in the first line of the *Metaphysics*, πάντες ἄνθρωποι τοῦ εἰδέναι ὀρέγονται φύσει.

44 III.8.3.21–3: "So its making has been revealed to us as contemplation, for it is a result of contemplation, and the contemplation stays unchanged and does not do anything else but makes by being contemplation." Note that there seems to be no distinction made between ποίησις and πρᾶξις. See also 4.39–40.

45 See III.8.7.18–22, where the production of forms by living things is analogous to the production of intelligibles by Intellect. In each case, this is a ποίησις and so θεωρία, not πρᾶξις. The production of forms is a weakening of the contemplation of Intellect, because the forms are images of intelligibles or Forms.

46 III.8.7.5–6: "the products of contemplation are directed to the perfecting of another form and object of contemplation." At IV.8.1.1 the personal description of the union with Intellect, "many times I have awakened into myself" (πολλάκις ἐγειρόμενος εἰς ἐμαυτὸν), is presumably to be understood as punctuating activities aimed at a repetition of consciousness of the union. It is not a union with the One other than via union with Intellect. See also VI.9.3.22–7, where the indispensable instrumentality of Intellect is stressed in attaining union with the One. At V.1.5.3 the unification with Intellect is described as "in a way becoming one" (οἷον ἓν γενομένη), which surely indicates a qualified union, and hence a qualified union with the One. See Atkinson (1983: 104–5). As Hadot (1987b: 12–16) points out, a number of other texts such as V.8.10.32–43; V.8.11.23–4; 33–4, as well as IV.8.1.1, indicate that this is the mode of mystical union Plotinus has in mind. O'Daly (1974: 159–69) does not persuade me that union with the One is attained other than through the instrumentality of Intellect. Nevertheless, in the light of texts such as III.8.9.29, V.5.6.17–21, and VI.9.11.35–51, we should perhaps lay some stress on the distinction between intelligibles as instrument of the recognition of the existence of the One and a further stage when one has a kind of erotic experience of the One οἷον ἐστὶ. The latter case would indicate mystical union, but not without (1) a residual distinction between knower and the One and (2) the literal unintelligibility of the One. It is an experience that the One is virtually the self, but there is no direct cognition of its nature. See Rist (1971: 83–5).

47 Seidl (1985: 263), in an important paper which distinguishes psychological, epistemological, and metaphysical unity, argues that Plotinus intends the first two and not the last. "Sans doute, l'âme extatique ressemble dans son unité simple à celle de l'Un divin mais elle en est cependent essentiellement distincte, du fait que son unité, à elle est une unité causée, opérée (par l'Un), tandis que l'Un opère comme unité causatrice." Seidl also notes that the repeated use of verbs indicating union with the prefixes συν and μετα (V.8.11.46; VI.9.9.25, 46; VI.9.11.32) strongly suggests a residual distinctness. Beierwaltes (1985: 144) aptly summarizes this view: "in der Einung sieht die Seele den Gott *und* sich selbst als Einheit, sie empfindet sich als mit dem Einen geeint, sie sieht sich als einem, der zugleich im Einen und in sich selbst oder *im* Einen in *sich selbst* ist," relying in particular on VI.9.11.38–40 and VI.9.9.56. See also Arnou (1967: 259), Eborowicz (1958: 70ff.), Rist (1967b: 213–30), (1989: 183–90), and Kremer (1981: 54–5), who argue similarly. O'Daly (1973: 85) says, "The self, we may say, is totally *one with the One*, but as a subject, as *itself*." I think O'Daly here fails to recognize the important distinctions made by Seidl. O'Daly goes on to say that the distinction between self and One is "logical," but this cannot be right.

48 See Trouillard (1961b: 436–8) for a refutation of the pantheistic interpretation of Plotinus' mysticism.

49 O'Daly (1974: 164–5) and Trouillard (1961b: 434) have similar interpretations.

50 I think this is the basis for Bussanich's argument (1988: 180–93) in favor of "monistic" mysticism, where the soul is actually identified with the One, thereby transcending the activity of Intellect. Meijer (1992: 294–325) provides a helpful survey of the evidence pertaining to mystical union. He holds (308) that "the conclusion that the soul of the mystic and the Supreme Entity are identical cannot be avoided." But then he proceeds to qualify this union so considerably that he must further conclude, "I do not believe that Plotinus' theory about the union is consistent" (318). The texts Meijer cites on behalf of absolute union can all bear the sense that when one has attained to Intellect, one has come as close as possible to the One. Indeed, then, there is "nothing between them, nor are there still two, but both are one" (VI.7.34.13–15. See also V.5.8.21; VI.9.10.15). I interpret the words "two, but both are one" according to the principle that the One is not an entity that is really related to anything, though we are really related to it. We and the One are not two, for then there would be a real relation. We and the One are one in so far as we recognize that it is virtually ourselves.

51 At V.5.6.19–21 Plotinus distinguishes between learning that the One is by means of Forms and learning what it is like (οἷον) by letting the Forms go. What would letting the Forms go mean for an eternal intellect? Nothing, in my opinion. It seems that this "letting go" is the precise focus of the mystical experience. Intuiting that the Good is One and virtually oneself is in contrast to desiring the Good and contemplating it as many, that is, as the Forms. I think this interpretation works equally well for the famous description Plotinus gives of his own experience at IV.8.1ff. Bussanich (1988: 234–6) argues that the "pre-noetic" state of Intellect is distinct from the state of mystical union. But this is also true for the former and the "final" state of Intellect, though they are in reality one.

Bibliography

Ancient Authors

Plotinus

Armstrong, A. H. (1966–88). *Plotinus*. 7 volumes. Loeb Classical Library. Cambridge, Mass.: Harvard University Press.

Bréhier, E. (1923–38). *Plotin Ennéades*. Paris: Les Belles Lettres. 6 tomes en 7 volumes.

Harder, R. (1956–71). *Plotins Schriften*. Neubearbeitung mit griechischem Lesetext und Anmerkungen fortgeführt von R. Beutler und W. Theiler. Hamburg: Felix Meiner.

Henry, P. and Schwyzer, H.-R. (1951, 1959, 1973). *Plotini Opera*. 3 volumes (*editio maior* = H-S$_1$) (v. 1, Bruxelles: Edition Universelle, *Enneads* I–III); (v. 2, Bruxelles: Editions Universelle and Paris: Desclée de Brouwer, *Enneads* IV–V); (v. 3, Paris: Desclée de Brouwer and Leiden: E. J. Brill, *Ennead* VI).

—— (1964, 1976, 1982). *Plotini Opera*. 3 volumes (*editio minor* = H-S$_2$). Oxford: Clarendon Press. (v. 1, *Enneads* I–III); (v. 2, *Enneads* IV–V); (v. 3, *Ennead* VI).

Plato

Burnet, J. (1900–7). *Platonis Opera*. 5 volumes. Oxford: Clarendon Press.

Aristotle

Minio-Paluello, L. (1949). *Aristotelis Categoriae et Liber de Interpretatione*. Oxford: Clarendon Press.

Ross, W. D. (1924). *Aristotle's Metaphysics*. 2 volumes. Oxford: Clarendon Press.

—— (1936). *Aristotle's Physics*. Oxford: Clarendon Press.

—— (1955). *Aristotelis Fragmenta Selecta*. Oxford: Clarendon Press.

—— (1961). *Aristotle. De Anima*. Oxford: Clarendon Press.

Epicurus

Usener, H. (1887). *Epicurea*. Leipzig: Teubner.

BIBLIOGRAPHY
Stoics

Von Arnim, J. (1903–24). *Stoicorum Veterum Fragmenta* (*SVF*). 4 volumes. Leipzig: Teubner.

Sextus Empiricus

Bury, R. G. (1933–49). *Outlines of Pyrrhonism* (v. 1); *Against the Logicians* (v. 2); *Against the Physicists*, *Against the Ethicists* (v. 3); *Against the Professors* (v. 4). Loeb Classical Library. Cambridge, Mass.: Harvard University Press.
Mutschmann, H. and Mau, J. *Sexti Empirici Opera*. (1912, 1914, 1954, 1962). 4 volumes, indices by K. Janácek. Leipzig: Teubner.

Alexander of Aphrodisias

Bruns, I. (1887). *De Anima Liber cum Mantissa*. Berlin: Reimer.
Hayduck, M. (1891). *In Aristotelis Metaphysica Commentaria*. Berlin: Reimer.

Proclus

Dodds, E. R. (1933, 2nd edition 1963). *The Elements of Theology*. Oxford: Clarendon Press.

Thomas Aquinas

Cathala, M.-R. and Spiazzi, M. (1977). *In Duodecim Libros Metaphysicorum Aristotelis Expositio*. 3rd edition. Turin: Marietti.
Maggiòlo, M. (1954). *In Octo Libros Physicorum Aristotelis Expositio*. Turin: Marietti.

Modern Authors

About, P. J. (1973). *Plotin et la quête de l'un*. Paris: Seghers.
Alfino, M. R. (1988). "Plotinus on the Possibility of Non-Propositional Thought," *Ancient Philosophy*, 8, 273–84.
Amado, E. (1953). "A propos des nombres nombrés et des nombres nombrants chez Plotin (Enn. VI.2.6)," *Revue Philosophique*, *143*, 423–5.
Anton, J. P. (1964). "Plotinus' Refutation of Beauty as Symmetry," *Journal of Aesthetics and Art Criticism*, *23*, 233–7.
—— (1967). "Plotinus' Conception of the Functions of the Artist," *Journal of Aesthetics and Art Criticism*, *26*, 91–101.
—— (1976). "Plotinus' Approach to Categorical Theory," in Harris (1976), 83–9.
—— (1977). "Some Logical Aspects of the Concept of Hypostasis in Plotinus," *Review of Metaphysics*, *31*, 258–71. Reprinted in Harris (1982a), 24–33.
Anton, J. P. and Preus, A. (1983). (eds) *Essays in Ancient Greek Philosophy*. V. 2. Albany, N.Y.: SUNY.
Aquilla, R. (1992). "On Plotinus and the 'Togetherness' of Consciousness," *Journal of the History of Philosophy*, *30*, 7–32.
Armstrong, A. H. (1936). "Plotinus and India," *Classical Quarterly*, *30*, 22–8. Reprinted in Armstrong (1979), I.

—— (1937). "Emanation in Plotinus," *Mind*, *46*, 61–6. Reprinted in Armstrong (1979), II.

—— (1938). "The Gods in Plato, Plotinus and Epicurus," *Classical Quarterly*, *32*, 190–6.

—— (1940). *The Architecture of the Intelligible Universe in the Philosophy of Plotinus*. Cambridge: Cambridge University Press.

—— (1954). "Spiritual or Intelligible Matter in Plotinus and St. Augustine," in *Augustinus Magister*, 277–83. Reprinted in Armstrong (1979), VII.

—— (1955). "Plotinus' Doctrine of the Infinite and its Significance for Christian Thought," *Downside Review*, *73*, 47–58. Reprinted in Armstrong (1979), V.

—— (1955–6). "Was Plotinus a Magician?," *Phronesis*, *1*, 73–9. Reprinted in Armstrong (1979), III.

—— (1957). "Salvation, Plotinian and Christian," *Downside Review*, *75*, 126–39. Reprinted in Armstrong (1979), VI.

—— (1960). "The Background of the Doctrine 'That the Intelligibles are not Outside the Intellect,'" in *Sources*, 393–413. Reprinted in Armstrong (1979), IV.

—— (1961). "Platonic Eros and Christian Agape," *Downside Review*, *79*, 105–21. Reprinted in Armstrong (1979), IX.

—— (1967a). (ed.) *The Cambridge History of Later Greek and Medieval Philosophy*. Cambridge: Cambridge University Press.

—— (1967b). "Plotinus," in Armstrong (1976a), 195–268.

—— (1971). "Eternity, Life and Movement in Plotinus' Accounts of Nous," in *Néoplatonisme*, 67–74. Reprinted in Armstrong (1979), XV.

—— (1972). "Neoplatonic Valuations of Nature, Body and Intellect," *Augustinian Studies*, *3*, 33–9.

—— (1973a). "Elements in the Thought of Plotinus at Variance with Classical Intellectualism," *Journal of Hellenic Studies*, *93*, 13–22. Reprinted in Armstrong (1979), XVI.

—— (1973b). "Man in the Cosmos: A Study of Some Differences Between Pagan Neoplatonism and Christianity," in den Boer et al. (1973), 171–94. Reprinted in Armstrong (1979), XXII.

—— (1974). "Tradition, Reason and Experience in the Thought of Plotinus," in *Plotino e il Neoplatonismo in Oriente e in Occidente*, 171–94. Reprinted in Armstrong (1979), XVII.

—— (1975a). "Beauty and the Discovery of Divinity in the Thought of Plotinus," in Mansfeld and de Rijk (1975), 155–63. Reprinted in Armstrong (1979), XIX.

—— (1975b). "The Escape of the One," in Livingston (1975), 77–89. Reprinted in Armstrong (1979), XXIII.

—— (1976). "The Apprehension of Divinity in the Self and Cosmos in Plotinus," in Harris (1976), 187–98. Reprinted in Armstrong (1979), XVIII.

—— (1977a). "Form, Individual, and Person in Plotinus," *Dionysius*, *1*, 49–58. Reprinted in Armstrong (1979), XX.

—— (1977b). "Negative Theology," *Downside Review*, *95*, 176–89. Reprinted in Armstrong (1979), XXIV.

—— (1979). *Plotinian and Christian Studies*. London: Variorum.

—— (1980). "Philosophy, Theology and Interpretation: The Interpretation of Interpretors," in *Eriguena*,7–14. Reprinted in Armstrong (1990), X.

—— (1981). "Some Advantages of Polytheism," *Dionysius*, *5*, 181–98. Reprinted in Armstrong (1990), I.

—— (1982a). "Negative Theology, Myth and Incarnation," in O'Meara (1982), 213–22. Reprinted in Armstrong (1990), VII.

—— (1982b). "Two Views of Freedom: A Christian Objection in Plotinus *Enneads* VI, 8(39), 7, 11–15," in Livingston (1982), 397–406.

—— (1983). "The Negative Theology of Nous in Later Neoplatonism," in Blume and Mann, 31–7. Reprinted in Armstrong (1990), III.

—— (1984a). "The Divine Enhancement of Earthly Beauties: The Hellenic and Platonic Tradition," *Eranos Jahrbuch*, *53*, 49–81. Reprinted in Armstrong (1990), IV.

—— (1984b). "Dualism Platonic, Gnostic, and Christian," in Runia (1984), 29–52. Reprinted in Armstrong (1990), XII.

—— (1984c). "Pagan and Christian Traditionalism in the First Three Centuries," *Studia Patristica 15*, pt 1, 414–31.

—— (1986) (ed.) *Classical Mediterranean Spirituality, Egyptian, Greek, Roman*. New York: Crossroad.

—— (1990). *Hellenic and Christian Studies*. London: Variorum.

—— (1991). "Aristotle in Plotinus: The Continuity and Discontinuity of *Psyche* and *Nous*," in H. J. Blumenthal and H. Robinson (1991), 117–27.

Arnou, R. (1921, 2nd edition 1967). *Le Désir de Dieu dans la philosophie de Plotin*. Rome: Presses de L'Université Grégorienne.

—— (1921, 2nd edition 1972). *Praxis et Theoria: Etude de détail sur le vocabulaire et la pensée des Ennéades de Plotin*. Rome: Presses de L'Université Grégorienne.

—— (1930). "La Séparation par simple altérité dans la 'Trinité' Plotinienne," *Gregorianum, 11*, 181–93.

Atherton, P. J. (1976). "The Neoplatonic 'One' and the Trinitarian 'Arche,'" in Harris (1976), 173–86.

Atkinson, M. (1983). *Ennead V.1: On the Three Principal Hypostases: A Commentary with Translation*. New York: Oxford University Press.

Aubenque, P. (1971). "Plotin et le dépassement de l'ontologie grecque classique," in *Néoplatonisme*, 101–8.

—— (1979). (ed.) *Actes du VIe Symposium Aristotelicum: études sur la métaphysique d'Aristote*. Paris: J. Vrin.

—— (1981). "Néoplatonisme et analogie de l'être," in *Néoplatonisme*, 63–76.

Aubin, P. (1953). "L' 'image' dans l'œuvre de Plotin," *Recherches de Sciences Religieuses, 41*, 348–79.

Audi, R. and Wainwright, W. J. (1986). (eds) *Rationality, Religious Belief and Moral Commitment*. Ithaca, N.Y.: Cornell University Press.

Augustinus Magister. (1955). Congrès international Augustinien (1954). Paris: Etudes Augustiniennes.

Baladi, N. (1970). *La Pensée de Plotin*. Paris: Presses Universitaires de France.

—— (1971). "Origine et signification de l'audace chez Plotin," in *Le Néoplatonisme*, 89–97.

Bales, E. F. (1982). "Plotinus' Theory of the One", in Harris (1982a), 40–50.

Barion, J. (1935). *Plotin und Augustin: Untersuchungen zum Gottesproblem*. Berlin: Junker & Dunnhaupt.

Barnes, J. and Mignucci, M. (1988). (eds) *Matter and Metaphysics*. Fourth Symposium Hellenisticum. Naples: Bibliopolis.

Barnes, T. D. (1976). "The Chronology of Plotinus' Life," *Greek, Roman and Byzantine Studies, 17*, 65–70.

Becker, O. (1940). *Plotin und das Problem der geistigen Aneignung*. Berlin: Walter de Gruyter.

Beierwaltes, W. (1961). "Die Metaphysik des Lichtes in der Philosophie Plotins," *Zeitschrift für Philosophische Forschung, 15*, 334–62.

—— (1967). *Plotin über Ewigkeit und Zeit (Enneade III.7)*. Frankfurt am Main: Vittorio Klostermann.

—— (1971). "Andersheit: Zur neuplatonischen Struktur einer Problemgeschichte," in *Néoplatonisme*, 365–72.

—— (1972). "Andersheit: Grundriss einer neuplatonischen Begriffsgeschichte", *Archiv für Begriffsgeschichte*, *16*, 166–97.

—— (1973). "Die Entfaltung der Einheit," *Theta-Pi*, *2*, 126–61.

—— (1977a). "Negati Affirmatio," *Dionysius*, *1*, 127–60.

—— (1977b). "Plotins Metaphysik des Lichtes," in Zintzen (1977), 75–15.

—— (1980). (ed.) *Eriugena: Studien zu seinen Quellen*. Vorträge des 3. Eriugena-Colloquiums 1979. Heidelberg: Carl Winter Universitäts Verlag.

—— (1985). *Denken des Einen: Studien zur neuplatonischen Philosophie und ihrer Wirkungsgeschichte*. Frankfurt am Main: Vittorio Klostermann.

Benz, E. (1931). *Die Entwicklung des abendländischen Willensbegriffs von Plotin bis Augustin*. Stuttgart: W. Kohlhammer.

Benz, H. (1990). *"Materie" und Wahrnehmung in der Philosophie Plotins*. Würzburg: Königshausen & Neumann.

Bertier, J., Brisson, L., Charles, A., Pépin, J., Saffrey, H.-D., Segonds, A.-Ph. (1980). *Traité sur les nombres (Ennéade 6,6[34])*. Paris: J. Vrin.

Blume, H.-D. and Mann, F. (1983). (eds) *Platonismus und Christentum: Festschrift für Heinrich Dörrie*. Münster: Aschendorffsche Verlagsbuchhandlung.

Blumenthal, H. J. (1966). "Did Plotinus Believe in Ideas of Individuals?," *Phronesis*, *11*, 61–80.

—— (1968). "Plotinus Ennead IV.3.20–1 and its Sources: Alexander, Aristotle and Others," *Archiv für Geschichte der Philosophie*, *50*, 254–61.

—— (1971a). "Soul, World-Soul and Individual Soul in Plotinus," in *Néoplatonisme*, 55–3.

—— (1971b). *Plotinus' Psychology: His Doctrine of the Embodied Soul*. The Hague: Martinus Nijhoff.

—— (1972). "Plotinus' Psychology: Aristotle in the Service of Platonism," *International Philosophical Quarterly*, *12*, 340–64.

—— (1974). "Nous and Soul in Plotinus: Some Problems of Demarcation," in *Plotino e il Neoplatonismo in Oriente e in Occidente*, 203–19.

—— (1976a). "Neoplatonic Elements in the De Anima Commentaries," *Phronesis*, *21*, 64–87.

—— (1976b). "Plotinus' Adaptation of Aristotle's Psychology: Sensation, Imagination and Memory," in Harris (1976), 41–8.

—— (1981). "Plotinus in Later Platonism," in Blumenthal and Markus (1981), 212–22.

—— (1983). "Some Problems About Body in Later Pagan Neoplatonism: Do They Follow a Pattern?," in Blume and Mann (1983), 75–84.

—— (1984). "Plotinus' 'Ennead' I,2,7,5: A Different Hapax," *Mnemosyne*, *37*, 89–93.

—— (1987). "Plotinus in the Light of Twenty Years' Scholarship 1951–1971," in Haase and Temporini (1987), *II.36.1*, 528–70.

—— (1992). Plotinus, *Enneads* V 3 (49). 3–4," in *Méthexis: Etudes néoplatoniciennes présentées au Professeur Evanghélos A. Moutsopoulos*. Athens: CIEPA, 140–52.

Blumenthal, H. J. and Lloyd, A. C. (1982). (eds) *Soul and the Structure of Being in Late Neoplatonism*. Liverpool: Liverpool University Press.

Blumenthal, H. J. and Markus, R. A. (1981). (eds) *Neoplatonism and Early Christian Thought: Essays in Honour of A. H. Armstrong*. London: Variorum.

Blumenthal, H. J. and Robinson, H. (1991). (eds) *Oxford Studies in Ancient Philosophy*. Supplementary Volume. *Aristotle and the Later Tradition*. Oxford: Clarendon Press.

Boas, G. (1921). "A Source of the Plotinian Mysticism," *Journal of Philosophy*, *18*, 326–32.

Bodéüs, R. (1983). "L'Autre Homme de Plotin," *Phronesis*, *28*, 256–64.

Boer, W. den *et al.* (1973). (eds) *Romanitas et Christianitas: Studia J. H. Waszink.* Amsterdam: North-Holland Publishing Co.

Bogen, J. and McGuire, J. E. (1984). (eds) *How Things Are: Studies in Predication and the History of Philosophy and Science.* Dordrecht: D. Reidel Publishing Co.

Bonetti, A. (1971). "Studi intorno alla filosofia di Plotino," *Rivista di filosofia neoscholastica, 63*, 487–511.

—— (1980). "Dialettica e religione nell'interpretazione Neoplatonica della prima ipotesi dell 'Parmenide' I," *Rivista di filosofia neoscholastica, 72*, 3–30; 195–223.

Boot, P. (1983). "Plotinus' On Providence (Ennead III.2–3): Three Interpretations," *Mnemosyne, 36*(4), 311–15.

Bos, A. P. (1984). "World-Views in Collision: Plotinus, Gnostics, and Christians," in Runia (1984), 11–28.

Bossier, F. and de Waechter, F. (1976). (eds) *Images of Man in Ancient and Medieval Thought.* Leuven: Leuven University Press.

Botros, S. (1985). "Freedom, Causality, Fatalism and Early Stoic Philosophy," *Phronesis, 30*, 274–304.

Bousquet, F. (1976). *L'Esprit de Plotin: l'itinéraire de l'âme vers Dieu.* Sherbrook, Quebec: Editions Naaman.

Boyancé, P. (1963) "Notes sur la froura platonicienne," *Revue de Philologie, 37*, 7–11.

Braga, G. C. (1932). "Il problema del rapporto fra le anime individuali e l'anima dell'universo nella filosofia di Platone," *Rivista di filosofia, 23*, 106–25.

Brague, R. and Courtine, J.-F. (1990). (eds) *Mélanges en hommage à Pierre Aubenque.* Paris: Presses Universitaires de France.

Bréhier, E. (1928). *La Philosophie de Plotin.* Paris: Boivin.

Breton, S. (1981). "Difficile néoplatonisme," in *Néoplatonisme*, 91–101.

—— (1985). "L'Un et l'être", *Revue Philosophique de Louvain, 83*, 5–13.

Brisson, L. (1991). "De quelle façon Plotin interprete-t-il les cinq genres du sophiste?", in *Etudes.*

Brisson, L., Goulet-Cazé, M. O., Goulet, R., O'Brien, D. (1982). *Porphyre. La Vie de Plotin I.* Paris: J. Vrin.

Bröcker, W. (1966). *Platonismus ohne Sokrates – ein Vortrag über Plotin.* Frankfurt am Main: Vittorio Klostermann.

Bruni, G. (1963). "Introduzione alla dottrina plotiniana della materia," *Giornale critico della filosofia italiana, 42*, 22–5.

Brunner, F. (1973a). "Création et émanation: fragment de philosophie comparée," *Studia Philosophia, 33*, 33–43.

—— (1973b). "Le Premier Traité de la cinquième 'Ennéade': 'Des trois hypostases principielles,'" *Revue de Théologie et de Philosophie, 23*, 135–72.

—— (1990). "L'Aspect Rationnel et l'aspect religieux de la philosophie de Plotin," *Revue Théologique et Philosophique, 122*, 417–30.

Brunschwig, J. (1988). "La Théorie stoïcienne du genre suprême et l'ontologie platonicienne," in Barnes and Mignucci (1988), 19–127.

Büchner, H. (1970). *Plotins Möglichkeitslehre.* Munich: Anton Pustet.

Burkert, W. (1975). "Plotin, Plutarch und die Interpretation von Heraklit und Empedocles," in Mansfeld and de Rijk (1975), 137–46.

Bussanich, J. R. (1987). "Plotinus on the Inner Life of the One," *Ancient Philosophy, 7*, 163–89.

—— (1988). *The One and its Relation to Intellect in Plotinus.* Leiden: E. J. Brill.

—— (1990). "The Invulnerability of Goodness: The Ethical and Psychological Theory of Plotinus," *Proceedings of the Boston Area Colloquium in Ancient Philosophy, 6*, 151–84.

Butchvarov, P. (1970). *The Concept of Knowledge.* Evanston, Ill.: Northwestern University Press.

—— (1979). *Being Qua Being*. Bloomington, Ind.: Indiana University Press.

Cadiou, R. (1959). "Esthétique et sensibilité au début du néoplatonisme," *Revue Philosophique, 149*, 71–8.

Calogero, G. (1974). "Plotino, Parmenide e il Parmenide," In *Plotino e il Neoplatonismo in Oriente e in Occidente*, 49–59.

Capitani, F. D. (1984). "Platone, Plotino, Porfirio e Sant'Agostino sull immortalità dell'anima intesa come vita," *Rivista di filosofia neoscholastica, 76*, 230–44.

Carbonara, C. (1954, 2nd edition 1964). *La filosofia di Plotino*. Naples: Libreria Scientifica Editrice.

Cardona, G. (1971). "E autentica la teoria aristotelica del primo motore immobile?," *Rivista critica di storia della filosofia, 26*, 243–70.

Carriere, G. (1950). "Man's Downfall in Plotinus," *New Scholasticism, 24*, 284–308.

—— (1951). "Plotinus' Quest of Happiness," *Thomist, 14*, 217–37.

Chaix-Ruy, J. (1976). "Plotino e la genesi dell'umanesimo interiore," *Archiv für Philosophie, 39*, 660–6.

Charles-Saget, A. (1982). *L'Architecture du divin: mathématique et philosophie chez Plotin et Proclus*. Paris: Les Belles Lettres.

Charrue, J. -M. (1978). *Plotin: Lecteur de Platon*. Paris: Les Belles Lettres.

Cherniss, H. F. (1944, 1962). *Aristotle's Criticism of Plato and the Academy*. New York: Russell & Russell.

Chisholm, R. M. (1982). *Brentano and Meinong Studies*. Atlantic Highlands, N.J.: Humanities Press.

Chrétien, J.-L. (1980). "Le Bien donne ce qu'il n'a pas," *Archive de Philosophie, 43*, 263–77.

Cilento, V. (1960). "Mito e poesia nelle Enneadi di Plotino," in *Sources*, 243–310.

—— (1961). "Psychè," *Parola del Passato, 16*, 190–211. Reprinted in Cilento (1973), 63–81.

—— (1963). "La radice metafisica della libertà nell'antignosi Plotiniana," *Parola del Passato, 18*, 94–122.

—— (1965). "Storia del testo di Plotino," *Rivista di filologia classica, 93*, 369–79. Reprinted in Cilento (1973), 335–48.

—— (1967). "Stile e linguaggio nella filosofia di Plotino," *Vichiana, 4*, 29–41.

—— (1969). "Tracce di dramma e di mimo nelle Enneadi di Plotino," *Dioniso, 43*, 277–94. Reprinted in Cilento (1973), 241–54.

—— (1971a). "Il genio religioso di Plotino tra misteri antichi e nuovi," *Filosofia, 22*, 149–64.

—— (1971b). *Paideia antignostica: Riconstruzione d'un unico scritto da Enneadi III.8, V.8, V.5, II.9*. Florence: F. Le Monnier.

—— (1971c). "Stile e sentimento tragico nella filosofia di Plotino," in *Le Néoplatonisme*, 37–42.

—— (1973). *Saggi su Plotino*. Milan: U. Mursia & Co.

—— (1974). "Presenza di Plotino nel mondo moderno," in *Plotino e il Neoplatonismo in Oriente e in Occidente*, 13–29.

Clark, G. H. (1942). "Plotinus' Theory of Sensation," *Philosophical Review, 51*, 357–82.

—— (1943). "Plotinus' Theory of Empirical Responsibility," *New Scholasticism, 17*, 16–1.

—— (1944). "The Theory of Time in Plotinus," *Philosophical Review, 53*, 337–58.

—— (1949). "Plotinus on the Eternity of the World," *Philosophical Review, 58*, 130–40.

Clarke, W. N. (1952). "The Limitation of Act by Potency," *New Scholasticism, 26*, 167–94.

—— (1959). "Infinity in Plotinus: A Reply," *Gregorianum, 40*, 75–98.

Code, A. (1984). 'On the Origins of Some Aristotelian Theses About Predication," in Bogen and McGuire (1984), 101–31.

Cole, E. B. (1992). "Plotinus on the Souls of Beasts," *The Journal of Neoplatonic Studies*, 63–90.

Combès, J. (1969). "Deux styles de libération: la nécessité stoïcienne et l'exigence plotinienne," *Revue Métaphysique et Morale*, 308–24.

—— (1989). *Etudes néoplatoniciennes*. Grenoble: Editions Jérome Millon.

Cornford, F. M. (1935). *Plato's Theory of Knowledge*. London: Routledge & Kegan Paul.

Corrigan, K. (1981). "The Internal Dimensions of the Sensible Object in the Thought of Plotinus and Aristotle," *Dionysius*, *5*, 98–126.

—— (1984). "A Philosophical Precursor to the Theory of Essence and Existence in Thomas Aquinas," *Thomist*, *48*, 219–40.

—— (1985a). "The Irreducible Opposition Between the Platonic and Aristotelian Concepts of the Soul and Body in Some Ancient and Mediaeval Thinkers," *Lával Théologique et Philosophique*, *41*, 391–401.

—— (1985b). "Body's Approach to Soul: An Examination of a Recurrent Theme in the Enneads," *Dionysius*, *9*, 37–52.

—— (1986a). "Is There More Than One Generation of Matter in the Enneads?," *Phronesis*, 167–81.

—— (1986b). "Plotinus' 'Enneads' 5,4(7),2 and Related Passages: A New Interpretation of the Status of the Intelligible Object," *Hermes*, *114*, 195–204.

—— (1987). "Amelius, Plotinus and Porphyry on Being, Intellect and the One," in Haase and Temporini (1987), *II.36.2*, 975–93.

Corrigan, K. and O'Cleirigh, P. (1987). "The Course of Plotinus Scholarship from 1971–1986," in Haase and Temporini (1987), *II.36.1*, 571–623.

De Corte, M. (1935). *Aristote et Plotin*. Paris: Desclée De Brouwer.

—— (1938). "Plotin et la nuit de l'esprit," *D'études carmélitaines*, *23*, 102–15.

Costello, E. B. (1967). "Is Plotinus Inconsistent on the Nature of Evil?," *International Philosophical Quarterly*, *7*, 483–97.

Covotti, A. (1935). *Da Aristotele ai Bizantini*. Naples: A. Rondinella.

Crocker, J. R. (1956). "The Freedom of Man in Plotinus," *Modern Schoolman*, *34*, 23–5.

D'Ancona, C. (1990). "Determinazione e indeterminazione nel sovrasensibile secondo Plotino," *Rivista di storia della filosofia*, *45*, 437–74.

D'Ancona Costa, C. (1992). ΑΜΟΡΦΟΝ ΚΑΙ ΑΝΕΙΔΕΟΝ. Causalité des formes et causalité de l'Un chez Plotin," *Revue de Philosophie Ancienne*, *10*, 69–113.

Deck, J. N. (1967). *Nature, Contemplation and the One: A Study in the Philosophy of Plotinus*. Toronto: University of Toronto Press.

—— (1982). "The One, or God, is not Properly Hypostasis: A Reply to Professor Anton," in Harris (1982a), 34–9.

Deck, J. N. and Armstrong, A. H. (1978). "A Discussion on Individuality and Personality," *Dionysius*, *2*, 93–9.

Deuse, W. (1983). *Untersuchungen zur mittelplatonischen und neuplatonischen Seelenlehre*. Mainz: Akademie der Wisssenschaften und der Literatur.

Dillon, J. (1976). "Image, Symbol and Analogy: Three Basic Concepts of Neoplatonic Allegorical Exegesis," in Harris (1976), 247–62.

—— (1983). "Plotinus, Philo and Origen on the Grades of Virtue," in Blume and Mann (1983), 92–105.

—— (1987). "The Mind of Plotinus," *Proceedings of the Boston Area Colloquium in Ancient Philosophy*, *3*, 338–58.

Dodds, E. R. (1928). "The Parmenides of Plato and the Origin of the Neoplatonic 'One,'" *Classical Quarterly*, *22*, 129–43.

—— (1956). "Notes on Plotinus, Ennead III.7," *Studia Italiana di Filologia Classica*, *27–8*, 108–13.

—— (1960a). "Numenius and Ammonius," in *Sources*, 3–32.

—— (1960b). "Tradition and Personal Achievement in the Philosophy of Plotinus," *Journal of Roman Studies*, *1*, 1–7.

—— (1965). *Pagan and Christian in an Age of Anxiety*. Cambridge: Cambridge University Press.

—— (1973). *The Ancient Concept of Progress*. Oxford: Clarendon Press. Includes reprint of (1960b).

Dombrowski, D. (1987). "Asceticism as Athletic Training in Plotinus," in Haase and Temporini (1987), *II 36.1*, 701–12.

Dörrie, H. (1954). "Zum Ursprung der neuplatonischen Hypostasenlehre," *Hermes*, *82*, 331–42.

—— (1955a). "Ammonius, der Lehrer Plotins," *Hermes*, *83*, 439–77.

—— (1955b). "Hypostasis: Wort und Bedeutungsgeschichte," *Nachrichten der Akademie der Wissenschaften in Göttingen*, 35–92. Reprinted in Dörrie (1976a), 13–69.

—— (1960). "Die Frage nach dem Transzendenten im Mittelplatonismus," in *Sources*, 193–223. Reprinted in Dörrie (1976a), 211–28.

—— (1963). "Plotin: Philosoph und Theologe," *Die Welt als Geschichte: Zeitschrift für Universalgeschichte*, *23*, 1–22. Reprinted in Dörrie (1976a), 361–74.

—— (1965). "Emanation: Ein unphilosophisches Wort im spätantiken Denken," in Flasch (1965), 119–41. Reprinted in Dörrie (1976a), 70–88.

—— (1970). "Der König: Ein platonisches Schlüsselwort, von Plotin mit neuem Sinn erfüllt," *Revue Internationale de Philosophie*, *24*, 217–35. Reprinted in Dörrie (1976a), 390–405.

—— (1974). "Plotino, tradizionalista o inventore?," in *Plotino e il Neoplatonismo in Oriente e in Occidente*, 195–201.

—— (1975). (ed.) *De Jamblique à Proclus*. Geneva: Fondation Hardt.

—— (1976a). *Platonica Minora*. Munich: Wilhelm Fink.

—— (1976b). "Tradition und Erneuern in Plotins Philosophieren," in Dörrie (1976a), 375–89.

Duméry, H. (1964). *The Problem of God in the Philosophy of Religion*. Evanston, Ill.: Northwestern University Press.

—— (1971). "Plotin de Joseph Moreau," *Revue de Synthèse*, *92*, 211–49.

—— (1974). "L'Etre et l'Un", in *Miscellanea Albert Dondeyne*, 331–50.

Dzohadze, D. V. (1974). "La dialettica di Plotino," in *Plotino e il Neoplatonismo in Oriente e in Occidente*, 91–108.

Eborowicz, W. (1957, 1958). "Le Sens de la contemplation chez Plotin," *Giornale di Metafisica*, *18*, 219–40.

Edman, E. (1925). "The Logic of Mysticism in Plotinus," *Studies in the History of Ideas*, *2*, 51–81.

Edwards, M. J. (1989). "Aidos in Plotinus: Enneads II.9.10," *Classical Quarterly*, *83*, 228–32.

Elsas, C. (1975). *Neuplatonische und gnostische Weltablehnung in der Schule Plotins*. Berlin and New York: Walter de Gruyter.

Emilsson, E. K. (1988). *Plotinus on Sense Perception*. Cambridge: Cambridge University Press.

—— (1991). "Plotinus on Soul–Body Dualism," in Everson (1991), 148–65.

Eon, A. (1970). "La Notion plotinienne d'exégèse," *Revue Internationale de Philosophie*, *92*, 252–89.

Etudes sur le Sophiste de Platon. (1991) Naples: Bibliopolis.

Evangeliou, C. (1982). "The Ontological Basis of Plotinus' Criticism of Aristotle's Theory of Categories," in Harris (1982a), 73–82.

Everson, S. (1991). (ed.) *Psychology*. Companions to Ancient Thought 2. Cambridge: Cambridge University Press.

Fabro, C. (1970). "Platonism, Neo-Platonism and Thomism: Convergencies and Divergencies," *New Scholasticism*, *44*, 69–100.

Ferwerda, R. (1965). *La Signification des images et des métaphors dans la pensée de Plotin*. Groningen: J. B. Wolters.

—— (1980). "L'Incertitude dans la philosophie de Plotin," *Mnemosyne*, *33*(4), 119–27.

—— (1982). "Plotinus on Sounds: An Interpretation of Plotinus' 'Enneads' V.5.5.19–27," *Dionysius*, *6*, 43–7.

—— (1984). "Pity in the Life and Thought of Plotinus," in Runia (1984), 53–62.

Fielder, J. (1976). "Chorismos and Emanation in the Philosophy of Plotinus," in Harris (1976), 101–20.

—— (1977). "Plotinus' Copy Theory," *Apeiron*, *11*, 1–11.

—— (1978a). "Plotinus' Reply to the Arguments of the Parmenides 130a–131d," *Apeiron*, *12*, 1–5.

—— (1978b). "Plotinus' Response to Two Problems of Immateriality," *Proceedings of the American Catholic Philosophical Association*, *52*, 98–101.

—— (1980). "A Plotinian View of Self-Predication and TMA," *Modern Schoolman*, *57*, 339–47.

—— (1982). "Plotinus and Self-Predication," in Harris (1982a), 83–9.

Findlay, J. N. (1974). *Plato: The Written and Unwritten Doctrines*. London: Routledge & Kegan Paul.

—— (1975). "The Three Hypostases of Plotinism," *Review of Metaphysics*, *28*, 660–80.

—— (1976). "The Neoplatonism of Plato," in Harris (1976), 23–40.

—— (1982). "The Logical Peculiarities of Neoplatonism," in Harris (1982a), 1–10.

Fine, G. (1993). *On Ideas*. Oxford: Clarendon Press.

Fischer, H. (1956). *Die Aktualität Plotins: Über die Konvergenz von Wissenschaft und Metaphysik*. Munich: C. H. Beck'sche Verlagsbuchhandlung.

Flasch, K. (1965). *Parusia: Studien zur Philosophie Platons und zur Problemgeschichte des Platonismus: Festgabe für Johannes Hirschberger*. Frankfurt am Main: Minerva.

Foss, L. (1982). "Are There Substances? Another Look at the Classical Doctrine," in O'Hara (1982), 69–88.

Fraisse, J. -C. (1980–1). "La Simplicité du beau selon Plotin," *Cahiers du Centre George-Radet 1*, 60–80.

—— (1985). *L'Intériorité sans retraite: lectures de Plotin*. Paris: J. Vrin.

Frankfurt, H. (1971). "Freedom of the Will and the Concept of a Person," *Journal of Philosophy*, *68*, 5–20.

Frenkian, A. M. (1943). "Les Origines de la théologie négative de Parménide à Plotin," *Rivista Classica*, *15*, 11–20.

—— (1964). "L'Enseignement oral dans l'école de Plotin," *Maia*, *16*, 353–66.

Früchtel, E. (1970). *Weltentwurf und Logos zur Metaphysik Plotins*. Frankfurt am Main: Vittorio Klostermann.

Fuller, B. A. G. (1912). *The Problem of Evil in Plotinus*. Cambridge: Cambridge University Press.

Gagnebin, C. (1963). "La Pensée de Plotin, et Philosophie de la vie spirituelle," *Revue de Théologie et de Philosophie*, *14*, 84–95.

Gandillac, M. D. (1952, 2nd edition 1966). *La Sagesse de Plotin*. Paris: Librairie Hachette.

—— (1979). "Plotin et la 'Métaphysique d'Aristote,'" in Aubenque (1979), 247–59.
Gatti, M. (1982). *Plotino e la metafisica della contemplazione*. Milan: Cooperativa universitaria studio e lavoro.
—— (1983). "Sulla teoria Plotiniana del numero e sui rapporti con alcuni aspetti della problematica delle 'dottrine non scritte' di Platone," *Rivista di filosofia neoscholastica*, *75*, 361–84.
Gelzer, T. (1982). "Plotins Interesse an den Vorsokratikern," *Museum Helveticum*, *39*, 101–31.
Gersh, S. E. (1973). *Kinesis Akinetos. A Study of Spiritual Motion in the Philosophy of Proclus*. Leiden: E. J. Brill.
Gerson, L. P. (1983). (ed.) *Graceful Reason: Essays in Ancient and Medieval Philosophy Presented to Joseph Owens*. Toronto: Pontifical Institute of Medieval Studies.
—— (1987). "Two Criticisms of the Principle of Sufficient Reason," *International Journal of the Philosophy of Religion*, *21*, 19–42.
—— (1990). *God and Greek Philosophy: Studies in the Early History of Natural Theology*. London: Routledge.
—— (1991). "Causality, Univocity, and First Philosophy in *Metaphysics* ii," *Ancient Philosophy*, *11*, 331–49.
Gilson, E. (1962). *L'Etre et l'essence*. 2nd edition. Paris: J. Vrin.
Gloy, K. (1989). "Die Struktur der Zeit in Plotins Zeittheorie," *Archiv für Geschichte der Philosophie*, *71*, 303–26.
Gorman, C. P. (1940). "Freedom in the God of Plotinus," *New Scholasticism*, *14*, 379–405.
Graeser, A. (1972a). *Plotinus and the Stoics. A Preliminary Study*. Leiden: E. J. Brill.
—— (1972b). "Vier Bücher über Plotin," *Göttingische Gelehrte Anzeigen*, *224*, 191–233.
Graham, D. W. (1987). *Aristotle's Two Systems*. Oxford: Clarendon Press.
Guerard, C. (1986). "L'Aspect neoplatonicien de la critique des idees par Aristote," *Revue Théologique et Philosophique*, *118*, 35–45.
Guidelli, C. (1988). "Note sul tema della memoria nella Enneadi di Plotino," *Elenchos*, *9*, 75–84.
Guitton, J. (1933, 4th edition 1971). *Le Temps et l'éternité chez Plotin et Saint Augustin*. Paris: J. Vrin.
Gurtler, G. M. (1984). "Sympathy in Plotinus," *International Philosophical Quarterly*, *24*, 395–406.
—— (1988a). *Plotinus. The Experience of Unity*. New York: Peter Lang.
—— (1988b). "The Origin of Genera: Ennead VI 2[43] 20," *Dionysius*, *12*, 3–15.
—— (1992). "Plotinus and the Platonic *Parmenides*," *International Philosophical Quarterly*, *32*, 443–57.
Haase, W. and Temporini, H. (1987). (eds) *Aufstieg und Niedergang der Römischen Welt* (*ANRW*), pt. II: *Principat*. vols. 36.1 and 2. New York: Walter De Gruyter.
Hadot, P. (1960). "Etre, vie, pensée chez Plotin et avant Plotin," in *Sources*, 107–41.
—— (1963, 2nd edition 1973). *Plotin ou La simplicité du regard*. Paris: Plon.
—— (1973). "L'Etre et l'étant dans le néoplatónisme," *Revue de Théologie et de Philosophie*, *23*(3), 101–13.
—— (1974). "L'Harmonie des philosophies de Plotin et d'Aristote selon Porphyre dans le commentaire de Dexippe sur les Catégories," in *Plotino e il Neoplatonismo in Oriente e in Occidente*, 31–47.
—— (1980). "Les Niveaux de conscience dans les états mystiques selon Plotin," *Journal de Psychologie*, *77*, 243–66.
—— (1981a). *Exercises Spirituels et Philosophie Antique*. Paris: Etudes augustiniennes.

—— (1981b). "Ouranos, Kronos and Zeus in Plotinus' Treatise Against the Gnostics," in Blumenthal and Markus (1981), 124–37.

—— (1987a). "Structure et thèmes du Traité 38 (VI,7) de Plotin," in Haase and Temporini (1987), *II.36.1*, 624–76.

—— (1987b). "L'Union de l'âme avec l'intellect divin dans l'expérience mystique plotinienne," in *Proclus et son influence*, 3–27.

—— (1988). *Plotin: Traité 38. VI,7.* Paris: Les Editions Du Cerf.

Hager, F.-P. (1962). "Die Materie und das Böse im antiken Platonismus," *Museum Helveticum, 19*, 85–103.

—— (1964). "Die Aristotelesinterpretation des Alexander von Aphrodisias und die Aristoteleskritik Plotins bezüglich der Lehre vom Geist," *Archiv für Geschichte der Philosophie, 46*, 174–87.

—— (1970). *Der Geist und das Eine: Untersuchungen zum Problem der Wesensbestimmung des höchsten Prinzips als Geist oder als Eines in der griechischen Philosophie.* Bern: Paul Haupt.

—— (1973). "Metaphysik und Menschenbild bei Plotin und bei Augustin," *Annuaire de la Société Suisse de Philosophie (Studia Philosophica), 33*, 85–11.

—— (1976). "Zum Problem der Originalität Plotins: Drei Probleme der 'neuplatonischen' Interpretation Platons," *Archiv für Geschichte der Philosophie, 58*, 10–22.

—— (1977). "Die Materie und das Böse im antiken Platonsmus," in Zintzen (1977), revision of 1962 article with 'Nachtrag 1973,' 469–74.

—— (1984). "La Société comme intermédiaire entre l'homme individuel et l'Absolu chez Platon et chez Plotin," *Diotima, 12*, 131–8.

—— (1987). *Gott und das Böse im antiken Platonismus.* Würzburg: Königshausen & Neumann.

Hankey, W. (1980). "Aquinas' First Principle: Being or Unity?," *Dionysius, 4*, 133–72.

Harder, R. (1960a). *Kleine Schriften.* Munich: C. H. Beck.

—— (1960b). "Zur Biographie Plotins," in Harder (1960a), 275–95.

Harris, R. B. (1976). (ed.) *The Significance of Neoplatonism.* Albany, N.Y.: International Society for Neoplatonic Studies.

—— (1982a). (ed.) *The Structure of Being: A Neoplatonic Approach.* Albany, N.Y.: International Society for Neoplatonic Studies.

—— (1982b). (ed.) *Neoplatonism and Indian Thought.* Albany, N.Y.: International Society for Neoplatonic Studies.

Hartshorne, C. (1967). *A Natural Theology for our Time.* La Salle, Ill.: Open Court.

Hathaway, R. F. (1969). "The Neoplatonist Interpretation of Plato: Remarks on its Decisive Characteristics," *Journal of the History of Philosophy, 7*, 19–26.

Heinemann, F. (1921, 2nd edition 1973). *Plotin: Forschungen über die plotinische Frage, Plotins Entwicklung und sein System.* Leipzig: Felix Meiner.

Heiser, J. (1991). *Logos and Language in the Philosophy of Plotinus.* Lewiston, N.Y.: Edwin Mellen Press.

Hellemann-Elgersma, W. (1980). *Soul-Sisters: A Commentary on Enneads IV,3[27],1–8 of Plotinus.* Amsterdam: Rodopi.

Helm, B. P. (1981). "Time as Power and Intentionality," *Idealistic Studies, 11*, 230–41.

Henry, P. (1931). "Le Problème de la liberté chez Plotin," *Revue Néo-scolastique de Philosophie, 33*, 50–79; 180–215; 318–39.

—— (1938, 1941, 2nd edition v. 2, 1948). *Etudes plotiniennes,* vol. 1: *Les Etats du texte de Plotin, Les Manuscrits des Ennéades.* Paris: Desclée de Brouwer.

—— (1960). "Une comparaison chez Aristote, Alexandre et Plotin," in *Sources,* 429–44.

—— (1982). "The Oral Teaching of Plotinus," *Dionysius, 6*, 4–12.

Himmerich, W. (1959). *Eudaimonia: Die Lehre des Plotin von der Selbstverwirklichung des Menschen.* Würzburg: K. Trilsch.

Hintikka, J. (1962). *Knowledge and Belief: An Introduction to the Logic of the Two Notions.* Ithaca, N.Y.: Cornell University Press.

Huber, G. (1955). *Das Sein und das Absolute: Studien zur Geschichte der ontologischen Problematik in der spätantiken Philosophie.* Basle: Verlag für Recht und Gesellschaft.

Hunt, D. P. (1981). "Contemplation and Hypostatic Process in Plotinus," *Apeiron, 15*, 71–9.

Igal, J. (1971a). "La genesis de la Inteligencia en un pasaje de las Eneades de Plotino (V.1.7.4–35)," *Emerita, 39*, 129–57.

—— (1971b). "Commentaria in Plotini 'De Bono sive de Uno' librum (Enn. VI, 9)," *Helmantica, 22*, 273–304.

—— (1973). "Observaciones al texto de Plotino," *Emerita, 41*, 75–98.

—— (1975). "Sobre Plotini Opera, III, de P. Henry y H.-R. Schwyzer," *Emerita, 43*, 169–96.

—— (1979). "Aristoteles y la evolución de la antropologia de Plotino," *Pensiamento, 35*, 315–46.

—— (1981). "The Gnostics and 'The Ancient Philosophy' in Plotinus," in Blumenthal and Markus (1981), 138–49.

Inge, W. R. (1929, 3rd edition 1968). *The Philosophy of Plotinus.* 2 volumes. London: Longmans, Green & Co.

Inwood, B. (1985). *Ethics and Human Action in Early Stoicism.* Oxford: Clarendon Press.

Jackson, B. D. (1967). "Plotinus and the Parmenides," *Journal of the History of Philosophy, 5*, 315–27.

Jansen, H. L. (1964). "Die Mystik Plotins," *Numen, 11*, 165–88.

Jerphagnon, L. (1971). "Plotin e la figure de ce monde," *Revue de Métaphysique et de Morale, 76*, 195–205.

—— (1974). "Exigences noétiques et objectivité dans la pensée de Plotin," *Revue de Métaphysique et de Morale, 79*, 411–16.

—— (1982). "Doux Plotin?," *Revue de Philosophie, 172*, 397–404.

Jevons, F. R. (1964). "Dequantification in Plotinus' Cosmology," *Phronesis, 9*, 64–71.

—— (1965). "'Lumping' in Plotinus' Thought," *Archiv für Geschichte der Philosophie, 47*, 132–40.

Jonas, H. (1964). "Plotins Tugendlehre: Analyse und Kritik," in Wiedmann (1964), 143–73.

—— (1971). "The Soul in Gnosticism and Plotinus," in *Le Néoplatonisme*, 45–53.

Katz, J. (1950). *Plotinus' Search for the Good.* New York: King's Crown Press.

—— (1954). "Plotinus and the Gnostics," *Journal of the History of Ideas, 15*, 289–98.

Kélessidou-Galanou, A. (1971). "L'Extase plotinienne et la problématique de la personne humaine," *Revue des Etudes Grecques, 84*, 384–96.

—— (1972). "Le Voyage érotique de l'âme dans la mystique plotinienne," *Platon, 24*, 88–101.

—— (1973). "Plotin et la dialectique platonicienne de l'absolu," *Philosophia, 3*, 307–38.

Kordig, C. R. (1982). "The Mathematics of Mysticism: Plotinus and Proclus," in Harris (1982a), 114–21.

Kostaras, G. P. (1983–4). "Die Natur als Schau in der Sicht Plotins," *Philosophia, 13–14*, 318–23.

Krämer, H. J. (1964, 2nd edition 1974). *Der Ursprung der Geistmetaphysik:*

Untersuchungen zur Geschichte des Platonismus zwischen Platon und Plotin. Amsterdam: B. R. Gruner.

—— (1969). "ΕΠΕΚΕΙΝΑ ΤΗΣ ΟΥΣΙΑΣ," *Archiv für Geschichte der Philosophie, 51,* 1–30.

Kremer, K. (1965). "Das 'Warum der Schöpfung': 'quia bonus' vel/et 'quia voluit'? Ein Beitrag zum Verhältnis von Neuplatonismus und Christentum an Hand des Prinzips 'bonum est diffusivum sui,'" in Flasch (1965), 241–64.

—— (1966). *Die neuplatonische Seinsphilosophie und ihre Wirkung auf Thomas von Aquin.* Leiden: E. J. Brill.

—— (1969). *Gott und Welt in der klassischen Metaphysik.* Stuttgart: W. Kohlhammer.

—— (1981). "Selbsterkenntnis als Gotteserkenntnis nach Plotins," *International Studies in Philosophy, 13,* 41–68.

—— (1987). "Bonum est diffusivum sui: Ein Beitrag zum Verhältnis von Neuplatonismus und Christentum," in Haase and Temporini (1987), II.36.1, 994–1032.

Kvanvig, J. L. and McCann, H. J. (1988). "Divine Conservation and the Natural World," in Morris (1988b), 13–49.

Lassègue, M. (1982). "Le Temps, image de l'éternité chez Plotin," *Revue Philosophique, 172,* 405–18.

—— (1982–3). "Note sur la signification de la notion d'image chez Plotin," *Revue de l'Enseignement Philosophique, 33,* 4–12.

Layton, B. (1980). (ed.) *The Rediscovery of Gnosticism: Proceedings of the International Conference on Gnosticism at Yale 1978.* Leiden: E. J. Brill.

Lee, J. S. (1979). "The Doctrine of Reception According to the Capacity of the Recipient in Ennead VI.4–5," *Dionysius, 3,* 79–97.

—— (1982). "Omnipotence and Eidetic Causation in Plotinus," in Harris (1982a), 90–103.

Leroux, G. (1974). "Logique et dialectique chez Plotin: Ennéade 1.3[20]," *Phoenix, 28,* 180–92.

—— (1990). *Plotin. Traité sur la liberté et la volonté de L'Un [Ennéade VI, 8 (39)].* Paris: J. Vrin.

—— (1992). La Trace et les signes," in ΣΟΦΙΗΣ ΜΑΙΗΤΟΡΕΣ. *Hommage à Jean Pépin.* Paris: Institut d'Etudes Augustiniennes, 245–61.

Letocha, D. (1978). "Le Statut de l'individualité chez Plotin ou le miroir de Dionysios," *Dionysius, 2,* 75–91.

Lieshout, H. V. (1926). *La Théorie plotinienne de la vertu.* Freiburg: Studia Friburgensia.

Link-Salinger, R. (1989). (ed.) *Of Scholars, Savants, and their Texts.* New York: Peter Lang.

Livingston, E. A. (1975). (ed.) *Studia Patristica XIII: Papers Presented to the International Conference on Patristic Studies.* Berlin: Akademie Verlag.

—— (1982). (ed.) *Studia Patristica XVII: Papers Presented to the Eighth International Conference on Patristic Studies, Oxford 1979.* New York: Pergamon, 329–44.

Lloyd, A. C. (1955). "Neoplatonic Logic and Aristotelian Logic," *Phronesis 1,* 58–79; 146–60.

—— (1964). "Nosce Teipsum and Conscientia," *Archiv für Geschichte der Philosophie, 46,* 188–200.

—— (1969–70). "Non-Discursive thought – An Enigma of Greek Philosophy," *Proceedings of the Aristotelian Society,* 261–74.

—— (1976). "The Principle that the Cause is Greater than its Effect," *Phronesis, 21,* 146–56.

—— (1986). "Non-Propositional Thought in Plotinus," *Phronesis, 31,* 258–65.

——— (1987). "Plotinus on the Genesis of Thought and Existence," *Oxford Studies in Ancient Philosophy*, 5, 155–86.

——— (1990). *The Anatomy of Neoplatonism*. Oxford: Clarendon Press.

Ludin, J. H. (1964). "Die Mystik Plotins," *Numen*, *11*, 165–88.

McCumber, J. (1978). "Anamnesis as Memory of Intelligibles in Plotinus," *Archiv für Geschichte der Philosophie*, *60*, 160–7.

Madigan, A. (1987). "Plotinus on Personal Individuality: The Early Period," *International Society for Neoplatonic Studies*, typescript, 5 folios.

Mamo, P. S. (1969). "Forms of Individuals in the Enneads," *Phronesis*, *14*, 77–86.

——— (1976). "Is Plotinian Mysticism Monistic?," in Harris (1976), 199–216.

Manchester, P. (1978). "Time and the Soul in Plotinus, III.7[45],11," *Dionysius*, *2*, 101–36.

Manno, A. G. (1984). "L'ineffabile di Plotino," *Rivista Rosminiana di Filosofia*, *78*, *79*, 147–59; 20–37.

Mansfeld, J. and de Rijk, L. M. (1975). (eds) *Kephalion: Studies in Greek Philosophy and its Continuation Offered to Professor C. J. de Vogel*. Assen: Van Gorcum.

Marien, B. (1949). *Bibliografia critica degli studi plotiniani*, in edition of *Enneads* by V. Cilento, V. III. Bari: Laterza & Figli, 389–662.

Martin, R. M. (1982). "On Logical Structure and the Plotinic Cosmos," in Harris (1982a), 11–23.

Martinich, A. (1970). "The Descent of the Soul in the Philosophy of Plotinus," *Kinesis*, *3*, 34–42.

Marucchi, P. (1935). "Studi Plotiniani, I: Metafisica della libertà. Commento a Enn. VI,8," *Atene e Roma*, *3*, 161–76.

Massagli, M. (1982). "Amelio neoplatonico e la metafisica del Nous," *Rivista di filosofia neoscholastica*, *74*, 225–43.

Matter, P. P. (1964). *Zum Einfluss des platonischen Timaios auf das Denken Plotins*. Winterthur: P. G. Keller.

Maurer, A. (1962, 2nd edition 1982). *Medieval Philosophy*. Toronto: Pontifical Institute of Medieval Studies Press.

Meijer, P.A. (1992). *Plotinus on the Good or the One (Enneads VI,9)*. Amsterdam: J. G. Gieben.

Merlan, P. (1953a, 3rd edition 1975). *From Platonism to Neoplatonism*. The Hague: Martinus Nijhoff.

——— (1953b). "Plotinus and Magic," *Isis*, *44*, 341–8.

——— (1963). *Monopsychism, Mysticism, Metaconsciousness: Problems of the Soul in the Neoaristotelian and Neoplatonic Tradition*. The Hague: Martinus Nijhoff.

——— (1964). "Aristotle, 'Met A 6, 987b20–35' and Plotinus, 'Enn V 4,2,8–9,'" *Phronesis*, *9*, 45–7.

Miller, C. L. (1977). "Union with the One, Ennead 6,9,8–11," *New Scholasticism*, *51*, 182–95.

Moreau, J. (1956). "L'Un et les êtres selon Plotin," *Giornale di metafisica*, *11*, 204–24.

——— (1970a). "Plotin et la tradition hellénique," *Revue Internationale de Philosophie*, *92*, 171–80.

——— (1970b). *Plotin ou la gloire de la philosophie antique*. Paris: J. Vrin.

——— (1981). "Origine et expressions du beau suivant Plotin", in *Néoplatonisme*, 249–63.

Morris, T. (1988a). (ed.) *Philosophy and the Christian Faith*. Notre Dame, Ind.: University of Notre Dame Press.

——— (1988b). (ed.) *Divine and Human Action*. Ithaca, N.Y.: Cornell University Press.

Mortley, R. (1975a). "Negative Theology and Abstraction in Plotinus," *American Journal of Philosophy*, *96*, 363–77.

—— (1975b). "Recent Work in Neoplatonism," *Prudentia*, 7, 47–52.

—— (1980). "Love in Plotinus," *Antichthon*, 14, 45–52.

Mossé-Bastide, R. (1972). *La Pensée philosophique de Plotin*. Paris: Bordas.

Moutsopoulos, E. (1971). "Sur la participation musicale chez Plotin," *Philosophia*, 1, 379–89.

—— (1976). "Dynamic Structuralism in the Plotinian Theory of the Imaginary," in Harris (1976), 235–46.

—— (1980). *Le Problème de l'imaginaire chez Plotin*. Athens: Société Hellénique des Etudes Philosophiques.

—— (1984). "Kairos and Kairic Activity in the Work of Plotinus," *Estudios Clásicos*, 26, 443–7.

Müller, H. F. (1913). "Ist die Metaphysik des Plotinos ein Emanationssystem?," *Hermes*, 48, 408–25.

—— (1914a). "Orientalisches bei Plotinos?," *Hermes*, 49, 70–9.

—— (1914b). "Plotinos über Notwendigkeit und Freiheit," *Neue Jahrbücher für das klassische Altertum*, 17, 462–88.

—— (1916a). "Enneade I.1: Peri tou ti to zwon kai ti o anthropos," *Hermes*, 51, 97–119.

—— (1916b). "Phusis bei Plotinos," *Rheinisches Museum für Philologie*, 71, 232–45.

—— (1917a). "Die Lehre vom Logos bei Plotin," *Archiv für Geschichte der Philosophie*, 30, 38–65.

—— (1917b). "Peri eudaimonias [Enn. 1.4]," *Hermes*, 52, 77–91.

—— (1917c). "Zur Ethik des Plotinos," *Hermes*, 52, 57–76.

Murray, J. S. (1951). "The Ascent of Plotinus to God," *Gregorianum*, 32, 223–46.

Myerscough, A. (1970). "The Nature of Man in Plotinus," *Studies in Philosophy and the History of Philosophy*, 5, 138–77.

Nagel, T. (1986). *The View From Nowhere*. New York: Oxford University Press.

Narbonne, J. -M. (1987). "Plotin et le problème de la génération de la matière; à propos d'un article récent," *Dionysius*, 11, 3–11.

Nebel, G. (1929). *Plotins Kategorien der intelligiblen Welt*. Tübingen: J. C. B. Mohr.

—— (1930). "Terminologische Untersuchungen zu Ousia und On bei Plotin," *Hermes*, 65, 422–45.

Le Néoplatonisme. (1971). Colloque de Royaumont 9–13 juin 1969. Paris: Centre Nationale de la Recherche Scientifique.

Néoplatonisme. (1981). *Mélanges offert à Jean Trouillard*. Fontenay-aux-Roses: Les Cahiers de Fontenay.

O'Brien, D. (1971). "Plotinus on Evil: A Study of Matter and the Soul in Plotinus' Conception of Human Evil," in *Le Néoplatonisme*, 113–46.

—— (1977). "Le Volontaire et la nécessité: réflexions sur la descente de l'âme dans la philosophie de Plotin," *Revue Philosophique*, 167, 401–22.

—— (1981). "Plotinus and the Gnostics on the Generation of Matter," in Blumenthal and Markus (1981), 108–23.

—— (1990). "The Origin of Matter and the Origin of Evil in Plotinus' Criticism of the Gnostics," in Brague and Courtine (1990), 181–202.

—— (1991). *Plotinus on the Origin of Matter*. Naples: Bibliopolis.

—— (1993). *Théodicée plotinienne, théodicée gnostique*. Leiden: E. J. Brill.

O'Daly, G. J. P. (1973). *Plotinus' Philosophy of the Self*. Shannon: Irish University Press.

—— (1974). "The Presence of the One in Plotinus," in *Plotino e il Neoplatonismo in Oriente e in Occidente*, 159–69.

O'Hara, M. L. (1982). (ed.) *Substances and Things: Aristotle's Doctrine of Physical Substance in Recent Essays*. Washington, D.C.: University Press of America.

O'Meara, D. J. (1974). "A propos d'un témoignage sur l'expérience mystique de Plotin (Enn. 1[6] 1,1–11)," *Mnemosyne, 27,* 238–44.
—— (1975). *Structures hiérarchiques dans la pensée de Plotin.* Leiden: E. J. Brill.
—— (1976). "Being in Numenius and Plotinus: Some Points of Comparison," *Phronesis, 21,* 120–9.
—— (1980a). "Gnosticism and the Making of the World in Plotinus," in Layton (1980), 365–78.
—— (1980b). "The Problem of Omnipresence in Plotinus, Ennead VI,4–5: A Reply," *Dionysius, 4,* 61–73.
—— (1982). (ed.) *Neoplatonism and Christian Thought.* Albany, N.Y: International Society for Neoplatonic Studies.
—— (1985a). (ed.) *Platonic Investigations.* Washington, D.C.: Catholic University of America Press.
—— (1985b). "Plotinus on How Soul Acts on Body," in O'Meara (1985a), 247–62.
—— (1990a). "Le Problème du discours sur l'indicible chez Plotin," *Revue Théologique et Philosophique, 122,* 145–56.
—— (1990b). "La Question de l'être et du non-être des objets mathématiques chez Plotin et Jamblique," *Revue Théologique et Philosophique, 122,* 405–16.
O'Neil, C. J. (1949). "Plotinus as Critic of the Aristotelian Soul," *Proceedings of the American Catholic Philosophical Association, 23,* 156–63.
Oosthout, H. (1991). *Modes of Knowledge and the Transcendental: An Introduction to Plotinus Ennead 5.3[49].* Amsterdam: B. R. Grüner.
Orsi, C. (1953). "La dottrina plotiniana del numero e le sue premesse storich," *Annali della Facoltà di Lettere e Filosofia dell'Università di Napoli, 2,* 137–74.
Palmer, R. B. and Hammerton-Kelly, J. B. (1971). (eds) *Philomathes: Studies and Essays in the Humanities in Memory of Philip Merlan.* The Hague: Martinus Nijhoff.
Paoli, U. (1990). *Der plotinische Begriff von* ΥΠΟΣΤΑΣΙΣ *und die augustinische Bestimmung Gottes als Subiectum.* Würzburg: Augustinus-Verlag.
Parfit, D. (1971). "Personal Identity," *Philosophical Review, 80,* 3–27.
Parma, C. (1971). *Pronoia und Providentia: Der Vorsehungsbegriff Plotins und Augustins.* Leiden: E. J. Brill.
Pazzi, A. (1979). "Alcuni aspetti della dottrina dell'anima in Plotino," *Rivista di filosofia neoscholastica, 71,* 290–305.
Pépin, J. (1950). "La Connaissance d'autrui chez Plotin et St. Augustin," *Revue Métaphysique et Morale, 55,* 128–48.
—— (1955). "Plotin et les mythes," *Rev. Philosophique de Louvain, 53,* 5–27.
—— (1956). "Eléments pour une histoire de la relation entre l'intelligence et l'intelligible chez Platon et dans le néoplatonisme," *Revue Philosophique, 146,* 39–64.
—— (1958). "La Connaissance d'autrui chez Plotin et St. Augustin," *Augustinus, 3,* 227–45.
—— (1971). *Idées grecques sur l'homme et sur Dieu.* Paris: Les Belles Lettres.
—— (1979). "Platonisme et antiplatonisme dans le traité de Plotin sur nombres, VI.6[34]," *Phronesis, 24,* 197–208.
Perler, O. (1931). *Der Nus bei Plotin und das Verbum bei Augustinus als vorbildliche Ursache der Welt.* Freiburg: Studia Friburgensia.
Phillips, J. F. (1981). "The Universe as Prophet: A Soteriological Formula in Plotinus," *Greek, Roman and Byzantine Studies, 22,* 269–81.
—— (1983). "Enneads V.1.2. Plotinus' Hymn to the World Soul and its Relation to Mystical Knowledge," *Symbolae Osloenses, 58,* 133–46.
—— (1987). "Stoic 'Common Notions' in Plotinus," *Dionysius, 11,* 33–52.
Pines, S. (1971). "The Problem of 'Otherness' in the Enneads," in *Le Néoplatonisme,* 77–8.

Pistorius, P. V. (1952). *Plotinus and Neoplatonism: An Introductory Study*. Cambridge: Bowes & Bowes.

Plantinga, A. (1974). *The Nature of Necessity*. Oxford: Clarendon Press.

—— (1980). *Does God Have a Nature?*. Milwaukee: Marquette University Press.

Plass, P. C. (1977). "Timeless Time in Neoplatonism," *Modern Schoolman*, *54*, 1–9.

—— (1982). "Plotinus' Ethical Theory," *Illinois Classical Studies*, *7*, 241–59.

Plotino e il Neoplatonismo in Oriente e in Occidente. (1974). Atti del Convengo Internazionale, Roma, 5–9 ottobre 1970. Rome: Accademia Nazionale dei Lincei.

Prini, P. (1968). *Plotino e la genesi dell' umanesimo interiore*. Rome: Edizioni Abete.

—— (1974). "Plotino e la genesi dell'umanesimo interiore," in *Plotino e il Neoplatonismo in Oriente e in Occidente*, 131–46.

Proclus et son influence. (1987). Actes du Colloque de Neuchâtel, juin 1985. Zurich: Editions Du Grand Midi.

Puech, H. C. (1960). "Plotin et les gnostiques," in *Sources*, 161–74.

Puelma, M. (1979). "Vorschläge zu Plotin Enn. VI.9," *Museum Helveticum*, *36*, 90–100.

—— (1980). "Zu Plotin Enn. VI.9: Ein Nachtrag," *Museum Helveticum*, *37*, 133–4.

Pugliese Carratelli, G. (1974). "Plotino e il problemi politici del suo tempo," in *Plotino e il Neoplatonismo in Oriente e in Occidente*, 61–70.

Randall, J. H. (1969). "The Intelligible Universe of Plotinus," *Journal of the History of Ideas*, *30*, 3–16.

Reale, G. (1983). "I fondamenti della metafisica di Plotino e la struttura della processione," in Gerson (1983), 153–75.

Remus, H. E. (1983). "Plotinus and Gnostic Thaumaturgy," *Laval Théologique et Philosophique*, *39*, 13–20.

Rich, A. N. M. (1954). "The Platonic Ideas as the Thoughts of God," *Mnemosyne*, *7*, 123–33.

—— (1957). "Reincarnation in Plotinus," *Mnemosyne*, *4*, 232–8.

—— (1960). "Plotinus and the Theory of Artistic Imitation," *Mnemosyne*, *13*, 233–9.

—— (1963). "Body and Soul in the Philosophy of Plotinus," *Journal of the History of Philosophy*, *1*, 1–5.

Rist, J. M. (1961). "Plotinus on Matter and Evil," *Phronesis*, *6*, 154–66.

—— (1962a). "The Indefinite Dyad and Intelligible Matter in Plotinus," *Classical Quarterly*, *12*, 99–107.

—— (1962b). "The Neoplatonic One and Plato's Parmenides," *Transactions of the American Philological Association*, *93*, 389–401.

—— (1962c). "Theos and the One in Some Texts of Plotinus," *Mediaeval Studies*, *24*, 169–80. Reprinted in Rist (1985), VII.

—— (1963a). "Forms of Individuals in Plotinus," *Classical Quarterly*, *13*, 223–31.

—— (1963b). "Plotinus and the Daimonion of Socrates," *Phoenix*, *17*, 13–14.

—— (1964a). *Eros and Psyche: Studies in Plato, Plotinus, and Origen*. Toronto: University of Toronto Press.

—— (1964b). "Mysticism and Transcendence in Later Neoplatonism," *Hermes*, *92*, 213–25. Reprinted in Rist (1985), XV.

—— (1965). "Monism. Plotinus and Some Predecessors," *Harvard Studies in Classical Philology*, *70*, 329–44.

—— (1966). "On Tracking Alexander of Aphrodisias," *Archiv für Geschichte der Philosophie*, *48*, 82–90.

—— (1967a). "Integration and the Undescended Soul in Plotinus," *American Journal of Philology*, *88*, 410–22.

—— (1967b). *Plotinus: The Road to Reality*. Cambridge: Cambridge University Press.

—— (1970). "Ideas of Individuals in Plotinus: A Reply to Dr. Blumenthal," *Revue Internationale de Philosophie*, *92*, 298–303.

—— (1971). "The Problem of 'Otherness' in the Enneads," in *Le Néoplatonisme*, 77–87. Reprinted in Rist (1985), VIII.

—— (1973). "The One of Plotinus and the God of Aristotle," *Review of Metaphysics*, *27*, 75–87. Reprinted in Rist (1985), IX.

—— (1974). "Plotinus and Augustine on Evil," In *Plotino e il Neoplatonismo in Oriente e in Occidente*, 495–508.

—— (1975). "Prohairesis: Proclus, Plotinus et alii," in Dörrie (1975), 103–17. Reprinted in Rist (1985), XIV.

—— (1976). "Plotinus on Moral Obligation," in Harris (1976), 217–34. Reprinted in Rist (1985), XI.

—— (1982). *Human Value: A Study in Ancient Philosophical Ethics*. Leiden: E. J. Brill.

—— (1983). "Metaphysics and Psychology in Plotinus' Treatment of the Soul," in Gerson (1983), 135–51. Reprinted in Rist (1985), X.

—— (1985). *Platonism and its Christian Heritage*. London: Variorum.

—— (1989). "Back to the Mysticism of Plotinus: Some More Specifics," *Journal of the History of Philosophy*, *27*, 183–97.

Roeser, T. P. (1945). "Emanation and Creation: The Doctrines of Plotinus and Augustinus on the Radical Origin of the Universe," *New Scholasticism*, *19*, 85–16.

Roloff, D. (1970). *Plotin: Die Großschrift III,8-V,8-V,5-II,9*. Berlin: Walter de Gruyter.

Romano, F. (1983). *Studi e Ricerche sul Neoplatonismo*. Naples: Guida Editori.

—— (1984). "La passione amorosa in Plotino," *Discorsi*, *4*(2), 190–202.

Ross, J. F. (1980). "Creation," *Journal of Philosophy*, *77*, 614–29.

—— (1986). "God, Creator of Kinds and Possibilities," in Audi and Wainwright (1986), 315–34.

—— (1988). "Eschatological Pragmatism," in Morris (1988a), 279–300.

—— (1989). "The Crash of Modal Metaphysics," *Review of Metaphysics*, *43*, 251–80.

—— (1990). "Aquinas's Exemplarism; Aquinas's Voluntarism," *American Catholic Philosophical Quarterly*, *64*, 171–98.

Rudberg, G. (1932). "Stilistisches zu Plotinos," in *Symbolae Philologicae. O. A. Daniellsson. Octogenario Dicalae*, 274–82. Uppsala: Almqvist & Wicksell.

Runia, D. T. (1984). (ed.) *Plotinus amid Gnostics and Christians*. Amsterdam: Free University Press.

Rutten, C. (1956). "La Doctrine des deux actes dans la philosophie de Plotin," *Revue Philosophique*, *146*, 100–6.

—— (1961). *Les Catégories du monde sensible dans les Ennéades de Plotin*. Paris: Les Belles Lettres.

Salmona, B. (1967). *La libertà in Plotino*. Milan: Marzorati.

Sambursky, S. (1978). "Das Gespenst des Vergänglichen," *Eranos-Jahrbuch*, *47*, 205–37.

Santa Cruz de Prunes, M. I. (1979a). *La Génèse du monde sensible dans la philosophie de Plotin*. Paris: Presses Universitaires de France.

—— (1979b). "Sobre la generacíon de la inteligencia en las Eneades de Plotino," *Helmantia*, *30*, 287–315.

Schall, J. V. (1985). "Plotinus and Political Philosophy," *Gregorianum*, *66*, 687–707.

Schibli, H. S. (1989). "Apprehending Our Happiness: Antilepsis and the Middle Soul in Plotinus, Ennead I.4.10," *Phronesis*, *34*, 205–19.

—— (1990). "Commentary on Bussanich," *Proceedings of the Boston Area Colloquium on Ancient Philosophy*, *6*, 185–92.

BIBLIOGRAPHY

Schiller, J. P. (1978). "Plotinus and Greek Rationalism," *Apeiron*, *12*, 37–50.

Schlette, H. (1966). *Das Eine und das Andere: Studien zur Problematik des Negativen in der Metaphysik Plotins*. Munich: Hueber Verlag.

Schoendorf, H. (1974). *Plotins Unformung der platonischen Lehre vom Schönen.* Bonn: Habelt.

Schofield, M. and Nussbaum, M. (1982). (eds) *Language and Logos: Studies in Ancient Greek Philosophy Presented to G. E. L. Owen.* Cambridge: Cambridge University Press.

Schroeder, F. M. (1978). "The Platonic Parmenides and Imitation in Plotinus," *Dionysius*, *2*, 51–73.

—— (1980). "Representation and Reflection in Plotinus," *Dionysius*, *4*, 37–59.

—— (1984). "Light and the Active Intellect in Alexander and Plotinus," *Hermes*, *112*, 238–48.

—— (1985). "Saying and Having in Plotinus," *Dionysius*, *9*, 75–82.

—— (1986a). "Conversion and Consciousness in Plotinus, 'Enneads' 5,1[10],7," *Hermes*, *114*, 186–95.

—— (1986b). "The Self in Ancient Religious Experience," in Armstrong (1986), 337–59.

—— (1987). "Synusia, Synais, Synesis. Presence and Dependence in the Plotinian Philosophy of Consciousness," in Haase and Temporini (1987), *II.36.1*, 677–99.

—— (1992). *Form and Transformation*. Montreal and Kingston: McGill-Queen's University Press.

Schubert, V. (1968). *Pronoia und Logos: Die Rechtfertigung der Weltordnung bei Plotin*. Munich: Verlag Anton Pustet.

Schürmann, R. (1982). "L'Hénologie comme dépassement de la métaphysique," *Etudes philosophiques*, *37*, 331–50.

Schuhl, P. M. (1973). "Descente métaphysique et ascension de l'âme dans la philosophie de Plotin," *Studi internazionale di filosofia*, *5*, 71–84.

Schwyzer, H.-R. (1944). "Die zweifache Sicht in der Philosophie Plotins," *Museum Helveticum*, *1*, 93–9.

—— (1951). "Plotinos," *Realencyclopädie der classischen Altertumswissenschaft* XXI.I, 471–592.

—— (1960). "Bewusst und Unbewusst bei Plotin," in *Sources*, 341–78.

—— (1970). "Plotin und Platons Philebus," *Revue International de Philosophie*, *92*, 181–93.

—— (1973). "Zu Plotins Deutung der sogenannten Platonischen Materie," in *Zetesis*, 266–80.

—— (1975). "The Intellect in Plotinus and the Archetypes of C. G. Jung," in Mansfeld and de Rijk (1975), 214–22.

Searle, J. (1992). *The Rediscovery of the Mind*. Cambridge, Mass.: MIT Press.

Seidl, H. (1985). "L'Union mystique dans l'explication philosophique de Plotin," *Revue Thomiste*, *85*, 253–64.

Sells, M. (1985). "Apophasis in Plotinus: A Critical Approach," *Harvard Theological Review*, *78*, 47–5.

Sharples, R. W. (1986). "Soft Determinism and Freedom in Early Stoicism," *Phronesis*, *31*, 266–79.

Sidorov, A. I. (1979). "Plotin et les gnostiques," *VDI*, 54–70.

Siegmann, G. (1990). *Plotins Philosophie des Guten. Eine Interpretation von Enneade V 27*, 238–44.

Siena, R. M. (1985). "Sull'impersonalismo teologico di Plotino," *Sapienza*, *38*, 319–26.

Simons, J. M. (1985). "Matter and Time in Plotinus," *Dionysius*, *9*, 53–74.

Singevin, C. (1969). *Essai sur l'Un*. Paris: Editions du Seuil.

Sinnige, T. G. (1975). "Metaphysical and Personal Religion in Plotinus," in Mansfeld and de Rijk (1975), 147–54.

—— (1984). "Gnostic Influences in the Early Works of Plotinus and Augustine," in Runia (1984), 73–7.

Sleeman, J. H. and Pollet, G. (1980). *Lexicon Plotinianum*. Leiden: E. J. Brill.

Smith, A. (1978). "Unconsciousness and Quasiconsciousness in Plotinus," *Phronesis*, *23*, 292–301.

—— (1981). "Potentiality and the Problem of Plurality in the Intelligible World," in Blumenthal and Markus (1981), 99–107.

Solignac, A. (1972). "Actualité du néoplatonisme," *Archive de Philosophie*, *35*, 571–80.

Sorabji, R. (1982). "Myths about Non-Propositional Thought," in Schofield and Nussbaum (1982), 295–314.

—— (1983). *Time, Creation & the Continuum*. Ithaca, N.Y.: Cornell University Press.

Les Sources de Plotin. (1960). Geneva: Fondation Hardt.

Stead, C. (1977). *Divine Substance*. Oxford: Clarendon Press.

Steel, C. G. (1978). *The Changing Self: A Study on the Soul in Later Neoplatonism*. Brussels: Paleis der Academien.

Straaten, M. V. (1975). "On Plotinus IV.7[2],8," in Mansfeld and de Rijk (1975), 164–70.

Strange, S. K. (1987). "Plotinus, Porphyry and the Neoplatonic Interpretation of the Categories," in Haase and Temporini (1987), *II 36.2*, 955–74.

—— (1992). Plotinus' Account of Participation in Ennead VI.4–5," *Journal of the History of Philosophy*, *30*, 479–96.

Stump, E. and Kretzmann, N. (1981). "Eternity," *Journal of Philosophy*, *78*, 429–58.

Sweeney, L. (1956). "Are 'Apeiria' and 'Aoristia' Synonyms?," *Modern Schoolman*, *33*, 270–9.

—— (1957). "Infinity in Plotinus," *Gregorianum*, *38*, 515–35; 713–32.

—— (1959). "Plotinus Revisited," *Gregorianum*, *40*, 327–31.

—— (1961a). "Another Interpretation of Enneads VI.7.32," *Modern Schoolman*, *38*, 289–303.

—— (1961b). "Basic Principles in Plotinus' Philosophy," *Gregorianum*, *42*, 506–15.

—— (1983). "Are Plotinus and Albertus Magnus Neoplatonists?," in Gerson (1983), 177–202.

Szlezák, T. A. (1979). *Platon und Aristoteles in der Nuslehre Plotins*. Basle: Schwabe & Co.

—— (1992). "L'Interpretazione di Plotino della teoria platonica dell'anima," *Rivista di filosofia neo-scolastica*, *84*, 325–39.

Telfer, W. (1957). "Autoexousia," *Journal of Theological Studies*, *7*, 123–9.

Theiler, W. (1944). "Plotin und die antike Philosophie," *Museum Helveticum*, *1*, 209–24.

—— (1960). "Plotin zwischen Platon und Stoa," in *Sources*, 63–6.

—— (1970). "Das Unbestimmte, Unbegrenzte bei Plotin," *Revue Internationale de Philosophie*, *92*, 290–7.

—— (1974). "Der Platonismus Plotins als Erfüllung der antiken Philosophie," in *Plotino e il Neoplatonismo in Oriente e in Occidente*, 147–58.

Thesleff, H. (1980). "Notes on unio mystica in Plotinus," *Arctos*, *14*, 101–14.

Tripathi, C. L. (1982). "The Influence of Indian Philosophy on Neoplatonism," in Harris (1982b), 273–92.

Trotta, A. (1992). "Interpretazione e critica di Plotino della concezione del tempo dei suoi predecessori," *Rivista di filosofia neo-scolastica*, *84*, 340–68.

Trouillard, J. (1953). "L'Impeccabilité de l'esprit selon Plotin," *Revue Histoire de Réligion, 143*, 19–29.

—— (1954). "La Présence de Dieu selon Plotin," *Revue Métaphysique et Morale, 59*, 38–45.

—— (1955a). "La Genèse du Plotinisme," *Revue Philosophique de Louvain, 53*, 469–81.

—— (1955b). *La Procession plotinienne.* Paris: Presses Universitaires de France.

—— (1955c). *La Purification plotinienne.* Paris: Presses Universitaires de France.

—— (1956). "La Méditation du verbe selon Plotin," *Revue Philosophique, 146*, 65–3.

—— (1961a). "The Logic of Attribution in Plotinus," *International Philosophical Quarterly, 1*, 125–38.

—— (1961b). "Valeur critique de la mystique plotinienne," *Revue Philosophique de Louvain, 59*, 431–44.

—— (1970). "L'Ame du Timée et l'un du Parménide dans la perspective néo-platonicienne," *Revue International de Philosophie, 92*, 236–51.

—— (1974). "Raison et mystique chez Plotin," *Revue des Etudes Augustiniennes, 20*, 3–14.

—— (1981). "Procession neoplatonicienne et création judeo-chrétienne," in *Neo-platonisme*, 1–31.

Turlot, F. (1985). "Logos in Plotinus," *Etudes philosophiques, 4*, 517–28.

Turnbull, R. G. (1984). "Zeno's Stricture and Predication in Plato, Aristotle, and Plotinus," in Bogen and McGuire (1984), 21–58.

Verbeke, G. (1971). "Les Critiques de Plotin contre l'entélechisme d'Aristote: essai d'interprétation de l'Enn. 4.7.8," in Palmer and Hammerton-Kelly (1971), 194–222.

—— (1973). "Le Statut ontologique du temps," in *Zetesis*, 188–205.

Verra, V. (1963). *Dialettica e filosofia in Plotino.* Pubblicazioni dell'Università degli Studi di Trieste, Facoltà di Magistero.

Vogel, C. J. de (1969a). *Philosophia*, part I. Assen: Van Gorcum.

—— (1969b). "The Monism of Plotinus," in de Vogel (1969a), 399–416.

—— (1971). "A propos de quelques aspects dits néoplatonisants du Platonisme de Platon," in *Le Néoplatonisme*, 8–14.

—— (1976). "Plotinus' Image of Man: Its Relationship to Plato as well as to Later Neoplatonism," in Bossier and de Waechter (1976), 147–68.

—— (1981). "The Soma–Sema Formula: Its Function in Plato and Plotinus Compared to Christian Writers," in Blumenthal and Markus (1981), 79–5.

—— (1985). "Platonism and Christianity: A Mere Antagonism or a Profound Common Ground?," *Vigiliana Christiana, 39*, 1–62.

Volkmann-Schluck, K.-H. (1941, 3rd edition 1966). *Plotin als Interpret der Ontologie Platons.* Frankfurt am Main: Vittorio Klostermann.

—— (1967–8). "Plotins Lehre vom Wesen und von der Herkunft des Schlechten (Enn 1.8)," *Philosophisches Jahrbuch, 75*, 1–11.

Wagner, H. (1956). "Die Schichtentheoreme bei Platon, Aristoteles und Plotin," *Studium Generale, 9*, 283–91.

Wagner, M. F. (1979). *Concepts and Causes. The Structure of Plotinus' Universe.* Dissertation. Ohio State University. Columbus, Ohio.

—— (1982a). "Plotinus' World," *Dionysius, 6*, 13–42.

—— (1982b). "Vertical Causation in Plotinus," in Harris (1982a), 51–72.

—— (1985). "Realism and the Foundation of Science in Plotinus," *Ancient Philosophy, 5*, 269–92.

—— (1986). "Plotinus' Idealism and the Problem of Matter in 'Enneads' VI.4 and 5," *Dionysius, 10*, 57–3.

Wald, G. (1990). *Self-Intellection and Identity in the Philosophy of Plotinus*. Frankfurt am Main: Peter Lang.

Wallis, R. T. (1972). *Neoplatonism*. London: Duckworth.

—— (1976). "Nous as Experience," in Harris (1976), 121–54.

—— (1981). "Divine Omniscience in Plotinus, Proclus and Aquinas," in Blumenthal and Markus (1981), 223–35.

—— (1983). "Plotinus and Paranormal Phenomena," in Anton and Preus (1983), 495–507.

—— (1987). "Scepticism and Neoplatonism," in Haase and Temporini (1987), *II.36.2*, 911–54.

Warren, E. W. (1964). "Consciousness in Plotinus," *Phronesis*, 9, 83–97.

—— (1965). "Memory in Plotinus," *Classical Quarterly*, 15, 252–60.

—— (1966). "Imagination in Plotinus," *Classical Quarterly*, 15, 277–85.

Westra, L. (1984). "The Soul's Noetic Ascent to the One in Plotinus and to God in Aquinas," *New Scholasticism*, 58, 99–126.

—— (1990). *Plotinus and Freedom: A Meditation on Ennead 6.8*. Lewiston: The Edwin Mellen Press.

White, M. J. (1985). *Agency and Integrality: Philosophical Themes in the Ancient Discussions of Determinism and Responsibility*. Dordrecht: D. Reidel.

Whittaker, J. (1975). "The Historical Background of Proclus' Doctrine of the Authupostata," in Dörrie (1975), 193–230. Reprinted in Whittaker (1984), XVI.

—— (1984). *Studies in Platonism and Patristic Thought*. London: Variorum.

Whittemore, R. C. (1966). "Panentheism in Neo-Platonism," *Tulane Studies in Phil.*, 4, 47–70.

Wiedmann, F. (1964). *Epimeleia: Die Sorge der Philosophie um den Menschen. Festschrift für Helmut Kuhn*. Munich: Verlag Anton Pustet.

Witt, R. E. (1931). "The Plotinian Logos and its Stoic Sources," *Classical Quarterly*, 25, 103–11.

Wolfson, H. (1952). "Albinus and Plotinus on Divine Attributes," *Harvard Theological Review*, 45, 115–30.

Wolters, A. M. (1982). "A Survey of Modern Scholarly Opinion on Plotinus and Indian Thought," in Harris (1982b), 293–308.

Wurm, K. (1973). *Substanz und Quälitat: Ein Beitrag zur Interpretation der plotinischen Traktate VI, 1, 2, und 3*. Berlin: Walter de Gruyter.

Zetesis. Festschrift E. de Strijcker. (1973). Antwerp: De Nederlandsche Boekhandel.

Zintzen, C. (1965). "Die Wertung von Mystik und Magie in der neoplatonischen Philosophie," *Rheinisches Museum für Altertumswissenschaft*, 108, 71–100.

—— (1977). (ed.) *Die Philosophie des Neuplatonismus*. Darmstadt: Wissenschaftliche Buchgesellschaft.

General Index

actions
  in our power 159
  not in our power 160
agent intellect 44, 52, 136, 172, 177, 180
Alfino, M. R. 278, 279
Anton, J. 232, 238, 257, 290, 291
apparent vs. true good 162
Aquinas, Thomas 27, 28, 29, 32, 33, 72, 241
Aristotelian essentialism 93–6, 112
  Plotinus' criticism 107
Armstrong, A. H. 228, 234, 236, 241, 243, 245, 250, 251, 255, 287
Arnou, R. 227, 273, 275, 280, 286, 289, 291, 292
Atkinson, M. 239, 243, 244, 288
Aubin, P. 261, 288

Baladi, N. 231, 272, 288
Bales 238
Beauty 212–18
  and error 215
  an imagery 214, 217
  and Intellect 212
  apparent and real 214
  artistic and natural 213, 214
  in souls 213, 214
  intelligible 215
  not symmetry 213
  property of Forms 212
Beierwaltes, W. 238, 245, 250, 252, 261, 266, 267, 287, 290, 292
Benz, H. 263, 276, 279
Bertier, J. 243
Blumenthal, H. 255, 268, 269, 272, 276, 278, 279, 280, 285
Bodéüs, R. 286, 287

Bonetti, A. 232
Botros, S. 274
Bousquet, F. 237, 271
Bréhier, E. 241, 246, 249
Brisson, L. 260
Brunner, F. 236
Brunschwig, J. 256
Büchner, H. 235, 236, 240, 246, 260
Bussanich, J. 234, 235, 238, 239, 244, 260, 283, 287, 293

categories 79–103
  Aristotle's theory 84–5
  Aristotle's theory criticized 84, 85, 90
  as kinds of being 79
  history of 79
  Plato's 97, 98
  Plotinian 96–103
  Stoic theory 81–3
  Stoic theory criticized 79–84
Charrue, J.-M. 232, 243, 269
Cherniss, H. 254
Chisholm, R. 229
Cilento, V. 249
Clark, G. H. 266, 276, 277
Clarke, W. N. 233
Code, A. 257, 262
cognition 170–84
  awareness of 172–3
  degrees of 164, 167, 170, 175, 176
  discursive 176, 177, 178
  imagery in 171, 172, 174
  impressions in 173, 174, 180
  non-representational 175
Cole, E. B. 289
Combès, J. 276
conglomerates 192
Cornford, F. M. 259

317

Index of Texts Cited